THE END OF THE COLD WAR ERA

To the Old Cold Warriors

THE END OF THE COLD WAR ERA

THE TRANSFORMATION OF THE GLOBAL SECURITY ORDER

SAKI RUTH DOCKRILL

Professor of Contemporary History and International Security
University of London

Hodder Arnold

A MEMBER OF THE HODDER HEADLINE GROUP

First published in Great Britain in 2005 by
Hodder Education, a member of the Hodder Headline Group,
338 Euston Road, London NW1 3BH

www.hoddereducation.com.

Distributed in the United States of America by
Oxford University Press Inc.
198 Madison Avenue, New York, NY10016

The advice and information in this book are believed to be true and
accurate at the date of going to press, but neither the author nor the publisher
can accept any legal responsibility or liability for any errors or omissions.

British Library Cataloguing in Publication Data
A catalogue record for this book is available from the British Library

Library of Congress Cataloging-in-Publication Data
A catalog record for this book is available from the Library of Congress

ISBN-10: 0–340–74032–9
ISBN-13: 978–0–340–74032–3

1 2 3 4 5 6 7 8 9 10

Typeset in 10/12pt Baskerville by Servis Filmsetting Ltd, Manchester
Printed and bound in Great Britain by CPI Bath

What do you think about this book? Or any other
Hodder Education title? Please send your comments to
the feedback section on www.hoddereducation.com.

Contents

List of Maps	vii
List of Tables	viii
Abbreviations	ix
Chronology (1945–2004)	xii
Preface and Acknowledgements	xxi

1. Introduction — 1
   - Dynamics of the Cold War — 2
   - The End of the Cold War Debate — 11
   - The Structure of the Book — 14

2. Gorbachev's New Thinking and the Breakup of the Soviet Union, 1985–1991 — 17
   - The Soviet Union and the World Prior to the Gorbachev Era — 17
   - Gorbachev in Power — 20
   - Acceleration, Glasnost and Perestroika, 1985–7 — 22
   - From Democratization to Fragmentation, 1988–90 — 27
   - The Worsening Economy and Society, 1989–91 — 33
   - The Disintegration of the Soviet Union, 1990–1 — 36
   - The Implications of Gorbachev's 'New Thinking' — 42

3. The Decline of Communism in Eastern Europe — 49
   - The Troubled Alliance: The Soviet Union and Eastern Europe — 49
   - Signs of Soviet Disengagement from Eastern Europe?: The Polish Crisis, 1980–1 — 54
   - Gorbachev's Policy Towards Europe, 1985–8 — 59
   - Gorbachev and Eastern Europe — 62

4. The Collapse of Communism in Eastern Europe and the Unification of Germany, 1989–1991 — 67
   - On the Eve of the Fall of the Berlin Wall — 67
   - The Fall of the Wall in November 1989 — 75
   - The Winds of Change in Eastern Europe — 79
   - The Unification of Germany in the Autumn of 1990 — 87
   - Post-Cold War Europe — 92

5. Reagan, Gorbachev and the Politics of Nuclear Security 99
   Three Outstanding Issues 100
   The Turning Point: Reagan and then Gorbachev, 1984–85 105
   Meeting of Minds – from Geneva to Reykjavik, 1985–6 109
   The Conclusion of the INF Treaty in December 1987 and After 113

6. The Demise of the Superpower Arms Race 121
   The Bush Administration and Gorbachev 121
   The Malta Summit in December 1989 124
   Baltic Clouds 126
   The Washington Summit, 30 May–3 June 1990 127
   The Red Army's Retreat from Europe, 1990–1 128
   The Conclusion of the START Treaty, 1991 130
   The Arms Reduction Race Continues After the August Coup – the
      Autumn of 1991 131
   Managing the End of the Cold War 134

7. Ideology and Great Power Politics in the Third World 141
   Patterns of Soviet Policy in the Colonial and Third World 142
   The Evolution of American Ideas Towards the Third World 147
   The Vietnam Syndrome and Moscow's 'Wheel of Fortune' in the
      Third World 155
   The Return of American Assertiveness: The Reagan Doctrine 162

8. The End of Superpower Competition in the Third World 167
   Gorbachev's 'New Thinking' and Regional Conflict 167
   Afghanistan 176
   Angola and Africa 185
   Nicaragua, Central America and Beyond 190
   From Rivalry to Cooperation in the Third World?: The First Gulf War,
      1990–1 198

9. The End of the Cold War and the Road to the War on Terror 203
   The End of the Cold War 203
   Different Visions of the End of the Cold War 205
   Entering the Post-Cold War Era 212
   Beyond the Cold War 213
   The West Becomes Assertive 216
   Post-Cold War American Grand Strategy – Setting the Agenda for
      the Future 218
   9:11 – The Return of the Hegemony to the Global Security Agenda 222

Notes 229
Select Bibliography 259
Index 275

List of Maps

1. Cold War Europe, 1945–89   50
2. Post-Cold War Europe   88
3. Cold War in the Far East (Korea and Vietnam)   152
4. Cold War in the Middle East and Central Asia   160
5. Cold War in Africa   187
6. Cold War in Central America   191

List of Maps

1. Cold War Europe, 1945–89 — 50
2. Post-Cold War Europe — 88
3. Cold War in the Far East (Korea and Vietnam) — 152
4. Cold War in the Middle East and Central Asia — 160
5. Cold War in Africa — 187
6. Cold War in Central America — 191

List of Tables

1. Military Expenditure – NATO and Warsaw Pact/Commonwealth of
   Independent States, 1989–9   94
2. INF Treaty Inspections and Eliminations   116
3. Strategic Nuclear Weapons – The USA and the USSR/Russia,
   1990–2004   137
4. US Public Opinion, 1993 – post-September 2001   223

Abbreviations

ABM	Anti Ballistic Missile
ACVs	Armoured Combat Vehicles
ASEAN	Association of South East Asian Nations
ATTU	From the Atlantic to the Urals
AWAC	Airborne Warning and Control System
BBC	British Broadcasting Corporation
BSP	Bulgarian Socialist Party
CC	Central Committee (of the Politburo)
CCP	Chinese Communist Parties
CFE	Conventional Armed Forces in Europe
CIA	Central Intelligence Agency
CIS	Commonwealth of Independent States
CJTF	Combined Joint Task Forces (NATO)
CMEA (COMECON)	Council of Mutual Economic Assistance
CNN	Cable News Network
COMINFORM	Communist Information Bureau
COMINTERN	Third Communist International
CPSU	Communist Party of the Soviet Union
CSCE	Conference on Security and Cooperation in Europe
CTBT	Comprehensive Test Ban Treaty
CWC	Chemical Weapons Convention
CWIHP	Cold War International History Project
DPA	Democratic Party of Albania
DPRK	Democratic People's Republic of Korea (North Korea)
EC	European Community
EDC	European Defence Community
EEC	European Economic Community
EMU	European Monetary Union
EU	European Union
FMLN	National Liberation Front (El Salvador)
FNLA	National Front for the Liberation of Angola
FRG	Federal Republic of Germany
FRUS	Foreign Relations of the United States
FSB	Russian International Security Service

FSLN	Sandinista National Liberation Front
G-7	Group of Seven Industrialized Nations
GATT	General Agreement on Tariffs and Trade
GDR	German Democratic Republic (East Germany)
GNP	Gross National Product
GOSPLAN	Soviet State Planning Committee
GRIT	Graduated and Reciprocated Initiatives in Tension Reduction
GRU	Soviet Military Intelligence Agency
GWP	Gross World Product
HDF	Hungarian Democratic Forum
ICBM	Intercontinental Ballistic Missile
IFOR	Implementation Force
IISS	International Institute for Strategic Studies
IMF	International Monetary Fund
INF	Intermediate-range Nuclear Forces
ISI	Inter-Services Intelligence Directorate (Pakistan)
IUAM	Islamic Union of Afghan Mujahidin
KAL	Korean Airlines
KFOR	Kosovo Peace Implementation Force
KGB	Soviet Committee of State Security (Secret Police)
KHAD	Afghanistan intelligence services
MBFR	Mutual and Balanced Force Reductions
MFN	Most Favoured Nations
MI6	Military Intelligence department concerned with espionage (UK)
MIRVs	Multiple Independently Targettable Re-entry Vehicles
MNF	Multinational Force
MPLA	Popular Movement for the Liberation of Angola
MX	Missile Experimental
NATO	North Atlantic Treaty Organization
NIE	National Intelligence Estimate (USA)
NMD	National Missile Defence
NSA	National Security Agency
NSC	National Security Council (USA)
NSDD	National Security Directive (USA)
NSF	National Salvation Front (Romania)
NPT	Non-Proliferation Treaty
OPEC	Organization of Petroleum Exporting Countries
OSCE	Organization of Security and Cooperation in Europe
PAV	Public Against Violence (Slovakia)
PDPA	People's Democratic Party of Afghanistan
PLO	Palestinian Liberation Organization
PUWP	Polish United Workers' Party
RENAMO	Mozambique National Resistance
RIIA	Royal Institute of International Affairs

ROK	Republic of Korea (South Korea)
RSFSR	Russian Federated Socialist Republic (Russian Federation)
SALT	Strategic Arms Limitation Talks
SAS	Special Air Service
SEATO	South East Asian Treaty Organization
SDI	Strategic Defense Initiative
SEA	Single European Act
SEATO	South East Asian Treaty Organization
SED	Socialist Unity Party of Germany (GDR)
SFOR	Stabilization Force
SINE	Soviet National Intelligence\Estimates
SLBM	Sea-Launched Ballistic Missile
SNF	Short-Range Nuclear Forces
SORT	Strategic Offensive Reductions Treaty
SPD	German Social Democratic Party
SRINF	Short-Range Intermediate Nuclear Forces
START	Strategic Arms Reduction Talks
STASI	East German Intelligence Service
SVR	Sluzhba Vneshnei Rasvedki (Russian foreign intelligence service)
SWAPO	South West Africa People's Organization
TWA	Trans World Airlines
TMD	Theatre Missile Defence
UAE	United Arab Emirates
UDF	Union of Democratic Forces (Bulgaria)
UDI	Unilateral Declaration of Independence
UN	United Nations
UNO	National Opposition Union (Nicaragua)
UNITA	Union for the Total Independence of Angola
USGPO	US Government Printing Office
USSR	Union of Soviet Socialist Republics
WMD	Weapons of Mass Destruction

Chronology (1945–2004)

1945	8 May	Surrender of Germany and the end of the Second World War in Europe
	26 June	United Nations charter and the creation of the UN
	16 July	First atomic bomb tested at Alamogordo
	17 July–2 August	Big Three at Potsdam conference
	6 August	Atomic bomb dropped on Hiroshima
	8 August	Soviets enters the (Asia)-Pacific War against Japan
	9 August	Atomic bombs dropped on Nagasaki
	15 August	Japan surrenders (formal VJ Day on 2 September)
	9 September	GRU (Soviet military intelligence agency) cipher clerk, Igor Gouzenko, defects from Soviet Embassy in Ottawa
1946	22 February	Kennan sends 'Long Telegram' from Moscow
	2 March	USA and Britain begin to press the Soviet Union to withdraw its troops from Iran
	5 March	Churchill's 'Iron Curtain' speech at Fulton, Missouri
	1 May	Allan Nunn May found guilty of giving atomic secrets to Soviet Union
	October	Greek Civil War starts (until October 1949)
	19/20 December	First Indochina War begins
1947	12 March	Truman Doctrine announced
	5 June	Marshall Plan to promote European recovery
	26 July	CIA and the NSC created by the National Security Act
	22/23 September	Cominform established by Soviet Union
	20 October	US House of Representatives' 'Un-American Activities Committee' investigates Communist influence in Hollywood
1948	19–25 February	Communist coup in Czechoslovakia
	14 May	United States recognizes Israel

	16 June	Emergency declared in Malaya in response to Communist insurgency
	24 June	Berlin blockade and airlift commences
	24 June	Yugoslavia expelled from the Cominform
	15 August	Republic of Korea (South Korea) proclaimed
	9 September	Democratic People's Republic of Korea (North Korea) proclaimed
	6 December	Whittaker Chambers and the 'Pumpkin Papers' case against Alger Hiss
1949	4 April	North Atlantic Treaty signed in Washington
	12 May	Berlin blockade ends
	13 July	Pope Pius XII's *Apostolic Acta* condemns Communism
	29 August	First Soviet atom bomb test
	15 September	Federal Republic of Germany established
	21 September	Mao Zedong proclaims the People's Republic of China
	7 October	German Democratic Republic established
	8 December	Chiang Kai-shek retreats to Taiwan
1950	25 January	Alger Hiss is condemned for perjury
	2 February	Klaus Fuchs arrested for spying
	9 February	Senator Joe McCarthy launches his crusade against Communism
	7 April	NSC 68 recommends American rearmament
	25 June	North Korea invades South Korea and begins Korean War
	29 September	UN forces cross 38th Parallel into North Korea
	30 September	Truman approves NSC 68 as NSC 68/2.
	26 October	China enters Korean War
1951	21 March	Julius and Ethel Rosenberg convicted of spying
	11 April	General MacArthur sacked by Truman after calling for attacks against China
	25 May	Guy Burgess and Donald Maclean defect to the Soviet Union
1952	15 February	Greece and Turkey accede to NATO
	10 March	Stalin Note calling for a reunified, neutral and rearmed Germany
	1 November	US explodes the first hydrogen bomb
	4 November	Dwight D. Eisenhower elected US President
1953	5 March	Death of Stalin
	19 June	Rosenbergs are executed

	27 July	Korean War ceasefire
	8 August	Soviet Union explodes its first hydrogen bomb
	19/20 August	CIA-backed coup to reinstate the Shah of Iran
	12 September	Khrushchev becomes General Secretary of the Soviet Communist Party
	22 December	Former Soviet security chief, Lavrenti Beria, executed as a spy
1954	7 May	Vietminh defeat French army at Dien Bien Phu
	27 June	Guatemalan coup against Arbenz organized by CIA
	21 July	Geneva Accords end First Indochina War; Vietnam is divided into North and South
	6–8 September	South East Asian Treaty Organization (SEATO) established
1955	8 May	West Germany joins NATO
	11–14 May	Warsaw Pact established
	18–24 July	Geneva summit talks between Britain, France, USA and USSR
1956	25 February	Khrushchev denounces Stalin's 'cult of personality' at the Twentieth Congress of the Soviet Communist Party
	18 April	End of the Cominform
	29 April	Disappearance of Commander Crabb while spying on Khrushchev's ship
	29 October	Start of Suez Crisis
	1–4 November	Soviet Union crushes uprising in Hungary
1957	5 January	Eisenhower Doctrine announced to defend Middle East
	25 March	Treaty of Rome establishes European Economic Community
	19 September	First US underground nuclear test in Nevada
	4 October	Soviet Union launches Sputnik I
1958	29 May	General de Gaulle forms new government in France to deal with Algeria
	31 July–3 August	Khrushchev meets Mao in Beijing
	10 November	Khrushchev initiates second Berlin Crisis
1959	2 January	Fidel Castro rises to power in Cuba
1960	1 May	U-2 spy plane shot down over Sverdlovsk in Soviet Union. Pilot Francis Gary Powers captured alive

	16 May	Paris Summit meeting collapses over U-2 incident
	13–14 July	United Nations intervenes in Congo crisis
	8 November	John F. Kennedy elected US President

1961   8 February 8   Patrice Lumumba reported murdered in the
                           Congo

        17–20 April   Bay of Pigs landing
        May   Kennedy sends Special Forces to South Vietnam
        3–4 June   Kennedy and Khrushchev summit in Vienna
        19–22 August   Berlin Wall built
        17 September   UN Secretary-General Dag Hammarskjöld killed in
                           air crash in Northern Rhodesia

1962   8 February   US Military Assistance Command established in
                           Vietnam

        10 February   Colonel Rudolph Abel exchanged for Francis Gary
                           Powers

        3 July   Algeria gains independence from France
        14–28 October   Cuban Missile Crisis

1963   5 August   Nuclear Test Ban Treaty signed between Britain, the
                           USA and USSR

        16 September   Indonesia starts a 'confrontation' with Malaysia
                           (until August 1966)

        22 November   Kennedy assassinated; Lyndon B. Johnson becomes
                           US President

1964   19 May   40 hidden microphones found in US Embassy in
                           Moscow

        5 August   Johnson orders first air strikes on North Vietnam
        14 October   Khrushchev replaced by Leonid Brezhnev
        16 October   China explodes its first atomic bomb

1965   8 March   First US combat troops sent to Vietnam
        30 April   US intervention in Dominican Republic

1967   5–10 June   Six Day War in Middle East
        July   Britain announces the decision to withdraw from
                           Singapore and Malaysia

1968   23 January   North Korea seizes the US Navy ship *Pueblo*,
                           charging crew with spying

        30–1 January   Tet Offensive in South Vietnam
        1 July   Nuclear Non-Proliferation Treaty (NPT) signed by
                           Britain, the USA, the USSR and 59 other
                           countries

	20 August	Soviet intervention in Czechoslovakia
	5 November	Richard Nixon elected US President
	23/24 December	*Pueblo* crew released
1969	25 July	Guam Doctrine. American troops start to withdraw from South Vietnam
	21 October	Willy Brandt becomes West German Chancellor. Policy of Ostpolitik
	17 November	Strategic Arms Limitation Talks (SALT) begin in Helsinki
1970	4 May	Kent State University shootings during anti-war protest
1971	15 June	Henry Kissinger secretly visits Beijing
	24 September	Britain expels 105 Soviet intelligence officers
	25 October	People's Republic of China admitted to the UN
1972	21–28 February	Nixon visits China and meets Mao Zedong
	22–26 May	Nixon visits Moscow. Nixon and Brezhnev sign ABM Treaty and SALT I Treaty
		Terrorists attack the Munich Olympics
	21 December	West and East Germany sign Basic Treaty
1973	27 January	USA, South Vietnam and North Vietnam agree to ceasefire
	11–12 September	Military coup in Chile overthrows President Salvador Allende
	6 October	Egypt attacks Israel and begins Yom Kippur War
1974	8 August	Nixon resigns as a result of Watergate scandal; Gerald R. Ford becomes US President
1975	30 April	North Vietnamese troops capture Saigon and the end of the Vietnam War
	1 August	Helsinki Accords signed
	11 November	Angolan civil war
	21 November	Church Committee reports on CIA assassination plots
	21 December	Carlos the Jackal and associates take hostages from the OPEC meeting in Vienna
	23 December	Publicly identified CIA station chief Richard Welch is murdered in Athens
1976	2 November	Jimmy Carter elected US President

1977	12 July	Congress funding for neutron bomb development
	1 October	Joint US–Soviet communiqué on Palestinian rights
1978	7 April	Neutron bomb production is deferred
1979	1 January	USA and China establish full diplomatic relations
	16 January	Shah of Iran overthrown
	15–18 June	Brezhnev and Carter sign SALT II Treaty at Vienna summit meeting
	17 July	Sandinistas seize power in Nicaragua
	4 November	Iranian students invade US Embassy in Tehran and take 52 US citizens hostage
	15 November	British government publicly identify Sir Anthony Blunt as the 'fourth man' of the Cambridge spy ring
	26 December	Soviet Union invades Afghanistan
1980	5 May	Iranian Embassy siege in London brought to an end by SAS
	22 September	Solidarity movement is formed in Poland
	4 November	Ronald Reagan elected US President
1981	20 January	American hostages in Tehran released
1982	29 June	Strategic Arms Reduction Talks (START) begin in Geneva
	10–12 November	Death of Brezhnev; Yuri Andropov becomes General Secretary
1983	9 March	Reagan describes Soviet Union as an 'evil empire'
	18 March	Hizballah suicide bomber blows up US Embassy in Beirut, killing 63 people, including CIA station
	23 March	Reagan announces Strategic Defense Initiative (SDI)
	1 September	Korean Airlines flight KAL 007 shot down by the Soviet Union
	23 October	Shiite suicide bombers destroy US barracks in Beirut, killing 241 Marines
	25 October	US intervention in Grenada
	22 November	West Germany decides to deploy Cruise and Pershing missiles
	23 November	INF talks collapse
	8 December	START talks collapse
1984	9 February	Death of Andropov; Konstantine Chernenko becomes General Secretary

1985	11 March	Death of Chernenko; Mikhail Gorbachev becomes General Secretary
	22 May	US sailor Michael Walker arrested for spying for the Soviet Union
	14 June	TWA flight 847 from Athens to Rome hijacked to Beirut
	July	KGB officer Oleg Gordievsky defects
	7 October	Hijacking of the Italian cruise ship *Achille Lauro*
	19–21 November	First Reagan–Gorbachev summit in Geneva
1986	5 April	Disco bombing in West Berlin
	15 April	In retaliation for disco bombing, US aircraft bomb Benghazi and Tripoli in Libya
	11–12 October	Reagan–Gorbachev summit in Reykjavik, Iceland
	3 November	Iran-Contra scandal revealed
1987	December 8	Reagan–Gorbachev summit in Washington; INF Treaty signed
1988	15 May	Soviet troops begin to withdraw from Afghanistan (completed on 15 February 1989)
	29 May–2 June	Reagan visits Moscow
	22 July	First Soviet SS-20 INF missile destroyed at Kapustin Yar
	8 September	First Pershing IA INF missile destroyed at Longhorn, Texas
	8 November	George Bush elected US President
	23 December	Pan Am flight 103 explodes over Lockerbie in Scotland
1989	18 June	Solidarity wins Polish parliamentary election
	10 November	Berlin Wall opened
	2–3 December	Bush–Gorbachev summit in Malta
	25 December	Nicolae Ceauşescu overthrown in Romania and executed
1990	22 May	Bush signs Biological Weapons Anti-Terrorism Act
	2 August	Iraq invades Kuwait
	3 October	West and East Germany unified
	24 October	Soviet Union conducts its last nuclear test
1991	16 January	First Gulf War begins
	31 July	Bush and Gorbachev sign START I Treaty
	24 August	Gorbachev resigns as general secretary
	6 November	KGB ceases to exist. Succeeded by FSB and SVR

	21 December	Soviet Union disbands and becomes the Commonwealth of Independent States
1992	23 September	USA conducts its last nuclear test
1993	3 January	Bush–Boris Yeltsin signing of START II
	13 January	USA signs the Chemical Weapons Convention
	26 February	New York's World Trade Center underground car park bombed, wounding 1042 people
1994	22 February	CIA officer Aldrich Ames charged with selling national security secrets to the Soviet Union
1995	19 April	Murrah Federal Building in Oklahoma City destroyed by car bomb, killing 168 people
	11 July	Decoded VENONA cables released by NSA show that Rosenbergs were guilty
	19 December	60,000 NATO troops enter Bosnia
1996	13 January	Deployment of Russian troops in support of NATO-led force IFOR in Bosnia and Herzegovina
	25 June	Truck bomb kills 19 US military and injures 240 at Dhahran, Saudi Arabia
	27 July	Pipe bomb explodes at Olympic Games in Atlanta
	20 December	Authority transferred from IFOR to SFOR
1997	28 May	NATO–Russia Permanent Joint Council created
1998	7 August	Terrorist bombs destroy US embassies in Nairobi and Dar-es-Salaam
	20 August	USA targets Afghanistan and Sudan with over 75 cruise missiles
	December	Air Campaign Desert Fox launched by US and UK forces against Iraq
1999	24 March	NATO launches air attacks against the Federal Republic of Yugoslavia
	23–25 May	NATO celebrates its 50th anniversary in Washington
	19 June	Russian troops join KFOR in Kosovo
2000	26 March	Vladimir Putin elected President of Russian Federation
	12 October	Terrorist attack on destroyer USS *Cole* in the port of Aden, Yemen
	13 December	George W. Bush elected US President

2001	6 July	FBI agent Robert Hanssen pleads guilty to 15 counts of espionage and conspiracy. Life imprisonment
	11 September	Two airliners crash into the twin towers of the World Trade Center in New York; a third crashes into the Pentagon; a fourth fails to reach Washington target but crashes outside Shanksville, PA. Fatalities exceed 3000
	7 October	US and UK forces launch attacks on Afghanistan
	13 November	Northern Alliance forces seize control of Kabul as Taliban forces retreat
	22 December	New Afghan government sworn in. Shoe bomber Richard Reid attempts to blow up American Airlines flight from Paris to Miami
2002	4 February	First NATO–Russia conference on role of military in combating terrorism
	24 May	Bush–Putin signing of SORT
	14 June	Russian troops leave NATO-led force SFOR in Bosnia and Herzegovina
	2 July	Russian troops leave NATO-led force KFOR in Kosovo
	23 October	Chechen rebels seize Moscow theatre. Over 100 hostages die when government forces storm the building, using gas
2003	19 March	Second Gulf War starts with US and coalition 'decapitation attack' attempt
	1 May	Bush says Iraq combat is over
2004	11 March	Terrorist bombing on Madrid commuter trains
	24 August	Chechen terrorists suspected in two near-simultaneous plane crashes in Russia
	1–3 September	Chechen terrorists seize a school in Beslan and hold 1100 schoolchildren, teachers and parents hostage. Government forces end siege with all terrorists and 335 hostages dead
	5 November	George W. Bush re-elected US President

Preface and Acknowledgements

The Cold War dominated the international system for nearly 45 years, and exerted a significant influence over the nature and scope of the many military and political conflicts that occurred during those years. The infrastructure of governments that participated in the Cold War in a major way has not yet been transformed into a new model suitable for a post-Cold War world. We still live in a transitional period.

The Cold War has ended and has become history. Probably because of its exceptional nature and because of its curious end, the Cold War has been subjected to considerable debate and attention from the media, political scientists and contemporary historians. The BBC and CNN broadcast a 24-part television series on the subject in 1998-9. The study of the Cold War benefits from the many accounts of insiders and memoirs by policy makers, as well as from the increasing number of published official archival sources that are available in Germany, the USA, the former Soviet Union/Russia, China, and the former socialist countries in Eastern Europe.[1] Students of the Cold War can now download official minutes, memoranda and working papers from the *Cold War International History Project (CWIHP)* at the Woodrow Wilson International Center for Scholars, Washington, DC and, more recently, from *the Parallel History Project on the Warsaw Pact and NATO (PHP).*[2] In addition, there are large collections of original studies on the Cold War published in the form of book series or in academic journals, which are dedicated solely to the subject.[3] The literature covering the end of the Cold War has expanded in recent years. The majority of books are devoted to a single subject, such as the unification of Germany, or to a key country such as France, Germany, China, the USA, or the Soviet Union.[4] Given the diversity of the issues involved, the current literature on the end of the Cold War is dominated by collections of essays by multiple authors. There are relatively few single-authored volumes: Raymond Garthoff's *The Great Transition: The End of the Cold War* (1994), Don Oberdorfer's *From the Cold War to a New Era: The United States and the Soviet Union, 1983-1991* (1991), and Michael Beschloss and Strobe Talbott's *At the Highest Levels: the Inside Story of the End of the Cold War* (1993) are detailed and comprehensive treatments of the end of the Cold War. However, they are all heavily focused on superpower relations. Oberdorfer, a diplomatic correspondent on the *Washington Post*, used interviews and press records. Beschloss and Talbott wrote 'the inside story', focusing on the years 1989–91. Garthoff, a now retired Senior Fellow at the Brookings Institution, has produced an outstanding, detailed, scholarly, and rather sympathetic account of Gorbachev's Soviet Union.

These sources now enable us to discern key trends and dynamics that shaped the end of the Cold War in three main areas, namely Europe, superpower relations and the Third World. This book is a single-authored synthesis based on available sources, including those mentioned above. It does not pretend to be a work of original research, but it draws on many published primary and secondary sources already available to researchers. It is an attempt to assess the causes, the development and the outcome of the end of the Cold War, and to place it in the wider context of the history of international relations. The book also explains post-Cold War developments of the key political, strategic and military dimensions up to the present.

My main argument is that, while Mikhail Gorbachev played a crucial role in taking the initiative in ending the Cold War, the terms of the East–West peace settlement were almost exclusively decided by the West and, by implication, by the USA. The key structures of the post-Cold War world were shaped by the West. During the Cold War, the bipolar system led by the superpowers was hardly relevant to other important global trends, such as the globalization of international economy and trade, information technology, and the growth of transnational actors and institutions. These trends were led by a group of Western industrialized nations with the USA as the key player. It can, therefore, be argued that the Cold War was part of the history of the growth of American hegemonic (or dominant) power, and of the process of America's expansion of its strategic frontier to a much greater extent than it had at the end of the Second World War. Except for the Soviet Union and the Communist countries in Central and Eastern Europe, by the end of the 1970s the rest of the world was more or less under informal USA strategic, military, political, economic and cultural influences. What is remarkable is that after the 11 September terrorist attack in 2001 (or 9:11), the USA further extended its strategic reach into Central Asia (which used to be within the Soviet Union), Eastern Europe (the former socialist countries), and Iraq (Moscow's former client state). As one American critic put it, 'our "security perimeter" has grown beyond recognition, and it continues to grow'.[5]

During the Cold War, the USA developed a sophisticated and sometimes convoluted infrastructure to deal with the global Communist threat. While some of the agencies were marginalized or curtailed after the end of the Cold War, the key structure remains intact. Many of those officials and policy makers who fought the Cold War are still alive. 9:11 galvanized the USA into reviewing the soft and hard structure of US national security policy.

The difference between the Cold War and the 11 September attack is immense, but the fundamental similarity is also stunning. 9:11 was a wake-up call for pushing 'national security' back to the forefront of the national political agenda, as it had been during the Cold War. 9:11 led the USA to prepare for a surprise attack wherever and whenever this might occur. When the world entered into the nuclear missile age in the 1950s, America's initial reaction was sombre. The Republican President, Dwight D. Eisenhower, reminded his close advisers in 1960 that 'For the first time in its history the United States is now fearful, the reason being, of course, the existence of a surprise attack capability on the part of the Russians.'[6] They knew then, of course, who their enemy was, and the bipolar system in Europe was more predictable than anywhere else. However, what the USA did not know was how difficult it would become, despite its superior technology, to eliminate the deadly Soviet Intercontinental Ballistic Missile (ICBM) threat to the nation. Equally, the enemy was illusive. The USA received virtually no advance warnings of the timing or the place of the next Communist advance, from which a surprise attack could easily have been made against the USA. Communism came as close to the USA as Cuba, Guatemala, Nicaragua and El Salvador. When Robert McNamara took up the post of Defense Secretary in 1961, he knew virtually nothing about Vietnam. Nor did he know just how much his public life would be taken up with that country.

This book is about how the world has evolved in recent years and how the recent past can be linked to the present. The future is unknown to all of us, but we might be better prepared for it if we can understand our recent past more fully. Given the limitations in time and space, I have had to sacrifice much detailed information in order to produce the broad picture.

It is always nice to acknowledge the people and institutions who have supported this project over the years. I am grateful to the Department of War Studies, King's College London, for the friendly environment in which I have been able to work over the last 15 years, and also to the Norwegian Nobel Institute, Oslo, for offering me a three-month senior research fellowship (February–April 2002) when I began this project in earnest. Special thanks should go to Professor Brian Holden Reid (Head of the Department of War Studies) and Professor Geir Lundestad (Director of the Norwegian Nobel Institute) for their warm support for this undertaking. I am also grateful to the two anonymous readers of this manuscript for their valuable suggestions and comments. Numerous friends, colleagues and students have discussed various topics related to this subject with me, which stimulated my thoughts. I would like to thank particularly Jimmy Athanassiou, Professor Günter Bischof, Professor Christoph Bluth, Professor Alexander O. Chubarian, Professor Michael Cox, Professor Ennio Di Nolfo, Benjamin Fischer, Professor Beth Fischer, Professor Sir Lawrence Freedman, Professor Jussi Hanhimaki, Professor Helga Haftendorn, Professor Beatrice Heuser, Dr Geraint Hughes, Dr Michael Kandiah, Dr Ann Lane, Professor Melvin Leffler, Professor Leopoldo Nutti, Professor Lawrence Kaplan, Professor Wolfgang Krieger, Professor Wilfried Loth, Professor Andrzej Paczkowski, Sir Michael Palliser, Dr Effie Pedaliu, Professor Anita Prazmowska, CWIHP Director Christian Ostermann, Professor Marie-Pierre Rey, Dr William Rosenau, Mrs Gillian Staerck, Professor Georges-Henri Soutou, Professor Antonio Varsori, Professor Natalia Yegorova, Professor John Young and Professor Odd Arne Westad. I also thank my publisher, Hodder Arnold, and especially Tiara Misquitta (Senior Desk Editor), for their patience in waiting for this project to be completed. I am grateful to Simon Moores and Pascal Barras for their research assistance, and my warm thanks go to postgraduate students at the Department of War Studies who took my optional course on the 'Rise and Fall of the Cold War' and, in particular, those students who have since formed an informal group called 'the Old Cold Warriors', who have critically and passionately discussed with me several key aspects of the Cold War and its end. Finally, my special thanks go to Michael for his love over the years and his unfailing support for my active academic life.

Saki R. Dockrill
London, March 2005

1

Introduction

Between 1989 and 1991 the world witnessed the most dramatic and traumatic changes in its post-1945 history: the end of Communism in Central and Eastern Europe, the unification of Germany, and the breakup of the Soviet Union. By then, the East–West competition in the Third World (Afghanistan, Angola and Nicaragua) had wound down. At the war's end, the superpowers were also able to agree, for the first time, to deep cuts in their respective nuclear arsenals. The end of the Cold War was much welcomed worldwide, while its peaceful termination surprised many.

The Cold War was fought very much on the assumption that 'if you are not with us, you are against us', an assumption that figured more prominently in American society than in its Western European counterparts. Propaganda activities, information gathering and spying were part and parcel of winning the hearts and minds of allies and potential allies. To varying degrees, the Cold War became an integral part of the domestic politics of many countries, such as in the form of McCarthyism or anti-nuclear movements in Europe. The main task of fighting the Cold War in Communist countries was on their home fronts. With the help of the KGB and its offspring in the Warsaw Pact countries, it was important for these countries to control their own societies through an intricate network of intelligence and spying. After all, the beginning of the end of the Cold War in Europe was effected by the eagerness of East Berliners to travel freely, and pushing open the Berlin Wall, a fact that brought home to us the importance of the domestic front, which helped to shape the scope and nature of Cold War fighting abroad.

The Cold War was not like the conventional wars that had been fought between the great powers before 1945, but nonetheless it was a global contest and a sort of war. The Cold War shared many of the characteristics of modern warfare: ideological differences, large numbers of weapons, war plans, operational manuals, covert operations and psychological warfare, the formation of alliances, economic and trade pressures, and the control of society. However, the Cold War, thankfully, did not end in the apocalyptic phase of the Third World War by nuclear weapons.[1]

The Cold War will be remembered as a lengthy period of antagonistic East–West relations, short of going to actual war, but there was no single factor responsible for the causes, development and the end of that war. At the core of the Cold War was the mutually perceived fear of a possible attack, a fear that was fed by mutual misperceptions and mutual lack of understanding of each other. This meant that each side had a tendency to depict the other in the worst possible light, which in turn created a situation whereby both sides misread each other's intentions and overestimated each other's capabilities. The possession of nuclear weapons by two superpowers made the confrontation deadly, while the East–West ideological competition added to the dynamic to expand, and intensify, the Cold War worldwide. Unlike conventional war, the Cold War had no clear cut beginning or ending. Before discussing the end of the Cold War and after in this book, it is worth noting the key aspects of the origins and development of the Cold War.

DYNAMICS OF THE COLD WAR

The Origins of the East–West Antagonism (1917–46)

As with most other international conflicts and wars, the Cold War also had a long period of gestation. To be sure, it was not until 1946/7 that the Cold War became a reality; however, in 1835 Alexis de Tocqueville, the French historian and politician, foresaw a possible future domination of the world by the USA and Russia. The USSR, which emerged after the Bolshevik Revolution of 1917 and the Russian civil war (1918–22), was a state-controlled socialist state that believed in its eventual victory over the Western capitalist and industrialized world. From the outset the Western powers received the Soviet Union with considerable suspicion and hostility. Britain and France had sided with the anti-Bolshevik forces and even sent troops – joined by Japanese and American military effectives – to Russia during the early part of the Russian civil war to prevent victory by the Communist revolutionaries, but without success. However, despite their ideological incompatibility, Moscow established diplomatic contacts with the outside world: with Germany, Britain, France, Japan and later, in the early 1930s, with the USA, Belgium, Spain and the newly emerged states in Eastern Europe, including Czechoslovakia, the Baltic states, Poland, Hungary and Yugoslavia.[2] Mutual hostility between the West and the Soviet Union was controlled during the interwar period for three main reasons: Josef Stalin (1928–53), the leader of the Soviet Union, was more interested in consolidating his power at home than exporting the Soviet socialist system abroad; the USA had retreated into isolationism after the First World War; and Western Europe became increasingly concerned about the potentially more menacing threat from fascism, led by Nazi Germany. The conclusion of the non-aggression pact between Nazi

Germany and the Soviet Union of August 1939 (following Moscow's two previous attempts to secure a reconciliation with Germany in 1918 and 1922) increased Anglo–French fears of a German–Russian combination threatening their security.

It was only Adolf Hitler's invasion of the Soviet Union in June 1941 that finally brought the Soviet Union onto the side of the USA and Britain. However, the Grand Alliance was nothing more than a marriage of convenience and the Soviet Union often felt ignored by the much closer Anglo–American alliance. Britain was more concerned than the USA about Soviet intentions in post-war Europe and, in advance of the war's end, Winston Churchill made percentage agreements with Stalin in 1944 whereby the Soviet Union would have a 90 per cent say over Romania, 75 per cent over Bulgaria, 50 per cent over Yugoslavia and Hungary, with Britain getting a 90 per cent influence over Greece, as opposed to Moscow's 10 per cent. At the end of the Second World War Stalin was satisfied with the broad acknowledgement by the USA and Britain of the 'gains' that the Soviet Union had made in Eastern Europe.[3]

In the immediate aftermath of the Second World War the USA and Britain still hoped to work with the Soviet Union through the newly created United Nations. None of these powers wanted to destroy the wartime alliance, but the confrontation in the Mediterranean and arguments over the occupation of Germany between the four occupying powers (Britain, France, the USA and the Soviet Union) eventually led to increasing tension between East and West by the end of 1946.

The Outbreak of the Cold War (1946–8)

Pressed by Britain to deal with Communist-led guerrilla movements in Greece and the Soviet threat to Turkey, the Truman administration announced 'it must be the policy of the United States, to support free peoples who are resisting attempted subjugation by armed minorities or by outside pressure' (a passage from the Truman Doctrine of March 1947), which was followed by the Marshall Plan to facilitate Europe's economic recovery to make it less vulnerable to the Communist threat. The defining moment of the Plan was to force the Soviet Union to choose whether or not it wanted to be included in it. Stalin eventually rejected it, as he decided that it was an American attempt to control Europe. The Marshall Plan was for Moscow a challenge that Stalin decided to counter with determined opposition.[4]

There were now two power blocs led by the USA and the Soviet Union, respectively. The USA, backed by an equally determined Britain, emerged from the Second World War as a powerful and energetic state. America was deeply security conscious for historical and cultural reasons, determined to safeguard its democratic values and freedom against the encroachment of Communism in the Western world. The Soviet Union, another security conscious state, was anxious to build buffer zones in Europe and the Far East against the West.

The Cold War Intensifies (1948–53)

Once the Cold War set in, the tempo quickened. Each event and confrontation deepened the mutual suspicions of each superpower and intensified the perceived threat of the other. The final breakup of the Council of Foreign Ministers at the end of 1947 was followed by a Communist coup d'état in Czechoslovakia in February 1948, the subsequent Norwegian fear that the Soviets were about to take over their country, and finally the Berlin crisis of 1948–9. These events helped Western Europe, led by Britain, to persuade the USA to be included in a peacetime alliance, leading to the conclusion in April 1949 of the treaty establishing the North Atlantic Treaty Organization (NATO).

Cold War pressures increased further during the following two years. The successful Soviet test explosion of an atomic bomb in August 1949 precipitated America's development of its hydrogen bomb programme. In the autumn, two German states were formed: the Federal Republic of Germany (FRG) led by the West, and the German Democratic Republic (GDR) under Soviet control. The expansion of Communist influence in Asia, with the establishment of the People's Republic of China under Mao Zedong in October 1949 and the outbreak of the Korean War in June 1950, globalized the Cold War. By then Eastern Europe (Yugoslavia rejected Stalin's exclusive control and seceded from the Communist Information Bureau, Cominform in June 1948) was in a Stalinist strait jacket.

The Korean War was regarded by the West as a sign of Soviet willingness to resort to the use of force to achieve its political goals, prompting NATO to embark on large rearmament programmes, including the decision to integrate West Germany in the abortive European Defence Community (EDC) and later into NATO. These moves were seen by Stalin as the West's shift from a political to a militant approach to the Cold War.[5] From this time on, the Cold War appeared to be no longer reversible and was regarded by the West as the central feature of the international system for some time to come, which it was.

Missed Opportunities?

No doubt future studies will examine why the Cold War was left unresolved for so long. One could even argue that the outbreak of the Cold War should have been avoided, given that Stalin did not have a blueprint for world domination.[6] More importantly, were any opportunities to end the Cold War missed, for example in 1952 (with Stalin's note offering a neutral, unified and rearmed Germany), 1953 (with the death of Stalin), 1955 (the short-term 'thaw' achieved by the Geneva Conference – the first post-war high level talks between the Soviet Union, France, Britain and the USA), 1963 (after the Berlin and Cuban missile crises), or in the early 1970s (Ostpolitik and the superpower détente with Moscow and Beijing)?

The German question remained the key to the shape of the Cold War in Europe throughout that war. Stalin offered in March 1952 to create a unified, rearmed and neutral Germany, thereby preparing to abandon East Germany if he could prevent the Federal Republic of Germany from being rearmed within

NATO. The West, haunted by the memories of the Rapallo Treaty of 1922 (the normalization of relations between the Soviet Union and Germany) with its perceived ganging up of the two countries against the West, as well as by the memories of the recent war against the Germans, vehemently objected to a neutral and unified Germany that might play off the East against the West. Whether or not Stalin's offer was genuine remains controversial today, but apparently he was aware that the West would reject his note. It seems that his offer was somewhat tentative and, as the West had suspected, had more to do with his anxiety to thwart NATO's plan of West German rearmament than with the pacification of Europe.[7]

The death of Stalin in March 1953 and the subsequent efforts by the new Kremlin leadership to create a mood of 'détente' appeared to present an opportunity to the West for a direct dialogue with Moscow. During this period the Korean War was brought to an end in July 1953 and the Austrian State Treaty was signed by the four occupying powers in May 1955. While the two superpowers had been engaged in a spiralling nuclear arms race for some time, the nuclear balance in the mid 1950s tilted decisively towards the USA. NATO was strengthened by the recent Korean War rearmament and by the inclusion of West Germany in its ranks in 1955, which was followed within a week by the formation of the Warsaw Pact in the East. Western leaders were initially cautious in responding to the Kremlin's overtures since, by that time, the Cold War had become a global phenomenon, with seemingly no immediate hope of a final resolution of the capitalist and Communist divide. Britain and France were, however, more anxious than the USA to discover whether they could persuade the Russians to agree to a unified Germany that would remain in NATO.

The Kremlin, now headed by Nikita Khrushchev, initially hoped to prevent the inclusion of West Germany in NATO. Failing that, Moscow had no desire to enter into further negotiations with the West over the unification of Germany and was prepared to accept the status quo, whereby the division of Germany would continue indefinitely. The Soviet Union was more interested in using the Geneva summit as an opportunity to enhance its international standing as a bona fide superpower.[8] The timing of the July 1955 Geneva summit coincided with growing world concern about the dangers of a nuclear war breaking out between the superpowers. Thus, both the USA and the Soviet Union wanted to impress the world that they were global peacemakers and not warmongers.

However, despite the talk of 'the spirit of Geneva' the Geneva summit did not break new ground in the Cold War. Nor did that 'spirit' last long. It was soon forgotten as a result of the crises during and after 1956: the Suez Crisis, the Hungarian uprising, the Soviet launch of Sputnik I, the subsequent 'missile gap' scare in the USA, the Berlin Crisis and the erection of the Berlin Wall in August 1961, and the Cuban Missile Crisis of 1962. The thaw certainly lessened the nuclear pressures of the Cold War and also helped to achieve stability in Europe by postponing the unification of Germany. Such a Cold War respite was needed by Khrushchev, who wanted to carry out domestic reforms to make the Soviet Union more economically competitive with the West. Beyond that, neither side believed that the other was genuinely willing to negotiate a peaceful settlement of the Cold War.

Backed by the stability in Europe, the Cold War in the 1960s moved on to the Third World and Soviet rearmament. Unlike Stalin, Khrushchev showed more interest in increasing contact with the newly emerging independent states outside Europe. In response, successive US presidents (Dwight D. Eisenhower, John F. Kennedy and Lyndon B. Johnson) took the challenge at face value and fought to win credibility and prestige in the areas where the USA hitherto had had little historical connection, such as in Vietnam. America's deep involvement in Vietnam allowed the Soviet Union to catch up in arms, both conventional and nuclear.

The 1970s détente was built around the regional détente in Europe and by a series of American initiatives designed to reduce US tensions with Communist China and the Soviet Union. In February 1972, President Richard Nixon surprised the world by visiting Beijing to meet the Chinese Communist leader, Mao Zedong. The meeting contributed to the subsequent Sino–US rapprochement, which led to a significant reduction of East–West tension in Asia. Three months later, in May, Nixon held a summit meeting with Leonid Brezhnev in Moscow, which culminated in the conclusion of the first superpower strategic arms control limitation talks, SALT I. The détente was a result of Nixon's skilful exploitation of the widening rift between Beijing and Moscow, and of the West's encirclement of Soviet Russia by bringing China into the Western bloc.

Western Europe's enhanced economic position was reflected in its increasing assertiveness in pursuing détente in Europe, which resulted in German Chancellor Willy Brandt's Ostpolitik. Ostpolitik stressed the normalization of West Germany's relations with the Soviet Union and the countries of Eastern Europe, including East Germany, and thus meant the renunciation of the Hallstein Doctrine of the 1950s. Ostpolitik confirmed the status quo of the two Germanies and the division of Europe and was, therefore, welcomed by the Soviet Union. The other aspect of Ostpolitik was an attempt to 'roll back' Communism in Eastern Europe in stages. The ensuing Europe-wide détente, which culminated in the Helsinki Accords of August 1975, showed Western Europe's inclusive approach to the question of reconciliation with the Eastern bloc through the increase of trade, cultural exchanges and dialogue. How these efforts would have ended remains an unanswerable question, as a result of the abrupt end of the Cold War in the 1980s, but it seems certain that the increased contact with the Eastern bloc ultimately helped to encourage the liberation of the Eastern European countries from Soviet tutelage in the late 1980s.[9]

The 1970s détente took place against a background whereby both superpowers felt that their power bases had begun to erode. While the superpowers continued to dominate the military and nuclear fields, their dominance had become less pronounced in other areas than in earlier decades. The economic rise of Western Europe and of East Asia during the 1960s meant that Britain, Germany, France and Japan were able to occupy crucial positions in international trade and finance. These changes demanded a new international financial system. In 1973, the USA decided to end the dollar's link to gold and to float the dollar against other major currencies. This marked the end of the Bretton Woods system. The superpower 1970 détente largely derived from America's anxiety to decouple Vietnam from the Cold War by appeasing the two Communist great powers,

China and the Soviet Union, while a relaxation of tension might help the USA to fight the Cold War more cheaply.

Détente provided the USSR with another opportunity to confirm its position as a superpower, and Moscow welcomed the West's recognition of the legitimacy of the Soviet Union and its security interests. The Soviet Union, while boasting of achieving strategic parity with the USA, was somewhat hamstrung diplomatically by the fact that it had to compete with both the USA and Communist China. It was also experiencing economic stagnation at home as well as in Eastern Europe. The American initiative on détente was beneficial to the Soviet Union: the SALT I Treaty gave the Soviet Union an advantage in certain areas and, economically, the Soviet Union received generous American credits and much-needed American grain imports. However, the détente remained limited to Europe and to superpower arms negotiations. It did not apply to the Soviet/Cuban activism in Africa, Central America, and elsewhere. It eventually disappeared altogether when the Soviet Union invaded Afghanistan in 1979.

Thus, mistrust, hostility, tension, cooperation and competition were the tidal patterns of the Cold War. Invariably a period of rising superpower tension was followed by a thaw, while often a thaw was followed by another tense period. For instance, the temporary respite of the Geneva summit in 1955 preceded the Berlin Crisis and the Cuban Missile Crisis, which were followed in turn by a relatively quiescent period in Europe in the 1960s and by détente in the early 1970s, which culminated in a further phase of rising superpower tension in the Third World by the mid 1970s. By the late 1970s, the cohesiveness of Western Europe was once more in disarray over the modernization of nuclear weapons, while the USA came to see that the superpowers' SALT agreement did not increase its national security. Once again, the Cold War was back on the front pages of major newspapers.

The Second Cold War? (1979–84)

If the popular image of the 1980s was anything to go by, the decade saw two major events: the return of the Cold War during 1979–84 and the end of the Cold War in the latter part of the same decade (1985–91). With his likable personality, Mikhail Gorbachev, the new Kremlin leader, emerged on the world scene in 1985 as a hero and ended the Cold War with a touch of magic.[10] Is this really what had happened?

On the surface of it, East–West relations had deteriorated significantly by the end of 1983. The Kremlin's optimism that détente would revive after the initial 'shock' of the Soviet–Afghan War had subsided was premature.[11] The Soviet Union had also hoped that the Red Army could withdraw as soon as the Communist Afghan government had been re-established and was in firm control of the country, but this, too, did not materialize. Instead, in February 1980 Kabul had to declare martial law in the face of the growing popular protest against the Soviet-sponsored communist government, and the Red Army intensified its military campaign in an effort to stabilize the worsening situation in Afghanistan (see chapters 7 and 8).

Moreover, it was unfortunate that Moscow had to deal with the newly elected and staunch anti-Communist and conservative Republican US President, Ronald Reagan, who entered the Oval Office in January 1981. In December 1979, the British Prime Minister, Margaret Thatcher, had predicted that the world was now facing 'the dangerous decade'. In her view, in the 1980s the 'challenges to our security and to our way of life may, if anything, be even more acute than in the 1970s', which would require the West to be 'firm, calm, and concerted'.[12] As it turned out, the new American President would react to this threat more strenuously than she could have bargained for.

Reagan, a former Governor of California, had led a successful anti-Communist campaign while he was the president of the Screen Actors' Guild during the height of McCarthyism. In California, he became renowned as a tough conservative, who did not shirk from arresting anti-war and civil rights protesters on university campuses. In 1981, Reagan became a 'most unashamedly ideological post-war president', surrounded by hard-line ideologues, such as William Casey (the director of the CIA) and Caspar Weinberger (Secretary of Defense).[13]

Reagan adopted a much tougher stance against the Soviet Union than had his predecessor, describing it as an 'evil empire', and embarking on a major rearmament programme. Jimmy Carter's universalist approach with its emphasis on human rights was replaced by national security as 'the diplomatic mantra'.[14] Almost echoing current US policy under George W. Bush, America's liberal internationalist stance was replaced by unilateralism. Reagan's angry and desperate mood was reflected not only in government circles but also in public opinion. The USA had been humiliated by the continued captivity of the American hostages in Iran, while America's backyard in Central America was also in turmoil. On the eve of the presidential elections in November 1980, a large majority of those polled were convinced that the USA now faced a deep and serious international crisis.[15] In his first press conference as President in January 1981, Reagan singled out the Soviet leadership as 'immoral', stating that the Soviets were 'willing to commit any crime, to lie and cheat',[16] and reverted to the tight bipolar system of the 1950s, regarding all conflicts in the world in terms of Soviet–American rivalry. As far as Reagan was concerned, it was the Soviet Union which had exploited America's willingness to achieve détente and arms control negotiations and, as a result, it must be countered from a position of strength.

At the core of Reagan's policy towards the Cold War was the fear of the growing Soviet expansionism in the Third World. The White House was equally alarmed by Moscow's ability to deliver nuclear strikes against Western European capitals, as well as the major cities in the USA, as a result of Moscow's recent modernization of its nuclear weapons; it was appreciated that the ongoing superpower negotiations were not reducing this dire Soviet threat to Western security. In 1983, Reagan launched the Strategic Defence Initiative (SDI) or Star Wars, an anti-ballistic missile defence system in space. A successful SDI would intercept and destroy incoming Soviet missiles before they reached the USA, thereby nullifying the nuclear deterrent power of the Soviet Union. The SDI deepened the

Kremlin's concern about the fate of future arms negotiations with the USA, which were in turn adversely affected by the Soviet shooting down of the South Korean Airlines flight (KAL 007) in September 1983.

In Europe, a nuclear crisis that began mainly as a result of the introduction of a new generation of Soviet missiles in Europe in the mid 1970s, divided the NATO powers. This situation was further complicated by the growing anti-nuclear movements in the major capitals in Western Europe. If the USA was unable to address the fear of a nuclear war in Europe by supplying American missiles to counter the Soviet Union's nuclear capabilities there, the White House feared that the situation might lead to 'Finlandization', the possibility that Western Europeans 'might well shrink from actions unpalatable to the Soviets'.[17] However, the superpower negotiations over the European missiles or the Intermediate-range Nuclear Forces in Europe (INF) had stalemated and NATO decided to go ahead with the deployment of new American missiles, which began to arrive in Europe in December 1983. In response, the Soviet Union walked out of the superpower nuclear arms negotiations talks. The deteriorating super-power relationship, in turn, heightened Moscow's fear of a possible military confrontation – the so-called 'war scare' of 1983 – as a result of NATO's 'Able Archer' exercise in November 1983.[18] In 1984 Reagan's re-election as President suggested that the West's confrontational approach was likely to continue, while the Soviet Union and its Eastern European satellite countries (except for Romania) declined to attend the Los Angeles Olympic Games.[19] Thus, the picture presented here suggests that the Cold War had once again become the fulcrum of deepening East–West mistrust and anxieties.

As this book will discuss later, in fact, the situation was not as bad as it appeared. Certainly there was no united view on the Soviet invasion of Afghanistan. Some commentators thought that it was a sign of Soviet 'weakness', rather than an attempt to expand its sphere of influence, reflecting 'a defence mentality'.[20] Reagan's tough approach towards Moscow was gradually softening as early as in 1983 (see chapter 5) and, once he had put his rearmament programme in train, he felt confident that he could deal with the Soviet Union. After all, the USA sought to reduce the fear of a Soviet surprise attack and this could not be attained if East–West relations remained strained.

Indeed, at the end of the 1970s Western Europeans were enjoying the fruits of the détente, increasing trade and cultural contacts with their Eastern European counterparts, and did not want to see détente collapse. They (with the possible exception of Mrs Thatcher) were apprehensive about Reagan's hard line approach to the Soviet Union. Most Eastern European leaders were struggling to cope with the worsening economic and social conditions in their countries and Hungary, East Germany and Poland, in particular, wanted to continue to develop economic and cultural ties with the West. Europe's desire for the continuation of détente was reflected in the convening of a conference on security and cooperation (CSCE) to uphold the Helsinki Accords in Madrid between 1980 and 1983, while another pan-European negotiation on the Mutual and Balanced Force Reductions (MBFR), which had begun in 1973 in an effort to reduce the threat of the Red Army in Eastern Europe, also continued during the

'Second Cold War' period, except for a brief interruption at the beginning of 1984. As for the Soviet Union, its aim was to catch up with, and equal, the USA in arms and influence, and détente in the 1970s facilitated this process. Moscow did not want to increase East–West tension either. The Kremlin wanted to disengage from Afghanistan when conditions there stabilized. It was more the consequence of Cuba's ambitions, rather than any Soviet initiative, that some of the Third World conflicts intensified in Central America, which had so alarmed many American conservatives in the early 1980s.

Thus, the Cold War intensified in the early 1980s against the will of all the key players. Most powers, including the USA, wanted to see the nuclear weapons possessed by both superpowers being reduced in number. The rise in tension, part of the tidal patterns of the Cold War, was mainly as a result of mutual misperceptions of each other's intentions. Nevertheless, there was no reversion to the High Cold War years of the 1950s. One could, therefore, argue that the era of negotiations and increasing contact that characterized the 1970s détente was not completely dead during the Second Cold War years. Hopes of maintaining the East–West détente remained strong in Europe, while Washington too, despite its rhetoric, was not prepared to fight the Cold War outright at the cost of undermining the credibility of America's global leadership. Reagan's new Cold War policy had its limits and was largely restrained by Congress and the American people, who still suffered from the 'Vietnam syndrome'. Reagan's rearmament programme, which was seen as a dangerous sign in Moscow, was also an effort to restore America's self-confidence as a superpower and not merely to counter the Soviet Union. In both blocs, there was a continuing interest in restoring détente, which had collapsed by the end of 1970s, or managing the Cold War to respect the 'legitimate interest of both sides'.[21]

The rise of the East–West tension in the early 1980s was also accompanied in the West by the emergence of a group of heavyweight but cool-headed political elites on both sides of the Atlantic: Reagan, Thatcher, François Mitterrand and Helmut Kohl. None of them were prepared to give in to the pressures from the Eastern bloc, whether this was to do with Soviet recalcitrant attitudes over nuclear weapons or their expansionist moves in the Third World. These Western leaders were in stark contrast to the two aging and feeble Soviet leaders (Yuri Andropov and Konstantine Chernenko) who came to power in the Kremlin after the death of Brezhnev and before the emergence of Gorbachev. The broad feature of this period was for the West to respond to the Eastern bloc firmly, but not at the cost of provoking the East unduly.

Thus, the dynamics of the Cold War as outlined above were supported by a degree of stability in the international system. In September 1989, Deputy Secretary of State Lawrence Eagleburger told an audience at Georgetown University that 'For all its risks and uncertainties, the Cold War was characterized by a remarkably stable and predictable set of relationships among the great powers.'[22] Despite the differences between its members over burden sharing and nuclear strategy, the North Atlantic Alliance was able to unite during Cold War crises against Moscow and demonstrated its determination not to provide the Kremlin with any opportunity of dividing the Alliance (especially between West

Germany and the other Western European allies, or between the USA and its Western European allies). The superpowers attempted to regulate their activities in the nuclear sphere and 'cooperated' in an effort to moderate the threat caused by their ability to destroy the world with their nuclear weapons. Moreover, they also competed with each other in waging 'peace' – an attempt to outdo each other by winning international support for their respective causes, as was instanced by a series of so-called peace offensives launched by the post-Stalin Kremlin leadership in the mid 1950s.[23] With some notable exceptions, they also refrained from meddling in each other's spheres of influence, for fear that this might provoke the other side to embark on a general war – indeed, the Cuban Missile Crisis demonstrated the extreme danger of such 'meddling'. Possession of megatons of nuclear weapons, for the most part, did impose caution and restraint on the behaviour of the two superpowers. Furthermore, Washington and Moscow had, to some extent, a shared political interest in avoiding responsibility for intensifying the Cold War, although they blamed each other for creating difficulties in the way of achieving world peace.

The Cold War can, therefore, be seen to be a series of partially successful efforts, such as détente, and often failed efforts by both the East and the West to resolve mutual ideological antagonism and geopolitical competition. At least both sides appreciated the need to avoid a final battle between the two blocs at the cost of the survival of the globe. However, for Moscow the Cold War had been a lengthy struggle to achieve its rightful place in a socialist-dominated international system. On the other hand, the West had long believed that the Soviet system would eventually decay and decline and that Western democratic capitalist values would eventually prevail. As far as the West was concerned, the Cold War was, in the main, a hell of a waiting game, thereby suggesting the length of time it took the West to end the Cold War. In 1985 the West finally faced a Soviet leader who would come to accept that Moscow's interests could be met more effectively by taking on the West's values and systems and by reducing East–West tensions. This book will discuss how the West's waiting game was ended by Gorbachev's new thinking and how the terms of the end of the Cold War were shaped by the West.

THE END OF THE COLD WAR DEBATE

Partly because of the quickened pace in which the international system has evolved since the end of the Cold War, culminating in the 9:11 terrorist attack on the USA in September 2001, the history of the Cold War looked to many like a remote episode in, and even an aberration from, the often messy international relations that characterized the world before and after the Cold War. However, from the point of view of historians and those policy makers who were engaged in the Cold War, the Cold War still remains a very recent phenomenon. For years to come, scholars and observers will debate how and why the Cold War ended in the way it did.

What we know so far is that nobody was on record as having foreseen the end of the Cold War, let alone the manner in which it finally ended. There are various views on the timing of the end of the Cold War. Writing in the spring 1989 issue of *Foreign Affairs*, Michael Mandelbaum stated that 'Ending the cold war requires ending the Soviet threat to Western Europe, which requires ending Soviet subjugation of Eastern Europe, which means allowing the people of that part of the world to decide freely how to govern themselves.'[24] This argument suggests that the collapse of the Soviet Union was not an essential requirement for the end of the Cold War. Alternatively, John Mueller maintains that the ending of the ideological conflict between liberal capitalism and state socialism was more important than the ending of the nuclear rivalry between East and West.[25] If this is true, the demise of the Cold War came about during 1988 when Gorbachev claimed to have 'completely discarded the old "revolution-ary–imperial" basis for Soviet foreign policy', including the concepts of 'class struggle' and 'bipolarity'.[26]

Furthermore, in 1988 the British Prime Minister, Margaret Thatcher, announced that 'we are not in a Cold War now'. George Shultz, the US Secretary of State during the Reagan administration, recalled that by the end of 1988 the Cold War 'was all over but the shouting'.[27] Brent Scowcroft, the National Security Adviser to American President George Bush, told his colleagues in February 1989 that 'the Marxist-Leninist threat is over as an ideological and economic challenge. We won that one . . .', while the Soviet Union was 'still a considerable military threat, but even that is changing'.[28] Bush himself declared the end of the Cold War just after the unification of Germany on 22 November 1990, but before the disintegration of the Soviet empire. A historian noted that the Cold War ended accidentally 'as a result of a simple administrative error' on 9 November 1989, which led to the collapse of the Berlin Wall.[29] But the Cold War was not, of course, confined only to Europe. James Baker, the US Secretary of State during the Bush years, believed that the end of the Cold War came in August 1990 when the USA and the USSR jointly protested against Saddam Hussein's attack on Kuwait. The USA did not conclude the START Treaty (the key superpower nuclear arms agreement) until July 1991, which indicated another benchmark for the end of the Cold War.

Who ended the Cold War and on whose terms? A sizable number of scholars pointed to Gorbachev's 'new thinking' in the Soviet Union after 1985 as the main factor in the final game of the Cold War.[30] However, it may be an exaggeration to argue that Gorbachev ended the Cold War, as the terms on which the Cold War ended were quite different from what he had hoped to achieve. By 1991, the Soviet Union itself had collapsed, and by then its Eastern European empire had also gone. Alternatively, some argue that the Cold War ended because of the hardline policies adopted by the new American President, Ronald Reagan, towards the Soviet Union, which finally brought the latter to its financial and economic nemesis.[31] As has been suggested in the previous section and will be discussed in detail in chapter 5, the USA was not directly responsible for the collapse of the Soviet empire. Nor did Reagan change his stance in favour of a dialogue with the Soviet Union because Gorbachev wanted him to do so. Reagan had already made his mind up about his future policy before Gorbachev came to power.[32]

Francis Fukuyama, on the other hand, saw the end of the Cold War in more definitive terms. The Cold War had both a geographical and an ideological dimension and Fukuyama saw its demise as the 'end of history', in the sense that the ideological conflict between the two world blocs was now over and that liberal democracy had finally prevailed over Communist state socialism.[33] Similarly, the end of the Cold War was the finale of a long period of rivalry between the Soviet Union and the USA, and it was the 'global expansion of American culture' that facilitated the 'decline of the closed, command economy of the Soviet Union'. John Lewis Gaddis also takes a similar view, in that the Western pursuit of stability through the policy of containment against 'authoritarian forces throughout the world' finally triumphed.[34] One could also argue that the whole process of the Cold War was influenced by a certain dynamic – the growth of the capitalist system – and, hence, it can also be argued that the Cold War did not 'so much collapse but it was bypassed'.[35]

In a direct challenge to such 'triumphalists' (many of whom are American), their Russian counterparts argue that the end of the Cold War was the result of 'relative decline of *both* superpowers'.[36] It is true that by the time the Reagan administration had left office in 1989, Reagan's deficit financing and attempts to tackle inflation by cutting output and employment did little to encourage confidence in America's future stability. The USA, which was the world's biggest creditor when Reagan came to power in the early 1980s, became the world's biggest debtor. Half of the US population was 'worse off' in real terms than it had been in 1980. If the capitalist world had been the victor in the Cold War, it did not seem to many at the time to be a rosy and prosperous world. The American capitalist system appeared to require a radical overhaul and, eventually, this became the main task of Bill Clinton's administration.[37] The well-being of the USA in the late 1980s was the subject of intense concern in the media and in academic circles, and Paul Kennedy's *The Rise and Fall of the Great Powers* certainly had a major impact on the 'America-in-decline' debate.

If ending the Cold War was about removing the Soviet threat, the end of the Cold War did not require the collapse of the Soviet Union as a precondition. There is no denying that the fall of the Soviet Union contributed significantly to the finale of the Cold War, but it was by no means the sine qua non for that end.[38] Gorbachev sought to end the Cold War and transform the hostility between the two superpowers into a more amicable 'special' relationship; if he had succeeded in this ambition, it would also have entailed the end of the Cold War.

Seen thus, there is no consensus yet amongst scholars and policy makers as to the prescribed requirements for the end of the Cold War or as to the exact timing of that end. These indicate the diversity and complexity of the Cold War. The Cold War may have overcome the Communist challenge to the Western global order, but mistrust, suspicion and hostility were critical in sustaining the mood of the Cold War. These feelings will not be dissipated overnight. Moreover, many of the regional conflicts in which the superpowers engaged were not necessarily resolved and, more often, conflict continued or recurred. There would be (we hope) no more nuclear stand-offs between the superpowers, but nuclear weapons after the Cold War were scattered around the new Soviet successor states. The Cold War ended in many places at different times and for different reasons and this book will explain why.

THE STRUCTURE OF THE BOOK

This book will assess the development and the end of the Cold War in three key areas: Europe (chapters 3 and 4), superpower relations and the arms race (chapters 5 and 6), and the Third World (chapters 7 and 8). Each of these subjects will be discussed in two chapters – the former will deal with the evolution and changes that took place before the final phase of the Cold War, while the latter is concerned both with the last years of the Cold War and further developments after the war's end. Together with the introduction and the concluding chapter, the book can therefore be read as the key aspects of international relations from 1945 to the present.

The West did not have any clear plan to end the Cold War, but it placed the onus of changing its attitudes towards the West on the Soviet Union as the first condition for the resolution of the Cold War. Nor did the West have any intention of entering into a premature agreement with the Eastern bloc at the cost of undermining Western values and beliefs. There was also no question of resolving the Cold War by attacking the Soviet Union militarily. Accordingly, chapter 2 will examine what changes were taking place in the Soviet Union roughly from the Brezhnev period to the end of the Gorbachev era.

Chapters 3 and 4 are concerned with Europe. Chapter 3 discusses the changes in Eastern Europe after the death of Stalin and its relations with the West during the 1970 détente, and also with the Soviet Union. In part, this is the history of Moscow's weakening grip on the Soviet satellite countries in Eastern Europe. It will explain why the Soviet Union was unable to deal with the Polish crisis of 1980–1 as decisively as it had dealt with the Hungarian uprising in 1956 or Czechoslovakia in 1968. This chapter also assesses Gorbachev's concept of a 'common European home' and his assumptions about the end of the Cold War in Europe.

Chapter 4 concentrates on the fall of the Berlin Wall, the unification of Germany, the end of Communism in Eastern Europe, and after. Both Britain and France were keen to engage with Gorbachev and were interested in re-establishing détente with the Soviet Union; why, then did these powers feel uncertain, even unhappy, with the sequence of events in Europe after 1989? The final section of chapter 4 will discuss post-Cold War key developments in Europe and ask whether Europe has really been transformed into something new, as many observers had expected in 1989.

Chapters 5 and 6 examine superpower relations and the security (conventional and nuclear) dimension of the Cold War. For both Moscow and Washington, arms control negotiations were quite important, perhaps more important than any other issue during the Cold War. How far nuclear deterrence and conventional forces could provide security that each respective country and its sphere of influence needed remained controversial throughout the Cold War. The resolution of this issue required the superpowers to adopt a certain amount of trust in each other, sufficient to enter into arms control agreements in good faith. Therefore, these chapters can also be read as the process of the normalization of relations between the Soviet Union and the USA from the late 1970s to the early 1990s. The major summit talks between the superpowers, such as Geneva, Reykjavik and Malta, are fully covered in these chapters. West European security was also dependent upon the credibility of America's nuclear deterrence and its readiness to maintain its conventional forces in Europe. The Cold War turned Europe into two divided armed camps. In the East, the cohesion of the Warsaw Pact powers hinged upon the presence and combat readiness of the Red Army and, also, on a close network between Eastern European Communist rulers and the Kremlin. The security dimension of the Cold War was, therefore, integral to our understanding of the Cold War.

Overall, superpower relations did not improve as quickly as was sometimes thought by contemporary observers. Suspicions about Gorbachev's intentions and the fear of a possible replacement of Gorbachev by a hardline leader in the Kremlin remained persistently in the minds of Washington's policy makers. It was true that Reagan eventually grew to like Gorbachev, but he remained suspicious of the Soviet Union until his last days in office. Gorbachev also retained a feeling of alienation from the Western world and was often at a loss as to how far he should meet the West's interests, in order to buy its good will, possibly in the form of substantial financial assistance, to prevent the Soviet Union from disintegrating. The final section of chapter 6 will examine the legacy of the Cold War in the field of nuclear weapons and how the proliferation of nuclear weapons has created a new security problem in the post-Cold War world.

Chapters 7 and 8 are about the Cold War in the Third World. Chapter 7 will examine the evolution of ideology, culture and ideas that both superpowers held before and during the Cold War. It will then survey the major sources of the Third World conflicts in the 1970s. Regional conflicts were by no means the determinant of the Cold War, but they helped to widen and complicate it. To this end, chapter 7 will deal with the 'Vietnam syndrome' and Soviet adventurism in Africa and elsewhere in the 1970s. Chapter 8 is concerned with the final phase of the Cold War. There were a number of key factors that shaped Gorbachev's dealings with the wider world. An examination of these factors will be followed by a more detailed analysis of three key regional conflicts in Afghanistan, Angola and Nicaragua. It must be noted that the failure to resolve these conflicts became a huge obstacle to the smooth ending of the Cold War. Chapter 8 will also deal with the First Gulf War (1990–1), which, while often viewed as an example of successful cooperation between the superpowers, also showed how difficult such cooperation was.

Chapter 9 'The End of the Cold War and the Road to the War on Terror' is the concluding chapter and the findings of each chapter will first be analysed and assessed. Secondly, the chapter will discuss further developments after the end of the Cold War, from the post-Cold War years to the 11 September terrorist attack and after. The discussion will be concerned with the relevance and irrelevance of the Cold War to other global trends that ran through the Cold War and after. In this context, a set of key global problems, which have emerged on the international agenda after the end of the Cold War, will be examined, including the issue of multilateral humanitarian intervention, post-Cold War American global security policy during the Clinton administration (1993–2000) and, finally, 9:11 and the return of America to global security leadership. Donald Rumsfeld, the US Defense Secretary, recently claimed that the current American armed forces 'resemble nothing so much as a smaller version of their Cold War selves, in many ways improved but hardly "transformed" '.[39] 9:11 prompted the need for change, but the implementation of detailed and sweeping changes is likely to become the main task of the second George W. Bush administration. The shadow of the Cold War has been a long and enduring one.

2

Gorbachev's New Thinking and the Breakup of the Soviet Union, 1985–1991

THE SOVIET UNION AND THE WORLD PRIOR TO THE GORBACHEV ERA

March 1985 saw Mikhail Gorbachev's accession to power as General Secretary of the Communist Party of the Soviet Union (CPSU). He landed the top job at the age of 54, the youngest member of the Politburo (the highest executive body in the CPSU),[1] and was highly conscious of the need to reform the Soviet system and its economic infrastructure.

The decay of the Soviet system had been well under way towards the end of the Brezhnev years. On the surface, however, Brezhnev's position looked stable: the 26th Party Congress in 1981 (a year before his death) applauded him as 'an ardent fighter for peace and communism'. The Brezhnev era (1964–82) is generally regarded as a period of stability at home and of growth of the Soviet Union's military and political strength. Ordinary Soviet citizens enjoyed better living conditions, with more hospital beds and more televisions. Moscow's influence also expanded worldwide: the Soviet Union had diplomatic relations with 139 nations, compared with 74 in 1960. It traded with more than 145 states in 1980, while in 1950 the number was only 45. The official history of Soviet foreign policy proudly claimed in the early 1980s that the Soviet Union was 'one of the great world powers . . . without whose participation not a single international problem can be resolved'.[2]

However, as Brezhnev's physical strength deteriorated after 1976, so did his mental capacity to govern the Soviet Union. His laid-back approach towards the Soviet ruling elites and his inclination towards acting as a chairperson or mediator, rather than providing firm leadership over party cadres, created a cosy environment for the nomenklatua. State bureaucrats and party elites grew increasingly complacent and lazy, resulting in endemic corruption, a swelling black market and the decline of such efficiency and vitality as had previously existed in the Soviet economy. In the early 1980s, the black market practically eliminated essential commodities and consumer goods from the shops and bread had to be rationed in some areas of the country. Many factories in the Soviet Union still relied on machines that had been built in the 1940s and 1950s, while Soviet society was experiencing a sharp rise in the death rate and in infant mortality.[3]

Any attempt to analyse Soviet economic data is rendered difficult by the fact that since the late 1920s, when Stalin controlled the Central Statistical Board, the Soviet Union had had no transparent and accurate statistics. In the late 1980s it was pointed out that officially published records ignored inflation rates, while greatly exaggerating Soviet economic growth. The West's adjusted records show that the Soviet Union's claims about its economic growth during the 1970s were completely fictitious: the Soviet Union's share of Gross World Product (GWP) between 1960 and 1980 was about 11–12 per cent, as opposed to 22–5 per cent in the case of the USA and 23–6 per cent in the case of the EEC. In terms of Gross National Product (GNP) per capita in 1980, the USA was three times, West Germany nearly four times, and both Japan and Great Britain about twice as prosperous than the USSR. The real downward shift in economic performance came some time in the mid 1970s and, in the agricultural sector, in 1979.[4]

While the USA was rather more constrained in its external activities as a result of its bitter experiences in Vietnam, the Soviet Union appeared to have extended its influence in the Third World in the 1970s. This did not, however, translate into an increase in the security of the Soviet Union. China remained hostile to the Soviet Union and there were frequent military clashes around their borders. In 1979 Beijing defiantly invaded Vietnam, a Soviet ally, while at the same time developing its ties with the USA and Japan in opposition to Moscow. In Central Asia, the Soviet Union became involved in what became a ten-year conflict within Afghanistan in 1979, initially with the aim of creating a stable, pro-Soviet government (see chapter 7). In Eastern Europe, Soviet satellites became restless, suffering as they were from economic hardship, poor management and the decline of community party leadership, with the Polish crisis of 1980–1 as a glaring example.

After the death of Brezhnev in November 1982 the Politburo chose Yuri Andropov (November 1982 to February 1984) as General Secretary. At the age of 68, he had served for 15 years as chief of the KGB (the Soviet Committee of State Security) under Brezhnev. The new General Secretary was a somewhat controversial figure. He had no hesitation in resorting to the use of military power to suppress anti-revolutionary elements: he had advocated Moscow's intervention in Hungary in 1956, Czechoslovakia in 1968, and Afghanistan in 1979. He also supported Moscow's expansion of power and influence in the Third World. On the other hand, he was anxious to modernize the Soviet system, allowing it to become more competitive with the West. For example, Andropov encouraged post-1956 Hungary to remain a reform-minded socialist state, in opposition to Mikhail Suslov who wanted to reduce Hungary to Moscow's 'puppet state'. During his long reign as head of the KGB, Andropov had modernized the agency and turned it into a mainly information processing centre, although it still remained a conservative body whose foremost purpose was to preserve the

Soviet system. Ambitious and calculating, Andropov also used the KGB machinery during the Brezhnev years to promote himself to become General Secretary after Brezhnev, partly in order to put himself in a position to initiate reforms. Andropov as General Secretary stressed discipline and the need to fight corruption, and was keen to improve Soviet society and economy.[5]

Gorbachev was Andropov's most trusted young apparatchik. Having been acquainted with Gorbachev in their same home town since the late 1960s, Andropov had already spotted him as the most capable and intelligent of the younger generation of Soviet leaders. Gorbachev's responsibilities grew under Andropov's reign and he became the latter's heir apparent. Andropov encouraged experts to come up with innovative ideas to reform the Soviet economic system through the promotion of science and technology. However, Andropov was never a radical or an imaginative reformer and his brief reign represented a combination of modernism and traditionalism. His continuous heart and kidney troubles increasingly eroded the quality of his leadership, which ended with his death in February 1984.

There were two contenders to be the next General Secretary: Brezhnev's protégé, Konstantine Chernenko (72 years old) and Andropov's favourite, Gorbachev. Chernenko, with his 30-year close working relationship with Brezhnev, lacked both personality and leadership qualities, and had failed to seize the opportunity of succeeding Brezhnev when the latter died. Chernenko, however, had increased his power during the frail leadership of Andropov. Much less experienced in foreign policy than Andropov, and already suffering from lung problems, the Politburo nevertheless opted for Chernenko as a more experienced and safer pair of hands than Gorbachev, but on condition that Gorbachev should act as deputy General Secretary.[6] The stability of Chernenko's leadership rested on a balancing act between the Brezhnevites and the younger and reform-minded Andropovian faction in the Politburo; as such, the Soviet Union was unable to adopt any clear-cut policies.

Chernenko's reign lasted only 390 days (February 1984–March 1985). During this period attempts were made, with some success, to open up a dialogue with the USA modelled on the Brezhnevite style of détente in the 1970s. However, Chernenko's initial months showed that the Soviet Union was tightening its belt in order to fight the Cold War with greater intensity. Soviet defence expenditure was set to increase considerably, while Andropov's austere approach to the CPSU ruling class was relaxed. The Soviet Union boycotted the Los Angeles Olympic Games in 1984, ostensibly in return for the West's refusal to attend the Moscow Olympic Games in the wake of the Soviet invasion of Afghanistan in 1980. The Kremlin also pressurised East Germany into cancelling a planned visit by the East German leader, Erich Honecker, to Bonn in September 1984. Meanwhile, the Soviet war scare propaganda grew in intensity: NATO's 'war plans' were published, while Reagan was depicted as an American version of Adolf Hitler.[7] In the end, Chernenko did not live long enough to see the outcome of his series of half-baked conservative initiatives and he passed away on the evening of 10 March 1985. The following day, Gorbachev was elected to the leadership of the Communist Party.

GORBACHEV IN POWER

After three funerals of the three ageing Soviet leaders in 1982, 1984 and 1985, the Soviet Union at last had a youthful, intelligent and well-educated man as its leader. This was by no means inevitable, but numerous favourable conditions and a degree of luck opened the way for Gorbachev. Born into a peasant family in the Stavropol region in 1931, an area that had been under German occupation for six months between 1942 and 1943, he had otherwise little direct experience of war or of Stalin's purges. Gorbachev joined the party in 1952 and developed his career as a regional Party secretary, attempting to achieve better harvests in his home region.

In 1978, he moved to Moscow to take up the post of Secretary of the Central Committee responsible for agriculture and in 1980 was made a full member of the Politburo. Gorbachev, a lawyer by training, and his wife, Raisa Maksimovna, a well-educated and trained sociologist, represented the 'modern Soviet intelligentsia' – those expanding groups of liberal thinkers, including specialists, professionals, intellectuals, writers, scientists and artists, who were, like Gorbachev, keen to see a radical reform of the Soviet system.[8]

Given Chernenko's quickly declining health, discussions about his possible successor had been underway for some months. Gorbachev's candidature was opposed by another ageing Brezhnevite, Viktor Grishin (First Secretary of the Moscow city Party Committee) and by the hardline Grigoriy Romanov, the Party Secretary for Defence. A substantial section of the Central Committee of the Party (consisting of high-ranking Party, government and military officials, top diplomats and prominent academics) had some misgivings about the selection of Gorbachev, but his candidacy was supported by Andrei Gromyko and two chief Andropovian officials (Yegor Ligachev and Viktor Chebrikov). The Central Committee and the Politburo eventually agreed by consensus on the nomination of Gorbachev to be the next Soviet leader. Gromyko was no modernizer, but knew enough about the corruption and decay of the Soviet system during the Brezhnev era to believe that reform of the system was essential. His nomination of Gorbachev, with his famous warning that Gorbachev had 'a nice smile but he had iron teeth', was 'fortuitous', especially in view of the death of Defence Minister, Marshal Dmitry Ustinov, in December 1984.[9] Ustinov was an influential figure in the armed forces and was respected by Gromyko and other senior Party officials. Although Gorbachev felt that his relations with Ustinov had become closer during the Chernenko years, other evidence suggests that Ustinov, a Stalinist conservative, did not reciprocate Gorbachev's warm feelings towards him. Ustinov's death cleared away the possible complications that may have emerged in the leadership contest. Moreover, Gorbachev, in carefully measured speeches, presented himself as one of the Andropovian moderate reformers, which helped to allay the old guard's suspicions of his intentions.[10]

Probably Gorbachev himself was unsure exactly what changes he was going to bring about in the Soviet Union at that time. Walking in the garden with Raisa at their Moscow apartment, Gorbachev discussed with her whether or not to take up the post. He recalled that 'if I really want to change something I would have to accept the nomination . . . *We cannot go on living like this.*'[11] His initial thoughts were focused on the much-needed improvement of the Soviet economy and his strong desire to cut back on Soviet arms expenditure. In doing so, he wished to create a favourable international atmosphere for the Soviet Union by opening up a dialogue with the West.[12]

The Soviet Union, one of the most ethnically diverse and heterogeneous countries in the world, was ruled by the Communist Party from Moscow. The state was the virtual owner of all property, land, buildings and machinery. On paper, there were two distinct organizations, the Party and the government, but in reality senior Party members occupied all key state and local government positions. The USSR State Planning Committee (Gosplan) was responsible for the entire country's planning and for the allocation of goods and resources. Party decisions were final and were above the law. Party officials were immune from civil prosecution, except for Party disciplinary action. The Soviet system, created by Lenin and Stalin, had no room for any accountability to its citizens and lacked flexibility in responding to the needs of lower levels. It was an undemocratic system, but was paradoxically called democratic centralism. Power, exclusively and entirely, resided with the CPSU. While this was obviously convenient for the ruling class, its increasing shortcomings were producing a 'pre-crisis' situation in economic and social terms. The Soviet Union, supposedly a superpower and the leader of the Eastern bloc, found itself in an embarrassing situation. Gorbachev was appalled to find that the real per capita income of the Soviet Union was the lowest of its fellow socialist countries, let alone the major industrial Western states.[13]

How could the Communist system be reformed without creating chaos? Richard Sakwa argues that 'communist reformism' is a contradiction in terms. Gorbachev's predecessors, Khrushchev, Kosygin and Andropov, tried to reform the system in varying degrees, but stopped short of upsetting the existing system itself. Gorbachev, too, aimed to improve the Soviet system and he remained committed to the Party until his last days in power. He also believed that the system could, and should, be reformed, rather than be replaced with something new. However, the Soviet system, in the words of Rachel Walker, 'was balanced like a house of cards – any movement in one card risked the collapse of the whole structure', but Gorbachev did not appreciate this.[14]

As he was aiming at reforming the Party from within, he needed to bring reform-minded allies into the Politburo. In April 1985, Gorbachev promoted three Andropovian colleagues, Viktor Mikhailovich Chebrikov (chairman of the KGB after 1982), Yegor Kuzmich Ligachev and Nikolai Ryzhkov, to full Politburo membership. Ligachev, now number two in Gorbachev's team, proved useful in strengthening Gorbachev's leadership during the initial years, but he was eventually to break his ties with Gorbachev. Ryzhkov, with his experience and knowledge of the Soviet economy, was important for Gorbachev's economic reforms. In September 1985, Ryzhkov was made Prime Minister (also known as the Chairman of the Council of Ministers).

Gorbachev also promoted a group of liberal thinkers to numerous key posts. Vladim Medvedev, a former director of the Academy of Social Sciences, was the theoretical exponent of Gorbachev's position. Having worked as the head of the Department of Science and Education for a few years, he was made a full Politburo member in 1988. After the demise of the Soviet Union, he continued to work with Gorbachev at the Gorbachev Foundation. In July 1985, Gorbachev surprised the Kremlin by appointing Eduard Shevardnadze, the then Georgian Party Secretary, who was probably the closest to Gorbachev's political outlook, as Foreign Minister. Shevardnadze, who had no experience of Soviet foreign affairs, replaced Gromyko, who was given the prestigious but powerless post of the President of the Presidium of the Supreme Soviet. Another major ally and intellectual companion of Gorbachev was Alexander Yakovlev, who had met Gorbachev in 1983, when he had been completing his ten-year assignment as Soviet ambassador to Canada. Yakovlev was one of the so-called Westernizers and a Europhile and in late 1985 Gorbachev asked him to take on the post of Central Committee Secretary for Ideology. Yakovlev was regarded as one of the strongest promoters of Glasnost and the democratization of Soviet society and he wrote most of Gorbachev's speeches concerning international affairs.[15] In 1987 he was promoted to a full Politburo member (until 1990). In 1986, another pro-Western diplomat, Anatoly Dobrynin, the long-serving ambassador to the USA, replaced Boris Ponomarev as head of the International Department.[16]

Within the inner circle of Gorbachev's confidants, it is worth mentioning two liberal thinkers, Anatoly Chernyaev and Georgy Shakhnazarov. Chernyaev, appointed Gorbachev's foreign policy aide in February 1986, remained one of his 'most reliable and faithful' assistants.[17] Chernyaev promoted the intellectual ideals behind Gorbachev's new thinking in foreign policy. Similarly, Shakhnazarov worked closely with Gorbachev from February 1988 as his aide on Eastern European affairs and also Gorbachev's domestic political reforms. Shakhnazarov, like Chernyaev, was attracted to social democratic thought; he had a similar working experience to that of Chernyaev in Prague, involved in publishing a Communist revisionist magazine, the *World Marxist Review,* and had contributed towards Gorbachev's drive towards achieving a 'humane, democratic, socialism'. Thus, Gorbachev surrounded himself with a group of pro-Western and liberal thinkers as his colleagues or assistants, who were to exert varying degrees of influence on the General Secretary when he set about reforming the Soviet Union, as well as changing the atmosphere of the Cold War.[18]

ACCELERATION, GLASNOST AND PERESTROIKA, 1985–7

Upon becoming General Secretary in April 1985, Gorbachev spoke to the Party Central Committee about the urgent need for 'the scientific and technological renewal of industry and the achievement of the labour productivity that is equal to that of the developed capitalist states'.[19] At the 27th Party Congress in February 1986, the 12th five-year economic plan (1986–90) was adopted, which aimed at doubling industrial output by 2000. Indeed, Gorbachev increased the target figures set by the Gosplan to almost unrealistic levels, as he believed that higher targets would help to galvanize the Soviet people into becoming a hard-working, self-disciplined and efficient labour force.[20]

However, the Soviet government did not possess sufficient resources to make these optimistic plans successful. No new investment in technology or in the training of the work force was on offer. The result was predictable. The new targets forced workers to work extended hours with no financial incentives and they eventually became exhausted and demoralized. Inspectors were rejecting more goods because of their poor quality and this, too, was affecting production levels.[21] The most damaging act of all during the initial 'acceleration' period was an anti-alcohol campaign. In April 1985, Gorbachev (who himself was a modest drinker) followed in Andropov's steps and launched a sweeping campaign against alcoholism to eradicate drunkenness and its related social problems. The campaign did much to reduce the quantity of alcohol available to the public, but did not cure the habit of drinking. Some turned to the black market or brewed strong home-made liquor. Others resorted to far more dangerous alternative drinks, including perfume and anti-freeze. The anti-alcohol campaign also harmed the state revenue, which recorded a loss of alcohol taxes of 12 per cent; to fill the gap, the government printed more bank notes, which increased inflation. Eventually, by 1988 the campaign faded away.[22]

These initial measures to accelerate the economy – really the continuation of Andropov's 'authoritarian perestroika' – backfired.[23] Gorbachev gradually realized that the Soviet economy could not be improved in the long run without undertaking a major political reform of the system of government and the modernization of Soviet society. To this end, Gorbachev launched the twin concepts of Glasnost (openness) and Perestroika (restructuring). Glasnost was designed to 'expose Soviet society to criticism and self-criticism' in the hope that this would help to root out corruption and economic mismanagement.[24] This meant increasing the circulation of information in society, loosening central political control over the media, and encouraging relatively free artistic and literary activities. Perestroika under Gorbachev came to mean reforming and improving all aspects of Soviet society, its economy and the Party-state political systems, and the term was used synonymously with Gorbachev's policy of reform.[25]

While Gorbachev had talked about these concepts before coming to power, they did not become the key elements of his policy until mid 1986. The Chernobyl nuclear disaster on 26 April 1986, which killed nearly 8000 people, exposed the weaknesses of the Soviet system to the world. The Kremlin acknowledged the incident only two days after it took place, after the Western media had reported the tragedy. Attempts to play down the scale of disaster by regional political authorities, and also to avoid public panic, were behind the causes of the late acknowledgement and the scarcity of factual information about the disaster; however, they were enough to convince Gorbachev of the need to accelerate Glasnost and to place it at the top of his political agenda.[26]

By the summer of 1986, there were signs that the media were circulating more information to the public, while the state censorship system was being relaxed, if not completely abolished. Andrei Sakharov and other dissidents were released from exile by the end of that year. Given his educational background, Gorbachev was especially keen to involve liberal intellectuals actively in the Glasnost movement. Within the following year, thousands of banned books were returned to public libraries and news reports became more accurate, now reporting corruption, crimes, drug taking, poverty and other social problems. It was also discovered that school history textbooks were far removed from the actual course of Soviet history and, as a result, Gorbachev ordered the cancellation of history examinations in schools in 1988 until more accurate textbooks became available.[27]

The Soviet past was re-examined critically. The corruption of Brezhnev's relatives and close associates was publicly scrutinized and his son-in-law was arrested in 1987 on a charge of bribery and sentenced to 12 years' imprisonment in a labour camp. Brezhnev's daughter, Galina, and other family members lost their special pensions and privileges. At the end of 1988, Brezhnev's name was removed from numerous places and buildings that had adopted his name.[28] Following de-Brezhnevization came de-Stalinization. Khrushchev was favourably regarded by Gorbachev, as the former had courageously denounced Stalinism in 1956. During a speech on the 70th anniversary of the revolution in November 1987, Gorbachev announced that a special committee would be set up to examine Stalin's crimes. In 1988 some 600 victims of Stalin's purges in the 1930s were cleared and their honours, some posthumously, restored. For example, Nikolai Bukharin's membership was restored and he was reinstated as a member of the Academy of Sciences.[29] Gorbachev was not prepared to denounce Lenin, whom he respected and, indeed, Gorbachev used Leninist theory and practice as his ideological base. While he eventually departed from Leninism he did so almost subconsciously as he later moved closer to democratic socialism. However, he continued to believe that the CPSU should take a leading role in making Glasnost and Perestroika successful. At the January 1987 Central Committee plenum[30] Gorbachev insisted on the need to democratize the political system and to introduce 'truly self-governing principles', which could be done, in Gorbachev's view, within the framework of Lenin's socialist ideas.[31]

Glasnost was intended as a form of public control over the state-party nomenklatura, who would become more accountable to the Soviet people.[32] At the end of the process, Gorbachev hoped, Party–state–public relations would improve, the country would begin to thrive, and this would strengthen public confidence in the Party's leadership. These expectations were ultimately to crumble, as the economic situation got worse, while his political reforms began to founder after 1989.

Glasnost did Soviet society some good, however. Previous leaders, including Lenin, Khrushchev and Brezhnev, had resorted to the limited and pragmatic use of Glasnost for their own purposes, but Gorbachev went much further than his predecessors would have done. In 1989 a large number of those polled answered that Glasnost was the most remarkable aspect of Gorbachev's initiatives, followed by economic reform, changes in the government and electoral reform. By the end of 1987 the country saw the rise of an increasing number of social and semi-political activists. While most were engaged in organizing entertainment events, a limited range of political activities was allowed to emerge by the formation of environmental lobby groups. Nearly half of Soviet citizens who had previously listened to Western radio broadcasts now switched to the Soviet media. By the end of 1988, official secrets were reduced by about one-third and, by then, the jamming of Western Russian-language stations, such as Radio Liberty, had also been abandoned. In the same year, the All-Union Centre for the Study of Public Opinion of Socio-Economic Problems was founded to provide a more reliable polling service.[33]

It was much more difficult to achieve economic reforms. The main purpose was to decentralize partially and at some local levels the Soviet economic command system. The Law on State Enterprise (1987) provided local farm and factory managers with more autonomy, while workers now elected their own managers. The Law on Co-operatives (1988) legalized small private businesses, mostly in the service sector. In reality, the limited introduction of a market economy with little knowledge of how the free-market system actually worked created confusion and difficulties. Soviet economic performance, in the meantime, was deteriorating: national income, industrial output and agricultural output all declined between 1986 and 1987. In October 1988, nearly 50 per cent of the state-owned enterprises recorded losses, while nearly 20 million people (out of a 135 million work force) were unemployed.[34]

Gorbachev took a middle of the road approach to Soviet economic policy and was willing to let various ideas be discussed before he acted on any of them. He somehow believed that a slow relaxation of the central management of the Soviet economy would yield dividends in the end. This rather laid-back approach was reflected in Gorbachev's slogan to '[m]ake the economy more economic'.[35] By 1987, Gorbachev's policy of reform (Perestroika) was being questioned increasingly by both factions: Party-state conservatives (including the Andropovian reformers, Ligachev and Cherbrikov), and radical reformers (led by Boris Yeltsin, who had been promoted to head the CPSU Central Committee Construction Department in April 1985 and then, in December of that year, to first secretary of the Moscow Party Committee). Conservatives increasingly suspected that Perestroika was, in fact, undermining the central authority of the CPSU and, with it, came the prospect of losing their perks and privileges. Radicals, on the other hand, worried whether the implementation of Perestroika was too slow and insufficient, for they believed that the Soviet Union should move more rapidly towards full public participation in politics and a free market economy.[36]

Yeltsin had been educated at a polytechnic, had become an engineer in the building trade, and had similar experiences in regional politics to those of Gorbachev. While both men (born in the same year, 1931) were ambitious reformers, they had completely different temperaments. Yeltsin was combative, impulsive and erratic at times, and had a tendency to risk 'brinkmanship' rather than engage in negotiations. Gorbachev, the more intellectual of the two, retained a confident and measured outlook as a man who disliked confrontational approaches to the problems he faced. Gorbachev had climbed up the career ladder more quickly than Yeltsin, who was promoted to a candidate member of the Politburo only in 1986 and whose frustration grew as Gorbachev did not take him into his inner political circuit, treatment which he considered unfair. The General Secretary found Yeltsin's manner crude and lacking in diplomacy and the tensions between the two intensified in 1986, as Gorbachev disliked the 'populist style' of Yeltsin's campaigns against corrupt party officials and civil servants in Moscow.[37] It was only a matter of time before the two became rivals rather than partners.

In October 1987, during a Central Committee plenum meeting, Yeltsin's 'long knives' were out against both Gorbachev and conservative officials. Yeltsin warned of the growing public disenchantment with Perestroika and also of glorifying a General Secretary (Gorbachev) who was immune from criticism or legal prosecution. During the meeting, Yeltsin announced his intended resignation both from the Politburo and from his post in the Moscow Party.[38] Gorbachev was furious and stormed out of the plenum for half an hour. On his return, he denounced Yeltsin's work in Moscow in an 'almost hysterical' tone.[39] This so-called Yeltsin affair developed further in a bizarre way. In early November, Gorbachev ordered Yeltsin, who was in hospital, to attend the plenum of the Moscow City Committee that would discuss his proposed resignation. The cause of Yeltsin's hospitalization has never been clarified – it was rumoured that he had attempted to commit suicide with scissors and was found covered with blood (as both Yeltsin's bodyguard and Gorbachev claimed) or that he had been taken to hospital 'with a severe headache and chest pains' (as Yeltsin explained).[40] According to Yeltsin, the doctors heavily sedated him, dragged him out of bed, (he felt like a 'robot') and put him into a car, which drove him to the Moscow City Committee to be dismissed. He was 'barely conscious' during the meeting, while his resignation was discussed and accepted by the Committee. The incident cast a long shadow over the future of the Gorbachev–Yeltsin relationship. Yeltsin felt humiliated by Gorbachev – the incident left 'a rotten taste' in Yeltsin's mouth for a long time to come. In February 1988 (by which time Yeltsin was out of hospital), the Central Committee plenum also accepted Yeltsin's resignation.[41]

Gorbachev, then, still commanded popularity and confidence at home and abroad. His earnest style of international diplomacy and his ideas of creating a less militant and more cooperative world were beginning to be taken seriously by American and Western European leaders. Gorbachev was steadily achieving a thaw in the Cold War, largely through unilateral concessions on the part of the Soviet Union. Following his call for the elimination of nuclear weapons from the world in January 1986, the General Secretary persuaded the Politburo, in February 1987, to agree to withdraw all medium-range nuclear missiles from Europe; later in April he also offered the Americans the destruction of all short-range Soviet missiles in Europe and in Asia (see chapters 5 and 6). The decision to withdraw from Afghanistan became public knowledge by 1988[42] (see chapter 8). In the USA, a number of summit talks with President Reagan established Gorbachev in American eyes as a popular international statesman. For example, in mid 1986, just over half of American poll respondents viewed Gorbachev favourably and the figure rose to over 70 per cent by the time of the Moscow summit in May 1988. Gorbachev's first book, *Perestroika and the New Way of Thinking for our Nation and the World* (published in November 1987), became an enormous success with sales of 5 million copies in 160 countries. Despite the growing divisions within the Soviet Communist Party and the slow and difficult progress of Perestroika, Gorbachev managed to integrate his diplomatic successes with his domestic politics and the Soviet public was genuinely pleased with the lessening of East–West tensions, for which Gorbachev's efforts were given due credit both within and outside the Soviet Union.[43]

FROM DEMOCRATIZATION TO FRAGMENTATION, 1988–90

By 1989 Gorbachev had become hostage to the reforms that he himself had initiated for his cause, for his Party and for his country. If Glasnost aimed at changing the mindset of the people and officialdom, Gorbachev's political reforms began to touch on the core of the Soviet problem, that is an attempt to democratize the Soviet system itself.

At the twice-postponed Central Committee plenum, which began in late January 1987, the General Secretary stressed that democratization of the political system was crucial to the socio-economic improvement of Soviet society. He openly criticized Party-state officials for their 'conservative sentiments, inertia, [and] a tendency to brush aside anything which did not fit into conventional patterns'. It was, in Gorbachev's words, 'either democracy or social inertia and conservatism'. A small step was taken in this direction. In the June 1987 local elections, for the first time in the Soviet system, 5 per cent of the constituencies allowed voters to choose from multiple candidates.[44]

The democratization of Soviet society had also opened up a Pandora's Box of increasing nationalism and separatism. The Soviet Union had a population of some 287 million, consisting of more than 100 different nationalities, with a large Muslim population in Central Asia. The country was a federation of 15 different Union Republics of various sizes and different historical, cultural, ethnic and religious orientations, with each republic containing various national groups. Russians made up 51 per cent of the entire population of the Soviet Union, 85 per cent of them lived in the Russian Republic, the largest of all the republics. The Russian Republic contains more than 100 other nationalities who represented, in 1989, half of the Republic's population. Russians, the dominant race in the Soviet Union, did not necessarily benefit from Moscow's control of the Union, as many non-Russian republics were receiving more subsidies than the Russian Republic. As Mark Galeotti states, the 'dominant group was not a race but a political class largely comprising Russians and other Slavs'.[45] According to the 1977 constitution, these Union Republics were incorporated into the Soviet Union on a 'voluntary basis' and they were guaranteed a right to conduct their own local and foreign affairs, each having its own parliament and government. In reality, however, the Soviet Union was 'national in form but socialist in content', held together under the principle of 'democratic centralism'. Accordingly, the Russian language and culture were imposed on the republics and the entire country was governed and controlled by the Politburo headed by the General Secretary.[46]

Nationalities and ethnicities had been a delicate and challenging problem for the Soviet Union, but they had always been controlled by the Party elites through the legitimacy of Communist ideology and, sometimes, by the use of force and terror, especially during the Stalin years. Glasnost also provided an opportunity to debate hitherto taboo issues, such as the crimes committed by Stalin.

The media engaged in a lengthy discussion about how many people Stalin had killed. A number of mass graves of Stalin's purges between 1937 and 1941 were found near Kiev, near Minsk, near Leningrad (renamed St Petersburg) and in Moscow. The 'secret protocols' contained in the Nazi–Soviet Pact of 1939, which led to the occupation of the Baltic Republics (Estonia, Lithuania and Latvia) by the Soviet Union in 1940, were published in the Baltic press in 1988 and in the following year the Kremlin acknowledged the existence of these documents.[47] Except for brief and failed attempts to democratize the country in the aftermath of the Russo-Japanese war in 1904–5 and during the first revolution in 1917, the Russian empire and the Soviet Union had never experienced democracy in the Western form. Gorbachev was the first Soviet leader to walk into such uncharted territory.[48] He took the view that democratization would improve state–Union relations, and believed that 'any nationalist chauvinistic trends' could be resisted only by 'consistent, sustained internationalism'.[49]

Moscow's effort to temper anti-Soviet and anti-Russian sentiments did not prevent a series of demonstrations and riots from breaking out in the republics. In December 1986, in the capital of the Kazakhstan Republic in Central Asia, crowds protested against the selection of a new Russian Party leader for the republic, which had a large Russian population (some 41 per cent). The Central Asian Republics are the most ecologically damaged and economically deprived regions of the country. Their inhabitants live in high mountainous areas and are heavily dependent upon the production of cotton and silk. The region was particularly affected by Stalin's mass deportations of people, who were transferred to other regions and abandoned there.[50]

Grievances against Stalin's repression also remained strong among the Crimean Tartar population within the Russian Republic, whom Stalin deported during the latter stages of the Second World War on suspicion of their having collaborated with the Germans. In the summer of 1987, some 700 Crimean Tartars demonstrated in Red Square, asserting their right to return to their Crimean homeland. In the same summer, thousands of Baltic people demonstrated on the anniversary of the Nazi–Soviet Pact on 12 August, protesting against the forceful annexation of their countries into the Soviet Union. In February 1988, nationalist tensions between Armenia and Azerbaijan took a violent form over a long-term territorial dispute concerning Nagorno-Karabakh, an autonomous region that had been transferred in 1921, by Stalin's order, from Armenia to Azerbaijan.[51]

Party Conservatives grew uneasy with Gorbachev's democratization of Soviet society. His reform initiatives, such as the anti-Stalin campaign, destroyed the myth about the glories of socialism and undermined the unity and credibility of the CPSU. Abroad, Gorbachev's peace offensives were reducing Soviet military power and political influence; the Soviet military were unhappy with reductions of conventional and nuclear weapons and were reluctant to withdraw from Afghanistan. The Nina Andreeva affair in March 1988 epitomized the conservatives' grievances against Perestroika/Glasnost.[52]

A conservative newspaper, *Sovetskaya Rossiya*, published a letter entitled 'I cannot go against my principles' written by Andreeva, a chemistry teacher in

Leningrad, apparently under Ligachev's influence. The letter lamented the excessive criticisms of Stalin and the dilution of the ideological tenet of the class struggle between capitalism and socialism, and criticized Perestroika as an anti-socialist phenomenon. This was the first direct attack against the leadership and Gorbachev took the letter as 'a frontal assault on the reform process', and secured a lengthy rebuttal in a *Pravda* editorial column three weeks later.[53]

Undeterred, Gorbachev was determined to press ahead with further radical reform programmes at the 19th Party Conference in July 1988 (which had been convened for the first time since 1941). The conference witnessed remarkable disagreements between conservatives and radicals, for the speakers were allowed to express their views by abandoning the traditional conference style. Gorbachev's ideals were high: he spoke of creating a 'democratic and humane' socialism by abandoning 'everything that deformed socialism in the 1930s and that led to its stagnation in the 1970s'.[54] The Soviet leader combined the essence of Lenin's call for 'people's power' with his acquired knowledge of the liberal democracy practised in the West. Thus, soviets (councils) would be empowered as legislative bodies to oversee the executive bodies of local and central governments, which were in turn to be monitored by an independent judicial system. His goal was to reduce the executive power of the CPSU and move towards a state governed by law. A series of resolutions Gorbachev put forward at the 19th Party Conference were accepted and further discussion followed in the autumn in the Politburo and the Central Committee. On 1 December 1988, the Soviet Union adopted a new electoral law and amended the 1977 constitution accordingly, by changing nearly one third of the articles contained in the Brezhnevite version. Political reform embraced the following three key aspects: the creation of the Congress of People's Deputies, the formation of a revamped and working parliament (the Supreme Soviet), and the 'democratization' of the Party's institutions.[55]

The Congress of People's Deputies would be made up of 2250 members, two thirds of whom would be elected nationally and on a regional basis. One third of the deputies would be nominated by various social organizations, in which the CPSU was to be guaranteed 100 seats. The Congress would in turn select a full-time Supreme Soviet (parliament), comprising 542 members, to replace the existing nominal Supreme Soviet. The new Supreme Soviet would elect its chair as the head of state (to be known as President), a title usually assumed by the General Secretary of the CPSU (i.e. Gorbachev). Under this system, the Supreme Soviet would meet more often than previously – now for three to four months twice a year – and would be empowered to oversee closely the work of the government.[56]

In parallel with this move, Gorbachev also downsized and simplified the CPSU apparatus as a step towards decoupling the functions of the government and of the Party. Not only was the number of Central Committee Departments reduced from 20 to 9, but the Secretariat of the Central Committee (an administrative body to implement the decisions made by the Politburo) was replaced by six new Central Committee Commissions. This shift was intended to give more power to Central Committee members to influence the decisions of the Politburo. The division between the executive and administrative branches within the Party apparatus would be blurred, with each Politburo member responsible for implementing specific policy decisions made by the Politburo – much like a 'traditional cabinet system'.[57]

Taking advantage of this series of political reforms, Gorbachev made further personnel changes to enhance his position within the Politburo in the autumn of 1988, with Yakovlev appointed as head of the new commission on international policy. Ligachev was put in charge of a difficult commission on agriculture, thereby effectively removing him from the centre of the policy-making process. Gorbachev's other colleague, Medvedev, succeeded Ligachev in heading the ideology commission, responsible for propaganda, culture and education. More controversial was Gorbachev's appointment of Vladimir Kryuchkov to be the head of the KGB. Kryuchkov proved to be more conservative than the former head, Chebrikov, and became one of the initiators of the 1991 coup. Chebrikov, like Ligachev, had become increasingly unhappy about Glasnost and Gorbachev moved Chebrikov from the KGB to become the chief of the new legal policy commission to oversee Gorbachev's legal reforms, although his incumbency was short-lived – in September 1989 Chebrikov resigned from the Politburo. Gorbachev's long-running concern was the composition of the Central Committee. At the time of the Party Congress in 1986, the Central Committee was largely filled with Brezhnevite traditionalists. Gorbachev used the April 1989 plenum to persuade some of them to retire before the next Congress (due to convene in 1991). Some 74 full members plus 24 candidate members departed from the Central Committee, including Gromyko. As a result, the total membership of full and candidate members was reduced by 21 per cent to 360.[58]

Altogether, the Party would now no longer exercise extensive control over the economic and social management of the country, but its guiding role as the beacon of the country would not disappear. This created an enormous contradiction in the reformed system. How would the CPSU retain its authority and function in a law-based society? The political reforms suffered a number of limitations and compromises and fell far short of the Western style of liberal democracy. Gorbachev was in fact treading very carefully on slippery ground. He was still General Secretary of the CPSU, and his reforms indicated that party officials would still remain influential in the new structure of the government. The election of the first People's Congress was set for March 1989, the process and outcome of which further revealed the weaknesses of the new political system.

First of all, the new Congress guaranteed 100 out of the total of 750 seats for the CPSU in the third chamber, which comprised deputies from the social organizations. Moreover, most of these organizations, such as the women's council and the Komsomol (the Lenin Young Communist League), were under the influence of the Party. The Party could exert influence over one third of the Congress and, by implication, retain the power to decide the membership of the Supreme Soviet. The rest of the Congress was made up of elected members, but the Party still retained substantial control over the process of the election. In order to be nominated as a candidate for deputy, he/she needed to be approved first by a selection committee in his/her constituency. Predictably, anti-Party candidates were unlikely to be nominated in the first place, or they had to go through extra hurdles and harassment if they were ever to be nominated. On the other hand, Party members could exploit loopholes easily and make their way on to the Supreme Soviet. As a result, the CPSU was able to secure Party candidates in more than a quarter of the constituencies. For example, the Academy of Sciences did not nominate Sakharov, the Nobel Prize winner, and it required a series of grass-root campaigns before this decision was reversed.[59]

The outcome was, therefore, rather a mixed bag. The CPSU dominated the new Congress by taking 87 per cent of the seats, a proportion that was higher than in the old Supreme Soviet (73 per cent) and more than half of these people were career bureaucrats. There were, however, notable defeats in the Baltic Republics, where popular fronts mounted serious challenges against conservative Communist elites. The Latvian Prime Minister was voted out and in Lithuania both its President and Prime Minister were defeated. A sizeable number of Communist regional and state party elites (34–38) were defeated throughout the country and they did not do well in the big cities, such as Moscow and Kiev. Nonetheless, Gorbachev was generally pleased with the outcome, which marked, in his eyes, 'a victory for Perestroika and a defeat for Conservatism'. The newly elected Congress included fewer workers and women deputies, but more professionals, prominent scientists like Sakharov, literary critics, and outspoken political commentators like Roy Medvedev. Yeltsin was, against pressure from CPSU conservatives, elected to the Congress with the largest number of popular votes amongst all the elected deputies.[60]

The 1989 nationwide contested elections elicited enormous popular enthusiasm, but the people were soon to be disillusioned by Gorbachev's political reforms. On 25 May 1989, the newly elected People's Congress began its first session, which was broadcast on TV and radio. The audience was surprised to see or hear how openly deputies admitted the basic economic and social problems of the country, and how openly they disagreed with each other about what should be done. Soviet workers stopped working, as they were glued to their TVs and radios, and labour productivity suffered. After a few days, the broadcasts were suspended. However, the message was clear. The first Congress not only exposed the weakness of the management of the Communist Party, but it also gave the impression that the newly empowered Congress, still dominated by conservative Communist deputies, would not do any better. Ordinary people expected something good to come out of the elections, such as more consumer goods or pay rises, but these outcomes seemed to be a long way off.[61]

A series of speeches made by new and often radical deputies were largely of a critical nature. The KGB was criticized for its past 'crimes' and they listed the 'victims' of human rights abuses. Yeltsin, still a CPSU member, made a powerful speech, pointing out that the state institutions were still in the hands of the old Communists, with Gorbachev presiding at the top as a new 'dictatorship'. Sakharov, who wanted to transform the USSR so that it was modelled on the Western style of liberal democracy, urged the deletion of the leading role of the CPSU from the constitution (Article 6). Thus, a small section of radical deputies (some 300) dominated the debates, but they were easily outvoted by the majority of conservative Communist deputies.[62]

The main task of the first Congress was to elect one fifth of the deputies to the Supreme Soviet (some 500 deputies). The election process was, however, based on 'negative voting', by crossing out those deputies who were regarded by the Party as undesirable, leaving ample opportunity for the Politburo to manipulate the final list of selected deputies. In the process, Yeltsin, the winner of the largest popular vote at the recent elections, failed to obtain a seat out of the 12 seats allocated to the Russian Republic. The incident made a mockery of so-called democratization and, to avoid further embarrassment, a Russian deputy was swiftly removed to allow Yeltsin a place on the Supreme Soviet. Gorbachev was duly elected unopposed and assumed the post of the first President of the Supreme Soviet for the next five years. The new President, in turn, chose his ally, Anatoly Lukyanov, as his Deputy Chair, and Ryzhkov remained in his post as Prime Minister. Radicals were acutely disappointed by the outcome and Yeltsin seized the opportunity to set up, at the end of July 1989, 'an inter-regional deputies' group,' a potentially destructive force in the re-structured parliament. In the same month, coal miners went on strike demanding radical economic improvements and called for the removal of the CPSU's leading role from the constitution.[63]

The whole process became a vicious circle. The more powerful Gorbachev's position became, the more fragmented became the political structure. Subsequent to the 1989 national elections, republic and local elections (except in Georgia and Armenia) were held in December 1989 and March 1990. Elections in the Baltic republics saw the overwhelming victory of the popular fronts, pushing the Communists into a minority. Gorbachev conceded to Lithuania's demand for the deletion of Article 6 from its republican constitution in January 1990. Similarly, the 'Democratic Russia' bloc made up of Russian nationalists and anti-Party radical reformers obtained more than half the seats in Moscow's city council and, in May 1990, Boris Yeltsin was elected chairman of the Supreme Soviet of the Russian Soviet Federated Socialist Republic (RSFSR), or the Russian Federation. Two months later, Yeltsin resigned from the CPSU.

The Baltic and Russian republics were rather exceptional, albeit important, ones. Most other opposition forces or non-Communist candidates in minor soviets lacked the experience, institutional backing and resources to organize themselves or acquire popular support. The authority of the CPSU was under-mined, but it still owned the country's industrial and cultural assets. Similarly, local Party organizations still retained enough power to control the management of these resources. The democratization process encouraged people to form various political groups, but Gorbachev remained reluctant to approve a multi-party system until late 1990. Under the circumstances, the emergent political forces and informal political activists were easily frustrated, fragmented and sometimes isolated.[64]

However, similar democratizations of political systems, encouraged by Gorbachev, were producing more powerful results in Eastern Europe. Poland, Hungary and Czechoslovakia succeeded in ousting their Communist govern-ments during the latter half of 1989. The Berlin Wall fell in the autumn of 1989, which unleashed the liberation of East Germany. A flood of refugees fled to

West Germany and elsewhere, calling for the unification of Germany, which, after a series of political negotiations by the powers concerned, took place in October 1990 (see chapter 4).

In Moscow, faced with the fragmentation of the political system, two important decisions were made in the spring of 1990. While Gorbachev still hoped that the CPSU would play a 'consolidating role' in society,[65] the democratization process meant separating the functions of the Party and state. The legislature was taken over by state and local soviets and it soon became clear that there was no point in clinging to the leading role of the CPSU; the Central Committee duly accepted the deletion of Article 6. Secondly, in an attempt to control the country and given the anxiety to avoid a repeat of the popular revolutions taking place in Eastern Europe, an executive presidency was set up at the top of the entire governing structure, modelled on the USA. On 15 March 1990 Gorbachev was elected unopposed to the new post with 71 per cent approval by the deputies who voted.[66]

In legal terms, Gorbachev's authority had never been stronger and, indeed, was stronger than Stalin's had been. Gorbachev's power now included the right to appoint the Prime Minister (the head of the Council of Ministers) and other government top officials, to veto legislation (a veto that could be overridden by the Supreme Soviet), to issue presidential decrees, and to dissolve the government and the USSR Supreme Soviet. He was also empowered to declare a state of emergency and to impose direct rule during a crisis. According to the initial plan, the President was to be popularly elected, thereby enhancing his credibility as leader, as in the USA. The USSR Congress, however, as an emergency measure, appointed Gorbachev to the post and, as such, demonstrated the sense of urgency felt by Soviet leaders about the need for firm leadership at the top to deal with the crisis. The establishment of the new presidency, however, was further to confuse the decision making process within the numerous institutions in the central government. It also blurred the separation of power between the legislature and the executive, with the result that the newly reformed USSR Congress and USSR Supreme Soviet were somewhat weakened.[67] Gorbachev was now forced to confront the problems arising from his reform programme almost single-handedly, as he now exercised expanded power, which entailed greater responsibility.

THE WORSENING ECONOMY AND SOCIETY, 1989–91

Perestroika was intended to allow the introduction of market forces and the relaxation of state controls over the economy. Years of neglect by the Soviet leadership in providing its people with adequate and good quality consumer goods had been a major feature of the Soviet economic system, but Perestroika made it worse. Gorbachev was a visionary, but he had few ideas about how to implement his ideals. Curiously, there was plenty of money in circulation but the distribution system collapsed. The Soviet economy was a halfway house – neither planned nor fully market based.[68]

By 1989, the rationing of basic consumer goods (sugar, bread, meat, vegetable, soap and cigarettes) had become a familiar feature of the people's daily lives. It was reported that nearly 90 per cent of the population were hoarding these scarce items to ensure their survival in case things became worse, thereby exacerbating the chaotic supply situation[69] – the shops were practically empty of merchandise. Some people resorted to stealing rabbits from the Moscow zoo for their meat, or spent all night in front of a shop to get their sausages in the morning. Others complained that it took them two years to find a pair of socks of the correct size. A popular image of this period was demonstrated by 'cartoons of Brezhnev covered in medals and Gorbachev covered in coupons'.[70] Perestroika was sometimes punned as Catastroika, meaning deteriorating work discipline, rampant street crime, a swelling black market, a growing gap between rich and poor, unemployment, disorderliness and drunkenness. Nearly half of the population polled at the end of 1990 replied that they did not expect the Soviet economy to recover within the next ten years. More than one in ten of the respondents of opinion polls, and nearly 20 per cent of younger people, replied that they would like to 'leave the USSR altogether if they could'. The rate of emigration in 1990 rose by 200 per cent compared with that of the previous year.[71]

The problems were many and complex. However, they can be reduced to three areas. First, radical economic reform was hampered by the fact that the Soviet Union covered a huge territory and the old system was far more ingrained into the infrastructure than Gorbachev had initially understood. Through Perestroika, the old central economic command system was weakened, but had not completely disappeared. The grossly unrealistic price of commodities, which had been unchanged for decades (for example, rents had remained the same since 1928, gas and electricity bills since 1946, the cost of bread since 1954, and meat and milk since 1964), put growing pressure on the state revenues to provide subsidies. In the late 1980s the government was spending nearly 24 times more in subsidizing the cost of foodstuffs compared with the mid 1960s. In effect, the retail price reflected less than one third of the production cost. Reform of prices was the key to the transition from a state socialist economy to a free-market economy. However, this meant in reality removing state subsidies and increasing the price of essential commodities. This policy, if handled badly, could be suicidal to the government and would create further chaos in the economy.[72]

Second, a new style of economic management was emerging, but it was not being regulated by a new economic system. With the progress of Perestroika, a number of self-financing enterprises and cooperatives (mostly small businesses dealing with domestic and catering services, or selling consumer goods) had significantly increased, but the old central planning apparatus was still largely in place in 1990–1. Even in 1990, state sectors and the ministries were still expected to achieve the targets set under the five-year economic plan introduced in 1986. There was, therefore, constant tension between reformers who sought to open up the market, and conservatives, who saw the rise of a nouveau riche as a threat to the state sector. Moreover, given their new-found autonomy, the new business owners tended to seek short-term profits, often ignoring government instructions when they conflicted with this aim. Some chose more lucrative production lines, while others decided to produce fewer goods and sell them at higher prices. All these factors increased inflationary pressures, but without, of course, balancing supply and demand.[73]

Finally, the economic crisis demanded something be done quickly. However, the central government was increasingly deprived of resources and the ability to address the problems. While it still retained its old responsibility for subsidizing essential commodities until 1991, its revenues were being reduced by the anti-alcohol campaigns (which were discussed earlier), by terrible accidents (the Chernobyl nuclear disaster and the Armenian earthquake), and by a fall in oil prices on the world market. The central government's ability to collect taxes was considerably reduced. In 1991, it obtained just over one third of the planned revenue.[74]

If anything, the Soviet leadership sought to achieve either ambitious goals or at best long-term solutions. Gorbachev wanted to continue to reduce tension with the West by cutting defence expenditure. For instance, in December 1988 the Soviet Union aimed to reduce defence expenditure by 14 per cent. For historical and political reasons, the Soviet Union had created a powerful military industrial complex. While Gorbachev sought to transform 'military industrial capacity to civilian purposes', downsizing the Soviet defence structure would have required a major and complex reorganization. There was, in fact, no quick and easy way of producing extra resources by cutting back on defence expenditure.[75]

Similarly, Gorbachev believed that Soviet economy should enter the world market (he announced this during his speech at the UN National Assembly in December 1988), in the hope that this would help to modernize the Soviet economy. In 1988, the government was already considering the creation of a stock market, and of making the rouble a convertible currency. In 1990, the Soviet Union obtained observer status at the General Agreement on Tariffs and Trade (GATT). All these changes symbolized a remarkable ideological shift from the traditional Soviet hostility towards the capitalist economy. However, the USSR's new-found enthusiasm for the integration of its fragile and vulnerable economy with the outside world created more problems, but with no immediate profitable returns.[76]

The bulk of Soviet exports was raw materials, but these represented a meagre portion (less than 10 per cent) of Soviet GNP. Foreign investors were naturally cautious about investing in the weak Soviet economy. The number of active foreign–Soviet joint companies was still small in 1990 and these were in fact importing more goods than they were exporting. Since the Soviet threat was receding, the West had less incentive to organize an economic aid package for the country unless the economy was fully market based, thus frustrating Gorbachev's desire to rely on the West's technology and economic prowess in return for his cooperation with the West. The full integration of the Soviet economy into the world market would be a long-term process and it would require, in the short term, a substantial devaluation of the rouble. For example, in November 1989 it was exchanged by tourists for one tenth of its nominal value.[77]

To stem the worsening economic conditions, the Soviet leadership began to discuss a 500-day economic programme, calling for a quick transition to the market economy based on a plan devised by Stanislav Shatalin, a member of the newly created USSR Presidential Council.[78] The Prime Minister, Ryzhkov, objected to the plan, fearing that it would reduce Soviet living standards even further and increase political instability in the country. In the end, a more conservative economic programme was adopted by the government in the autumn of 1990, which, unsurprisingly, did little to abate the deepening economic and social crisis.[79]

Almost as a final and desperate measure, Gorbachev, after the autumn of 1990, turned to the right, deciding to rely on the experience of the conservatives and put a brake on Glasnost and Perestroika. In January 1991, Valentin Pavlov (a conservative who would become a leading planner of the August 1991 coup against Gorbachev) had replaced Ryzhkov. The new Prime Minister almost immediately began to tackle the hugely inflated economy – inflation had risen to at least 150–200 per cent in 1990. Pavlov ordered the withdrawal of all high denomination bank notes from circulation at a week's notice. In the spring of 1991, the government launched a price reform, which resulted in a sharp increase (70–90 per cent) in state retail prices. These measures wiped out the savings of ordinary people, who were, at the same time, confronted with a higher cost of living.[80]

By 1991, the effects of the haphazard process of Gorbachev's economic reforms resulted in an all-round negative Soviet economic performance: industrial output fell by 7.8 per cent, agricultural output by 7.0 per cent, and the Soviet GNP by 15 per cent. The price changes contributed to the increasing number of people (25 per cent of the population) who lived in poverty. The majority of Soviet workers felt that the transfer to a market economy would create more problems in society, and were against private ownership. At the end of 1990, nearly 60 per cent of the Soviet public did not have much of an idea what a market economy actually entailed.[81] This loss of direction was mirrored by the loss of public support for the Soviet Communist Party. It had a membership of 19 million in 1985, but in 1990/1, 4 million members had left the Party.[82] Gorbachev's popularity was steadily declining. The celebration of the Communist Party May Day in 1990 was greeted with a growing clamour for Gorbachev's resignation. Yeltsin exploited the opportunity skilfully and emerged as the most popular politician in the country.[83]

THE DISINTEGRATION OF THE SOVIET UNION, 1990–1

During this final stage of the Soviet Union's existence, Gorbachev's choices became extremely limited. Even his loyal aides became doubtful about his domestic policy. 'Nothing was working out the way Gorbachev intended', Chernyaev wrote, 'much less how it really ought to have.'[84] Bad as conditions were, the Soviet Union might still have maintained its unitary federation if Gorbachev had carefully reformed the relations between the centre and the republics in the earlier stages of Perestroika. He believed that his reform initiatives would lead to a freer, less centralized and more efficient Soviet Federation. Instead, they unravelled the 'nationality' question and led to increased tensions between the centre and the republics. The Kremlin occasionally resorted to the use of force in an attempt to suppress separatist disturbances. While Gorbachev was abroad in April 1989 the Red Army was sent into Tbilisi, the capital of Georgia, in an attempt to break up demonstrations. Similarly, Soviet troops were sent to Baku, capital of Azerbaijan, in January 1990 and, later, into the Baltic Republics in 1991. However the use of force only inflamed local hostility to the central government and to Gorbachev himself.[85]

In 1988 and 1989 the republics had not sought to gain full independence from the Soviet Federation, but wanted autonomy within it and expected a fair distribution of power between the centre and the republics. The fact that the economies of the republics had long been integrated into the Soviet central economic system suggested that independence would be a costly and risky undertaking. Moreover, premature independence would create problems for nearly 60 million people who lived outside their home republics. Their common status as Soviet citizens had so far minimized the problem of ethnic and national conflicts within, and across, the republics.[86] To their great disappointment, Gorbachev's Perestroika and Glasnost barely touched upon the freedom of the republics, but his economic reforms eventually required the Soviet leader to grant more power to them. In the spring of 1990, the republics were given greater autonomy in the fields of taxation, finance, investment and trading. Gorbachev also promised the drafting of a new Union treaty, which would allow the republics to become sovereign states within the restructured Soviet Federation.[87]

These measures did not arrest the problems of the republics. The Russian Republic under Yeltsin was now complaining that the Republic owned only 15 per cent of its oil and controlled 30 per cent of its industrial output, with the rest going to finance the other republics.[88] During 1990, all the 15 republics declared that their laws would take primacy over the laws of the USSR. By implication, the republics could now reject Gorbachev's presidential decrees unless they were first approved by the republican parliaments. Alternatively, the republics could refuse to enrol their eligible manpower for Soviet national service and, by early 1991, several republics did just that, creating considerable problems for the organization of the Soviet armed forces. In addition, the republics now declared that their economic and financial contributions to the central government revenue would be cut drastically, threatening the economic viability of the central government.[89] Upon becoming the popularly elected President of the Russian Federation in May 1991, Yeltsin declared the full autonomy of the Russian Republic, which would mean a considerable loss of the central government's financial reserves and spelled the death knell of the Soviet Union.[90] The CPSU's authorities were equally challenged when the Lithuanian Communist Party seceded from the central Party in December 1989, followed, a year later, by the Georgian Party, and by the Moldavian Party in early 1991.[91] The worsening Soviet economy strengthened republican determination to manage their economic affairs for the sake of their own survival, thereby quickening the pace of the collapse of the traditional centre–republican relationship.

The central government responses to the increasingly restive republics were rather slow and far from consistent. In the summer of 1990, Gorbachev agreed to negotiate a new Union Treaty, but by this time, the Baltic Republics were already determined to obtain complete independence from the Soviet Union. The rest of the republics wanted full autonomous power within the Soviet Federation, with the central government acting merely as a coordinating body. Gorbachev, however, still insisted on the importance of maintaining the socialist Soviet Union as a unitary state. The gap between the republics and the centre became too wide to bridge. The draft Union Treaty, published in November 1990, fell far short of the expectations of the republics. Although it was approved in principle by the Soviet Union Congress of People's Deputies in December 1990, the Union decision was unlikely to carry any weight, as numerous republican representatives (the Baltic Republics declined to join the negotiations from the outset) were absent from the Congress.[92] Sadly, it showed that the new political structure, which Gorbachev had proposed in the summer of 1988, was no longer a workable institution.

The choice Gorbachev could now take was either to take sides with the remaining, but still strong conservatives, or to push his radical reforms at further cost to the interests of the Soviet Union. A rumour of a military coup against Gorbachev in the autumn of 1990, when Gorbachev was supposed to have moved some airborne forces to protect Moscow before the opening of the Supreme Soviet, was also a factor in helping sway Gorbachev to line up with the conservatives, forming the so-called 'Winter alliance' with them. The interior ministry was now headed by a hardliner, Boris Pugo. In December 1990, the Foreign Minister, Shevardnadze, resigned in protest against this 'advance of dictatorship'.[93]

The Baltic Republics' aspirations for complete independence troubled the Soviet leader most. In response to Lithuania's unilateral declaration of independence from the Soviet Union in April 1990, Gorbachev imposed economic sanctions on the republic, which, together with the West's efforts to defuse the crisis, persuaded Lithuania to suspend outright independence. The nationalist drive to oust anti-Communist governments in the Baltics grew stronger and, in January 1991, Soviet forces were used in an attempt to restore the central authorities to power in Lithuania and Latvia. Sunday 13 January 1991 turned into a 'bloody Sunday' when the Soviet military units clashed with the local population, resulting in the deaths of 17 civilians in Vilnius, the capital of Lithuania. Behind this tragedy were two generals (who became two of the plotters in the August coup), who acted, apparently, without Gorbachev's knowledge. In any case, the Lithuanians went ahead with their own referendum and they overwhelmingly voted for their independence from the Soviet Union in February 1991, followed in March by Latvia and Estonia.[94]

Gorbachev did not, of course, want to resolve the nationality question with the use of force and sought to settle the nationality problem by negotiations. To this end, in March 1991 a referendum was held on the nationality question. Those who were polled were asked whether it was necessary to 'preserve the Union of Soviet Socialist Republics as a renewed federation of equal sovereign republics', and the majority answered in the affirmative (76.4 per cent). The referendum did not address the problem fully and several republics (including the three Baltic states) refused to participate in it altogether. Those republics who did participate in the referendum remained unhappy with another revised draft treaty in March 1991, which still maintained 'central' control over the Union's defence and foreign policy. As a result, Gorbachev realized that this 'Winter alliance' had not done him any good. He decided to work secretly with nine republics (those that had participated in the March referendum) in the so-called 9 + 1 talks (also known as the 'Novo-Ogarevo process'), in order to reach agreement on a new Union Treaty. The KGB soon found out about Gorbachev's reversion to reformism and this alienated the conservatives, who were becoming increasingly concerned about the fate of the Soviet Union.[95]

On 24 July 1991, a further revised Union Treaty, which entailed considerable concessions on the part of the USSR government in favour of the interests of the republics, was ready for signature. It called for the creation of the 'Union of Soviet Sovereign Republics' by omitting the word 'Socialist' from the country's title, and the treaty was based on voluntary republican membership. Under the new treaty, the central government would lose the power to collect taxes, while all decisions concerning Union institutions would be made jointly with the republics. It also accepted the primacy of the republics' laws over all Union law. In short, the Soviet Union would lose its governing authority over the republics and it appeared to the conservative ministers that the new treaty would make their continued existence redundant. The treaty was to be signed on 20 August by the Russian Republic, Kazakhstan, Uzbekistan, Tajikistan and Belorussia, while Ukraine remained undecided.[96] In early August Gorbachev went on his summer holiday to the Crimean coast. The reformists grew uneasy: Yakovlev (who had not been re-elected as a member of the Central Committee at the 28th Congress in the summer of 1990), and Shevardnadze both anticipated an imminent 'right-wing coup'.[97]

On 18 August, five officials arrived at Gorbachev's holiday villa in the Crimea. They urged Gorbachev to issue either a presidential decree declaring a state of emergency, or transfer his powers to his Vice-President, Gennady Ivanovich Yanayev. Gorbachev rejected both requests and was then placed under 'house arrest'. On 19 August, the State Emergency Committee, headed by the Vice-President, took over the country and immediately imposed controls over TV and radio stations, and newspapers. The plotters announced that Gorbachev was incapacitated due to illness, which many doubted, as he had looked fit and well before he left for the Crimea just two weeks before. They made it clear that they wanted to block the ratification of the new Union Treaty, in order to save the Soviet Union and improve the economic condition of the country. The majority of the initiators were leading members of the government, whom Gorbachev himself had appointed, including the Vice-President (Yanayev), the Prime Minister (Pavlov), the Defence Minister (Dmitri Yasov), the Chairman of the KGB (Kryuchkov), the Interior Minister (Pugo), and the Deputy Chairman of the Defence Council (Oleg Baklanov).[98]

Apparently, plans for emergency action of this kind had been in place for some time and, ironically, Gorbachev himself had been responsible for increasing the power of the KGB and the Ministry of Internal Affairs after he became the President in March 1990, ostensibly because of the need to restore law and order in the face of an increasingly fragmented and chaotic Soviet society. There were several ominous indications beforehand that a coup was imminent. In June 1991, the US secret services obtained information about an imminent coup against Gorbachev and this message was passed to Gorbachev by the American ambassador, Jack Matlock. Gorbachev did not take the warning seriously, dismissing it as a 'load of rubbish'.[99] Leading Soviet conservatives wrote to *Sovetskaya Rossiya* in July, urging 'a national and patriotic unity'.

There is some evidence to prove that Gorbachev was already planning to remove the anti-reformist conservatives from key posts, such as the KGB chief, as soon as the new Union Treaty was signed on 20 August. Gorbachev mentioned these ideas to President Bush during the Moscow summit between 29 July and 1 August, and again during the negotiations with Yeltsin over a new Union Treaty before he set off for his summer holiday. These conversations were bugged by the KGB, which strengthened the plotters' determination to launch the August coup. According to Oberdorfer, at the KGB hotel-spa in Moscow on 17 August, Kryuchkov discussed his plans with a few colleagues, including Pavlov and Yazov, while having a steam bath with vodka and Scotch. This account supports the view that Gorbachev was taken by surprise by the plotters, and he continued to blame them for 'disrupting' the completion of the new Union Treaty.[100]

The coup was, however, badly prosecuted. The plan to arrest Yeltsin was implemented too late and the Russian President and his officials managed to escape into the Russian parliament (the White House) behind the barricades. Soviet tanks were sent into the Moscow streets, but without any specific instructions as to what they were supposed to do. Meanwhile, the plotters were embroiled in angry debates among themselves and spent most of the time during the coup drinking heavily. Yeltsin came out as the first and foremost opponent of the coup, denouncing the Committee as 'reactionary and unconstitutional'. By 20 August, pro-reformers in Moscow mounted huge demonstrations – among the demonstrators were Andrei Sakharov's widow, Shevardnadze and even the Patriarch of the Russian Orthodox Church. By that evening, nearly 70,000 people gathered around the Russian parliament building face to face with the armed forces sent in by the plotters. Confronted with this unexpected resistance, the coup quickly crumbled.[101] Many young military officers decided not to support the coup, while the anti-terrorist forces defied orders from the Emergency Committee to crush the demonstrators.[102] One of the coup initiators, Boris Pugo, committed suicide. Only three demonstrators were killed, but the pro-coup forces had no stomach for an attack on the Russian parliament, an action that might provoke a civil war. In the early hours of 22 August, Gorbachev had safely returned to Moscow with a Russian delegation despatched under the authority of the Russian parliament.

The failed coup demonstrated Gorbachev's inability to control his own government, but it is also interesting to ask, as did Andrey Grachev (Gorbachev's informal adviser and later his press secretary), 'how many possible coups d'état did Gorbachev manage to avoid in the years before the unsuccessful August 1991 putsch?'[103] Walking a tightrope, he and his handful of loyal new thinkers pushed through a series of reforms in an effort to improve the Soviet Union.

In the end, it was the August coup and Yeltsin who shaped the final outcome of Perestroika. Immediately upon returning to Moscow after the coup, the Soviet leader still talked about the need to revitalize the Communist Party of the Soviet Union, but its already declining authority had been lost completely after the coup. Gorbachev soon realized this and resigned from the post of General Secretary of the CPSU on 24 August. He subsequently instructed the nationalization of all party properties and called for the dissolution of the Party Central Committee. The USSR Supreme Soviet passed a resolution underwriting these instructions.

Secondly, just as the CPSU was becoming a spent force, Yeltsin also made sure that he maximized 'his own political power and the role of Russia'.[104] His immediate denunciation of the coup captured the minds of pro-democrats, and his dynamic actions, such as addressing both the soldiers and the demonstrators from the top of one of the tanks situated near the Russian parliament, were widely regarded as courageous. However, Yeltsin also took advantage of the fateful hours of uncertainty during the coup: the President of the Russian Republic issued a series of decrees against the orders of the State Emergency Committee. He placed all the armed forces and all the institutions on Russian soil under the control of the Russian government. Upon returning to Moscow, Gorbachev was publicly humiliated by this display of Yeltsin's leadership and the former had to accept that Yeltsin's decrees during the coup were legal, including the transfer of authority from the Soviet Union to the Russian Republic. Yeltsin then banned all CPSU activities within the Republic and, by the end of August, the USSR Ministry of Finance, the USSR State Bank and the Bank for Foreign Economic Relations were all placed under the control of the Russian Republic. The non-Russian republics began to see Yeltsin as 'a new dictatorial "Russian-centre" replacing the 'old dictatorial Soviet "centre"'.[105]

The key ministers of the government who had instigated the coup were either arrested or sacked by Gorbachev. The machinery of the central administration, that is, Gorbachev's power base, was considerably weakened. The post-coup situation made the republics even more responsible for their own affairs. In the capital, Moscow, where many state buildings were located within the Russian Republic, the situation was even more confused, as a de-facto division of power had been created after the coup between the White House (the Russian parliament) and the Kremlin (the Soviet government).

Thus, the August coup led to the domination of Yeltsin and of his Russian Republic over the Soviet central authority and this was to have a further significant impact on the fate of the new Union Treaty. Within a matter of a week after the coup, the Baltic Republics declared their complete independence and were recognized by the international community, including the European Union. Ukraine also overwhelmingly voted to become an independent republic (which was to be ratified by a referendum later), followed by Moldova and Azerbaijan. The Russian Republic was also moving towards becoming an independent Republic, although it intended to remain within the Union. There was now little chance the Union could be preserved in any meaningful way. Gorbachev, however, continued negotiations with the remaining nine republics and on 14 November 1991 they agreed to form a 'confederative union state', with its central authority limited to the areas specified by the members of the Union.[106]

However, Yeltsin prevaricated. He wanted to reserve the final decision prior to its discussion by the Russian Supreme Soviet. Gorbachev's last hope of re-establishing a new unitary state was completely shattered by a referendum in Ukraine, the second most powerful republic in the Union, on 1 December 1991. Over 90 per cent of the population voted for full independence from the Union. Gorbachev had already publicly stated that he could not 'imagine the Union Treaty without Ukraine'.[107] Yeltsin moved quickly. He met the two other leaders of the Slav republics (Ukraine and Belarus – previously known as Belorussia) in Minsk and came up with the idea of creating a 'Commonwealth of Independent States', a loose organization of independent states with no central government. It was open to the other Soviet republics to join, but Gorbachev was furious about the way Yeltsin had outmanoeuvred him. After all, the creation of the CIS meant the demise of the Soviet Union and the end of Gorbachev's presidency. On 21 December 1991, 11 republics agreed to join the CIS. The three Baltic states and Georgia remained aloof, although Georgia has since become a member of the CIS. Yelstin and Gorbachev then met for the last time on 23 December, when they agreed that the Soviet Union was to cease to exist at the end of 1991. Yeltsin showed no mercy towards Gorbachev and everything was hurried in advance of the formal end of Gorbachev's official status. On 25 December, even before Gorbachev made his final television address, his presidential apartment in Moscow had been sealed, and he and his family were ordered to leave the property within 24 hours. Gorbachev's office was already being used by Yelstin by 27 December. The red flag was lowered from the Kremlin within an hour after Gorbachev's resignation speech, to be replaced with the flag of the Russian Federation. Yeltsin, who was somehow displeased by Gorbachev's resignation speech, failed to turn up for the final ceremony handing over power to the Russian President, including the right to use nuclear weapons. A few days later, on 31 December, the Soviet Union was formally dissolved.[108]

THE IMPLICATIONS OF GORBACHEV'S 'NEW THINKING'

The Gorbachev era left a paradoxical legacy – it was both a 'resounding failure' and a 'triumphant success'.[109] His Perestroika finally demolished the old centre of the Soviet system, but at the cost of the collapse of the Soviet Union itself. The rivalry and hatred between the two powerful reformist leaders, Gorbachev and Yeltsin, facilitated the process of Gorbachev's Perestroika to a degree (his policy for the democratization of the Soviet political system after 1988 was what Yeltsin had been pushing for), but resulted in the decline of Gorbachev's authority. In addition, the relatively weaker, but continuing resistance from conservatives, who launched the failed August coup, made Perestroika and Glasnost a much more political affair than liberating and improving the economic and political systems of the Soviet Union. Behind these power struggles, the Soviet people had become disenchanted with Perestroika, which had simply meant 'mass unemployment and a rationing system'. The Soviet leader was described as 'hypocritical, weak and lacking in self-confidence', and 'indifferent to human suffering'. Externally, however, Gorbachev's 'new thinking' was welcomed by the international community. *Time* magazine made Gorbachev 'Man of the Year' in 1987, and *Der Spiegel* and Britain's independent television credited him in the same manner in 1988 and 1989, respectively. In 1990, he became 'Man of the Year' in France, and was awarded the Nobel Peace Prize.[110]

This final section will examine the major themes contained in the so-called new thinking, and its implications for international politics and for the fate of the Soviet Union. Gorbachev, himself a keen student of international relations, had, since the 1970s, forged close ties with liberal Soviet intellectuals in Moscow, and had developed an interest in transforming the Soviet Union into a Western-style social democratic system. Gorbachev soon realized that the traditional sense of isolation and insecurity, which characterized the history of the Soviet Union, was exacerbated by the lengthy Cold War. Soviet preoccupation with competition with the USA in the Third World and in nuclear arsenals, resulted in the isolation of the Soviet Union from the modern industrial states in Western Europe and East Asia. Moreover, Gorbachev noted that the Kremlin's decades-old commitment to waging the Cold War left the country economically inefficient, technologically incompetent, and socially underdeveloped. The purpose of Gorbachev's Perestroika was to reverse all these trends and to renew the Soviet Union as a reformed and modern socialist country.[111]

Gorbachev's new political thinking was underpinned by his anxiety to improve the economy of the Soviet Union. Appreciating the close connection between domestic and foreign policy, Gorbachev gave priority to domestic reforms over Soviet foreign policy and, to achieve this, he needed to create a peaceful and cooperative international environment.[112] Gorbachev did everything to advance his ideas. He surrounded himself with writers and academics at home, while he enjoyed exchanges of views with politicians like the Spanish Prime Minister, Felipe González, and the British Prime Minister, Margaret Thatcher. Gorbachev was not only a bold and progressive thinker, but he also symbolized the rise of the pro-Western intellectuals in the Soviet establishment.

Gorbachev's 'new thinking' was characterized by de-emphasizing the ideological struggle between capitalism and socialism in favour of globalism, universalism and interdependence. These themes were already made explicit in his speech before the 27th Party Congress in February 1986. Gorbachev pointed out that global problems, including the ecological issue and the distribution of natural resources, could only be resolved by international cooperation. The ideological division in fact prevented the people from exchanging information and ideas in the arts and sciences. In his book on Perestroika, Gorbachev urged his readers to see the 'realities by removing the ideological edge from interstate relations'.[113]

From this thinking Gorbachev developed the concept of humanistic universalism – all human beings had a right to defend their 'personal, political and social rights', and 'there was a need for non-intervention in other peoples' affairs'. The exposition of these views indicated that Gorbachev was in fact moving away from Marxist-Leninist orthodoxy.[114] Behind this was Gorbachev's acceptance of progressive capitalism and its dominance in the world. In his speech on the anniversary of the Russian revolution in 1987, the Soviet leader contended that capitalist society was not necessarily aggressive, and imperialism could be contained through peaceful negotiations. Regardless of the differences of systems, Gorbachev insisted that states could cooperate to resolve global issues, just as the Soviet Union was able to work together with the USA during the war against Fascism.[115] By the end of 1988 the ideological tenets of Soviet foreign policy had all but disappeared.[116]

This admission of the progress, rather than the decline, of capitalism was accompanied by a sombre recognition of the state of Soviet socialism. In 1961 Khrushchev had raised hopes by stating that Soviet socialism was now so advanced that, by the end of the next decade, the Soviet Union, having surpassed the USA in terms of overall production, would be constructing a Communist society. Twenty years later, Brezhnev had to tone down this rosy picture and the assumption then was that Soviet society was 'proceeding to communism through the stage of "developed socialism"'. By 1987, any reference to 'developed socialism' was dropped, to be replaced by 'developing socialism', suggesting that the transition to a Communist society remained a long way off.[117]

Thus, the need for interdependence, the development of capitalism and the decline of socialism together led to the modification of the idea of the inevitability of war between the two different systems. Khrushchev had replaced this concept with the notion of 'peaceful coexistence' in the mid 1950s, but the Kremlin used this notion to intensify the class struggle and East–West rivalry.[118] Gorbachev considered a peaceful and constructive cooperation between the East and West, instead of 'peaceful co-existence', to be beneficial to the Soviet Union.

Dialogue, instead of war, was reinforced by Gorbachev's acceptance of the dangers of nuclear weapons. The nuclear arms race was one factor that stood in the way of cooperative Soviet–US relations, while wasting an enormous quantity of Soviet resources and technological prowess, which could otherwise be utilized for the civilian sector.[119] Upon his accession to power in April 1985, he froze the installation of SS-20 missiles in Europe. On the anniversary of Hiroshima in August of the same year, the Soviet Union began a five-month nuclear testing moratorium, which was later extended to February 1987. In January 1986, Gorbachev called for the elimination of all nuclear weapons by the year 2000 and, in his 'Delhi declaration' in November 1986, the Soviet leader took his stand upon a 'non-violent and nuclear-free world'.[120]

Moreover, the Soviet leader stressed the importance of disarmament and arms control as the major instruments for peace, and dismissed the arms race with the capitalist countries as a wasteful and futile exercise. This was reflected in a new guideline called 'reasonable sufficiency', which was adopted at the 27th Party Congress and, subsequently, by the Warsaw Pact. Under this concept, the Soviet Union was to adopt a defensive strategy and abandon the first use of nuclear weapons. The strategy indicated the 'possibility of asymmetric force reductions' and was followed in December 1988 by Gorbachev's announcement that the

Soviet Union would unilaterally withdraw nearly half a million troops from Europe and Asia.[121]

In parallel with this much less militant posture was Gorbachev's increasing vigour for personal diplomacy worldwide. His charm offensives succeeded in creating a new image of a cooperative and more friendly Soviet Union and led to a surge of 'Gorbymania' abroad. Gorbachev's new emphasis on Europe was reflected in his concept of 'a common European home', which he mentioned during his visit to Britain in December 1984 (see chapter 3).[122] The scheme for creating a common home was also developed in the Asia-Pacific region, where he talked about creating a common Pacific home, or in Scandinavia in the form of 'the sub-arctic, our common home'.[123] Widening Soviet foreign relations – other than superpower relations – was his central theme for global dialogue. His trips to foreign countries were extensive – from Western Europe to Latin America, Japan, South Korea, Israel, Ireland and South Africa and, on 1 December 1989, he made the first state visit of a Soviet leader to the Vatican, at the invitation of the Pope.[124] Soviet relations with Yugoslavia and with China had also improved (see chapter 8).

To the conservatives, the new thinking was demolishing everything they had fought for during and after the Second World War. Marshal Sergei Fedorovich Akhromeyev, who had been Gorbachev's trusted Chief of General Staff and also the First Deputy Defence Minister (1984–8), initially admired Gorbachev for his courageous opposition to the arms race with the USA and he helped Gorbachev by keeping the armed forces united behind the latter's new thinking. However, by 1988 he had lost confidence in Gorbachev's policy and resigned after Gorbachev's UN speech promising a Soviet withdrawal from Eastern Europe.[125] Troop withdrawals from Eastern Europe began after 1989, but the returning soldiers found the domestic situation appalling. They had lost the relatively privileged lifestyle that they enjoyed in Eastern Europe and were, on their return home, re-housed in 'tents, converted bath houses and barns' with little prospect of a future career.[126] By the autumn of 1990, the armed forces and the right-wing officials in the Party were all criticizing Gorbachev's conduct of domestic and external affairs. Deeply disappointed, Akhromeyev supported the August coup, committing suicide in the wake of its failure. Thus, Gorbachev's new thinking in foreign policy eventually increased the opposition to his reforms at home, encouraged Eastern Europeans and the Baltic Republics to opt for independence from the Soviet Union, and precipitated the collapse of the Soviet Union. Rachel Walker summed up the situation thus: 'Gorbachev behaved in the classic fashion of the CPSU General Secretary: very good at grand gestures but utterly indifferent to the domestic problems of implementation and the *real* planning involved in their solution.'[127]

Externally, Gorbachev's active personal initiatives can be seen as a means of managing Soviet decline or, in the words of Stephen White, the 'diplomacy of decline'. The Soviet Union's influence was largely confined to the developing countries, while the USA took the most developed and major international players under its wing. In the late 1950s, nearly 30 per cent of the world population and 9 per cent of the world's GNP (except the USSR itself) were under

Soviet influence; however, by the end of the 1970s the corresponding figures fell to 6 per cent of the world population and 5 per cent of world GNP.[128] Gorbachev judged that cooperation with the most advanced nations in the world would be rewarded by their granting economic and technological assistance to the ailing Soviet Union. With the Soviet Union's modifications of its foreign policy, Gorbachev anticipated that the Cold War could be turned into a collaborative alliance between the two superpowers. During the Malta summit in December 1989, Gorbachev proposed to the US President, George Bush, the setting up of a 'Soviet–American condominium' since the USSR and the USA were 'doomed to dialogue, coordination and cooperation'. He concluded that 'there is no other choice'.[129]

However, Gorbachev's foreign policy achievements were bound to be affected by his dismal results at home, and vice versa. If the Soviet Union wanted to maintain its global power status, Gorbachev's new thinking suggested a cheaper and economically rewarding alternative to the continuation of the Cold War. The irony was that if he wanted to be seen to be committed to the new thinking abroad, he had no alternative but to pursue this course in his domestic reforms and thus develop Glasnost into democratization. However, much as he was attached to the Soviet Union as a unitary state, his domestic reforms were intended to demonstrate to the outside world that his new foreign policy was serious and genuine, not a propaganda tool. In this process, his second priority (improving relations with the West) called for progress in his domestic reforms, which had initially been his first priority, and this was where his weakness and failures stood out in comparison with his foreign policy achievements. However, in his final years, his domestic failures also began to erode his reputation in foreign affairs. In July 1990, Gorbachev appreciated an invitation to a G-7 economic summit meeting, which could be said to be the culmination of his efforts to open up the Soviet Union to the world economy, but he had to return to Moscow virtually empty handed, except for a few conditional financial promises. The G-7 states were by then appalled by the magnitude of Gorbachev's failure to tackle the economic chaos in the Soviet Union and his inability to handle the growing separatist sentiments in his own country.[130]

His successful contribution to the end of the Cold War was not accompanied by the same degree of success at home. Perhaps the August coup and the rise of Yeltsin's Russian Republic killed the prospect of preserving the Soviet Union, as Gorbachev himself implied.[131] Alternatively, Chernyaev, Gorbachev's aide, points out the tardiness of the West's recognition of the urgency attached to Gorbachev's request for some financial assistance to help salvage the Soviet Union's deepening economic crisis. This was despite the fact that Gorbachev, during the July meeting, questioned why the West could find about $100 billion 'instantaneously' for the Gulf War, but not for the USSR. Chernyaev wondered if, had the West had offered immediate financial assistance, say, by the spring of 1991, things might have developed differently.[132]

One must remember that Gorbachev had to work under the enormous pressure of time – events took on their own momentum with much greater speed than

Gorbachev had originally anticipated, overtaking his Perestroika and Glasnost. One could come up with various alternative paths the Soviet Union could have taken if Gorbachev had not been elected as General Secretary of the CPSU. An Andropovian type of reform might have saved the Union for the time being. Alternatively, a conservative leadership may have pursued economic reforms 'with extreme authoritarianism', modelled on China's reforms.[133] However, Gorbachev chose not to take China's path to reform, that is the regeneration of the Chinese economy before making gradual changes to its socio-political system. He did not believe that economic reforms would be tolerated in the Soviet Union if the political structure remained the same, as it was difficult to separate the two.[134] In the light of the steady decline of Soviet power and influence at home and abroad, Moscow would have probably tried to reduce its expensive foreign commitments, notably in Afghanistan, although the timing and terms of Moscow's disengagement from the Third World could well have been difficult, with or without Gorbachev in power.

In summary, prior to Gorbachev, the Soviet Union had been experiencing a continuing process of relative decline vis-à-vis the developed Western world. There had also been numerous attempts, notably under Khrushchev and Andropov, to make the Soviet Union more competitive, but not at the cost of undertaking drastic political reforms at the top, as Gorbachev eventually attempted to achieve. The result was that, by the mid 1980s, Soviet society was suppressed, depressed, and frustrated, and the Soviet state was unable to serve as the motor of an engine that would provide the power to ensure a better future for the country. At the same time, the Soviet Union was not totally unaffected by global trends, such as the development of technology and information systems led by the West. With the added impetus of détente and its consequent increasing contacts with the West, some Soviet intellectuals, as well as political elites, aspired to create a more dynamic Soviet society with a more competent management style at its apex. The chances were, therefore, that the Soviet Union would produce a politician like Gorbachev in the top post of the country, who was selected by the old Soviet ruling class as a man who, they thought, knew how to renew the country.

However, the decay and decline of the Soviet system did not immediately lead to its collapse. After all, the Soviet Union was not equal in economic and industrial terms to the USA in 1945, and Soviet sacrifices during the Second World War further disadvantaged the Soviet Union relative to the USA, which came out of the war much stronger and much richer. Gorbachev's thinking and his methods of reform had, therefore, played a crucial part in leading the country onto the path it eventually took. His preoccupation with securing peaceful collaboration with the West eventually allowed Gorbachev to go beyond the limits of the Soviet Union's national interests. If these national interests suggested the unity of the Soviet Union and the maintenance of its sphere of influence in Eastern Europe, the new leadership grossly underestimated the Soviet Union's traditional source of power, ideology and coercion (military and economic), which had sustained the whole fabric of the Soviet Union and its empire. One can, therefore, argue that Gorbachev was the first

Soviet leader to boldly set out a comprehensive overhaul of the country; however, in doing so, he failed to articulate the Soviet Union's national interests. In other words, Gorbachev wanted to change the Soviet Union for the better and also wanted to change the world for the better, but his ambitions to do both at the cost of underestimating Soviet national interests led to the collapse of the Soviet Union and its empire.

3

The Decline of Communism in Eastern Europe

Ben Fowkes contends that 'Revolutions have often been preceded by a collapse of morale among the former rulers, which renders them incapable of acting decisively.'[1] This contention applied not only to the Eastern European leaders but also to the Soviet attitude towards the region in the 1980s. This chapter will first explain the decline of Communism in Eastern Europe before Gorbachev came to power, then examine how Gorbachev developed his European policy and his concept of a 'common European home'.

THE TROUBLED ALLIANCE: THE SOVIET UNION AND EASTERN EUROPE

Moscow's relations with the Communist countries in Eastern Europe had long been troublesome. The Kremlin leadership had been challenged by a defiant Yugoslavia in 1948, by the East German uprising in 1953, by the 1956 uprisings in Poland and Hungary, and in Czechoslovakia by the Dubček regime in 1968. The Red Army invaded and suppressed the revolts in Hungary in 1956 and in Czechoslovakia in 1968. In 1968, Brezhnev also announced that the Soviet Union had the right to intervene in the affairs of any of the Communist bloc countries to suppress counter revolution (the Brezhnev Doctrine). Throughout the post-Stalin era the Kremlin experienced severe difficulties in keeping its Eastern European satellites united. Yugoslavia continued to move on its own reformist path, with the reduction of the central power of the Party, and in 1961 it was the only Eastern European state to attend a conference of non-aligned nations. At the end of 1961 Albania, 'Stalin's most loyal ally', chose to align itself with Communist China and it formally withdrew from the Warsaw Pact in September 1968. Romania also adopted a separatist path after 1956 and resisted Moscow's attempts to control the Romanian domestic economy.[2] All this demonstrated that

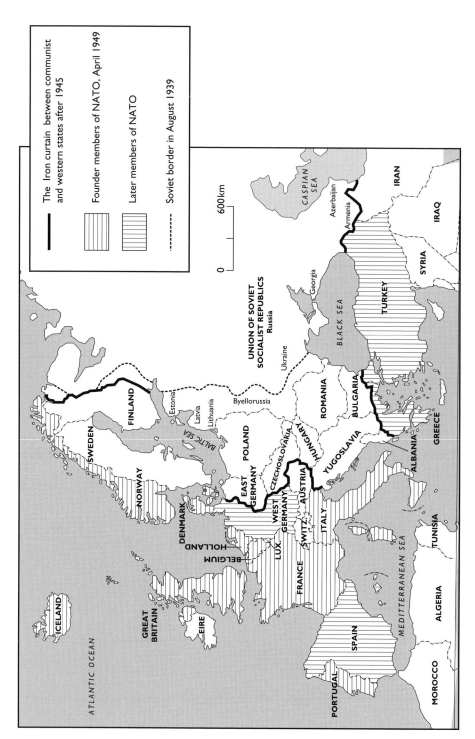

1. Cold War Europe, 1945–89

the Soviet grip on the Eastern European countries was steadily declining. The problems inherent in democratic centralism adopted in Eastern Europe were essentially similar to those experienced in the Soviet Union. However, the Eastern European regimes were more fragile than that of Moscow, for the survival of their rulers hinged upon the quality of the Soviet leadership and, by implication, the strength of Soviet military power and influence. The sense of vulnerability was muted by the determination of the Kremlin under Brezhnev to maintain 'the Soviet security buffers acquired after the Second World War'.[3]

By the middle of the 1960s, it was clear the socialist economic system adopted in Eastern European countries had seen better days. While the less developed and more autocratic Balkan countries (Bulgaria, Romania and Albania) were still showing some economic growth (for example, Romania actually increased its annual rate of growth from 6.6 per cent in 1956 to 9.1 per cent by 1965), in the major Eastern European countries – Hungary, Poland, the German Democratic Republic and Czechoslovakia – economic growth declined between 1956 and 1965. With the launch of the second de-Stalinization process by Khrushchev after 1961, the Kremlin indicated that it would tolerate gradual reforms in Eastern Europe. A limited range of political and economic reforms were introduced in Hungary, Poland and the GDR in the 1960s, but any excessive degree of reform, as in the case of Czechoslovakia, was condemned by the Kremlin as a counter-revolutionary activity, thereby increasing the troubled relationship between Moscow and Eastern Europe.[4]

With the Kremlin's encouragement of reform after 1961, Czechoslovakia, which had been under a conservative Stalinist ruler, Antonin Novotný, was compelled to introduce a degree of relaxation, moving away from the Stalinization of the past. This involved an examination of the purges that had been launched against the Slovaks, the role of the Communist Party in a repressive society, and the stagnation of the Czechoslovakian economy. However, reforms soon strengthened the hands of the anti-conservative section of the Party and made Novotný's position difficult. The tension within the Party establishment sharpened at the time of the six-day Arab–Israeli war in 1967. The war created a division between those liberals who supported Israel and the conservatives who loyally followed the Kremlin's pro-Arab position. Novotný had been Khrushchev's favourite and, partly because of this, Brezhnev had never warmed to the Czech leader, who was now seeking help from Moscow to restore his faltering leadership. 'It's your affair', Brezhnev told Novotný, which made his position in his party untenable. In January 1968, he was replaced by Alexander Dubček.[5]

Dubček had joined the Presidium of the Czechoslovak Communist Party in 1962 as the first Slovak politician who had successfully climbed to a senior post in the country. Dubček was chosen as Novotný's successor, as a moderate and populist figure acceptable both to the conservatives and liberal wings of the Party. In effect, Dubček became instrumental in promoting 'Socialism with a Human face' – a precursor of Euro-Communism in the 1970s. By the summer of 1968, Czechoslovakian Perestroika and Glasnost were gaining their own momentum and pressures for change spread to nearly every corner of the country. The Czechs and Slovaks were hoping to improve the position of the Slovak minority, and to come to terms with their two different historical cultures through devolution. Dubček sought to reform Czechoslovakia, but he had no intention of breaking away from the Soviet Union. However, other Czech reformist Party officials were willing to go further, by reducing Party control over the Church, parliament, censorship and the economy, as in Gorbachev's Perestroika. The dilution of the Party's role in Czech social, political and economic affairs became the main aim of the Prague Spring.[6]

Czechoslovakia's liberation movement, however, caused other Eastern European rulers much anxiety. Walter Ulbricht of East Germany and Wldyslaw Gomulka of Poland were increasingly concerned about the ripple effects of changes in Czechoslovakia on the stability of their own regimes.[7] Moscow grew uneasy, too. Unlike Romania, Poland and Hungary, Czechoslovakia was traditionally pro-Russian. Although in late July 1968 the Soviet leadership was infuriated by a reformist Czech general's remarks about the need to improve the Warsaw Pact's 'inequalities', it is known that the news about 'the infamous Gen. Prchlík' came 'too late' to have any impact on the Soviet decision to smash the Prague Spring.[8] The crisis in Czechoslovakia presented an enormous challenge to the Kremlin leadership. The country was a major producer of advanced weapons and uranium for Moscow's military-industrial complex and, as such, was too important to be allowed to leave the Soviet orbit. Nevertheless, Brezhnev was reluctant to resort to repressive measures against Prague, which might, he feared, provoke the West into war against Moscow. Andrei Gromyko, the Soviet Foreign Minister, and Andropov, the Chief of the KGB, both apparently persuaded an indecisive Brezhnev to take the decision to intervene. During the crisis, Brezhnev began to take heavy sedative tablets, which became a permanent habit. There was also the fear that once Czechoslovakia fell into the hands of counter-revolutionaries, the rest of the Warsaw Pact powers might follow suit. It was important for Moscow to nip 'the Prague Spring' in the bud.[9]

On the night of 20/21 August 1968, the Soviet Union, with the help of other Warsaw Pact countries (the GDR, Poland, Hungary and Bulgaria), mounted a huge military operation, twice as large as Moscow's intervention in Hungary in 1956, and with it the Prague Spring ended abruptly. The Soviet military intervention shocked Dubček and other Czechoslovakian reformers and they were reluctantly forced to accept that Marxist-Leninist theory was, in fact, 'incompatible with a genuine, modern, democratic, economic and political system' and, even worse, the system was not 'even open to reform'.[10]

The death of the Prague Spring marked the decline of the legitimacy of Communist rule throughout Eastern Europe, while the Soviet Communist Party had lost its appeal to its fellow Communists in Western Europe. The younger generation of Eastern European intellectuals began to search for a 'European' identity as an alternative to subordination to Moscow, although many of their rulers had no choice but to return to conservatism (or 'normalization') by closing the doors to the modernization of the Communist socio-economic systems, a situation that persisted into the middle of the 1970s.[11] The Kremlin, having found that there had been no violent reactions from the West to the crushing of the 'Prague Spring', became more confident about the ability of the Soviet Union to defend its own interests. This sense of confidence was reinforced by Soviet military and nuclear strength, which had been built up during the 1960s. The Soviet Union was now ready to enter into more peaceful international relations, despite the remaining ideological differences, with the Western bloc. Détente was simply, for Moscow, the West's recognition of the Soviet Union's equality with the USA in terms of power and influence in the world.[12]

The détente in 1970 created a measure of at least surface stability in Eastern Europe. The signature of the Helsinki Act by 33 Eastern (except Albania) and Western European countries, as well as the USA and Canada, represented the culmination of European détente, which began in the late 1960s. The détente provided Western Europe with the potential to melt down the Iron Curtain by stealth: increasing trade, cultural and human contacts with its Eastern counterparts would expose Eastern Europeans to Western democratic and liberal ideas, better consumer goods, and more sophisticated technology, thereby loosening the cohesion of the Soviet bloc. The West hoped that the easing of East–West tensions in Europe would make both Eastern and Western Europe less concerned about building up their armaments, increase their freedom of action, liberate them from intervention by both superpowers, and would altogether provide the West with a feasible way of disarming the enemy in stages. The West rested its hope of breaking down East–West barriers in Basket III of the Helsinki Act, which contained a joint East–West pledge to respect human rights in individual countries. The Soviets accepted the provision, assuming that 'no one could seriously expect them to honour' it, but Czech intellectuals tried to persuade the government to defend the human rights of individuals. They produced their manifesto in January 1977, *Charter '77*. The Czech police force suppressed the supporters of *Charter '77*, but signatories to the Charter grew by nearly four times by 1980, with the total number reaching 1000.[13]

Closer economic and cultural links with the West encouraged by détente eased Eastern Europeans' access to Western markets and technology, but it also helped to accentuate the economic problems and the contradictions in the Communist systems in the region. By then, the majority of Eastern Europeans were believed to have shifted from the period of 'socialist construction' to a more advanced stage, such as developed socialism, which was meant to be closer to the ultimate goal of achieving Communism. In an effort to improve their economies and living standards and to create 'consumer Communism', Eastern European leaders imported Western technology and raised loans from Western banks as a 'means of buying off public opinion and delaying the harsh impact of structural change in the state social economy'.[14]

However, the rulers would soon learn that their assumptions were incorrect. The rise in world oil prices between 1973 and 1978 affected the economies of the advanced Western countries, on which the economies of Eastern Europe were now dependent. Superpower relations grew worse, with the threat of a renewed Cold War in Europe towards the end of the 1970s. Accordingly, the Eastern European states found the prices of imported commodities rising, interest rates increasing and trade with the West contracting. Moreover, the oil crisis compelled the Soviet Union to increase its own oil prices, which piled further significant economic burdens on many Eastern European states. Their difficulties were compounded by the fact that Eastern Europe was losing out in competition in exports with the newly industrializing and cheap-labour countries of Asia and Latin America. Reliance on Western technology did not help to make Eastern European countries any more competitive either, for the rigid structure of their command economies was not conducive to the adaptation of technology in the production of quality goods. The Eastern European economies began to decline after 1975 with no sign of recovery and, by 1981, many Eastern European states were borrowing more money to finance their accumulating debts to the USA and Western Europe, debts that increased ten-fold between 1971 and 1980.[15] Ironically, the more liberated and industrialized countries, like Hungary and Poland, suffered more as a result of their steady integration into the world market, as their leaders felt a greater need to provide the public with better services than did the more repressive and conservative socialist states. For example, the economy of Hungary became insolvent in 1981, which compelled Budapest to join the International Monetary Fund (IMF) and the World Bank.[16] Overall, the growing contradictions between the reality and the goals of socialism were glaringly clear to the ordinary populations, as the failure of consumer Communism was increasingly evident across Eastern Europe.

SIGNS OF SOVIET DISENGAGEMENT FROM EASTERN EUROPE?: THE POLISH CRISIS, 1980–1

Nowhere was the decline of confidence in the party leadership more significant than in Poland. This resulted in the 1980–1 crisis when, for the third time, Polish workers revolted against their Communist leadership. Following the 1956 uprising, in December 1970 on the eve of the Christmas festivities, the Polish government under the hardline, but nationalist Wladyslaw Gomulka, increased the price of food stuffs, which provoked angry protests from the workers in the Lenin shipyard in Gdansk. Despite Moscow's opposition to the use of force, the Polish leader brutally suppressed the strikers, which cost 75 lives. The military solution provoked anguished responses from workers elsewhere in the country, which caused Gomulka to use force more often and more aggressively in an effort to maintain national stability. This repression resulted in the loss of his credibility and he was replaced by Edvard Gierek. Gierek's subsequent effort to placate the population was with promises of achieving a socialist utopia by means of a number of economic reforms; however, further loans from the West led to a deterioration in Poland's economic and social situation by the late 1970s. The election of the Polish Pope John Paul II in 1978 strengthened Polish nationalism and helped to unite the non-Party intellectuals and the Roman Catholic Church in support of the discontented peasants and workers.

In the latter half of the 1970s, Poland was faced with mounting debt and nearly 90 per cent of the earnings from Poland's exports were used to repay its debts to the West. Greater numbers of Poles were travelling to the West in the

1970s, where they experienced at first hand the growing gap between the economies of East and West. The population was increasingly disenchanted with the government's mismanagement of the country, let alone its failure to establish a genuinely prosperous socialist utopia. Housing and health services were particularly poor and the ordinary people lived in appalling conditions. This, in turn, increased popular resentment against the high-ranking Communist officials, who enjoyed perks and special favours at the cost of the majority of the workers.[17]

In July 1980, a rise in meat prices led to a series of strikes which, in September, was followed by the founding of the Solidarity movement, led by Lech Wałęsa, an electrician from the Lenin shipyards in Gdansk. Solidarity, once described as Europe's 'first genuine workers' revolution since the Paris Commune of 1871,' was a mass national movement. It was not initially intended to replace the current Communist government, but was created as an organization that would mount a strong political protest against the weakened and divided Polish regime.[18] How to respond to this latest crisis tormented both Moscow and Warsaw. There was no clear prescription for a solution to the crisis and the outcome was not deliberately planned in either capital. Moscow, initially and somewhat reluctantly, agreed to a military solution and then postponed it at the end of 1980, finally abandoning it in 1981.

Hearing of the outbreak of the Polish crisis, Brezhnev initially resorted to the usual method of creating a Soviet threat to intervene militarily, by calling up Soviet reservists and by putting the Red Army on alert. With his health rapidly failing, he appeared to be still guided by his interventionist doctrine, but he also pressed the Polish leadership to act decisively against Solidarity. However, behind the scenes, a group of top Soviet leaders, including Suslov, Andropov and Ustinov (who made the decision to invade Afghanistan in 1979), were not entirely convinced of the need for military intervention in Poland, although they were united in the view that Moscow 'cannot and must not lose Poland'.[19]

The other Eastern European leaders, in East Germany, Czechoslovakia and Bulgaria, fearing that the crisis might affect the stability of their own regimes, urged Moscow to intervene in Poland. By December 1980, the Soviet Union and the Warsaw Pact powers had drawn up a military plan, which envisaged an invasion force comprising 15 Soviet, one East German and two Czechoslovak divisions, under the cover of a joint military exercise. The Warsaw Pact forces would occupy Polish areas close to the major towns and industrial sectors, in order to exert the maximum pressure to avert the worsening crisis. Unlike the Czech invasion by the Warsaw Pact, the Polish leadership was informed of the upcoming intervention, which was to occur between 8 and 21 December 1980. Three days prior to the planned action, the Polish party leader, Stanislaw Kania (who had replaced Gierek in the wake of the August crisis), warned Brezhnev that if there were another intervention similar to that against Czechoslovakia in 1968, 'there would be a national uprising. Even if angels entered Poland they would be treated as bloodthirsty vampires and the socialist ideas would be swimming in blood.' Brezhnev was apparently persuaded by this warning, responding that 'OK, we will not go in, although if complications occur we would. But without you we won't go in.'[20] Subsequently, the Soviet Union stood aside from the deepening Polish crisis.

In February 1981, General Wojciech Jaruzelski, the Minister of Defence, became Prime Minister, and in October 1981 he also took over Party leadership from Kania. Jaruzolski's power base was now formidable and, since the autumn of 1980 (before the Warsaw operation had been cancelled), he had been working with other military officials to prepare for an 'administrative' action against Solidarity, in the form of martial law.[21] In the autumn of 1981, Poland was drifting into chaos and it appeared that neither the government nor Solidarity could control the situation through political negotiations.[22]

In mid October 1981, Jaruzelski was compelled to request Soviet military help in the event that the Polish security forces proved inadequate to bring the situation under control. In response, the Kremlin leadership agreed only to apply economic sanctions if necessary, but declined to provide Soviet military assistance. The position was subsequently confirmed in a Politburo meeting on 10 December 1981, which stated 'there can be no consideration at all of sending in troops'. Even the right wing ideologist, Suslov, agreed that Soviet military action would lead to a 'catastrophe'.[23] The Polish leadership received neither the assurance of any military assistance, nor any gesture of cooperation from the Warsaw Pact. It is, therefore, arguable whether Jaruzelski was, as he claimed, forced to choose the military option *in order* to forestall an imminent intervention. Recent evidence suggests that it was Jaruzelski who wanted Moscow's assurance of military help if things had gone badly, and the Kremlin was rather put out by the persistence with which he entreated Moscow for military intervention.[24] On the night of 13/14 December, Jaruzelski declared martial law, sealed the Polish borders, and placed the country under military control. The leading members of Solidarity and leaders of the strikers were arrested and imprisoned. Within a year, Wałęsa was released and martial law was partially suspended, but Jaruzelski and his military officials remained in full control of the country.

After the Polish crisis, a semblance of uniformity appeared to have been restored to Eastern Europe, but, in reality, the differences between the various countries increased. Poland and Hungary were prepared to be more tolerant in dealing with dissidents, in order to avoid further crises. Their more conservative counterparts (Czechoslovakia and the GDR) and the relatively underdeveloped Balkan countries (Romania, Bulgaria and Albania) remained under the tight control of their rulers. Yugoslavia remained in a unique situation and was prepared to be more magnanimous towards its democratic elements than its conservative peers in the Balkans. The failure of Yugoslavia's economic reforms in the 1960s had led to the growth of nationalism in the various republics. The rise of Croatian nationalism, which characterized the 1970–1 crisis, was overcome by purging the Croatian Party leadership and by strengthening Party discipline. However, the unity of Yugoslavia was further threatened by its continuing economic failure (by 1984, the Yugoslav population had to put up with a decline of some 30 per cent in living standards) and by the death of Marshal Tito in 1980. These conditions led to the eruption of another ethnic crisis, this time over Kosovo (an autonomous province within the Serbian Republic since

1963, the inhabitants of which were predominantly Albanian). The region was regarded by the Serbians as 'the holy place of all Serbs' – it had been the centre of the Serbian Empire in the Middle Ages. By 1981, Kosovo's living standards had deteriorated further in relation to the rest of Yugoslavia, and it now demanded the upgrading of its province to an independent republic, equal to Slovenia, Croatia and Serbia. The Kosovan conflict continued and between 1981 and 1987 the predominantly Serbian police force arrested more than 5000 Kosovar Albanians.[25]

By the early 1980s, the German Democratic Republic led by Erich Honecker was regarded as the most rigid socialist country, and the most thriving economically. In reality, the situation in the Republic replicated that of the other Communist states in Eastern Europe. West German Chancellor Willy Brandt's Ostpolitik in the early 1970s led to the international acceptance of the GDR as a separate socialist state and it, together with the Federal Republic of Germany, acquired full membership of the UN in September 1973. The conclusion of the Basic Treaty with the FRG in 1972 encouraged 68 countries to recognize the GDR within the next 12 months. For West Germany, Ostpolitik was intended to remove barriers to inter-German contacts, leading eventually to national reconciliation and the unification of Germany. For example, with the conclusion of the Basic Treaty, the number of West German travellers to East Germany more than doubled in 1983, while West Berliners were also able to travel more easily to East Berlin and the GDR, thanks to the inter-German transit agreement in the spring of 1972. Postal and telephone communications between the two Germanies significantly increased and so did cooperation in sport, medicine and healthcare. The size of the GDR's trade with the West increased by 6 per cent in the 1970, at the expense of its trade with the Soviet Union.[26]

While Honecker appreciated the benefits of financial cooperation with the West, he was afraid that the East German population might succumb to the pressures from the West. Hence, while Ostpolitik began to reduce some aspects of the German–German barrier, East Germany was careful to maintain its state as a separate entity by emphasizing 'the differences between the GDR and FRG, and their lack of any commonality'.[27] Honecker gave priority to the tightening of central economic management and, in the spring of 1972, ordered the nationalization of what remained of the private and semi-private sectors of the economy, comprising 15 per cent of the entire industrial workforce. The school curriculum was also revised, with more emphasis on the teaching of Marxism-Leninism rather than classical German literature.[28] All in all, East Germany sought to become a more Soviet-style socialist country in the 1970s and, despite some relaxation of travel to the West, its system remained militant and repressive. After 1975, East Germany's economy, while benefiting from its 'indirect subsidies' from the FRG, began to deteriorate rapidly. Increased Soviet oil prices (which rose nearly three times between 1975 and 1980) hit the industrialized East Germany particularly hard, while its foreign debt grew by eight times.[29]

Elsewhere in Eastern Europe, signs of economic and social decline were becoming increasingly visible to the population, and the rulers were running out of methods of salvaging the situation. If anything, a strong Soviet leadership could have helped to restore some coherence to the region, but the Polish crisis revealed the fluctuations in the determination of the Soviet leadership to act decisively. Moscow ultimately judged that a Soviet military intervention would further exacerbate East–West relations, while it was unconvinced that an intervention would help to unite and pacify Poland either. Andropov, then the Chief of the KGB under the Brezhnev regime, was most adamant against taking an interventionist course:

> I don't know how things will turn out in Poland, but even if Poland falls under the control of 'Solidarity', that is the way it will be. And if the capitalist countries pounce on the Soviet Union, and you know they have already reached agreement on a variety of economic and political sanctions, that will be very burdensome for us. We must be concerned above all with our own country and about the strengthening of the Soviet Union. That is our main line.[30]

Thus, the Kremlin feared the intensification of the Cold War more than the possible loss of Poland to the anti-government forces. This in itself indicated a decline in the ability and willingness of the Soviet Union to sustain its own sphere of influence in Eastern Europe, a precursor to Gorbachev's subsequent approach to that region.

All these developments were not quite discernible in the West. Western intelligence gave inconsistent estimates of the situation during the Polish crisis, which was hardly surprising given that both Moscow and the Polish leadership were vacillating as to what policy to follow. Moreover, two months prior to the imposition of martial law, Colonel Ryczard Kuklinski on the Polish General Staff, a CIA operative, had been moved out of Poland by the Agency for fear of detection by the KGB. The West, therefore, continued to expect Moscow's military intervention in the Polish crisis and was surprised at the internal crackdown in the absence of Soviet tanks and the Red Army.[31]

The USA took the Polish crisis extremely seriously. Within a couple of weeks of the declaration of martial law in December 1981, Washington, without consulting its European allies in advance, announced its intention of imposing sanctions not only on Poland, but also on the Soviet Union. Reagan (unlike Bonn) continued to believe that the Soviet Union would intervene even after the imposition of martial law in Poland, since he regarded Jaruzelski as the Kremlin's 'puppet'.[32] West Germany was even more reluctant than its Western European allies to damage Ostpolitik by intensifying the Cold War against Moscow over the Polish crisis, and European leaders were annoyed with America's openly confrontational and unilateral approach to the crisis. Although the Western Europeans followed the USA in imposing some limited economic sanctions against Poland and the Soviet Union, they eventually persuaded Washington to continue with the planned oil pipelines connecting Siberia with seven Western European countries.[33]

The West believed that some pressure on Poland was necessary, since this might, they believed, compel the Polish government to continue with reforms and democratization. In March 1982, Reagan signed a presidential directive, NSDD-32, confirming the American policy of liberation and psychological warfare, which had been adopted at the inception of the Cold War. In doing so,

Washington hoped to 'weaken Soviet influence and strengthen indigenous forces for freedom in the region'. In response to the Polish crisis, the President asked the CIA to help Solidarity covertly by providing 'money, communication equipment, and intelligence information' in order to keep the opposition alive and well.[34] However, none of the leaders in Europe or in Washington then foresaw that the deepening crisis in Eastern Europe, combined with Moscow's reluctance to restore order in its Eastern European satellites, would eventually clear the way for the revolutionary changes that were to sweep the region in 1989.

GORBACHEV'S POLICY TOWARDS EUROPE, 1985-8

As with his internal reforms, Gorbachev's policy towards Europe evolved in stages during the period. His main foreign policy concerns initially focused on the need to improve superpower relations in the field of arms negotiations. After 1987, the Gorbachev leadership began to engage seriously in Europe and in that year he spelled out the idea of creating a 'common European home' by 'transcending the division of Europe'.[35] Between 1987 and 1988, the greater part of Gorbachev's international meetings were with Western European leaders. After a meeting with the British Prime Minister, Margaret Thatcher, in the spring of 1987, Gorbachev felt that 'we study Europe badly and we know it badly'.[36] In early 1988, the Institute of Europe in the Soviet Academy of Sciences was created to undertake research and consultation on the whole of Europe and, as such, became a useful think tank to clarify the 'common European concept' for the Soviet leadership. In mid 1986, Gorbachev had warned the Ministry of Foreign Affairs that the Soviet Union 'must not see Europe "through the prism of its relations with the United States of America"', for Europe needed to be treated as an independent entity. The Soviet leader was also seeking to change Soviet relations with the Eastern European countries, which should involve 'less smugness on the Soviet side'.[37] In the spring of 1988, some significant institutional changes were made to reflect Gorbachev's aspiration to deal with Europe as a whole. The Central Committee's department in charge of Soviet relations with 'ruling Communist parties' was dissolved and merged with the International Department. CPSU's exclusive relations with Eastern European Communist Parties were also transferred to the Foreign Ministry of the Soviet government.[38]

However, Gorbachev, Shevardnadze and Yakovlev, the three individuals who shaped Soviet foreign policy towards Europe, were not seeking a genuinely united Europe, as they assumed that Eastern European countries would remain socialist, as opposed to the West's capitalist counterparts. Nor did they foresee that Eastern European countries would seek total independence from the Soviet Union. Rather, the division of Europe into two blocs would be gradually reduced over time, eventually, it was hoped, leaping to a rapprochement between the capitalist Western European and the socialist Eastern European countries. In this context, Gorbachev was intrigued by the Spanish social democratic model and believed it applicable to Eastern Europe. Overall, the Soviet leadership was much less clear about what the ultimate shape of a common European home would be, let alone how to create it.[39]

What, then, were Gorbachev's views on a European rapprochement? It appears that Moscow envisaged its finalization at three levels – military, institutional and socio-political.[40] At the military level, the Kremlin saw the accumulation of armaments in Europe as the source of mistrust and hostility between the two blocs, and regarded the elimination of nuclear weapons and reductions of conventional forces as useful steps towards reducing the threat of the Cold War. While Western European leaders generally supported a less militant Europe, they were suspicious of any signs of a slackening of the US security effort, nuclear and conventional, in Western Europe. Thus, an improvement in superpower relations was not necessarily welcome news to the main Western European capitals. The 1986 superpower summit in Reykjavik was one such case. When Reagan and Gorbachev nearly agreed to eliminate all nuclear weapons and to achieve bona fide nuclear disarmament, this sent a shock wave through many Western European capitals.[41]

Gorbachev himself was somewhat ambiguous about the nature of military reconciliation. In his memoirs, he states that 'we had to face the realities and accept the existing structures (NATO and the Warsaw Pact), pushing them at the same time towards co-operation – and hence towards a gradual transformation of both NATO and the Warsaw Pact, their relations shifting away from tension towards eventual stability'.[42] While the impact of the arms negotiations on European security will be considered in chapters 5 and 6, it proved a challenging task to reduce military tensions by making changes to Western Europe's post-war security structure. The Soviet leadership viewed the resumption of the Conference on Security and Cooperation in Europe (CSCE) in late 1986 as a positive move towards resolving the mutual distrust between the two blocs. Possibly by 2000, as envisaged by Moscow's Institute of Europe, a pan-European security structure could be constructed on the basis of the CSCE.[43]

As for the second level of East–West conciliation, Gorbachev, as early as 1985, hoped that some institutional cooperation between the European Economic Community (EEC) and the Council of Mutual Economic Assistance (CMEA, known as COMECON in the West) would be possible. However, the CMEA had been established by Stalin in order to maximize Soviet economic control over the Communist countries in Eastern Europe and, as such, was an 'artificial multilateral formation', which lacked the degree of integration achieved by the EEC. Moreover, under Stalin each Communist country was compelled to follow the Soviet economic style by giving priority to heavy industry at the cost of developing the consumer sector and light industry. As a result of these factors, the CMEA neither achieved genuine international cooperation, nor facilitated economic growth within the Eastern European bloc.[44]

Gorbachev urged the CMEA to strengthen its economic integration, as he thought that this would make the idea of economic cooperation with Western European countries more feasible. However, the two blocs were operating on a totally different footing – the free market economic system in the West and the centrally planned command system in the East. Although the Soviet leadership encouraged Eastern Europe to undertake economic reforms, it often increased the differences between, rather than the integration of, their economies, as the level and nature of these reforms varied from country to country. Moreover, the EEC was expanding further into the southern flank of Europe (Spain and Portugal became full members of the Community in 1986) and was also strengthening its central institutions. In 1987 the Single European Act (SEA) was ratified, which would allow free movement of goods, capital and labour within the Community, as a step towards achieving a single economic market within the following five years.

Clearly, there was the problem of the widening gap between a successful Western EEC and an inefficient and technologically backward CMEA. Moreover, economically stricken Eastern Europe and the Soviet Union could not undertake much in the way of investment and radical reform necessary to make the CMEA a thriving concern. Nor was the EEC particularly keen to extend an equal institutional status to the CMEA. This all meant that the economic fusion between the two blocs was fraught with practical and ideological obstacles. It was not until June 1988 that the two institutions officially recognized each other and, in August, the Soviet Union and EEC established 'a full diplomatic relationship'.[45]

Probably the most difficult, but most important, level of cooperation would be at the socio-political level. How could these two societies live together without the Iron Curtain? The Gorbachev leadership was aware that the 'nature of the regimes in the USSR and Eastern Europe' was the main obstacle to East–West cooperation in Europe and foresaw that the democratization of the socialist systems should facilitate such cooperation. At the end of 1988, the Soviet reformers were considering converging the two different systems through mutual compromise between East and West. For example, they envisaged that Western Europe could come closer to Eastern Europe by adopting a system of 'socialist capitalism', while Eastern European countries were introducing more democracy into their socialist system.

The idea of mutual transformation by renouncing the notion of victory over the enemy had been adopted by the Italian Communist Party in the middle of the 1970s, was seconded by the West German Social Democratic Party and, as such, was not completely new to Europe. Some Soviet officials even contemplated that building socialism in the whole of Germany was 'an integral part of the common European home's foundation'.[46] The notion was, however, at odds with the West's concept of détente with Eastern Europe, which envisaged a peaceful way of transforming the Eastern European authoritarian socialist system into a liberal democratic capitalist system.

Indeed, the Soviet leaders did not expect a radical alteration in Eastern Europe's political systems. Gorbachev's idea of promoting pluralism and democracy existed in his mind within the framework of a socialist one-party system. During the Malta summit in December 1989, Gorbachev protested about a US statement describing the Eastern European countries as changing 'political orientations "on the basis of Western values"', as arrogant. Gorbachev retorted that democracy and freedom were not synonymous with Western values, but that they were 'universal human values' applicable to other different political systems.[47]

In total, the notion of a common European home must be flexible enough to accommodate two different Europes in one home, yet robust enough to transcend the obvious difficulties and differences. The leaders in major Western capitals were all familiar with the Soviet Union's pan-European approach. The concept was first raised in 1954 and was expanded during the Geneva summit conference in July 1955. In 1966, the Warsaw Pact also called for creating a similar pan-European security system, which eventually led to the Helsinki process in the 1970s. The West saw in these Eastern initiatives 'the same old girl in a new dress'; that is, a rehashed attempt by Moscow to extract from the West recognition of the legitimacy of the Soviet bloc, while encouraging the West to liquidate their alliance systems. It also appeared that a common European home was an extension of Khrushchev's 'peaceful co-existence' of the two separate blocs, although Gorbachev's common European home emphasized cooperation or a 'degree of integrity' between East and West, rather than continuing with the East–West rivalry.[48] However, such cooperation implied that the West should respect and, if necessary, guarantee 'the political status quo of Eastern Europe'. Thus, the projected 'home' would be advantageous for the Soviet Union in many ways. Moscow would benefit from Western Europe's technological and scientific superiority, which could be extended to Eastern Europe without the latter being absorbed into the Western bloc. These were the same concepts that in the 1970s Moscow calculated would enable the East to benefit from the East–West détente. Viewed cynically, a common European home could mean the delegation of the Soviet Union's responsibility for Eastern Europe in material and economic terms to Western Europe, without losing Moscow's political leadership over its sphere of influence.

Another issue that remained vague was the future role of the USA in a common European home. Initially, Gorbachev stressed Europe's greatness and uniqueness, describing Europe as one of the most economically developed and politically sophisticated regions of the world, while the USA had 'abducted' Western Europe as part of its satellite sphere of influence.[49] It was inevitable, therefore, that the common European home was received with some caution, even hostility, in Western Europe, as a traditional Soviet ploy to drive a wedge between Western Europe and the USA.[50] However, the superpower relationship had considerably improved by 1988 and, when Moscow realized that any attempts to decouple Western Europe from the USA were counter-productive, the Soviet Union began to see the USA's role in Europe in a more positive light. After 1988, Soviet intellectuals saw the inclusion of the USA in the common European home as also beneficial to the interests of the Soviet Union. It was hoped that the USA's presence in Western Europe would help to reduce the remaining Soviet threat to Europe, provide Europe with an opportunity to exert some influence on US foreign policy generally, and serve ultimately as 'guarantors of the Warsaw Pact's stability and of the Soviet Union's role in it'.[51] Apart from the question of whether this was indeed a feasible solution to the end of the Cold War in Europe, it remained uncertain as to whether this notion of a common European home would be acceptable to the Eastern Europeans.

GORBACHEV AND EASTERN EUROPE

Gorbachev's European policy was constructed upon an improvement in Soviet–Western European relations, and his policy towards Eastern Europe in the process remained in limbo. As soon as he became General Secretary in 1985, he told the Eastern European Communist leaders that, from then on, they were responsible for dealing with the problems in their own countries. Gorbachev's close adviser, Chernyaev, recalled that there was no doubt in Gorbachev's mind about pursuing his 'non-intervention' policy in Eastern Europe, even if this meant that the Soviet Union might lose its 'imperial image' as a result.[52] Indeed, Gorbachev stuck to his policy of non-intervention to the end of the collapse of Communism in Eastern Europe.

Apart from this, no real changes took place in Soviet–Eastern relations between 1985 and 1988. Even after the Soviet Union embraced Glasnost and Perestroika wholeheartedly, Moscow did not appear to have any policy of transforming the Eastern European countries into more democratic entities, or any serious attempt to cajole the more conservative countries (i.e. Romania, Czechoslovakia and East Germany) into following the examples of reformist Hungary and Poland.[53] In contrast with Gorbachev's cordial and friendly relationship with the Western European leaders, his attitude towards the Eastern European counterparts from the outset was somewhat coloured with a sense of helplessness and suspicion about their intentions. For Gorbachev, argues Vladislav Zubok, Eastern European affairs 'could be a bottomless pit, and the communist apparatchiks there were too far below him for him to want to be bothered with them'. This apparent lowly status accorded to the Soviet Eastern European alliance was by no means unusual for a Soviet leader, since Gorbachev's predecessors had equally not been troubled by the need to consult their Eastern European comrades over questions that might directly concern them.[54]

Gorbachev's Soviet policy also reflected a degree of loss of Soviet leadership over the Warsaw Pact countries. After the 1968 crisis in Czechoslovakia, the Soviets began to reorganize and revamp the Warsaw Pact, partially modelled on NATO. During the 1970s, the Pact had become a bona fide military organization. Aside from Romania, the rest of the Warsaw Pact signatory members were willing to use the opportunity to increase their roles in the organization and to make it an 'alliance of equals'. For a time, the reformed Warsaw Pact served Soviet purposes. Top military officials of the Warsaw Pact were educated in Moscow and they became loyal to the Warsaw Pact and to the Kremlin. In 1980, the Pact accepted the subordination of their military forces to the Soviet High Command in time of war. However, modernization also served to increase the power of the Warsaw Pact countries to resist the Soviet leadership.[55] East Germany had resented the deployment of Soviet missiles on its soil and, in the mid 1980s, East Berlin was convinced that 'nothing could be learnt any more from the Soviet Union – not industry, nor in agriculture, nor ideology'.[56] The lack of respect and trust between Moscow and the Eastern European capitals was also reflected in the Kremlin's conclusion in 1985 that the situation in Eastern Europe had become 'a mess', which might require some disciplinary action, as 'Kádár was doing whatever he wanted, Honecker was hiding something from us; the Poles flirted with the Americans and planned to purchase Boeings instead of our airplanes'.[57]

Gorbachev's attitude was not to discipline these leaders, but let them do what they thought was necessary to improve conditions in their own countries. It was no coincidence that Gorbachev showed some sympathy towards the less conservative, more reform-minded leaders of the Eastern European countries, notably Poland and Hungary. Among them, General Jaruzelski became Gorbachev's favourite Eastern European leader, who, after the 1980/81 crisis, had adopted a middle of the road approach to anti-government opposition forces. Solidarity's previous anti-government activities were pardoned in 1986, indicating that the government was no longer prepared or even able to suppress the opposition. In the same year, Gorbachev allowed Jaruzelski to make an official visit to Lithuania, part of the old Polish kingdom, to help to strengthen the General's image in Poland as a patriotic leader.[58]

In 1985, Hungary was the most developed country in Eastern Europe, as János Kádár continued to deliver economic and political reforms. In May 1985, the government introduced a new electoral law, which allowed independent candidates to compete with their Communist counterparts. However, Kádárism had reached its nadir by 1987, since the country's economy had been deteriorating for some time, and Kádár (who was then 76 years old) was also becoming critical of Gorbachev's reform policy and was seeking to cooperate with the more conservative forces in the Kremlin. By 1987, the relationship between Gorbachev and the Hungarian leader had further deteriorated, especially as the latter was becoming an opponent of the advancement of Perestroika and Glasnost in Hungary. Gorbachev, however, refused to become embroiled with Hungarian politics, even though Kádár's possible successor, Károly Grósz, needed Gorbachev's backing to remove Kádár from power.[59] Meanwhile, Hungarian democratization was to develop faster than that of the Soviet Union, as a result of which the Communist leaderships in Moscow and Budapest could not do anything to control events after 1989.

If Gorbachev did not unite or coordinate reformist policies in the Communist countries with those of the Soviet Union, he also remained on the sidelines in dealing with the more conservative Eastern European countries. Czechoslovakia's leader, Gustáv Husák, was ageing and suffered from poor health, thus providing an opportunity for a reformist Party official to replace Husák. During his visit to Czechoslovakia, Gorbachev neither showed any sympathy towards the 1968 Prague Spring, nor sided with the conservative forces. Moscow's passivity failed the democratizing forces in Czechoslovakia and, as a result, the post-Husák regime fell into the hands of conservatives.[60] Although Gorbachev did talk frankly about the need for democratization in Romania, it remained doubtful how much, if any, of Gorbachev's advice had been taken into consideration by its dictator, Ceauşescu, who had been, for some time, isolated from the main stream of the Warsaw Pact and was openly critical of Gorbachev's Perestroika. Nor did Gorbachev cut much ice with the German Democratic leader, Honecker, who was at first receptive to Gorbachev's idea of East–West relaxation through arms control, but resented Soviet Perestroika and its impact on his regime.[61]

Consequently, the politics of Eastern Europe were increasingly placed at the mercy of their own domestic conditions, an outcome which hinged upon the ability and skills of the leadership of each Eastern European state. Having said this, Eastern European countries were not immune from the impact of the

Gorbachevian reforms in the Soviet Union and his efforts to end the Cold War. Romania imposed strict restraints on the flow of information (all typewriters were required to be registered with the government to limit clandestine publications by anti-governmental groups), but the Romanians managed, in any case, to obtain the information by turning to Hungarian television. It was well known to the East German leadership that the population was watching West German television, and the Czechs enjoyed Austrian and West German broadcasts. This circulation of information, together with the increased contact with the West after the 1970 détente, helped to undermine the hardline and anti-Gorbachevian Eastern European regimes, while, under more tolerant regimes, the Poles and the Hungarians exploited the new changes in Moscow to advance their cause against their rulers at home.[62]

In January 1989, Gorbachev asked the newly created Foreign Policy Commission of the Politburo (led by Yakovlev) to examine future developments in Eastern Europe. The majority of study papers, produced by Soviet analysts and academics, foresaw 'an overall crisis of the alliance'. Some argued that Eastern European allies were 'already quietly rejecting "socialism" and were "in a powerful magnetic field" of the West'. The prognoses were gloomy, but almost all advisers rejected any form of Soviet intervention, which was believed to be counterproductive, a view with which Gorbachev agreed. The Soviet reformers thought Moscow's intervention might precipitate a major crisis in Eastern Europe, would ruin Perestroika and Glasnost at home, and lose the West's confidence in Moscow. They hoped that reforms would eventually improve the conditions of Eastern Europe, which would allow them to do business with their Western counterparts on an equal basis. While the Soviet leadership was aware of the fragility and weaknesses of the Communist regimes in Eastern Europe, they were convinced that Eastern Europe could only survive if it undertook genuine political and economic reforms. Accordingly, the Soviet reformers rejected the advice and pleas from those conservatives in the Soviet Union and Eastern Europe that reform would open up a Pandora's Box, which could precipitate the collapse of state socialism in these countries.[63]

Gorbachev initially adopted a 'wait and see position' on Eastern Europe with regard to reform, but by 1988 he was getting impatient with the lack of progress or even willingness of many Eastern European countries to follow in the steps of Soviet Perestroika and Glasnost. In December 1988, he publicly announced the repudiation of the Brezhnev Doctrine and promised reductions of Soviet troops in Eastern Europe. The declaration was designed to remind conservative Eastern European leaders of 'Soviet disengagement from Eastern Europe', with the result that the opposition forces in those countries were likely to have their hands strengthened against the existing regimes. It was hardly surprising that the Czechs and East Germans were opposed to Gorbachev's pledges at the UN.[64] The other side of the coin was for the Soviet Union to reduce or even abrogate the means of exerting Soviet influence over Eastern Europe. By rejecting intervention, Gorbachev hoped to use his persuasive skills to demonstrate to Eastern Europe the success of what was then hoped to be Perestroika in his country. However, after 1989, the domestic situation took a turn for the worse, taking up much of Gorbachev's time and energy, and he became even more eager to achieve a rapprochement with the West, to salvage his faltering leadership at home. His critics argued that Gorbachev '"surrendered" Eastern Europe to the West in exchange for his international stardom and the mantle of a "new thinker"'. In this process, in Moscow's priorities Eastern Europe remained low, with its attitude characterized by 'immoblism'.[65]

The irony was that no one in Moscow wanted to abandon Eastern Europe, including Gorbachev. He was perhaps so optimistic and confident about the region staying in the Soviet orbit, that he virtually turned a deaf ear to the warnings about the problems occurring in many Eastern European countries. Zubok emphasized Gorbachev's 'aversion' to the use of military force, which also limited Gorbachev's choice, but he believed in the 'third way, socialism with a human face', which could be an option for Eastern Europe 'between old style communism and capitalism'.[66] This proved illusory after 1989.

4

The Collapse of Communism in Eastern Europe and the Unification of Germany, 1989–1991

During the late 1980s and early 1990s, the world witnessed 'revolutions' in Eastern Europe. Just how quickly and relatively smoothly the transition of power from Communist to more liberal regimes took place in these countries surprised the Western world. As it happened, the fall of the Berlin Wall, the subsequent weakening of the position of the existing Communist rulers in Eastern Europe, the rapid unification of Germany between November 1989 and October 1990, and the deteriorating socio-economic condition of the Soviet Union, all contributed to the demise of Communism in Eastern Europe. As this chapter will show, the cardinal element in the changes in Eastern Europe in its final stages lay in the lack of any Soviet will to intervene in the region. By the end of 1991, Germany had been united and included in NATO, while the Warsaw Pact had been disbanded.

ON THE EVE OF THE FALL OF THE BERLIN WALL

On the night of 9 November 1989, crowds of East Germans were gathering around the Berlin Wall and at about 11.30 p.m. the East German passport controllers and border guards were literally forced to abandon their duties, and open the gates. As a result, the Berlin Wall fell. Like the August coup in the USSR, the fall of the Berlin Wall quickened the tempo of transforming a Cold War Europe into something new.

The year 1989 started relatively peacefully. Europe was still divided, the Soviet Union was not yet disintegrating, and Gorbachev felt he had achieved much in ending the Cold War against the West. At the end of December 1988, Gorbachev confidently reported to the Politburo about his recently well-received speech at the UN: 'our initiatives pulled the rug out from under the feet of those who had been prattling . . . that new political thinking is just about words . . . the unilateral reduction left a huge impression and created an entirely different background for perceptions of our politics and the Soviet Union as a whole.' What concerned the Soviet leadership most was how far the incoming George Bush Republican administration would accept the seriousness of the Soviet intention of ending the Cold War. Gorbachev correctly depicted Bush as a 'very cautious politician', who would be surrounded in his administration by Conservative traditionalists who had lived most of their lives under Cold War conditions. Under the circumstances, continued Gorbachev, 'we should have a thoughtful, dynamic, practical policy' to ensure that the new American administration should not 'take a protracted time out and slow down the tempo of our political offensive'.[1]

Washington DC

George Bush came to power when the popularity of Gorbachev was rising fast in the USA and elsewhere in the world. In the face of Gorbachev's series of proposals, the West looked defensive and, in American eyes, Gorbachev's peace offensive 'undermined the US leadership'. Bush, a former director of the CIA and Vice-President during the Reagan years, was well versed in American foreign affairs. He appointed his like-minded and pragmatic conservative friends and colleagues to key decision-making posts, including James Baker as Secretary of State, Dick Cheney as Secretary of Defense, and Brent Scowcroft as his National Security Adviser.[2] These men were not likely to be lured by the 'Soviet smile', as the American Ambassador to Moscow, Jack Matlock, put it. Moscow's seemingly conciliatory attitude was seen as a tactical manoeuvre, aimed at maintaining its 'great power position' at less cost to the Soviet Union, rather than an actual change of Moscow's thinking or strategy towards the West. Overall, the main actors of the Bush administration had not been closely involved in dealing with the Kremlin leadership during the Reagan years (even Bush's direct experience with Gorbachev as Vice-President remained modest), and personal and political trust between the elites both in Moscow and Washington had to be rebuilt.[3] Moreover, Bush was mindful of the need to 'move out of Reagan's shadow',[4] and the White House did not contemplate immediately following up the series of summit talks with Gorbachev, which had characterized the second term of the Reagan administration.

For these reasons, the administration wanted to take a 'pause' during its initial few months, in order to review America's foreign policy towards Moscow. While the issues of the Third World (see chapters 7 and 8) and of the arms control negotiations (see chapters 5 and 6) remained unresolved between the superpowers, it appeared to Washington that Europe could be an area to explore further, to see whether Moscow was willing to translate Gorbachev's recent pledge, to reduce the size of the Red Army in Eastern Europe, into action.[5] In the early months of 1989, Poland and Hungary were making progress with their political and economic reforms. When the Polish government legalized Solidarity in April 1989, the Bush administration decided to offer economic assistance to Warsaw as a sign of the West's appreciation of Poland's democratization. However, Washington's position on the liberation of Eastern Europe was inevitably limited: while the USA wanted to see the region becoming free and democratic, it did not want to incite the anti-government movements unduly, since to do so might aggravate the domestic turmoil in Poland and elsewhere in Eastern Europe. Bush, like Gorbachev, wanted to see gradual changes, not radical revolutions, which might affect the security of Western Europe or undermine Washington's relations with Moscow.[6] In April, the initial policy review concluded that US policy should be neither 'to help [n]or hurt Gorbachev'.[7]

The fluidity of the situation made it difficult for the new administration to adopt a bold initiative for the future of Europe, although Henry Kissinger came up with the idea that the stability and freedom of Eastern European countries could be guaranteed, possibly secretly, by both superpowers; that is, for Moscow to allow the Eastern Europeans to liberate themselves and for Washington, in return, to refrain from exploiting the situation at the cost of the USSR's interests. Kissinger raised the idea with Gorbachev in Moscow in early 1989, when the former Secretary of State delivered 'a courteous letter of greeting' from the new American President. While Gorbachev was not greatly interested in such a proposed secret deal with Washington, the State Department regarded the Kissinger proposal as 'dangerous' and it was eventually dropped by Baker.[8]

The problem with a divided Europe was that, while it was not an ideal situation, it had been relatively stable, especially after the German Social Democratic (SPD) Chancellor, Willy Brandt, took the initiative of recognizing two Germanies of different political and social orientations. The Bush administration was not unanimous about how to overcome the division of Europe: the National Security Council urged the President to take the German question as central to US policy for Europe in the final phase of the Cold War, while the State Department demurred, correctly assuming that there was no point in opening such a Pandora's Box, as none of its European allies, including the FRG, were anxious to revisit the issue of German unification. Bush himself was uncertain and did not feel strongly the need to 'push the matter' at that time. While the 'pause' continued, Gorbachev, the media and the world were all becoming impatient about the lack of any positive initiatives coming from the Bush administration.[9]

In May, the new administration was at last ready to put forward a number of broad ideas about US foreign policy. The Bush administration would take Gorbachev's European initiative seriously and help to push this forward. In a speech at Texas A & M University on 12 May 1989, the President stated that 'it is time to move beyond containment, to a new policy for the 1990s', and to integrate the Soviet Union 'into the community of the nations'. Towards the end of that month in Mainz, Germany, the President also hinted at possible moves to end the division of Europe: 'The world had waited long enough. The time is right. Let Europe be whole and free', although he implied that the unification of Germany would be for the Germans to decide, and would not be dictated by Washington.[10] West Germany was placed at the centre of US Western European policy, with Washington describing Bonn as now 'partners in leadership', moving away, to the annoyance of Mrs Thatcher, from the Anglo–US special relationship of the Reagan years. At the NATO summit on 29 May in Brussels, Bush also proposed, partly in response to Gorbachev's troop reduction speech in December 1988, a cut in numbers of both American and Russian troops in Europe, in order to allow a much less militant Europe to emerge. In retrospect, Bush's 'pause' was not wasted. The administration was able to put the necessary measures in place in a cautious manner.[11]

London and Paris

Britain wanted to keep the cost of fighting the Cold War to a minimum and appreciated the relaxation of tension between East and West. Britain, together with other European powers, believed that increasing contact with the Soviet Union was the best way of disarming the Soviet fear of the West, thereby loosening Moscow's ties with its Eastern European satellite countries. In the process, the solution to a divided Germany would proceed in stages, but this was, London hoped, a long-term project. Given that the Cold War could not be resolved militarily, Britain had often played enthusiastically the role of international statesman vis-à-vis the Soviet Union, ever since Winston Churchill's call for summit talks with Moscow in the 1950s.

As early as December 1984, the British Prime Minister, Margaret Thatcher, had struck a responsive chord with Gorbachev, with whom, after her meeting with him in December 1984, she thought she could do 'business'.[12] However, the long history of hostile relations between Britain and the Soviet Union (and the Russian Empire before), meant that London was not easily swayed by Gorbachev's 'wishful' new thinking about foreign policy. Thatcher told Gorbachev in April 1987 that Britain was not yet convinced that a new Soviet Union was emerging, until Moscow took 'the steps necessary to translate words into deeds'. Similarly, London received Gorbachev's plans for arms control cautiously – as the British Foreign Secretary stated in January 1989, 'we must not confuse hope or even expectation with reality. . . .The Soviet Union had a well-stocked hat full of well-armed rabbits and . . . will be able to go on surprising us by drawing rabbits from that hat for many years to come.'[13] The British expected that Communism would eventually be defeated by the strength of liberal democracy. Thatcher claimed that she had already foreseen this possibility in 1988, when some Eastern European countries began to move towards reformist socialism, although she had not then anticipated how thoroughly Gorbachev would renounce the Brezhnev Doctrine when faced with the actual demise of the Eastern European Communist leaders by the end of 1989.[14] Britain was a status quo power in Europe and Thatcher regarded Gorbachev as a potentially important ally in bringing about gradually a 'balanced East-West relationship', which would not affect the transatlantic relationship.[15]

For different reasons, London's cautious sentiments were shared by Paris. Both powers were aware that West Germany was the most vulnerable to the new opportunities emerging from the restructuring of Europe. France was also particularly concerned about a possible change of the status of West Germany when East–West relations were undergoing a transformation.[16] Like Thatcher, the French President, François Mitterrand, soon appreciated how serious the new Soviet leader was about changing the Soviet Union, when Gorbachev made his first official visit to Paris in October 1985. The arrival of Gorbachev presented Mitterrand with the opportunity of asserting France's leadership in engineering the end of the Cold War in Europe, as Charles De Gaulle had sought to do two decades before, although Mitterrand would soon discover that France's other European allies – Italy, Britain and West Germany – were also keen to explore Gorbachev's new thinking, thereby making France's détente diplomacy less distinctive than it might otherwise have been. Paris was not entirely convinced of the genuine nature of Gorbachev's Perestroika, since it appeared to be merely making cosmetic changes to the existing Communist system. Nor was France any more enthusiastic about Gorbachev's concept of a common European home than was Britain, dismissing it as a half-baked idea.[17]

When superpower relations became more friendly by 1987, France sought to deepen its ties with West Germany, and to strengthen Western European cooperation in defence, political and economic matters, in order to protect France's national security interests. The declining value of superpower nuclear deterrence in Europe would also diminish the importance attached by Paris to upholding France's *force de frappe*. A stronger and more integrated Western Europe would help the French to overcome the Yalta nightmare: the war-time conference that led, in the French view, to the division of Europe under two hegemonies, the USA and the Soviet Union. The idea, however, proved insufficient once Gorbachev's new approach to Europe raised the prospect of confronting a new and united Europe.[18]

France, however, could not afford to resign itself to becoming a mere onlooker. It increased its security and political ties with West Germany by pushing forward the project for a European Monetary Union (EMU) in June 1988 and, in the same year, by creating a Franco-German Brigade. With the re-election of Mitterrand as President in May 1988, France appeared willing to develop its Ostpolitik jointly with West Germany. France had agreed to set up a bilateral working group with West Germany to formulate a common policy towards Eastern Europe and, by the autumn of 1988, the two powers were arranging joint visits by their officials to the East (although France's interest in Ostpolitik lessened somewhat in 1989). France's attitude towards the Soviet Union also softened, especially after Gorbachev's speech at the UN in December 1988. Mitterrand was particularly keen to develop a warm personal relationship with Gorbachev, while encouraging the West to provide Moscow with much-needed financial and economic help. While the liberation of Eastern Europe had remained a 'pious wish' for several decades, neither Paris nor London wished to see turmoil taking place in Eastern Europe, with its possible adverse implications for Gorbachev's position at home and for the future balance of Europe, which might be disadvantageous for Britain and France.[19] There existed a sense of unease about future developments in London and Paris in the early months of 1989.

Moscow

The place of two Germanies in the proposed common European home was not considered in any detail by the Gorbachevian reformers. This did not mean that they ignored the issue, but given the sensitivity attached to it, Moscow hoped that the question could be postponed. As early as November 1987, Vyacheslav Dashichev, a researcher at the Institute of the Economy of the World Socialist System, argued that the division of Germany was the key to the division of Europe and that, without resolving the former, it would be difficult to achieve an East–West rapprochement, let alone the construction of a common European home. The Soviet Union could opt for a unified and neutral Germany, which would entail West Germany's withdrawal from the NATO alliance. If this happened, and the Warsaw Pact was disbanded, it would mean the end of the two bloc alliances. Dashichev added that the unification of the two German states might encourage West Germans to look more favourably on socialist ideas, which, in turn, might help to strengthen socialism across Europe. Alternatively, the two Germanies could become confederated. Dashichev's main concern was the growing economic and social gap between the two German states and, unless East Germany undertook radical reforms to bridge this gap, unification might not be feasible. A unified Germany with a possibly socialist orientation was not far from the concept that Stalin had put forward in the early 1950s, but since then East Germany had become a core part of the Soviet sphere of influence in Eastern Europe.[20]

In any case, the reformers, including Gorbachev, believed that Ostpolitik and the Helsinki Accords had settled the German question once and for all. That there were two German states with two different social systems was a historical reality and, during a meeting with the West German President, Richard von Weizsacker, in 1987, Gorbachev stated that 'history would decide what would happen in a hundred years'.[21] He agreed with the view expressed by the West German Social Democrats that the settlement of the German question should be postponed until a comprehensive security structure was established for the whole of Europe.[22] In other words, Gorbachev preferred the ending of the Cold War in Europe and the construction of a common European home first, although he assumed that a reformed East Germany might strengthen its links with West Germany during that process.[23]

In April 1989, Dashichev sent a revised proposal on the subject to Gorbachev and Shevardnadze. The 1989 proposal suggested approaching the unity of the two Germanies in stages. First of all, East Germany should be encouraged to initiate radical reforms, a process that could be assisted by West German financial help. As a result, a reformed East Germany would have a much better chance of achieving a 'rapprochement' with West Germany. This would, in turn, lead to a confederation of the two German states or other types of cooperation. He continued to insist that increasing German cooperation would open the way to a common European home, and that a reformed East Germany could work as the 'principal agent for bringing the two Europes close together'.[24] There was no response from the Soviet leaders to the 1989 proposal, but the subject was certainly on their minds. In January 1989, during a meeting with Kissinger, Gorbachev stated that 'My view is that we should keep an eye on Germany and by that I mean both Germanies, . . .We must not do anything to unsettle Europe into a crisis.'[25] By the summer of 1989, the highest political circles in Moscow were giving some thought to a possible confederation of the two Germanies and to the need for a rapprochement between the SPD and the Socialist Unity Party of (East) Germany (SED) (to fulfil the 'Euro-left' dream held by the Italian Communist Party). By then, developments in Eastern Europe were becoming uneven and there was a new urgency on the part of the Soviet leadership to persuade the more conservative countries, including East Germany, to undertake radical reform. Gorbachev realized that, without the transformation of Eastern Europe into a new form of revamped socialism, his European policy was likely to collapse.[26]

East Berlin and Bonn

The Soviet Union increasingly found Honecker's resistance to Perestroika a hindrance to the progress of Gorbachev's Europe policy. When Gorbachev came to power, he thought East Germany's relative economic and technological prowess vis-à-vis the other Eastern European countries could be used to improve Eastern Europe's competitiveness. Of course, this assumption collapsed, given Moscow's realization that East Germany was surpassed by West Germany by 40 per cent in terms of productivity, and by 50 per cent in real income. By 1989, these gaps were increasing.[27] For their part, the SED leaders were at first receptive to Gorbachev's idea of the relaxation of East–West tensions through arms control, but they came to resent, then to criticize, Gorbachev's efforts to undermine the ideological legitimacy of the Socialist system, let alone his launching of Glasnost and democratization.[28]

Moscow was aware that the apparent stability of East Germany was sustained by its increasing economic dependence on Bonn for hard currency and trade. Honecker's visit to Bonn in 1987 made the Kremlin uneasy about the possibility of an improvement in German–German relations occurring over its head. Moscow's dealing with the GDR characterized Gorbachev's dilemma in dealing with the USSR's Eastern European allies. On the one hand, the Soviet leader felt that Moscow should respect the sovereignty of its Eastern European allies, and told the Warsaw Pact members in the summer of 1989 that Moscow's future relations with them would be based on 'equality, independence and the right of each country to arrive at its own political position . . . without interference from an outside party'.[29] On the other hand, Moscow assumed, still in 1989, that its Eastern European allies would follow the example of the Soviet Union's reforms and regenerate their socialist states.[30]

The East German leader was becoming increasingly concerned by the effects on his own country of the reforms taking place in Poland and Hungary. The contradictions of the Stalinist model were stark, and the GDR had been living beyond its means for some time. East German anti-government critics found it impossible to challenge the regime from within, as they were either repressed by the huge Stasi intelligence service or forced to leave the country.[31] The country continued to benefit from trading East German immigrants for West Germany's money. The year 1984 alone saw 32,000 East Germans leave their homes; some 4.9 million East Germans escaped to West Germany between 1950 and 1989. This in itself demonstrated the dangerous tensions between the regime and its citizens.[32]

Honecker observed that Gorbachev's common European home was a sure way of hastening the revival of the German question.[33] The East German leader believed that the existence of East Germany was a historical fact, which could not be altered, and that all talk of German unification was simply a recipe for the collapse of his regime. In fact, Gorbachev's idea of requiring economic and social reforms to reduce the differences with Western Europe was to challenge directly the *raison d'être* of the GDR. Under the circumstances, there would be no 'justification' for two German states 'once ideology no longer separated them', an assumption that West Germany could also accept.[34]

While the SED party stuck to the preservation of its own regime, West Germany's relationship with Moscow improved steadily after 1988. After all, the existence of two Germanies had been the main outcome of the Cold War. West Germany could be said to be the least satisfied with the Cold War status quo within the Western alliance. On the other hand, Bonn had held fast to the idea of integrating itself into Western Europe since its birth in 1949, and it had successfully projected its power and influence throughout the Atlantic Alliance community. Given this long-standing reality of living with a divided Germany, the idea of a united one had been neglected in both Germanies. Although the notion continued to exist at philosophical, personal and cultural levels, it was no longer given much consideration in the context of territorial unification.[35] However, if a realistic opportunity for political changes in Europe emerged, it was suspected in Western Europe that Bonn could become the weakest link in the Atlantic Alliance.

When Gorbachev came to power, the West German Chancellor, Helmut Kohl, had dismissed Perestroika and Glasnost as propaganda, comparing Gorbachev to Joseph Goebbels. This inevitably angered the Soviet leader. Bonn's attitude towards the Soviet Union, however, began to change more quickly than did the attitudes of London and Paris. Gorbachev was willing to reduce Soviet nuclear and conventional forces, if necessary unilaterally, as in the INF Treaty of 1987 (see chapter 5). The credibility of the Soviet leadership was enhanced by his UN speech in December 1988 and by the decision not to intervene to prevent the changes occurring in Poland and Hungary in the first half of 1989. When Gorbachev visited Bonn in June 1989 (following the first Kohl–Gorbachev meeting in the autumn of 1988), his popularity there was enormous. Nearly half the number of West Germans who responded to an opinion poll put the Soviet Union as the chief architect of 'world peace', as opposed to 22 per cent given to the USA.[36] The new-found Soviet–West German accord produced numerous agreements, including the establishment of a hotline between Bonn and Moscow. Kohl had spoken publicly about his hopes for eventual German unity, but he was careful not to elevate the issue over the improvement of Soviet–West German bilateral relations. Kohl and Gorbachev broadly agreed that the question of German unification should not be forced on the two peoples by their rulers, but must await a natural resolution. Both leaders announced that West Germany and the Soviet Union would work together to 'overcome the division of

Europe'. Gorbachev welcomed West Germany's endorsement of his European policy, while Kohl responded positively to Gorbachev's request for financial help, if there were an economic crisis in the Soviet Union. The German Chancellor felt a 'decisive moment [had arrived] on the road to German unity'.[37]

THE FALL OF THE WALL IN NOVEMBER 1989

The fall of the Berlin Wall began as the result of a series of refugee crises. On 2 May 1989, Hungary took down the barbed wire from its border with Austria, in order to allow the Hungarians to travel freely to the West. This was part of the Hungarian government's Glasnost and it was also in accord with the recent agreement upholding the 'right of the individual to travel from any country', which was concluded between the Eastern and Western Europeans at the end of the Conference on Security and Cooperation in Europe in Vienna in January 1989.[38] The irony was that it was the East Germans who made the most of the Hungarian travel concessions. During the summer of 1989, hundreds, then thousands, of East Germans travelled to Hungary in order to try to escape via the Hungarian-Austrian borders to the West. Those East Germans who failed to secure entry into West Germany began gathering in the West German embassy in Budapest, asking for asylum. By August, the number of East German asylum seekers reached nearly 65,000, a situation that became intolerable for both Bonn and Budapest. According to a Hungarian-GDR agreement of 1969, the Hungarian government was obliged to prevent East Germans from travelling, without proper visas, through its territory to the West; however, due to the increasing numbers of East Germans pouring into Hungary, Budapest had to soften its policy and began to allow East German refugees to cross into Austria. This, in turn, resulted in a further increase in the number of East Germans travelling to Hungary to take advantage of the new Hungarian generosity.[39]

West Germany, too, found it difficult to abide by the existing agreement with East Berlin, whereby Bonn was required to repatriate East German asylum seekers to East Germany and would then make payments to East Berlin to secure their departure to West Germany. The Federal Republic government now began to admit the East German refugees into the country, and asked Hungary to allow them to leave for the West immediately.[40]

By late summer, the Soviet leadership was faced with mounting crises. Poland was moving towards forming a non-Communist government, while at home Gorbachev was struggling with a host of domestic troubles (the economy, nationality questions and his waning popularity). Moscow also underestimated the magnitude of the refugee problem. The Soviet Foreign Ministry thought that the crisis might be a blessing in disguise, since it might give East Berlin the impetus to embark on much-needed reforms. When Budapest asked Moscow for advice about what to do about the increasing number of refugees, Shevardnadze simply replied that 'This is an affair that concerns Hungary, the GDR, and FRG.' By implication, this was not a matter in which Moscow would interfere.[41] Accordingly, on 10 September the Hungarian government formally lifted its travel restrictions on the East German refugees, who could now travel legally from Hungary to the

West. This triggered probably one of the most remarkable human movements of recent times, as every day thousands of East Germans left their homes to go to the West. Within three days of Hungary opening up the Austrian border to the East Germans, some 12,000 East Germans had crossed into the West, with the number increasing every day. The refugee crisis soon spread to Czechoslovakia, as the Honecker government began to restrict East Germans from travelling to Hungary. Soon, the West German embassy in Prague was occupied by swelling numbers of East German refugees who wanted to go to the West and, as a result, Honecker now had to close the East German borders to Czechoslovakia.[42]

Honecker's authority was further undermined by the first public demonstration against the regime in East Germany, in Berlin in June 1989. From then, the 'political culture of demonstrations' gained currency in East Germany, and public protests spread to Leipzig, Dresden and elsewhere throughout the country by the autumn of 1989. Following in the footsteps of the Perestroika and Glasnost movements in Hungary and Poland, the East German public took to the streets to urge the government to introduce reforms. The SED authorities were undecided about how to deal with this wave of public protests, while the numbers of protesters in the city of Leipzig, for example, rose rapidly in the autumn from 5000 to 20,000, to 70,000 in October.[43] The government did not resort to the use of force until the autumn, when a demonstration on 7 October in Leipzig was dealt with by the SED security forces. Two days later, another large demonstration in the same city tested the nerve of the regime. The Stasi was preparing a detailed plan for a possible armed crackdown, while the Defence Ministry was reported to have ordered live ammunition to be made available for such an occasion. Even local hospitals were putting up extra beds for possible casualties. The GDR authorities had publicly commended China's massacre of protesters at Tiananmen Square on 4 June 1989, and it was expected that similar methods would be used against the Leipzig demonstrators. The East German Politburo was, however, divided, and Honecker's hardline approach was not supported unanimously. More importantly, Moscow advised Berlin against the use of violence. There were 19 Red Army divisions in East Germany, but the Soviet leadership made it clear to East Germany that Soviet troops would not back up 'any move against unarmed demonstrators'. Accordingly, the Party decided against the use of force, for fear of inflaming the anti-government forces even further. The Leipzig demonstration on 9 October went off peacefully, as did subsequent public protests.[44]

It was in this desperate climate that East Germany organized the official ceremony commemorating the 40th anniversary of the formation of the GDR on 6 October, which was attended by Gorbachev. During a meeting with Honecker, Gorbachev warned him that 'life punishes those who come too late'. Moscow still believed that the problem was with Honecker, and Gorbachev expressed to the other SED leaders his utmost confidence in the East German Socialist Party, which was, in his view, more solid and reliable than the Communist Parties in Hungary or Poland. Gorbachev's message almost immediately ended Politburo support for Honecker, who resigned on 17 October 1989.[45]

Nevertheless, the crisis in East Germany escalated. The new leader, Egon Krenz, who had been closely associated with Honecker (Krenz regarded the latter as his 'political mentor'),[46] had no credibility or plans for radical reform. His regime was soon challenged by even larger and more organized forms of anti-government protests, by the increasing scale of the human exodus into the West (57,000 people in October), and by the deepening economic crisis.[47] In desperation, East Berlin approached Bonn for economic assistance, but the West German Chancellor insisted on reforms in East Germany as the precondition for more comprehensive German–German relations, including financial aid. Kohl, like Gorbachev, but for different reasons, thought that a democratized East Germany would enable the two Germanies to come closer together. On 1 November, Krenz met Gorbachev in Moscow. This well-known meeting demonstrated how little the Soviet Union was prepared to do for the East Germans. Gorbachev was 'astonished' by the size of East Germany's financial deficit. It was living more than three times beyond its means. Gorbachev asked Krenz whether 'these numbers were exact'. The Soviet leader confessed that 'he had not imagined the situation to be so precarious'. East Germany was desperately seeking new loans to service its old debts, but the advice Gorbachev gave was not very helpful: he encouraged Krenz to tell the population 'the full truth'.[48] No immediate help was forthcoming either from Bonn or Moscow. As a result, the already battered Krenz government could not continue. On 7 November, the Krenz government stepped down, followed, the day after, by the collective resignation of the Politburo. A group of Party leaders, including Egon Krenz, took over the regime, with Hans Morrow as Prime Minister. This hotchpotch operation soon proved unable to arrest the decline of the SED party.[49]

Meanwhile, the East German government was hastily compelled to implement part of a new draft travel law on the morning of 10 November, instead of December that year, as had been originally planned. The new draft proposal was intended to permit emigrants to cross at 'any border crossing between the GDR, the FRG, and West Berlin' subject to a final decision by the Council of Ministers of the GDR government.[50] In the early evening of 9 November, party spokesman, Gunter Schabowski, who had wrongly thought the decision had been made by the government on that day, announced the proposal at an international press conference, which was broadcast live. Asked when the decision was to be implemented, he responded 'immediately, without delay'. The effect was almost instantaneous: vast crowds formed around the Berlin Wall, which was unexpectedly opened before midnight.[51] As Gorbachev himself described in his memoirs, the Berlin Wall was a 'symbol of the divided post-war world' and its fall, and the manner in which it fell, was to cast a much wider political shadow over the end of the Cold War in Europe.[52]

Over the next three days, more than half the entire East German population travelled to West Berlin. While most returned home after family reunion parties, or shopping, or just strolling around West Berlin, the whole nation of Germans, East and West, had experienced an extraordinarily moving and magical moment; as an East German put it, 'they began to speak their minds. . . .the sick will get up from their hospital beds'.[53] The West German national anthem was played spontaneously in the Federal Bundestag with the news of the fall of the Berlin Wall. Chancellor Kohl cut short a visit to Poland in order to travel to Berlin and he, too, was emotionally overwhelmed, declaring 'A free German fatherland lives! A free, united Europe lives.'[54] The long-suppressed feelings of German 'nationhood' were to become the theme of Kohl's subsequent politics.

It can be argued that the Berlin Wall would, sooner or later, have been opened up, for the East German leadership was already moving towards easing travel restrictions. However, the fact that the Wall was opened almost accidentally through administrative confusion, suggested the fragility of the SED party leadership (some officials in the Kremlin described Krenz as 'a dead man on vacation'),[55] and possibly the premature death of Gorbachev's common European home. Moscow was completely taken by surprise by the fall of the Wall, as were the other major capitals in Europe, and Washington, DC.

Moscow's reactions were complex. Gorbachev wanted to preserve the already much weakened GDR as a separate entity as long as he could. There would be no German unification before the GDR transformed itself into a reformed socialist country and before his common European home was constructed. In all, the Soviet Union wanted to keep the issue of German unification as a useful bargaining counter to achieve its political goals in Europe. To this end, Gorbachev used three different approaches to three different actors. In order to encourage the continued existence of the GDR, Gorbachev sent a message praising Krenz for what he had achieved (the fall of the Berlin Wall) 'in the correct fashion', encouraging him to continue with his reforms. To the Western powers, Gorbachev raised his concerns about Kohl's self-expressed interest in German unity and warned of its possibly dangerous consequences for the future of Europe. The Soviet leadership proposed the opening of consultations between the former occupying powers of defeated Germany (Britain, France, the USA and the Soviet Union) to discuss the question of German unification, in order to ensure 'the events do not take an undesirable path [to an early unification of Germany]'. Finally, Gorbachev urged Kohl to support stability in Europe and allow the GDR sufficient time to develop its reforms. Gorbachev gently reminded Kohl that 'under no circumstances . . . should the developments be forced in an unforeseen direction, turned towards chaos'.[56]

The fall of the Wall entirely destroyed the remaining legitimacy of the SED leadership: not only did the event melt away the sense of division between the Germans, but it also deprived the party of a crucial weapon, the Wall, the opening of which could have been traded for West Germany's economic assistance.[57] Krenz remained adamant that unification was not on the political agenda, for he did not want to see East Germany being absorbed into a stronger West Germany.

Kohl's approach was two-fold. On one level, he continued to insist that radical reforms in East Germany, including free elections and a free market, were prerequisites for West German aid to East Germany, thereby compelling the SED leadership to reform or die. On another level, Kohl emphasized the East German people's right of self-determination, in the belief that they would choose unity, if given the choice between that and the continuation of the GDR. Kohl's bold approach was, no doubt, facilitated by the knowledge that the Soviet Union would not attempt a forcible return to the former status quo in Germany. The 350,000 Soviet troops stationed in East Germany remained in their barracks when the Berlin gates were opened. After the fall of the Wall, Gorbachev and Shevardnadze opted not to resort to the use of force, deciding instead to face up to the new and uncomfortable reality. Gorbachev advised the East German government to ensure a 'peaceful' transition and this information was passed on to Bonn via Scowcroft.[58] Thus, from the outset, West Germany had the upper hand over East Germany, as well as over Gorbachev.

The three former occupying powers of the Western zones of Germany were aware, and had said so publicly many times in the preceding decades, that the unification of Germany was their ultimate political goal, since the post-war settlement of Germany had been frustrated by the outbreak, and the continuation, of the Cold War. Britain and France both welcomed the opening of the Berlin Wall, but they were concerned about its effect on Gorbachev's domestic position, since without him, as Thatcher told Bush in mid November, there would be no 'possibility of democracy in the Soviet Union'. Any rush towards German unification might either provoke the Soviet Union, or ruin the unity of the European community. Bush's initial reaction to the fall of the Wall was cautious, but he was ready to deal with the question of German unification when the opportunity arose, and when the Germans themselves decided on what to do.[59]

It soon became clear that Kohl's 'self-determination' approach was working. Support for unification in East Germany was gathering momentum. From mid November onwards, popular slogans were moving away from extolling the virtues of a democratic socialist country under the slogan of 'Wir sind das Volk!' (We are the people) towards German unity, with an increasing number of banners proclaiming 'Wir sind ein Volk!' (We are one people) appearing on the streets of East Berlin.[60] After the opening of the Wall, increasing numbers of West Germans were turning towards Germany's unity as their most favoured option, and the numbers supporting this view further increased towards the end of that year. Meanwhile, the Moscow government was confronted with the ever-worsening condition of East Germany. Timing was becoming an important factor for the Kohl government. The exodus from East Germany into the West escalated after the fall of the Wall.[61] Kohl wanted to translate the euphoria felt at the time of the fall of the Berlin Wall into reality. On 28 November 1989, the German Chancellor presented to the West German parliament a ten-point programme, culminating in a German federation. After 40 years of formal separation, the question of Germany' unity emerged on the international scene as a practical possibility.

THE WINDS OF CHANGE IN EASTERN EUROPE

It was not just the fall of the Berlin Wall that made the year 1989 memorable. The winds of change were raging in almost every corner of Eastern Europe. In most cases, the Communist rulers had been left with few cards to play. Defending the status quo, as we have seen in the case of the fall of the Honecker regime, became increasingly difficult, while attempts at reforming the Communist system, as in the case of the USSR, could be a recipe for the political suicide of the leadership. Frankly, it would have been a miracle if the leaders had survived this turmoil, whether they were conservative or reform minded.

In Poland, General Jaruzelski's economic reforms had encountered fierce popular protests in mid 1988, which compelled the Polish leadership to reconcile itself with Solidarity. Gorbachev was enthusiastic when the General broke the subject to him in the summer of 1988; the Soviet attitude helped Jaruzelski overcome the strong opposition to any rapprochement with Solidarity, expressed by the Central Committee of the Polish United Workers' Party (PUWP) in January 1989. Subsequently, round-table talks began between the government and Solidarity and, on 7 April 1989, both parties signed various accords, which included the re-legalization of Solidarity, a series of economic reform programmes, and Solidarity's participation in the general elections, which would be partially free, and which would take place in the summer.[62]

The Jaruzelski government calculated that such orderly and gradual steps towards democratization should help to neutralize the opposition forces and increase the credibility of the government. The Soviet Union saw the Polish reforms as the 'most desirable and exemplary model for Eastern Europe . . .'[63] However, Moscow's optimism soon gave way to a sense of unease, when the results of the elections were announced on 4 June 1989. Solidarity triumphed, despite its organizational disadvantages during the election campaign. Solidarity, originally a trade union, became by 1989 a loosely organized anti-Communist organization, joined by Poles from all walks of life, including doctors, engineers, journalist and teachers. The union no longer retained the kind of 'exuberant dynamism' displayed in the early 1980s and its popular appeal had been declining since then, which, of course, was one of the reasons why Jaruzelski gambled on radical economic reforms in 1988. The Polish people were becoming tired of domestic political infighting, which hindered any improvement in the continuing economic malaise from which they were suffering. Another reason was the lack of popular confidence in Lech Wałęsa, Solidarity's leader, whose autocratic leadership style and his 'Bolshevik methods' were well known inside the movement. Solidarity was not yet a fully fledged party organization and its leaders preferred incremental steps towards building democracy in Poland, possibly over a four-year period. On the other hand, the Communist Party still controlled the vital organs of the country, including the army, while the main administrative structure of the country was maintained by Party officials. In any case, it was part of the round-table agreement that Jaruzelski should remain as the head of state.[64]

The newly elected parliament was to elect a president in mid July, but numerous small parties, who used to cooperate with the PUWP, were now refusing to play a subservient role to the weakened Communist Party. The Solidarity deputies were expected to vote against the Communist candidate. There was thus a strong possibility that the General might be voted out in the forthcoming presidential election. Accordingly, a few Solidarity members intentionally abstained or cast invalid votes and the General was narrowly elected president by a majority of one.[65] The game was not yet over.

The next step was to form a new coalition government, but Solidarity prevaricated, with Wałęsa refusing to enter any government that contained Communist ministers. Then, on 7 August, Tadeusz Mazowiecki, a Solidarity journalist who was chosen as the new Prime Minister, was prevented from taking up this position because of Wałęsa's continued opposition to working with Communists in the new government. Ugly political infighting followed and the Soviet press began to accuse Wałęsa of seeking a 'coup d'état'.[66] In the end, Solidarity compromised and agreed to include four Communist ministers within the government. Assurances were also given to Moscow, mainly to allay Soviet sensitivities, that Poland would remain in the Warsaw Pact. This halfway reformed socialist system did not last much longer, as the Communist Party could not survive the pressures arising from the fall of the Berlin Wall. In December 1989, the Polish parliament approved the deletion of the 'leading role' of the Communist Party from the constitution, and the country ceased to be a socialist state by renaming itself 'The Republic of Poland'. In January 1990, the Communist Party was dissolved. Under the Mazowiecki government, Poland embarked on radical and often painful economic and other reforms, in an effort to create a democratic and free-market society. In December 1990, a nationwide election chose Lech Wałęsa to replace General Jaruzelski as President of Poland.

In Hungary, the position of Károly Grósz, who took over the post-Kádár regime in 1988, was somewhat akin to that of General Jaruzelski. Grósz was determined to maintain the leading position of the Hungarian Communist Party, while gradually democratizing the country. By 1989, Grósz's conservative faction was steadily outmanoeuvred by the reformist Communists within the party, led by Imre Pozsgay. Pozsgay had close contacts with the key opposition group, the Hungarian Democratic Forum (HDF), which had been established in 1987. In January 1989 Pozsgay publicly stated that the 1956 Hungarian uprising had not been a 'counter revolution', as it had been interpreted, but 'a popular insurrection against an oligarchical power', thereby challenging the legitimacy of the Hungarian Communist Party. The Party Central Committee agreed in March 1989 to delete the Party's leading role from the constitution and approved a multi-party system and free elections. Grósz realized that the democratization of Hungary on this scale was bound to destroy the Party itself, and frequently asked Moscow for help, only to be ignored by Gorbachev. Meanwhile, the Hungarian Communist reformers were moving towards a social democratic system and, in May 1989, the Party agreed that the cabinet should be responsible to parliament and not to the Party. In June, there was a Hungarian national ceremony to rebury Imre Nagy, who had been executed by the Soviet Union 31 years before, after the 1956 uprising. The ceremony was organized by the opposition, but the Communist reformers were allowed to attend. In early October, the reformers (who were by then in a majority) left the Communist Party altogether and formed the Hungarian Socialist Party. Round-table negotiations between the government and the opposition groups created a new and non-Communist Hungary. On 23 October 1989, the country was renamed the Hungarian Republic. By then, the political legitimacy of the Communist Party had all but disappeared and the former Communist reformers then hoped to retain power through political persuasion, and by pushing Pozsgay into the presidency.[67]

The shock of the fall of the Berlin Wall destroyed all the expectations of the former Communist reformers that they would still play a major role in the new

Hungary. In March–April 1990, the first free elections since 1945 took place and the country saw the creation of the first non-Communist coalition government led by the Hungarian Democratic Forum.[68]

Even conservative Czechoslovakia could not escape the winds of change. Under President Gustáv Husák, the country had seen the gradual resurgence of liberal democratic forces, led by the 'Prague Spring veterans'. Václav Havel (a prominent dissident and one of the founders of the Charter '77 group) was released from jail in May 1989 and the government announced moderate reform plans during the summer.[69] The Party was unable to prevent thousands of people from taking to the streets to protest against the Soviet invasion of 1968. Moscow endorsed the demonstrations by broadcasting an interview with Alexander Dubček on Soviet television. By the autumn of 1989, the Soviet leadership showed increasing impatience with a lack of willingness on the part of Czechoslovakia to jump on the radical reform bandwagon, and feared that if there were no changes, the situation might become 'explosive'.[70]

In Prague, the people reacted to the change in Berlin more swiftly than the government did. On 17 November, the Czech police force killed a student demonstrator, which provoked huge anti-government protests. The preservation of the Husák regime was becoming increasingly questionable, with the result that the Party Central Committee secured the resignation of the General Secretary, Miloš Jakeš. Within a week after 17 November, the rest of the Politburo resigned.[71] The government also began discussions with the recently formed opposition group, Civic Forum, which had evolved from the Charter '77 group. The forum was joined by Havel, Dubček and other opposition leaders. The Slovaks followed their example by creating an organization called the 'Public Against Violence' (PAV). Although Dubček remained a popular figure, he still believed in reformed socialism as the ultimate goal. It was, therefore, Havel who began to capture the minds of the public in the post-Berlin Wall atmosphere. By mid December 1989, more relaxed East–West relations emerged after the Bush–Gorbachev summit meeting in Malta (see chapter 6) and, after Moscow declared that those Warsaw Pact countries that had suppressed the 1968 Prague Spring were prepared to apologize, the Czech Communist conservatives saw that the writing was on the wall. Within the next few days, Husák resigned from the presidency and his Communist regime collapsed. On 29 December – the day of the so-called 'velvet revolution' – Havel was elected to the presidency of Czechoslovakia.[72]

The defeated Czech Communists believed that Gorbachev had abandoned Czechoslovakia by refusing to offer any help in sustaining their regime. The Kremlin explained that the 1968 invasion had 'burnt Soviet fingers', with the result that Gorbachev's Soviet Union had decided to take a more cautious attitude towards the internal politics of Czechoslovakia. In any case, by late 1989 Gorbachev was losing control over events, and any political intervention by Moscow in Czechoslovakia at that stage would probably have made no difference to the outcome. Alternatively, if the Warsaw Pact's official apology for the 1968 invasion had come earlier than the end of 1989, the conservative Communists would have been greatly weakened, allowing the pro-democratic Communists to develop a reformist programme, thereby following in the footsteps of Hungary and Poland.[73] Instead, once the Communist leadership had become discredited, the changes in Czechoslovakia took place rapidly during the last months of 1989. The experiences of the 1968 Prague Spring meant that the determination to move forwards to a liberal and democratic society had long existed, even if it had been suppressed. This may explain why the 'velvet revolution' was possible in the case of Czechoslovakia.

A new Czechoslovakia under Havel came into being in 1990, with the release of nearly 160,000 political prisoners. In March 1990, constitutional amendments granted the Slovaks' long-standing demand for equality of status with the Czechs, and the country was renamed the Czech and Slovak Federal Republic.[74] The general elections of June 1990 confirmed the rise of the non-Communist forces: a majority voted for Civil Forum and PVA, while only 13 per cent of the voters supported Communist candidates. Once liberated from Communist rule, the country was faced with the historical divide between the Czechs and Slovaks. Radical economic reform and the restructuring of the country increased the nationalist sentiments of Slovak politicians. Although it was reported that a majority of both Czechs and Slovaks were against the breakup of the federation, both parties agreed in November 1992, on the abandonment of the federation; on 1 January 1993, the Czech Republic and the Slovak Republic came into being. This finalized the 'velvet divorce'.[75]

The Balkans – Bulgaria, Romania and Albania – were all slower to respond to the winds of change than their Central and Eastern European counterparts. This was because of the combination of the ability of their existing conservative Communist rulers to hold on to power, and of the relative weakness of the non-Communist opposition groups in the region.[76] Bulgaria had been the most subservient and the most loyal of the satellites to Moscow for a number of historical and economic reasons. However, as with other Communist countries in Europe, Bulgaria's economy had worsened since the 1970s and, with the beginning of Gorbachev's reform plans at home, Bulgaria could not expect the relatively generous subsidies that Moscow had provided in the past. Todor Zhivkov, the long-term party leader of the Bulgarian Communist Party had, therefore, no great difficulty in adopting the slogans of Perestroika in Bulgaria, but Zhivkov was unwilling to introduce Glasnost. In 1987, he aimed at creating a new type of socialism *à la Zhivkov*, meaning no fundamental changes to his power or to the central role of the Communist Party. However, under his radical Party reforms, thousands of officials were forced to resign from their posts. He also encouraged the growth of free enterprise and attempts were made to adopt a free market economy. The outcome of these less than fundamental economic and political reforms produced administrative confusion and economic dislocation, and the bulk of the Bulgarian population turned against their undemocratic ruler.[77]

Zhivkov's credibility was further tested by his decision to step up the policy of the Bulgarization of the Turkish minority (comprising 20 per cent of the total Bulgarian population), in an effort to unite the country by revising Bulgarian memories of the hated Turkish domination of the country in previous centuries. As a result, during the summer of 1989, nearly 200,000 ethnic Turkish people left Bulgaria and fled to Turkey. This incident damaged Bulgaria's standing in the international community, provoked anti-government demonstrations, and reduced further Moscow's confidence in Zhivkov.[78]

One day after the fall of the Berlin Wall, the Bulgarian leader was ousted by an internally organized coup, and the Central Committee of the Party swiftly replaced Zhivkov by his Foreign Minister, Petar Mladenov. Under the new leadership, the country moved to political pluralism (with the formation of the Union of Democratic Forces (UDF) in opposition to the Communist Party in December 1989), while efforts were also made to separate the Party from the state. The Communist reformist government then granted the status of equality to all Muslims living in Bulgaria. In January 1990, the leading role of the Communist Party was removed from the constitution, and three months later the party was renamed the Bulgarian Socialist Party (BSP). Bulgaria then launched what proved to be painful economic reforms, but by July 1991, the BSP remained a strong political force in post-Berlin Wall Bulgarian politics. It was in October 1991 that the UDF managed to form the first non-Communist government with the help of other political organizations. Post-totalitarian politics in Bulgaria were far from stable, with the return of the BSP to power in the 1994 elections, but this belongs to post-Communist history.[79]

Romania was an estranged partner of Moscow's imperial league in Eastern Europe, and quite the opposite of the dutiful Bulgaria. The regime of Nicolae Ceauşescu, a Stalinist dictator, was fiercely repressive, and consciously distanced itself from Gorbachev's reform-minded Soviet Union. These factors explain why Romania was apparently unaffected by the winds of change and, even after the fall of the Berlin Wall, Ceauşescu safely staged the 40th Party Congress. Beneath the surface, anger and grievance among those ruled had long been simmering and, by the mid 1980s, Ceauşescu's domestic support had dwindled to a group of elite security guards.[80]

Romania's oil production had been declining for a long time and its oil reserves were now depleted. From 1984, Bucharest began to import oil from the Soviet Union and the West. Some effort was made to switch to coal production, but without much success, and the population had to rely on the less than perfect electrical generating system as the main energy source.[81] Romania's lack of economic competitiveness meant that its exports had stagnated, but Ceauşescu's anxiety to keep Romania independent drove him in 1989 to impose severe austerity measures on the population, in order to pay off its foreign debts.[82] In March and September 1989, the reformist Communists tried to organize, unsuccessfully, anti-Ceauşescu forces to remove the leader. Meanwhile, its neighbour, Hungary, launched a series of reforms and opened up its border with Austria, which increased Romania's concern about the flood of people (including many ethnic Hungarians from Romania) fleeing to Hungary.[83] By the end of 1989, Ceauşescu's regime was just about sustained, by the use of terror by a large secret police force. Thus, while apparently quiet, the country seethed with suppressed discontent, which was to lead to an explosive outcome.

In December 1989, a bloody revolt broke out, which led to the execution of Ceauşescu and his wife. The crisis was triggered by the regime's attack on the Hungarian minority in Romania, and especially over its attempt to deport an ethnic Hungarian pastor from the country. On 16 December, popular protests against the deportation developed into huge anti-government demonstrations in Timişoara, which the security forces tried to suppress, using live ammunition. By 21 December, the demonstrations had spread to the capital and, the next day, Ceauşescu was compelled to flee from the top of the party headquarters building by helicopter. Within the next few hours, the army decided to support the demonstrators. Thereafter, bloody fighting ensued between the army and the Securitate (Ceauşescu's special security force), which continued until after the dictator was captured and shot on Christmas Day.[84]

Whether or not the KGB helped to organize the December coup d'état has been debated by scholars, but we will have to wait for more definite evidence to become available in order to resolve the myths surrounding the sudden demise of the Ceauşescus.[85] The Soviet–US Malta summit in early December, which proclaimed the end of the Cold War, made it impossible for the Kremlin to intervene in a country whose leader Gorbachev, in any case, despised. It was, nevertheless, tempting to think that the Soviet Union, in the final stage of the violence in Romanian in December, might have offered some help to anti-Ceauşescu forces (who declared themselves to be the National Salvation Front – NSF). The NSF requested help from Moscow and from the West on 23 December (two days before the demise of the Romanian leader), as they were suffering from shortages of ammunition and were unable to defeat the pro-Ceauşescu security forces. France offered to send a volunteer brigade and appealed to Moscow to intervene. The USA also felt that, as Baker intimated on the TV on 24 December, it was of the utmost importance to Moscow and Washington for the democratic forces in Romania to destroy the Ceauşescu loyalists. The fact that the Soviets did not intervene was taken in the West to mean that the Brezhnev Doctrine was dead or, as Gorbachev's spokesman put it, it meant the replacement of the Brezhnev Doctrine by the 'Frank Sinatra Doctrine', dubbing his famous song, 'My Way'.[86]

The dramatic fall of the Ceauşescu regime was followed by an interim government, organized by the NSF, largely comprising reformist Communists led by Ion Iliescu, who had studied in the same university in Moscow as Gorbachev, in the 1950s. The NSF was initially eager to achieve reformed socialism: on 28 December the country was officially renamed 'Romania' instead of the Socialist Republic of Romania, but the progress of democratization and economic reforms in Romania remained slow.[87]

Albania, like Romania, was governed by a Stalinist dictator. It was also the poorest Eastern European state. The country, which had lived under the shadow of potential Yugoslavian domination, was extremely wary of the hegemonic powers. Albania had broken off diplomatic relations with Moscow, in favour of Beijing, in 1961, and had also withdrawn from the Warsaw Pact in 1968, after the invasion of Czechoslovakia. In the wake of the Sino-US rapprochement in the 1970s, the relationship with China had cooled considerably and Albania began to take a more rational approach to its former enemy neighbours, Yugoslavia and Greece. Because of these unique developments, Albania should have had no reason to fear the Gorbachev factor. However, the sweeping changes occurring in Central and Eastern Europe eventually impacted on Albania itself. In early 1989, the Party announced its intention of launching structural reforms and, after the fall of the Berlin Wall, the government resorted to granting amnesty to some political prisoners. These softening attitudes were met by increasing demands from the population for the introduction of democracy, with growing numbers of anti-government demonstrations. The Albanian leadership eventually agreed to legalize the opposition parties, which led to the formation of the Democratic Party of Albania (DPA) on 12 December 1990. The political upheaval coincided with the worsening of economic conditions in Albania and the reformist Communists steadily lost their credibility, as they failed to save the country from the prospect of bankruptcy. In March 1992, general elections produced a huge victory for the DPA, which effectively removed the Communists from the government.[88]

Another unique Communist country in the Balkans was Yugoslavia, long estranged from the Soviet Union. The basic problems confronting the Yugoslavian Federation (consisting of Serbia, Croatia, Slovenia, Macedonia, Montenegro and Bosnia-Herzegovina) were similar to those that the other Eastern European neighbours faced in the 1980s: the declining legitimacy of Communism was accompanied by worsening economic and social conditions, as well as increasing foreign indebtedness. In addition, the question of nationalism arising from the Kosovo conflict (the origins of which were discussed in chapter 3) complicated Yugoslavia's politics. The Serbs, the dominant population in Yugoslavia, complained that Tito's efforts to secure devolution for the other nationalities had contributed to the deterioration of the Communist system by inflaming nationalist feelings. Non-Serbs, however, condemned Communism for its failure to achieve a satisfactory solution to the nationality question. In 1986, Slobodan Milošević was elected leader of the Serbian League of Communists of Yugoslavia and, in 1989, he became the president of Serbia. Milošević sought to maximize the Kosovo issue, in order to preserve the Communist system to the advantage of the Serbs. Unlike Yeltsin, who also exploited Russian nationalism for his own benefit, Milošević opened a Pandora's Box by declaring, in 1987, that he would not only 'liberate' the Serbs in Kosovo, but also all ethnic Serbs through-out Yugoslavia.[89] As a result, separatist and nationalist feelings in the republics within the Federation escalated.

In September 1989, the Slovene Assembly (still dominated by Communists) declared its independence from the Federation and also removed the leading role of the League of Communists of Yugoslavia from its constitution, thereby setting the stage for the disintegration of Yugoslavia. By the end of 1990, all six republics had held elections and, as a result, Serbia, Slovenia and Croatia adopted new constitutions. In June 1991, Slovenia and Croatia declared their full independence from the Federation and the Serbs thereupon despatched Federal forces (in which the Serbs predominated) to those republics to suppress their independence movements. Slovenia was a small and largely homogenous republic, which contained few Serbs and possessed its own republican defence force. Milošević in effect conceded Slovenia's independence, but opposed that of Croatia, a much larger republic than Slovenia, which contained a large Serb population of 600,000. Serbs had occupied one third of Croatia before a UN peacekeeping force intervened to broker a ceasefire in early January 1992. By that time, military confrontation was also taking place in Bosnia-Herzegovina, and Yugoslavia had practically ceased to exist, with the Federation consisting only of Serbia and Montenegro. This outcome was strongly resisted by the Serbs, who, under the slogan of 'ethnic cleansing', embarked on bloody inter-ethnic military conflicts in Bosnia, Macedonia and Kosovo in the following decade.[90]

Regardless of their proximity to, or their relationship with, the Soviet Union, all the existing Communist regimes in Eastern Europe collapsed between 1989 and 1991. In most cases, the Communist rulers were compelled to resign as a result of the actions of the reformist Communists or anti-government forces, who then succeeded them. With the exception of Romania (where some 600 deaths were recorded during the December coup d'état)[91] and Yugoslavia, the transition of power was relatively peaceful, although the economic problems facing the new leaders remained daunting, with rising unemployment and inflation, and consequently worsening social conditions. In that process, in Hungary and Poland, some former or reformist Communists were returned to power in order to try to regain the stability of their countries, albeit in a considerably changed political culture. In Bulgaria and Romania, on the other hand, ex-Communists clung to power for a number of years after the end of the Cold War, showing little enthusiasm for radical reform.[92] However diversified the post-Cold War political and economic structures of the former Communist countries may have been, Communism as the predominant ideological and political force in these countries had bankrupted itself in the years 1989 and 1991. The fall of the Berlin Wall served to show how much the Soviet Union had lost its authority over its Eastern European satellites. The lack of Soviet intervention during the crisis was praised by the West: Bush told the Soviet leader during the Malta summit in December 1989 that 'we have a high opinion of your personal reaction and the reaction of the Soviet Union as a whole to these dynamic and at the same time fundamental changes'.[93] The Hungarian Communist, Grósz, however, reminds us that 'it is not the collapse of the East European regimes that led to the collapse of the USSR. It is because, in its essence, the Soviet regime had already collapsed that the East European regimes fell.'[94]

THE UNIFICATION OF GERMANY IN THE AUTUMN OF 1990

The final stage of the end of the Cold War in Europe was concerned with the fate of East Germany and its consequent implications for a post-Cold War Europe. In the text, the 'unification', rather than 'reunification', of Germany, is used: the final shape of a unified Germany was based on the existing borders after 1945, which meant the loss of territories east of the Oder–Neisse rivers, which had been lost to Poland, as well as East Prussia, which had been divided between Poland and the Soviet Union, both at the end of the Second World War.

It was Helmut Kohl and his Christian Democratic Party who seized the psychological moment of the time when, on 28 November 1989, some three weeks after the fall of the Berlin Wall, he presented to the Bundestag his ten-point programme for the unification of Germany.[95] Kohl's plan envisaged a gradual process of merging the two German states, first into a contractual community,

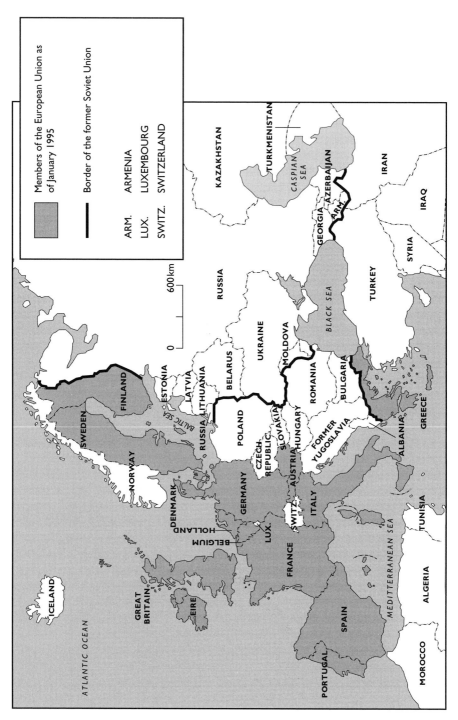

2. Post-Cold War Europe

Members of the European Union as of January 1995

Border of the former Soviet Union

ARM. ARMENIA
LUX. LUXEMBOURG
SWITZ. SWITZERLAND

then into a confederation, and eventually into 'one state', possibly within the following decade. In preparing his speech, the Chancellor did not consult his Foreign Minister, Hans-Dietrich Genscher, who belonged to the Free Democratic Party. West Germany's European allies were surprised and irritated by Bonn's solo diplomacy over such an important issue as the German question. Kohl calculated that Bonn would need America's backing, which would help to overcome the possible differences arising with Bonn's Western European allies and with Gorbachev. Bush was informed of Kohl's unification plan at the same time as it was being announced in the Bundestag.[96]

The USA was happy to support Kohl's drive towards unification, provided that a united Germany would be included in NATO. The NATO solution had been the long-established consensus within the transatlantic alliance since the 1950s.[97] West Germany, now a trusted and powerful ally in the Atlantic Alliance, was well aware of the imagined or actual fears of the West confronting the increased power of a united Germany and, as a result, Kohl assured Bush of Bonn's 'unequivocal loyalty' to NATO. It was clear to Washington that Bonn was not trying to achieve 'the national goal of the Germans independently'. Thereafter, until the unification was completed, the Bush administration made steadfast efforts to transform the Chancellor's dream into reality.[98]

During the NATO summit meeting in Brussels on 4 December 1989, the USA encouraged its Western European allies to look towards a gradual and peaceful unification, which would satisfy Germany's right of self-determination and ensure its continued membership of NATO. West Germany also tried to mitigate possible fears about altering the *status quo ante* in Europe by the unification of Germany: Bonn, jointly with Paris, enthusiastically supported the deeper integration of the European Community of Western Europe, confirmed Germany's intention of staying in NATO after unification, and also promised to help the Soviet Union economically. While other Western European allies, including Britain, France, Italy and the Netherlands, remained alarmed about the prospect of a united and stronger Germany in Europe, in the end they accepted America's position on the subject. With this, German unification was now put at the centre of the West's political agenda.[99]

Kohl's surprise initiative angered Gorbachev, especially as the German Chancellor had assured the Soviet leader on the phone just after the fall of the Berlin Wall that West Germany would not exploit the uncertain situation or take steps that 'might trigger an avalanche'. Gorbachev vented his anger in early December 1989 when he met Genscher, describing Kohl's ten-point proposal as 'the conditions of an ultimatum'. By that time, most of the Eastern European countries were slipping away from Moscow's control, but Gorbachev still hoped to build a 'common European home' before considering the fate of the two Germanies. The Soviet leader also apprehended that Kohl's proposal might quicken the pace of East Germany's collapse, which might result in a West German takeover of the country.[100] On the other hand, Gorbachev appreciated that Moscow's continued opposition to German unification might damage Moscow's new and friendly relationship with the West. The Soviet Union wanted to slow down the process and relied on the opponents of unification in the West to support its aim. Moreover, the Modrow government, weakened considerably after November, had been compelled to bring forward the timing of the promised free elections in March by three months. At the end of January 1990, the Soviet Union and East Germany agreed that the two Germanies could form a 'contractual community' leading to a neutral confederation between the two states.[101] This was a significant adjustment to the dynamic of events: the Soviet Union now agreed to German unification in principle.

The crucial questions remained as to the timing and the terms of German unification. A sense of urgency now prevailed in the West, as East Germany was on the verge of complete collapse and it was also important to resolve the question while Gorbachev was still in power.[102] In mid February 1990, the USA persuaded its NATO allies and Moscow to agree to use the '2 plus 4 formula' – originally suggested by French Foreign Minister Michel Jobert, and developed by the US State Department – that is, that the two German states and the four occupying powers (USA, France, Britain and the Soviet Union) would discuss the terms of unification, especially on the relationship between a unified Germany and NATO.[103] The formula was presented to the Germans as a more acceptable method of solving the problem, and as a better way of discussing the subject within a small conference, rather than in a wider political gathering, such as a CSCE conference, which was the course preferred by Moscow and France. Subsequently, Bonn and Washington agreed to quicken the pace of unification. Instead of a confederation of the two German states, Bonn now aimed at establishing a monetary union with East Germany after the 18 March election; that is, a unified Germany was no longer envisaged as merging the two states into one, but as West Germany taking over the Eastern state altogether.[104]

Meanwhile, Kohl deployed his 'Deutschmark' diplomacy in Moscow to the best of his ability. During a meeting with Gorbachev on 10 February 1990, the German Chancellor suggested that Germany would renounce its claims on the lost eastern territories beyond the current eastern border of the GDR, while the current GDR territory could well remain outside NATO. Kohl offered economic assistance to the ailing Soviet Union and promised to take on the GDR's economic 'obligations' to the Soviet Union. Kohl thought that the meeting went very well, as Gorbachev seemed to endorse the idea of Germany's self-determination.[105] Thereafter, Kohl continued to use his economic and financial pledges as a means of extracting from Gorbachev Moscow's gradual acceptance of the West's terms of unification of Germany.

The general election in East Germany on 18 March (with a 93 per cent turnout rate), demonstrated an unequivocal vote for unification. Those who opposed the West German–US fast track unification plan had formulated no new policy or initiative to take its place. Mitterrand and Thatcher tried to work out a plan to slow down the process of unification, but without success. Kohl, facing a difficult election at the end of 1990, wanted time to enable him to attract more conservative voters at home. Partly because of this, Bonn did not clarify, until March 1990, its acceptance of a unified Germany consisting of the existing post-1945 territories, which had contributed to the uneasiness of the likely consequence of unification in Western Europe, Poland, Czechoslovakia and the Soviet Union.[106]

After March 1990, the unity of the Atlantic Alliance between West Germany and its allies solidified, while the 2 plus 4 negotiations began to make slow progress. The key remaining question was now how to overcome Moscow's remaining opposition to the prospective membership of a unified Germany in NATO. If NATO was now to keep within its ranks a unified Germany, this would significantly undermine the *raison d'être* of the Warsaw Pact and, with it, the remaining vestiges of Soviet influence over Eastern Europe would completely disappear. Consequently, the Soviet Union would be 'marginalized' in post-Cold War Europe. The conservatives in the Kremlin were angered by Gorbachev's weak stance on Germany: in addition to agreeing to a united Germany, Moscow was now confronting the prospect of its inclusion in NATO.[107] Gorbachev, therefore, stuck to his guns and refused to consider the NATO solution. On the other hand, the alternative ideas that the Soviet Union offered were neither realistic, nor immediately applicable. They included the simultaneous inclusion of a unified Germany both in NATO and in the Warsaw Pact (whose function was considerably weakened after 1989), or the creation of a pan-European security system (which would, by implication, hold up the unification of Germany until such a system was formed), or decoupling the unification process from the question of Germany's membership of any external organizations. As Gorbachev's expectations of obtaining Western economic assistance were high on his agenda, he had been left with few cards to play if he wanted to prevent a united Germany from joining NATO.[108]

The West tried to allay the potential Soviet fears of an enlarged NATO containing a united Germany by suggesting numerous safeguards to ensure the Soviet Union's future security, echoing similar attempts made by the West in the middle of the 1950s, such as the Eden plan at the Berlin conference in January 1954 and another at the Geneva summit meeting in July 1955. However, in the late 1980s, the Bonn republic took a leading role, together with the USA, in making the NATO solution acceptable to Moscow. The Kohl government offered a friendship treaty with Moscow to keep German–Soviet relations on an even keel after unification, promised numerous financial credits to Moscow to sustain Gorbachev's Perestroika, and also agreed to underwrite the cost of the Red Army's withdrawal from East Germany, all of which were designed to accelerate the path to eventual unification without upsetting Moscow unduly.[109] When Gorbachev, probably inadvertently, agreed with Bush in May 1990 that it was a united Germany, and not Moscow or Washington, which should determine its external relations, Moscow's opposition to the NATO solution became unsustainable.

After the formation of an economic union between West and East Germany on 1 July, the final phase of the unification of Germany began to unfold rapidly. Meanwhile, the West never slackened its efforts to make a unified Germany more palatable to Moscow. The July NATO summit stressed the political, rather than military, aspects of the NATO alliance and promised to revise its forward defence posture. The subsequent G-7 meeting also promised an economic aid package to Moscow, in part as a reward for Moscow's agreement on the unification of Germany. These concessions helped to save Gorbachev's face, although they did not, in the end, have much impact on arresting the economic and social decline at home.[110] Further and more substantial technical and financial assistance was offered when Kohl met Gorbachev in the Caucasus on 15–16 July. At this meeting, Gorbachev agreed to the restoration of full sovereignty of Germany, its membership of NATO on condition that no NATO troops would enter the former GDR territory during the period when the Red Army was being withdrawn (he, however, conceded that the Soviet Union would shorten the withdrawal period to three to four years, while Kohl agreed that the ban on the stationing of NATO troops in the former GDR territory should be extended even after the withdrawal of the Red Army), and the end of the allied occupation rights in Berlin and Germany at the time of the conclusion of the 2 plus 4 Treaty (the Soviets conceded on this point from their earlier insistence on a gradual renunciation of the four power rights). These concessions were secured after Kohl offered a generous financial package to the Soviet Union during the meeting. In reality, West German military effectives, which were not under NATO's command, would enter the former GDR territory after unification, and so NATO's security guarantee over the whole of Germany would become effective from the first day of a united Germany. Thus, to Kohl's surprise, the Soviet Union accepted the unification of Germany on Western terms. Within the Kremlin, there was last-minute resistance to Gorbachev's acceptance of a unified Germany, but he told the dissidents 'the train has already left'.[111]

On 12 September 1990, in Moscow the 2 plus 4 Treaty was signed, whereby a new united Germany agreed to reduce its armed forces to 370,000 personnel by 1994, and confirmed its intention of not manufacturing or deploying weapons of mass destruction. It was also agreed that the Soviet Union would withdraw its troops from East Germany by 1994 and, after that, only German armed forces (and not other NATO forces) would be stationed in the former East German state, as long as Germany remained in NATO.[112] On 3 October, East and West Germany were formally united as one state. It heralded the end of the post-war era in Europe and, in December 1990, Kohl was elected the first Chancellor of the new Germany.

POST-COLD WAR EUROPE

In retrospect, the formation of a united Germany firmly anchored in the two key Western Organizations – NATO and the European Community – demonstrated the resilience of the Western system, and the fragility of the Soviet/Russian leadership in Europe in post-Cold War Europe. Despite Moscow's lingering enthusiasm about creating a pan-European security system under the banner of the CSCE, the importance and usefulness of the process was now almost non-existent. On 17–19 November 1990 at a CSCE summit conference in Paris, the NATO and the Warsaw Pact members signed a treaty concerning Conventional Forces in Europe (CFE), which promised massive reductions of military hardware in each alliance and, in practical terms, the Soviet Union agreed to scrap more weapons than the USA to meet the agreed military ceiling under the treaty (see chapter 6). The two alliances also agreed to develop 'new partnerships and friendly cooperation', and formally acknowledged the end of the Cold War in

Europe. All the 34 nations participating in the Paris conference signed the 'Charter of Paris for a New Europe', and a few steps were taken to give the CSCE an institutional apparatus, which included annual meetings of foreign ministers, a small secretarial headquarters in Prague, a Conflict Prevention Centre in Vienna, and an Office for Free Elections in Warsaw.[113]

All these would have been welcomed as the historic end of the Cold War, if they had happened before the fall of the Berlin Wall and prior to German unification. However, the USA was now preoccupied by the war in Iraq and was less concerned about Europe. The Warsaw Pact had, for some months, ceased to be viable as a military organization. Out of the six remaining members, Hungary and Czechoslovakia, two major members of the Pact, had already requested Moscow to withdraw the Red Army from their territories in early 1990. Under the recent agreement on a unified Germany, Moscow was also committed to the withdrawal of the Red Army from the former East Germany by 1994. East Germany had ceased to be a member of the Warsaw Pact. Similarly, Poland's security concerns about the existing borders with a united Germany had been assuaged by the unification treaty, and Poland had now little reason to require the presence of the Red Army in its territory.[114]

It would have been rather inconvenient for the West if the Warsaw Pact had disappeared quickly, before the treaty for the CFE had been signed by the two alliances. However, for the new Eastern European leaders, the Warsaw Pact was now nothing more than the symbol of Soviet imperial leadership in the region. After a unified Germany was securely in NATO and after the CFE Treaty was signed, Poland, Hungary and Czechoslovakia requested, in January 1991, the immediate dissolution of the Warsaw Pact; otherwise, they warned Moscow, they would unilaterally withdraw from the organization. In February 1991, to avoid a further humiliation to Soviet prestige, Gorbachev finally agreed to dissolve the Pact. The Warsaw Pact countries met for the last time in July 1991 to disband the organization – the Soviet representative was understandably absent from the proceedings.[115]

The disappearance of the Warsaw Pact left Moscow with only the CSCE as a political means of keeping Soviet power and influence in post-Cold War Europe, which might eventually replace NATO, as Khrushchev had wanted in the 1950s.[116] However, the CSCE was a huge and cumbersome body, which could not function without the approval of all its signatories. After the end of the Cold War, the CSCE sought a pan-European organization on the basis of the concept of cooperative collective security. In 1994, it was renamed the Organization of Security and Cooperation in Europe (OSCE), involving 53 member countries, including Canada and the USA. Russia, which emerged after the demise of the Soviet Union, soon revived its interest in the organization, which might prevent NATO from becoming the sole European security organization. However, during the last days of the Soviet Union, Moscow refused to discuss its military intervention in the Baltic states in early 1991, while Yeltsin resented the OSCE meddling in Chechnya. The failure to act during the crisis over Kosovo further deepened Russia's disappointment with the organization. Moreover, the diversity of threats perceived by the main actors, and the pressure for globalization in the post-Cold War world, meant that the idea of building a pan-European organization that could provide common security remained illusory. By the mid 1990s, the OSCE transformed itself into a machine dealing with preventive diplomacy and conflict avoidance.[117]

In the end, it was NATO that came out of the Cold War in remarkably good shape. Many suspected that, with the end of the Cold War, the USA might with-draw from Europe altogether and the *raison d'être* of the North Atlantic Alliance would disappear. Certainly the size of America's military presence, nuclear and conventional, was to become smaller, but Washington continued to play the dom-inant role in the post-war Atlantic Alliance over the crises in the Persian Gulf, in Bosnia and Kosovo, and served, in technological and military terms, as the ultim-ate security provider for Europe. During the Rome summit in November 1991, NATO approved a 'New Strategic Concept', which proclaimed that 'we no longer face the old threat of a massive attack', thereby allowing NATO forces to be 'smaller and more flexible'; otherwise the organization would continue to 'provide security for the West', which was 'still very relevant' in a post-Cold War world, as General Colin Powell (then the Chairman of the Joint Chiefs of Staff) put it.[118] For its existing Western members, NATO remained a vital mechanism for ensuring the continued American engagement in European security affairs, to contain a unified Germany, and to provide security in the face of a weakened, but unpredictable Russia.[119]

TABLE 1 – MILITARY EXPENDITURE – NATO AND WARSAW PACT/COMMONWEALTH OF INDEPENDENT STATES, 1989–9

Year	Military Expenditure		Armed Forces		Gross National Product		Population		Military Expenditure per capita		Gross National Product per capita	
	Constant 1999 $bn		Thousands		Constant 1999 $bn		Millions		Constant 1999 $		Constant 1999 $	
	NATO	WP/CIS	NATO	WP/CIS	NATO	WP/CIS	NATO	WP/CIS	NATO	WP/CIS	NATO	WP/CIS
1989	589	447	5860	4950	13,900	4280	655	401	898	1120	21,200	10,700
1990	578	394	5780	4400	14,200	4070	678	403	853	978	21,000	10,100
1991	532	324	5590	3850	14,500	3580	684	389	779	834	21,200	9200
1992	544	87	5150	2630	14,800	1580	689	284	789	306	21,500	5580
1993	522	75	4900	2200	15,000	1420	695	285	751	264	21,600	5000
1994	500	72	4900	2000	15,500	1210	700	285	714	253	22,100	4270
1995	476	50	4690	2080	15,900	1130	705	285	675	175	22,600	3990
1996	463	46	4620	2030	16,300	1090	710	284	653	163	23,000	3840
1997	461	52	4510	1850	16,900	1100	715	284	645	181	23,700	3870
1998	457	40	4370	1700	17,500	1060	720	284	635	139	24,300	3730
1999	475	45	4580	1580	18,600	1070	783	284	607	160	23,800	3770

WP/CIS = Warsaw Pact/Commonwealth of Independent States
Source: *World Military Expenditures and Arms Transfers (WMEAT)*, US Arms Control and Disarmament Agency, now published by the Bureau of Verification and Compliance of the US State Department. 28th Edition (2003).

Moreover, it can be argued that from the outset the West put the onus of change in the Soviet system as the main condition for the end of the Cold War. However desirable it was to see the end of the Cold War in Europe, there were of course limits to what the West could have done to secure this. For the sake of ending the Cold War, the West was not prepared to alter its values, ideology and institutions. It was, therefore, the Soviet Union who held the key to the end of the Cold War in Europe, but in an actual sense, it was the Soviet Union who *had* to come around to adopting Western values if it sought friendship, rather than confrontation, with the West. This was why the West was not enthusiastic about Gorbachev's 'common European home', which, in effect, demanded the end of the Cold War 'symmetrically' through mutual concessions, and an equal role for the Soviet Union with the USA in Europe.[120] The sinews of the bipolar system meant that the solution to the division of Europe could not be found in the establishment of a halfway house. When the Cold War ended peacefully and largely on Western terms, there was to be no reason to assume that their political systems, including the Atlantic Alliance, would suffer as a result (apart from the task of adjusting to the new situation). In that sense the continuation of the alliance was hardly surprising.

One can also point out that, while the Atlantic Alliance may not have been formed without the pressure of the Cold War, and while it was meant initially to be a military alliance, Western Europe had been as much concerned to develop its relations with the USA as with containing the Soviet threat. In the process, NATO became more of a liberal democratic institution than a military alliance. The disappearance of one main cause (such as the Soviet threat) does not necessarily turn the clock back to where it was originally. Over the last four decades, the major Western European powers have built a closely integrated European Community to achieve stability, to prove to the USA the economic viability of post-war Europe, to develop a European identity, and also to contain the Soviet Union. If Western Europe came to be regarded as the show-case for the capitalist democratic system, this magnified the failure of Soviet leadership in Eastern Europe and in the Soviet Union itself. Western Europe was also to gain increasingly from its strength and from its skills in developing a degree of interdependence with the USA. The pressures of the Cold War often reminded the US leadership of the need to temper disagreements with Europe, in order to uphold the solidarity of the Western Alliance. This attitude was shared by Western European leaders during numerous Cold War crises. Even when the USA enjoyed economic preponderance during the first two decades after the Second World War, it was debatable whether the USA wielded hegemony commensurate with the size of its economic power.[121] Within Western Europe, American leadership was received with a degree of reluctance and resistance. By the 1960s, the 'Americanization debates' had tended to peter out in Western Europe, showing that the Europeans had learned to develop their own identities and strength within the framework of the Western Alliance.[122]

In the end, the transatlantic relationship that had underwritten the security of Western Europe survived the Cold War. The need for a transatlantic alliance remained, and it still remains today, despite the frequent and familiar arguments about US deterrence, détente, burden sharing, and 'out of area' issues, arguments which have been endemic since 1949. The Cold War may have 'arranged' the marriage between Western Europe and the USA, initially for convenience, but the success of Western Europe was eventually structured around the transatlantic relationship.[123] Both the Bush administration and the Thatcher government were determined to put NATO at the forefront of the post-Cold War organizations over the pan-European CSCE process. The response was mutual: Western Europe renewed its 'invitations' to the USA to remain involved in the region.[124]

In parallel with this confirmation of Atlanticism, Western Europe also proceeded, as had been planned before the end of the Cold War, to the deeper integration of the (Western) European Community. In February 1992, the Maastricht Treaty was concluded and the Community was transformed into the European Union, which also included the formation of a Common Foreign and Security Policy. The closer Franco-German defence cooperation (which emerged in the mid 1980s) was given further impetus to move forward because of Germany's increased status as a result of the unification, in the form of the Eurocorps created in 1994. The Bush administration was perhaps more concerned than the succeeding Clinton administration about the more assertive and economically stronger Western Europe, which might become a new rival to the USA. However, in economic terms (in which Clinton appeared more interested than foreign policy, when he was sworn into office), Washington always welcomed 'hegemony on the cheap' in Europe.[125]

Overall, the fundamental structure of Western Europe had hardly undergone any major change in the immediate aftermath of the end of the Cold War. The plans that were put in place before that end were implemented without major alterations and, while the richest country, Germany, was beset with severe problems in its efforts to absorb eastern Germany into the former Bonn Republic, there was no major upheaval in Western Europe as a result of the unification of Germany. On the contrary, this even helped to give additional momentum to the French and German leadership to 'strengthen EC institutions', thereby allowing for more progress in this direction.[126]

Compared with the unity and consolidation of Western Europe, the situation in the former Eastern European area was quite different. Bush proclaimed in May 1989 that 'the Cold War began with the division of Europe. It can only end when Europe is whole', but at the end of the Cold War Europe was certainly not whole, nor transformed into one entity. The end of the Cold War brought about the unification of Germany, thereby completing the task left over from the end of the Second World War. The newly united Germany then relatively quickly established a much delayed rapprochement with its 'eastern neighbours', who were now inclined to view Germany as 'a partner' rather than as 'a potential opponent'.[127] However, this did not lead to the immediate unification of Europe – on the contrary, the West was confronted with the traumatic phase of the disintegration of the former Soviet sphere of influence. The dissolution of the Warsaw Pact was part and parcel of this process and it happened as a result of the Eastern Europeans' own decisions, 'possibly before it was thought even desirable' by the West.[128] Because of the disappearance of the Iron Curtain, the division and the differences between Eastern and Western Europe looked even more stark than had been imagined, thanks to the Western media's penetration into countries that had previously been in Moscow's sphere of influence. These differences were not only limited to those between East and West. Within Eastern Europe, the group of states that are termed collectively as Central Europe, including the Baltic States, Hungary, Poland and the Czech Republic, wanted to develop their identities and obtain their security require-ments through integration into the Western community. However, in the Balkans, and in the other former Soviet republics, the notion of a 'security community' was 'alien amid the rivalries and inter-state conflicts'. The collapse of the former Yugoslavia continued to inflame the region after the end of the Cold War. When Bosnia declared its independence in March 1992, horrendous open warfare took place in Bosnia between Serbs, Croats, and Bosnian Muslims. Faced with the first military conflict on a scale not seen since the end of the Second World War, NATO was initially unable to deal with a situation outside its area – 'perhaps the worst dispute in its history'. Eventually, a USA-led NATO force responded to the crisis and developed, subsequently, the concept of the Combined Joint Task Forces (CJTF) to deal with similar crisis situations in the future.[129]

Thus, the end of the Cold War left the problem that, while the former Warsaw Pact countries did not object to the continuation of NATO, they were left outside it.[130] Despite the Eastern Europeans' euphoria just after their liberation from Soviet tutelage, the new leaders lacked both the experience and the ability to govern their own countries democratically, in the face of the often worsening economic and social conditions after the end of the Cold War.[131] It proved to be an arduous process before the previous system could be reformed and assimi-lated into the Western systems. All these factors led to a much slower and more gradual process of the West's peace settlement with the disappointed former Soviet bloc countries. Equally important for NATO was to take account of Russia's sensibilities, suspicious as Moscow was of the West's advances into the East.[132] This required the West to tread carefully the path towards expansion to the East.

It was not until 1994 (nearly half a decade after the end of the Cold War) that some practical steps began to be taken towards creating a new and united Europe. NATO approved the 'Partnership for Peace', which extended its secur-ity cooperation into the former Communist states in Europe, and paved the way for NATO enlargement, despite Russia's continuing resistance. In May 1997, NATO and the Russian Federation signed an agreement, whereby both parties were to cooperate with each other on the question of European peace and secu-rity; subsequently, in July the NATO Madrid summit invited Poland, Hungary and the Czech Republic to join NATO. In 2002, NATO–Russian relations were further strengthened under the term of 'NATO at 20', and in March 2003, a further seven countries – Bulgaria, Estonia, Latvia, Lithuania, Romania, Slovakia and Slovenia – were invited to apply for NATO membership; the alliance now comprised 26 countries. Apart from Bulgaria and Romania, these countries joined the EU, together with Poland, Hungary, the Czech Republic, Cyprus and Malta in 2004.[133] The end of the Cold War brought with it the domination of the Western order across Europe, not through the West's insistence, but largely through invitations extended by their former Soviet satellites. The latter's anxiety to be part of the Western community played no small part in transforming the transatlantic alliance into a post-Cold War apparatus.

5

Reagan, Gorbachev and the Politics of Nuclear Security

The previous chapter has shown that a less dangerous environment was being created in Europe after the fall of the Berlin Wall. It would, however, be difficult to accept that the Cold War had ended, while the two superpowers still retained massive quantities of nuclear weapons. The possession of large stockpiles of weapons of mass destruction by the two superpowers placed the Cold War world 'under the shadow of global nuclear battles'.[1] This was not because these superpowers were willing to use them against each other, but the signs in the early 1980s suggested that, despite their pledges to regulate nuclear weapons through negotiations, they did not appear to make the world any safer than before.

With the shock of the Cuban Missile Crisis in 1962, the superpowers began to regulate their activities in the nuclear sphere and to cooperate, in an effort to moderate the threat caused by their ability to destroy the world. Following the conclusion in 1963 of the Nuclear Partial Test Ban Treaty, came the signature of the Nuclear Non-Proliferation Treaty (NPT) in 1968 between the USA, Britain and the Soviet Union, which was eventually joined by 59 countries. The two superpowers then agreed to achieve a 'stable mutual strategic deterrence' by entering into the Strategic Arms Limitations Talks (SALT) in 1969.[2] The SALT I agreement in 1972 included an ABM Treaty limiting both sides' anti-Ballistic Missile system to two sites, and also an interim agreement freezing the existing number of long-range (strategic) nuclear missile launchers. The subsequent SALT II agreements (signed by Carter and Brezhnev in June 1979) set an equal ceiling (2400) of long-range strategic weapons, with further sub-limits imposed on the number of missiles that could carry multiple warheads. However, SALT II was unable to address the problem of controlling the qualitative arms race effectively, as each power continued to produce more complicated weapons systems, some of which were not verifiable. The Soviet Union, nevertheless, ratified the treaty swiftly, but the US Senate suspended its approval of SALT II, as the majority of Senators interpreted the treaty as allowing the Soviet Union to retain its heavy ICBMs and Backfire bombers, which could hit the USA. In the remaining Carter years, the superpowers, nevertheless, agreed to abide by the terms of SALT II, and had started preliminary SALT III talks on the Intermediate-range Nuclear Forces in Europe (INF). The new Republican President, Ronald Reagan, called the SALT II Treaty 'fatally flawed' and expressed no interest in resuming SALT negotiations with Moscow. Washington's priority was now given to a military build up, not arms control negotiations, and to confrontation, instead of détente, with Moscow.[3]

The advancement of technology and capabilities meant that both superpowers acquired, by the mid 1960s, a global nuclear ability to destroy the world instantaneously, and their reluctance to see the proliferation of nuclear weapons in the hands of the lesser powers helped to sustain the 'image' of a bipolar system on the basis of superpower nuclear deterrence well into the 1980s.[4] Thus, the bipolar system and the superpower nuclear arms race were closely connected and any significant changes to the latter were likely to affect the maintenance of the former. After 1985, the superpowers seemed keen to eliminate the bulk of their strategic and tactical nuclear weapons, to downgrade the importance of nuclear deterrence in the realm of international relations, and to achieve 'cooperative denuclearisation'.[5]

THREE OUTSTANDING ISSUES

When the two leaders of the superpowers met for the first time since 1979, at Geneva in November 1985, President Reagan, told the new Soviet General Secretary, Gorbachev, that:

> Here you and I are, two men in a room, probably the only two men in the world who could perhaps bring about peace in the world . . . Mr General Secretary, we don't mistrust each other because we are armed; we are armed because we mistrust each other.[6]

For the Soviet Union its relationship with the USA had always been the key to its foreign and military policy considerations during the Cold War. Gorbachev was no exception to this. Prior to the Geneva summit, he thought that the 'military rivalry' with the USA was the most difficult factor inhibiting the creation of a new order ending the Cold War.[7]

Before the Gorbachev–Reagan Geneva summit, there remained three main areas of difficulty in achieving a breakthrough in the negotiations. They were the INF talks concerning nuclear weapons in Europe after the deployment of Soviet SS-20s in the latter half of the 1970s; the question of actually reducing the number of superpower strategic nuclear weapons and their delivery system under the Strategic Arms Reductions Talks (START); and Moscow's opposition to Reagan's Strategic Defence Initiative (SDI) or Star Wars.

Western Europe's concern about the reliability of America's security commitment to Europe had been apparent ever since the 1950s, and it became more pronounced when, by the mid 1970s, the Soviet Union achieved a rough parity with Washington in the field of strategic nuclear weapons through the SALT negotiations. This suggested that America's extended nuclear deterrence over Western Europe had become problematic.[8] Furthermore, the Soviet Union decided to modernize its theatre nuclear weaponry by deploying SS-20s from 1977 to replace the older SS-4s and SS-5s. The land-based, solid fuelled and more advanced SS-20s, with three warheads attached to each missile, were capable of hitting all the Western European capitals. From Moscow's point of view, the intro-duction of the SS-20s was intended to enhance Soviet nuclear deterrent power in Europe, to counter America's forward-based systems and the British and French nuclear weapons, and, eventually, to achieve nuclear parity with the Western bloc in Europe.[9] Western Europe, led by Helmut Schmidt, Chancellor of the Federal Republic of Germany, however, saw that SS-20s destabilized the European nuclear balance, increased the possibility of a Soviet nuclear surprise attack, and reduced further the credibility of America's extended deterrence. The Carter administra-tion's responses to the new security problem in Europe had been slow and confus-ing. Carter first decided to impose the notorious 'neutron bombs' on Europe, which the European public opposed. However, when Schmidt finally came to support the deployment of the bombs, the American President (who had never liked the idea in the first place) abandoned it altogether.

In response to Western Europe's anxieties, President Carter eventually accepted that similar nuclear weapons to the SS-20s should be installed in Europe and, in December 1979, NATO agreed to a 'dual track' policy, by which American Cruise and Pershing II missiles were to be deployed in Western Europe. NATO also expressed its readiness to begin negotiations with Moscow over the future of INF in Europe. These new American missiles would be deployed in several European countries, including West Germany, Italy, Britain, the Netherlands and Belgium, and it would help to strengthen nuclear deterrence in Europe vis-à-vis the Soviet Union. As always, deterrence (a concept largely founded on psychological consid-erations) was a double-edged sword: nuclear deterrence can be enhanced by the modernization of existing weapons systems, or by the introduction of new types of weapons, but such measures would often contribute to the escalation of the arms race. Indeed, a majority of Western Europeans did not welcome the deployment of new American missiles, which were regarded as making nuclear war more, rather than less, likely in Europe. Accordingly, the 1979 NATO dual track deci-sion assumed that the INF negotiations, if successful, might obliterate the need for the new Euro missiles, or that the Soviets might be persuaded to scrap the SS-20s altogether. By implication, the 1979 decision was intended to put pressure on the Soviet Union to begin arms control talks with Washington on the INF, as otherwise NATO would have to deploy American missiles in Europe.[10]

Just as the deployment of the SS-20s upset the stability of the Western European nuclear deterrent, the proposed American deployment of Euro mis-siles constituted a new security problem for the Soviet Union. Throughout the negotiations with the USA over strategic nuclear arms, Moscow upheld its notion of achieving 'equal security' with the West. Indeed, the West's idea of Euro mis-siles to be distinguished from superpower strategic nuclear weapons (which would be used to 'attack by United States or Soviet forces on opposing home-lands'), was alien to Moscow, as the Soviet Union regarded any nuclear weapons (theatre or strategic), capable of hitting targets in the Soviet Union directly, either from the American homeland or from American forward bases in Europe, or by British and French nuclear forces, as strategic.[11] Moscow now insisted that the American forward based system be taken into consideration in any nego-tiations over the INF, and the prospects for nuclear arms negotiations were further diminished by the renewed Cold War in the late 1970s.[12]

Western Europeans wanted to maintain European détente with Moscow as long as they could and viewed with growing concern President Reagan's tough talk about the Russians, his readiness to use military forces to resolve Third World conflicts such as the 1983 invasion of Grenada, and the US military build-up. Moreover, soon after he came to power, Reagan stated repeatedly that a limited nuclear war could be confined to Europe, which fuelled further European fears about the decoupling of American nuclear deterrence from the security of Western Europe. In the meantime, peace, anti-nuclear and anti-American movements were growing in strength in Europe, reflecting the increasing public concern about the danger of the uncontrolled expansion of nuclear weaponry. By early 1981, the Helmut Schmidt government, under intense pressure from its peace movements, was moving towards opposing the deployment of the Cruise and Pershing II missiles on its territory.[13]

Reagan's militant and confrontational approach to the Soviet Union also increased fears in the Kremlin that the USA was now prepared to attack the Soviet Union, and this, together with the information about NATO's war plans obtained by the East German Intelligence Service (Stasi), contributed to the 1983 war scare in Moscow.[14] The Soviets were particularly concerned about the possi-ble deployment of the Pershing II missiles as a real threat to the security of the Soviet Union, as they believed that the high-precision missiles would be capable of hitting the country and destroying its missile silos in a few minutes. A recent study claims that the Politburo did not overestimate the power of the Western peace movements to prevent the deployment of the American INF missiles in Western Europe, for Moscow was convinced that the US deployments would take place. In any case, Moscow's ability to exploit the division in the North Atlantic Alliance was reduced by the Polish crisis, and also by its persecution of the peace movements in Eastern Europe.[15] All this meant that neither Western Europe nor the Soviet Union wanted more nuclear weapons in Europe.

Reagan aimed at enhancing America's global leadership by rebuilding the country's military power as 'the motor of international authority'. Inherited from Carter's defence build-up in 1980, National Security Directive 32 in May 1982 called for the acceleration of US rearmament, the expansion of allied defence programmes, economic pressures on the USSR and its satellite coun-tries, and psychological warfare aimed at weaning the Soviet satellites away from Moscow. Reagan's military spending in real terms increased by 50 per cent between 1980 and 1985, but how this in fact strengthened the USA has long been debated.[16] Supporters claimed that Reagan's rearmament facilitated the USA's 'spectacular military performance' during the 1991 Gulf War, and also helped to persuade Gorbachev that the idea of competing with Washington militarily was untenable.

However, despite its renunciation of the SALT II Treaty, the Reagan administration's strategic arms build-up did not exceed that allowed under the unratified SALT II, and it made only a few alterations to the rearmament measures put in place during the final years of the Carter administration. Reagan decided to go ahead with the controversial B-1 strategic bomber (a $28 billion plane), which had been cancelled by the Carter administration, but the aircraft did not meet the strategic requirements of those who supported the programme.[17] As weapons systems became technologically more complex, it became increasingly difficult to obtain support from a Congress bemused by the very sophistication of these weapons. One congressman wondered whether these missiles, equipped with ultra-complicated guidance systems, would 'hit Washington or Moscow if we get into a war'.[18] Congress, while suspicious of SALT II, did not, however, wish to see an investment of tens of thousands of dollars in new mobile ICBMs (to reduce America's ICBM vulnerabilities), as had been requested by the Carter administration. The original plan to deploy 200 MXs (or Missile Experimental) to meet the Soviets' heavy and multiple-vehicle missiles, was frustrated because of the high costs involved, the technical uncertainties and as a result of pressure from conservative political elites and environmentalist groups. The Reagan administration was forced to review the scheme and adopted the temporary palliative of putting the MX into the Minutemen silos until 1984.[19] Critics pointed out that Reagan's defence programme was based on an exaggerated view of the 'nation's strategic vulnerability', and later in 1983 the Scowcroft commission came to the conclusion that there existed no such 'windows of vulnerabilities' in US nuclear strategic armed forces.[20]

Behind Reagan's rhetoric was his belief in the danger of the accumulation of nuclear weapons; he was deeply troubled by a possible accidental nuclear war, a feeling reinforced when Moscow shot down a South Korean airliner in 1983. In Reagan's view, the previous strategic nuclear weapons talks had not served the interests of America's national security, the Russians could not be trusted, and the arms race was 'moving ahead at a pell-mell pace' based on the Mutual Assured Destruction Doctrine. That nuclear weapons were morally repugnant was also gaining currency in Europe, as well as in the USA.[21]

In an effort to resolve these dilemmas, Reagan called for the reduction, rather than the mere limitation, of the number of nuclear weapons in the superpowers' arsenals, and in November 1981 announced the so-called 'zero' option. The proposal (privately agreed at the NATO Nuclear Planning Group in October 1981) expressed America's readiness to abandon the planned deployment of 572 (Cruise and the Pershing II) missiles in Europe scheduled for 1983, in return for Soviet dismantling of their INF forces already deployed in Europe (SS-20s, SS-4s and SS-5s). The idea of cancelling the additional deployment of Soviet missiles had been advocated by Brezhnev in early 1981 and the issue had also been discussed between West Germany and Moscow. But Reagan's zero option went further, calling for not only Moscow's abandonment of new deployments of SS-20s, but also all existing intermediate-range missiles, some of which were nearly 20 years old. Moreover, the proposal excluded American sea-based missiles, aircraft, and the British and French nuclear weapons. The Reagan administration calculated that, since the proposal would have no chance of being accepted by the Soviets *in toto*, Washington could safely precede to the deployment of its Euro missiles as planned. The zero option, if adopted, might not serve Europe's strategic interests either, as it meant once again decoupling America's strategic nuclear forces from its conventional and tactical nuclear weapons stationed in Europe. However, in terms of propaganda, the zero option appealed to various segments of anti-nuclear protesters in Europe and the USA.[22]

When the two superpowers resumed their negotiations on the INF in November 1981, the Soviet Union, as expected, turned down the zero option. Instead, Moscow came up with numerous ideas for reducing the number of the INF forces in order to deter the planned deployment of American missiles in Europe, but without success. In early February 1982 Moscow suggested the mutual reduction of INF forces by two thirds, which was, however, rejected by the USA, because the Soviets could mobilize those deployed in Asia (where the Soviet Union placed 110 SS-20s out of 350 in total) to attack Europe.[23] During the summer of 1982, the two chief arms control negotiators (Paul Nitze and Yuli Kvitsinskiy) walked in the woods outside Geneva and produced a proposal which would impose an equal ceiling of INF forces of 75; however, neither Moscow nor Washington was willing to countenance a compromise that might undermine their respective military positions in Europe. In November 1983, the die was cast in West Germany. The newly elected Christian Democrat Chancellor, Helmut Kohl, resurrected the FRG's pro-Atlantic posture and secured a 'yes' vote in the Bundestag on 22 November in favour of the deployment of the new Pershing missiles on its soil. As a result, on the following day the Soviet delegation walked out of the Geneva conference on the INF.[24]

In the field of strategic nuclear weapons, Reagan also took a bold stance. Instead of limiting the number of them, in May 1982 he called on the Strategic Arms Reduction Talks (START) to consider a reduction of the number of warheads by one third, and a reduction of the number of ICBMs to an equal ceiling. The latter required the Soviet Union to destroy more missiles than the USA. Moreover, the new weapons systems, the MX, the B-1 bomber, and the Trident submarine-launched ballistic systems, were not included in the proposal. Again, the START proposal did not appeal to the Soviet Union as a useful basis for negotiations and superpower negotiations were also suspended in December 1983.[25]

Probably the most imaginative, yet disturbing, challenge to the superpower arms control negotiations was Reagan's SDI or Star Wars. In March 1983, the President surprised the world and many in his administration, by announcing the decision to set up a space-based defensive shield against incoming missiles. His initiative was soon dubbed 'Star Wars', originating from the popular 1977 film *Star Wars*, and its 1980 sequel *The Empire Strikes Back*. Reagan succeeded in shifting the image of the Cold War into fighting in space, far away from the USA.[26] The President resented nuclear weapons and, even more, resented the fact that the USA had had to suffer from a threat of nuclear annihilation. It seemed, therefore, clear to him that the offensive nuclear arms control negotiations between the superpowers were failing to reduce this threat, and he was convinced that SDI would achieve this instead. He was even prophetic, especially in the light of the post-September 2001 world, when he stated that 'We all know how to make the missiles. One day a madman could come along and make the missiles and blackmail all of us – but not if we have a defense against them.' Reagan was quite happy for the USA to share its SDI technology with other powers who were ready to give up their nuclear weapons.[27]

Two related motives were behind the Star Wars programme: the declining value attached to strategic nuclear deterrence and aspirations towards the de-nuclearization of the world.[28] A successful SDI programme would make nuclear weapons utterly irrelevant to superpower competition, although many officials in the Pentagon and scientists in the USA doubted whether SDI was technically feasible and financially acceptable. However, the Secretary of Defense, Caspar Weinberger (1981–87), was a keen supporter of the project.[29] The European allies received Reagan's new initiative nervously – it meant undercutting European security and decreasing the deterrent value of British and French nuclear weapons, if the Soviet Union resorted to a similar initiative, decoupling the defence of Europe from that of the USA.[30]

The Star Wars project also unsettled the Soviet Union. Moscow regarded it as an attempt to destabilize the superpower arms control negotiations to make the Soviet nuclear arsenal obsolete, to expose Soviet technological weakness if it was unable to counter it, and to strengthen America's incentive to strike the Soviet Union first, without worrying about a Soviet retaliatory attack. More than any-thing else, the Soviet Union contended that SDI violated the ABM Treaty, which at least kept the issue of ballistic missile defence separate from the superpower arms control negotiations. While Moscow also suspected that Reagan was pursu-ing an 'unrealistic task', his statement was seen to be encouraging the arms race in space and affecting Soviet space-based satellites and other communication systems. In fact, neither of the superpowers was free of blame in this space-defence field. In the mid 1970s the USSR had also embarked on research into space-based weapons similar to the SDI, which had not gone unnoticed by Washington. Subsequently, in 1979, the Soviet Union decided to construct a large early warning radar station at Krasnoyarsk in Siberia and, in July 1983, an American reconnaissance satellite camera took a photograph of the construction site which offered clear evidence of Moscow's violation of the ABM Treaty. Nevertheless, Moscow felt that, after having finally caught up with the Americans in the field of offensive nuclear weapons, SDI was a further challenge to Soviet technical and economic resources, as well as an attempt to disarm the Soviet Union 'in the face of the American nuclear threat'.[31] Overall, 1983, the golden anniversary of the US recognition of the Soviet Union, marked one of the lowest points in superpower relations during the Cold War.

THE TURNING POINT: REAGAN AND THEN GORBACHEV, 1984–5

Reagan's conviction that 'if we were going to get them (the Soviets) to sue for peace, we had to do it from a position of strength', suggests that 1984, his presidential re-election year, would be a good time to start reversing his earlier hardline rhetoric.[32] By then, the USA had launched a five-year research and development programme on Star Wars costing the nation $26 billion. Reagan's other rearmament programmes were also in place. There were earlier signs that the US President was willing to establish good relations with the Soviet leadership, such as during his meeting with the Soviet Ambassador to the USA, Anatoly Dobrynin, in February 1983. The Soviet Union reciprocated Reagan's overture by permitting the Pentecostal Christians from Siberia, who had been living in the basement of the US Embassy in Moscow, to leave the country. The Soviet war scare in the autumn of 1983 also persuaded Washington to soften its approach to Moscow.[33] In a speech in January 1984, Reagan publicly shifted his approach from confrontation to rapprochement with the Soviet Union. The President now called for the beginning of superpower dialogue, arms reductions and confidence building measures in the Third World.

The Soviet Union, however, suffered from a succession of frail leaders at the top in the aftermath of the death of Brezhnev in November 1982. Jack Matlock warned Washington that the USA was unlikely to see any substantial response to Reagan's recent overtures in the foreseeable future.[34] Overall, 1984 was marked by only the hesitant beginning of superpower rapprochement In the summer of 1984, the superpower hotline communications system was upgraded. In September 1984, Reagan (then 73 years old) met Gromyko (who was two years senior to the President) for the first time. The meeting was arranged by George Shultz (1982–8), who in June 1982 replaced Alexander Haig, Reagan's maverick first Secretary of State. The two-hour Reagan–Gromyko conversation in the Oval Office did not produce anything substantive: neither side was willing to make any tangible concessions on specific issues. Gromyko found Reagan courteous, but the meeting was confrontational and the conversation 'edgy'. Reagan found Gromyko conservative, inflexible and 'as hard as granite'.[35] Within the Washington administration, Shultz was more disposed to negotiations with Moscow than Reagan's more conservative advisers – Casper Weinberger, his deputy Richard Perle, and Richard Allen (Reagan's National Security Adviser). While the Soviets appreciated Reagan's aspiration to achieve a nuclear-free world, they demanded the end of his Star Wars programme and an agreement on the non-first use of nuclear weapons as conditions for re-opening the superpower arms negotiations, neither of which Washington was prepared to accept.[36]

Despite this mixed progress with superpower relations, Reagan's second term (following his landslide victory in the November 1984 presidential re-election) began with further efforts to improve relations with Moscow.[37] At the beginning of 1985, Shultz and Gromyko met to discuss a possible resumption of arms control talks. SDI remained an impediment to such a step, Gromyko arguing that 'you just want superiority in order to blackmail us', but Shultz's patience eventually paid off. It was finally agreed that three sets of talks would take place in Geneva in March 1985, one on strategic offensive arms reduction talks (START), the second on intermediate range nuclear forces (INF), and the third on SDI.[38]

By the time Gorbachev came to power in the spring of 1985, the stage was set for the commencement of arms control talks. The timing could not have been more ideal. The Soviet Union chose for its top job a man who wanted diplomacy, negotiations and reconciliation with the capitalist bloc, and who knew that the Soviet Union could not afford the cost of the worsening of the Cold War. Both Reagan and Gorbachev disliked nuclear weapons, wanted to get rid of them if they could, and sought a dynamic change in superpower relations. Gorbachev was an astute politician who knew how to maximize his charms to achieve his goals. Reagan's close aides also noted that, while the President was against everything that the Soviet Union stood for, he had an 'unbounded confidence' in his capacity to convert others to his position. The former Hollywood actor obviously knew how to project himself.[39]

Within three months after Gorbachev came to the Kremlin, Reagan and Gorbachev agreed to meet on the shores of Lake Geneva in November 1985. Gorbachev quickly impressed Shultz (who met the new leader during Chernenko's funeral in March) as an 'entirely different kind of leader in the Soviet Union'. Shevardnadze, who replaced Gromyko in the summer of that year, came across to his American counterpart as a more flexible and personable individual than the old guard. In late September 1985, the US President invited the Georgian diplomat to his Oval Office, and Shultz was surprised to find Shevardnadze laughing at Reagan's jokes about Communists. However, as the Secretary of State put it, 'the US-Soviet relationship is not just about personalities'.[40] The superpower rivalry had been the central feature of the international system for decades and it was difficult to dispel the long-standing mistrust and scepticism between the two capitals through a few friendly top-level talks. The Soviet Union still wanted to achieve 'strategic parity', which was, in Gorbachev's view, the 'natural state of Soviet-American relations'.[41] The chance of reconciliation, in Moscow's view, depended upon the SDI: Gorbachev thought that the American project would complicate superpower arms reductions negotiations and would invite a new arms race in space. It should, therefore, be abandoned. In other words, SDI increased Gorbachev's incentive to seek a summit with Reagan.[42]

The Reagan administration approached the Geneva summit differently from Moscow. It appreciated that the Soviet Union was moving towards the reduction of nuclear armaments, but believed that Moscow's moderation was a result of American pressure through its rearmament programme. While Moscow placed emphasis on nuclear arms control negotiations as the means of ending the Cold War with the USA, Washington wanted to examine the overall aspects of bilateral relations: the USA openly criticized the Soviet Union for its continuing encouragement and assistance to the Communist regimes in Afghanistan, Nicaragua and other Third World countries, and for its violations of the human rights provisions of the Helsinki Final Act. On the occasion of celebrating the tenth anniversary of the CSCE Final Act at the end of July 1985, Shultz delivered a 'hard hitting' speech, condemning Moscow for suppressing personal freedoms, such as travelling, speech and access to wider information.[43] The USA focused on changing the Soviet system or regime change, as 'the problem in arms control was not the arms, but who controlled them'.[44]

The road to the Geneva summit was by no means smooth. The Reagan administration suspected that the Soviet Union had already violated the SALT II

Treaty, and Weinberger insisted that the USA abandon its current restraint and ignore the limitations imposed by the treaty, which was, in any case, due to expire at the end of 1985. The State Department took account of diplomatic niceties and suggested that the USA should maintain 'interim restraint', pending the negotiations on the START Treaty. Eventually, Reagan came up with a compromise in June 1985, stating that the USA would continue to comply with the limitations imposed by the SALT II Treaty by scrapping older weapons, although it would keep open the option of abandoning the treaty.[45]

SDI divided the administration. There were those, led by Weinberger, who wanted to speed up research on the Star Wars programme by abandoning the ABM Treaty, while others, led by Robert McFarlane, Reagan's third National Security Adviser, sought to use the project as a bargaining chip to extract concessions from the Soviet Union. McFarlane surprised a TV audience on 6 October by stating that research, testing and development of SDI was, in fact, permissible under the 1972 ABM Treaty. This interpretation was disputed even within the administration, and was also criticized by Britain and West Germany.[46] In any case, the Secretary of State doubted that the project would become operative before the mid 1990s. Given this situation, the USA could continue with the current level of research on SDI for the next few years, within the confines of the ABM Treaty (the British Prime Minister also advised Reagan on similar lines when she met him at Camp David in December 1984).[47] However, any suggestion of abandoning the ABM Treaty would fuel controversy in Congress, annoy America's allies and, of course, strain Washington's relations with Moscow. Central to the SDI controversy was the fact that the project had 'enormous potential' to be used by the Americans to extract concessions from Moscow, but the administration could not agree on how to maximize that potential.[48]

Moscow's intense preoccupation with SDI was evident: the subject was brought up many times in Gorbachev's letters to Reagan, during Shultz's meetings with Shevardnadze, and in Moscow's proposal in September 1985 calling for a 50 per cent reduction of offensive strategic weapons in return for the USA's abandonment of the project. Prior to the Geneva summit, when Shultz met Gorbachev in Moscow, the Soviet leader criticized the programme at considerable length, to the extent that Dobrynin became concerned that Gorbachev was 'overdoing it . . . because that would merely reinforce Reagan's belief in its (SDI's) importance'.[49] Indeed, Shultz believed that SDI made Gorbachev anxious to reach agreement with the USA, and he (Shultz) agreed with Reagan that the Star Wars programme should be kept intact and not bargained away.[50]

The prospects for a successful Geneva summit were further undermined by a series of espionage revelations prior to the conference. In March, a US military liaison officer, Major Arthur Nicholson, was killed by the Red Army in East Germany, and the USA reacted angrily by expelling a Soviet army officer from Washington and also by cancelling a visit by members of the Naval War College to Moscow. Oleg Gordievsky, the KGB chief in London, defected to Britain in July and two months later his revelations to MI6 led Thatcher to expel 31 Soviet spies from Britain. In August, the USA accused Moscow of Soviet efforts to monitor and spy on American diplomats serving in the country, by using a potentially harmful chemical (which was later disproved). The media dubbed the incident 'Spy Dust on the Summit Road.'[51]

MEETING OF MINDS – FROM GENEVA TO REYKJAVIK, 1985–6

At the Geneva summit on 19–20 November some 3500 journalists assembled, eagerly awaiting the first top level superpower talks since 1979. Gorbachev and Reagan spent nearly 15 hours together in private discussions, which were, in Gorbachev's words, 'constructive, frank, and increasingly friendly'.[52] Both found each other tough, but Reagan 'grew to like' Gorbachev, who could be 'warm and outgoing in a social setting'.[53] Unsurprisingly, however, SDI became the main source of disagreement between the two. While they agreed, in principle, to deep cuts in strategic offensive weapons and separate negotiations on the INF missiles, the agreement was dependent upon America's abandonment of the SDI project. Gorbachev argued that 'if nuclear missiles were destroyed, there would be no need for a Star Wars defense against them'. In response, Reagan offered to share America's SDI technology with Moscow, although the idea had already been criticized in Washington when Reagan first announced it during the presidential election campaign in the autumn of 1984. Gorbachev rightly pointed out why he could not take Reagan's offer seriously, since the American President was not persuaded by Soviet insistence that Moscow would never attack the USA.[54] The summit thus ended without any agreement on arms control issues.

Reagan was, however, pleased with the fact that he had not made any concession to the Soviet leader and, in any case, the USA was not in a hurry. As long as the Soviet Union was unwilling to change its system and reverse its opposition to SDI, the USA was not prepared to make any hasty concessions. By comparison, the Soviet Union was in an unfavourable position to negotiate with the USA. Gorbachev sought to block SDI, but had offered nothing in return to compel the USA to do so. He simply concluded in a letter to the American President that 'we had managed to overcome a serious psychological barrier' at Geneva.[55] The Geneva summit certainly restored the Soviet Union into the media spotlight as one of the two superpowers and Gorbachev proudly reported to the Politburo that the summit was 'an important event not only in our bilateral relations, but in world politics as a whole'.[56] The Geneva summit proved to be the first step towards détente – both sides agreed to resume cultural exchanges, restore some civilian aircraft services and to establish new consulates.

The year 1986 opened with Gorbachev's bold arms control proposal. On 15 January, he called for the removal of all INF missiles from Europe, a similar suggestion to Reagan's 1981 zero option proposal (which, however, had included a proposal for withdrawing Soviet INF missiles from Asia as well). Moscow also proposed nuclear disarmament which was to be achieved by 2000, and announced an extension of the unilateral moratorium on Soviet nuclear testing. Gorbachev's pledges were still linked to America's renunciation of the SDI project and, as such, were largely regarded in Washington as propaganda.[57] Shultz noted that if Gorbachev shared Reagan's idea of eliminating nuclear weapons from the world, Washington might be able to persuade the Soviet Union to reduce its large numbers of strategic offensive weapons. The US Secretary of State still felt that Gorbachev was merely trying to '*repair*' the Communist system at home, and 'not *replace* it'.[58]

The post-Geneva months witnessed a worsening of superpower relations. Despite Reagan's request in February 1986, Gorbachev refused to set a definite date for another summit unless the USA changed its mind about SDI. When the Soviets did suggest a meeting to discuss the nuclear testing ban in March, Washington turned it down. In the same month, the USA demanded that Moscow make large cuts in the number of Soviet officials working for the UN, as they were suspected of espionage. In retaliation, the Kremlin expelled an American official working in Moscow, on suspicion of spying. Meanwhile, the Soviet Union protested against an incursion by America's nuclear-armed cruiser into Soviet territorial waters near the Crimea and, also in April, in retaliation for the US bombing of Libya, Shevardnadze cancelled a visit to Washington in May. Gorbachev's handling of the Chernobyl disaster in late April was another source of outrage in Washington. Reagan attacked the Soviet Union for 'its stubborn refusal to provide a full account'. In return, Gorbachev accused the USA of initiating an anti-Soviet campaign in an effort to 'sow new seeds of mistrust and suspicion towards the socialist countries'.[59] In May, the President in turn criticized the Soviet Union for violating the SALT II Treaty (which had expired at the end of the previous year), and stated that the USA would ignore the limitations imposed by the treaty 'unless the Soviets were prepared to make massive concessions'.[60]

This series of 'tit for tat' reprisals did not, however, lead to a return to the Cold War of Reagan's earlier days. Gorbachev showed himself to be accommodating and agreed, in April, to meet the American President without any strings attached (thereby dropping his earlier demand for America's abandonment of the SDI project). Moscow also accepted that the INF negotiations should be held independently of the START, which the USA had been seeking for some time.[61] Reagan responded to Moscow's climb down favourably and, when Shevardnadze visited Washington to deliver Gorbachev's letter to the President on 19 September, Reagan opted for Reykjavik as the venue for the next meeting with the Soviet leader.

Another round of spy incidents after August threatened the opening of the Reykjavik summit in the autumn. America's arrest of Genmady Zakharov, a KGB agent, on 23 August was followed, a week later, by the Soviet arrest of Nicholas Daniloff, an American journalist who had become inadvertently involved in CIA operations. Zakharov's arrest (which had been decided at lower levels, without the knowledge of either Reagan or Shultz) angered Gorbachev, who instructed the KGB to arrest Daniloff to 'balance the scales'. The Daniloff arrest became a huge public relations issue in the USA. Reagan was outraged, but the two men were eventually released in succession on 29 and 30 September. Meanwhile, the Reagan administration expelled nearly 250 Soviet officials who were suspected of being KGB operatives. Moscow retaliated with equal vigour by withdrawing 260 Soviet employees working in the US Embassy in Moscow. It was only in mid October that both sides decided to put an end to the battle of spies.[62]

The Reykjavik summit (11–12 October) was hurriedly prepared at the same time as the espionage affair, but this summit was to be remembered by many as the most dramatic of them all. There were different levels of preparations and expectations on the two sides: the USA was more relaxed and much less well prepared, since Reykjavik was intended to be a preliminary meeting, before a substantive summit scheduled to be held in Washington in 1987. The President was expecting to discuss Euro missiles and nuclear testing, but was not willing to give in to the Soviet leader over Star Wars. Simply, the USA intended to hold on to its existing position and if the Soviet Union refused to accept it, so be it.

Gorbachev was under pressure from his colleagues in the Politburo to make a substantive agreement with the USA at Reykjavik. He brought with him to the summit a troop of officials and senior advisers.[63] Gorbachev's aim was to delay America's research on SDI in return for Soviet concessions on their nuclear offensive weapons. Even if this did not work, the Soviet Union could demonstrate to the world that SDI (and not Soviet intransigence) was 'the main obstacle to an agreement' on nuclear arms control negotiations.[64] At Reykjavik, Gorbachev was keen to do business with Reagan, finding the latter 'not quite prepared for detailed talks', and he looked irritated by a monologue by the President about the creation of an America free of nuclear threats.[65]

The two-day summit meeting took place in the dining room of Hofdi House, once occupied by the British ambassador to Iceland. It was reported to be haunted and because of this it was sold by the British government in 1952. From the outset, Gorbachev took the initiative by laying out his comprehensive arms control proposals in front of the American delegation. The Soviet Union was ready to agree to a 50 per cent cut in the three areas of strategic offensive weapons: intercontinental ballistic missiles (ICBM), sea-launched ballistic missiles (SLBM), and heavy bombers, which also included for the first time Soviet heavy ICBMs, the main threat to US national security. With reference to the INF missiles, the Soviet Union agreed to eliminate all long-range INF missiles in Europe, and was willing to discuss a limit on its INF in Soviet Asia. Moscow would no longer ask for British and French nuclear forces to be included or frozen at existing levels. Gorbachev also accepted any necessary verification measures, including on-site inspections, which marked a remarkable shift from the previous Soviet position on the subject. In the field of space and defensive systems, Gorbachev abandoned his pressure for the cancellation of SDI, but he now asked the USA to commit itself to a ten-year non-withdrawal from the ABM Treaty. During that period, it was suggested that the USA would be allowed to proceed with a limited level of research on SDI.

Overall, the Soviet proposal showed a significant move towards the American position, by presenting a series of concessions in many important areas of the arms control negotiations on American terms. Gorbachev, in Shultz's words, 'was laying gifts at our feet'. Even Richard Perle, usually a hardliner and currently assistant Secretary of Defense, was impressed with the proposal. Thereafter, Paul Nitze, a senior expert on US arms control negotiations, and his American working group, acted together with their Soviet counterparts headed by General Akhromeyev (the Soviet Chief of the General Staff), to close the differences between both sides or, from the American point of view, to bring the Soviet Union even closer to their position. Nitze found Akhromeyev a 'challenging negotiator with a clear, well-informed mind'.[66] The two teams did take occasional breaks between their night time debates to engage in private conversations. They almost enjoyed each other's company. A significant by-product of the Reykjavik summit was the opportunity for the Americans to catch a glimpse of the changes Gorbachev was making in the Soviet Union. America's previous experience often went: 'You knew you were talking to someone who wasn't a real human being. You were talking to a programmed mind of someone doing something for some reason other than what an individual human being would do on his own hook.'[67] Now, in Reykjavik, the Americans were surprised to discover that their negotiating partners were humane, chatty and even sound.

In the early part of the second day of the summit, the Americans were pocketing more and more concessions from the Russians. In the START, Nitze managed to persuade Akhromeyev to agree to equal outcomes, rather than an equal number of reductions. This would require 'unequal reductions where the current levels favoured one side', but it was progress, nonetheless, towards reducing the threat of Soviet ballistic missiles, an area where the USA felt it was behind.[68] In addition, Gorbachev now agreed to limit Soviet INF missiles in Asia to 100 warheads, to be balanced by the same number of American counterparts to be deployed in the USA (probably in Alaska targeting the eastern part of the Soviet Union). However, there had been no progress over the question of SDI. Gorbachev expressed his dissatisfaction and Shevardnadze also looked tense – it was as though the earlier mood of excitement prevailing in Hofdi House had been a propaganda ploy by the acclaimed ghosts.

During the afternoon of the second day, both sides went backwards and forwards over what each party believed had been achieved so far. Reagan was disposed to agree a ten-year commitment to the ABM Treaty, as Gorbachev had requested, on the understanding that during that time the USA could freely research, test and develop the Star Wars systems. At the end of the ten-year period, when the ABM Treaty expired, both superpowers could then freely deploy their defence systems. Reagan could accept this outcome as it would not affect the scope and nature of his SDI programme at all. During the proposed ten years of commitment to the ABM Treaty (1986–96), the superpowers also accepted, in principle, substantial cuts in their respective nuclear arsenals. The American plan called for a 50 per cent cut of strategic nuclear weapons (bombers, ICBMs and SLBMs) within the first five years (1986–91), followed by the total elimination of ballistic missiles (Soviet and American) during the second five-year period. At the end of the ten-year period, 'with all offensive ballistic missiles eliminated, either side would be free to deploy defences'. In other words, the USA could close the so-called window of vulnerability by eliminating the Soviet ballistic missiles during the second stage of arms reductions (1991–6). After 1996, Reagan hoped that a successful SDI would replace the strategic arms race and provide the USA with a protective shield against incoming nuclear missiles.[69]

During the final meeting, starting at 5.30 p.m. (the meeting was originally scheduled to end at noon), both sides felt that they had made considerable progress, and jubilant feelings returned to the house. Reagan finally realized that 'Hell. He (Gorbachev) doesn't want to set up a summit. He wants to have a summit. Right here.' Gorbachev then asked why the both countries could not completely eliminate all strategic nuclear weapons, and not just the ballistic missiles. 'It would be fine with me', replied Reagan, 'if we eliminated all nuclear weapons', and both agreed: 'We can do that. Let's eliminate them. We can eliminate them.'[70] However, Gorbachev added that 'This all depends, of course, on you giving up SDI.' All the Soviet proposals, continued Gorbachev, were tied to the SDI project, on which research should be confined to 'laboratories' for the next ten years, in accordance with the more strict interpretations of the ABM Treaty. To Reagan, this meant killing his SDI project slowly and he rejected Gorbachev's proposal. The meeting broke up and an acute sense of disappointment and frustration overwhelmed the two leaders. Reykjavik proved that the superpowers could come very close to an accord, but could not clinch the deal.[71]

THE CONCLUSION OF THE INF TREATY IN DECEMBER 1987 AND AFTER

Most of the press accused Reagan's preoccupation with SDI as the cause of the breakdown of the Reykjavik summit. The Politburo, too, concluded on 14 October that SDI, and not Gorbachev, was the main cause of the failure.[72] Shultz was, however, personally impressed that SDI drove Gorbachev to come so close to the American negotiating position on nuclear strategic weapons. The good news was that the superpowers had not reached an agreement on nuclear disarmament. The Reykjavik summit disturbed many Western Europeans and the meeting *nearly* showed how the USA would and could unilaterally determine nuclear issues without consulting its European allies. The collapse of the summit pleased many officials in the State Department and in the Pentagon, who feared the possible undesirable consequences for the administration in Congress and amongst America's allies if the 'potentially historic' agreements had gone ahead.[73]

Nevertheless, the Reykjavik talks did help to put a human face on Soviet–US relations and it proved to be a stepping stone for successive arms control negotiations. In Iceland, the provision of human rights was now firmly placed on the subsequent negotiating agenda, the terms of INF agreements had been worked out, and the essence of the START agreement was laid down. Despite the deadlock, Reagan spoke warmly of Gorbachev afterwards, while Gorbachev developed his confidence in the American President.[74] The seeds of the meeting of minds were sown in Reykjavik.

The Soviet leader was, by then, deeply committed to his far-reaching Perestroika and Glasnost. In order for his domestic reforms to succeed, Gorbachev needed cooperative relations with the outside world, which might assist his reform programme financially and keep Eastern Europe solvent in his projected 'common European home'. Moscow also remained anxious to remove the Pershing II missiles from Germany. Gorbachev thus had a number of powerful reasons to seek swift results from the INF negotiations. In part, he had overvalued the propaganda effect of SDI on the USA and Western Europe: he calculated that once the Soviet Union proved to the world that SDI was the main obstacle to the superpower arms control negotiations, anti-nuclear movements in the USA and Western Europe would pressurize their governments to make concessions. However, as was shown earlier, while SDI divided the Western European allies, it did not cause a breakdown of the transatlantic relationship. While the Mitterrand government was determined to lead a European space project, *Eureka,* to counter SDI, French firms were allowed to enter into contracts with the American sponsored research agency on SDI. Britain, West Germany and Italy signed collaborative research projects with the USA on SDI between 1985 and 1986. Equally, the prospect of removing Soviet and American nuclear missiles from Europe was received with some misgivings in NATO, for this raised the need to deal with other imbalances, notably in the fields of conventional and chemical weapons.[75]

After Reykjavik, the Reagan administration suffered from setbacks at home. The Republicans lost control of the Senate after the 1986 mid-term elections. Moreover, the White House-led covert operation, the Iran-Contra affair, came to the surface in the autumn of 1986 (see chapter 8). As a result, the credibility of the Reagan administration was called into question and his popularity dwindled. A number of officials were implicated in the Iran-Contra scandal. Admiral Poindexter, the National Security Adviser, was sacked, together with his NSC staff associate, Colonel Oliver North. The CIA director, Bill Casey, was also deeply involved, and was forced to resign through illness in January 1987.[76] The Iran-Contra affair, rather than superpower relations, now dominated American politics. There was no exchange of New Year greetings between the two leaders, but both felt that something had to be done in the disarmament field.

In early 1987, Gorbachev decided to tone down his obsession with SDI (as his Western friends and experts on arms negotiations were urging him to do, if he wished to achieve success in arms control negotiations with Washington), and he began to shower the West with a series of nuclear arms control proposals.[77] In February 1987, when Casper Weinberger was about to take the initiative in authorizing the deployment of the first portion of the SDI system (which, in the end was pigeonholed in the light of the furore from the American public, Congress and European allies), the Soviet leader announced that he was now willing to eliminate all medium-range missiles in Europe without linking this to SDI (the Europe zero option). In April, when Shultz visited Gorbachev in Moscow, the latter offered to scrap all shorter-range – from 500 to 1000 km – INF (SRINF) missiles (the double zero option). The Soviet Union at that time possessed some 900 SRINF, with 390 already deployed, but the Americans had no equivalent weapons in Europe. These Soviet short-range missiles were placed in Eastern Europe in response to America's decision to deploy the INF weapons in Europe in 1983. In theory, if the USA was to scrap its INF weapons as part of a superpower agreement, then there would be no need for the Soviet SRINF to stay. Having said this, the decision to scrap nearly 900 missiles unilaterally was unheard of in the history of superpower arms control negotiations. Shultz and Reagan were both delighted with the progress at the Moscow meeting.[78]

The Soviet military leadership, while appreciating the removal of the US INF forces from Europe, was shocked by Gorbachev's offer to remove the SRINFs altogether.[79] Finally, in July, Gorbachev announced the 'global double zero option', by proposing to eliminate the medium-range INF missiles deployed in Asia in addition to the ones in Europe, as well as destroying all shorter-range INF missiles elsewhere.

In 1987 Gorbachev also began to engage actively with Western Europe with his 'common European home' initiative (see chapters 3 and 4). His nuclear disarmament proposals for Europe should have reinforced the impression that Gorbachev was indeed serious about overcoming the division of Europe. Indeed, public opinion in the key countries (Britain, Italy and West Germany in Europe, where American missiles were currently based) welcomed the superpowers' move to reduce the number of nuclear weapons on European soil. However, their political leaders and senior NATO officials were divided over Gorbachev's new proposals. Britain feared that the double zero option might lead to a third zero, with the disappearance of all American nuclear weapons from Europe, and urged Washington to suspend nuclear disarmament until agreement had been reached about reductions in conventional and chemical weapons. The Federal Republic of Germany, with its central geographical position in the Western Alliance, had founded its ultimate security on the physical presence of US nuclear weapons. Bonn was seriously concerned about the implications of the INF Treaty and would accept it only if there were further reductions in the American and Soviet short-range (between 0 and 500 km) nuclear forces (SNF), thus decreasing the possibility of the outbreak of a nuclear war centred on West Germany. France was worried about any steps that might 'weaken' its nuclear deterrence power in Europe.[80] Critics also argued that the INF Treaty would undermine NATO's flexible response strategy, while the reduction of American nuclear weapons would also highlight the strength of the Warsaw Pact in conventional forces, which might in turn lead to a 'pax Sovietica'. These alarmist views surprised Gorbachev, bringing home to him how difficult it was for Western Europe to 'part with American nuclear weapons'. In the end, Reagan supported the double zero option (i.e. removal of both INF and SRINF from Europe), and NATO endorsed it in June 1987.[81]

There was one issue remaining, however. While Gorbachev had become more flexible, and decided not to include the French and British nuclear weapons in the INF agreement, the Soviet military was particularly unhappy over the exclusion of the German Pershing IA missiles from the US–Soviet treaty. These missiles were owned by West Germany, although their warheads belonged to the USA. The Kohl government welcomed the double zero option, but insisted that West Germany keep its Pershing missiles as Bonn's only remaining nuclear deterrent. As far as the Soviet Union was concerned, they were part of the US nuclear arsenal and must, therefore, be included in the INF Treaty. Behind the scenes, the USA and Britain pressed Bonn to change its mind and, in August, the Kohl government reluctantly announced its decision to dispose of its 72 Pershing launchers. The USA subsequently agreed to withdraw the warheads from these missiles when the Germans dismantled the missiles.[82]

Gorbachev and Reagan signed the INF Treaty on 8 December 1987 at 1.45 p.m. precisely, as instructed by Nancy Reagan's astrologer. The treaty required the two superpowers to destroy all their intermediate missiles within the next three years. It meant that the USA had to dismantle a total of 283 deployed and non-deployed launchers, and 867 missiles, while the figures for the Soviet Union were 851 and 1836, respectively. In addition, the Soviet Union would unilaterally liquidate over 900 SRINF missiles. Numerous critics were quick to point out that the INF Treaty would reduce by only a small percentage (some 5 per cent) the nuclear weapons on both sides. However, under the INF Treaty for the first time an entire category of nuclear weapons in their respective arsenals was to be destroyed, including modern nuclear weapons. The Soviet Union agreed to, even invited, a deal which required Moscow to eliminate many more missiles than the USA, while at the same time accepting intrusive verification measures. It will be recalled that the key provisions of the INF Treaty had been proposed by Reagan in 1981. These appeared totally unrealistic then, but by 1987 they became part of the agreement supported by Moscow, given the impetus of Gorbachev's new thinking about Soviet foreign policy.

TABLE 2 – INF TREATY INSPECTIONS AND ELIMINATIONS

	Number of US inspections in Soviet Union	Number of Soviet INF missiles eliminated	Number of Soviet inspections in the US	Number of US INF missiles eliminated
31 May 1989	244	945	96	324
31 May 1990	102	701	46	171
31 May 1991	75	200	65	351
Totals	**421**	**1846**	**207**	**846**

	Type of Soviet INF missile	Number eliminated	Type of US INF missile	Number eliminated
	SS-20	654	Pershing II	234
	SS-4	149	Ground-Launched	
	SS-23	239	Cruise Missile	
	SS-12	718	BGM-109	443
	SSC-X-4	80	Pershing IA	169
	SS-5	6		
Totals		**1846**		**846**

Source: Federation of American Scientists.

At the same time, the American fear that disagreement on SDI might block the final conclusion of the INF Treaty did not materialize. At the beginning of November, Weinberger resigned and was replaced by Frank Carlucci. Colin Powell took Carlucci's place as Reagan's new National Security Adviser. The White House was now surrounded by more moderate and pragmatic advisers, which also helped to reduce the pressure of SDI on the Washington summit. The Soviet Union was also aware that, apart from the US President, Congress and his new advisers did not embrace Star Wars with great enthusiasm. On the eve of the Washington meeting, Congress cut Reagan's budget for the SDI by one third and imposed limitations on the testing of the SDI, so that it was in line with the stricter interpretation of the ABM Treaty, as Gorbachev had been urging. During the summit, Reagan nevertheless boasted of his confidence in turning SDI into a 'workable concept', but Gorbachev responded lightly that 'I think you're wasting money. I don't think it will work. But if that's what you want to do, go ahead.' Surely by then Gorbachev had realized that there would be no quick fix on the SDI project, and that the Soviet Union should act in accordance with its national interests if and when the SDI proved to be operational.[83]

Overall, the Washington meeting was, in Reagan's words 'the best summit we've ever had with the Soviet Union'. Gorbachev and Reagan established a personal rapport of a kind in Washington, and both sides gained prestige from the success of the summit. For Gorbachev, his success in arms control negotiations, albeit mainly through his unilateral concessions, was reflected in his popularity at home and abroad. The Soviet leader quickly became a 'PR genius' in Washington during his visit: with his disarming smiles and friendly manner, he helped to change considerably the American public perception of the Soviet Union. Reagan's handling of the Soviet Union scored the highest rating of 77 per cent, up 11 per cent from the pre-Washington summit polls, while his overall popularity also rose, overcoming the setback of the Iran-Contra affair.[84]

Compared with the eventful previous years, Reagan's last year, 1988, was less remarkable in terms of the promotion of superpower relations. Although the two leaders at the Washington summit agreed that the next goal was to achieve a 50 per cent reduction in their respective nuclear strategic arms weapons, it soon became clear that START negotiations were more complicated than the INF agreements, and that there would be too little time left before the two sides could prepare a workable package at the next summit in Moscow in May 1988. It should also be pointed out here that the US Senate found it difficult to approve the INF Treaty quickly, since some die-hard conservatives objected to nuclear disarmament altogether and, as a result, the delay in the INF Treaty ratification had an adverse impact on progress with START.[85] Reagan still believed that the recent improvement in superpower relations was mainly due to America's tough talking with the Soviet leader, based on his rapid rearmament programme. A US national security strategy document of January 1988 continued to regard Gorbachev's Soviet Union with some caution: despite Moscow's new image, it concluded, Washington failed to see 'any slackening of the growth of Soviet military power or abandonment of expansionist aspirations'.[86] In any case, Reagan was under no pressure to produce another tangible success in the arms control sphere. By contrast, Gorbachev's domestic policy was increasingly under attack from both his radical and conservative critics after 1988. He was a man in a hurry – he wanted to achieve further successes abroad to bolster his position at home, and it was rather unfortunate that the Soviet leader had to meet a new set of American leaders after the 1988 presidential election. Gorbachev probably meant it when he told Shultz in February 1988 that 'I wish we could sort of postpone all of this (i.e. dealing with a new administration) for three or four years so that we could keep working in a quiet setting.'[87]

As will be discussed in chapter 8, 1988 had seen some significant superpower agreements on Afghanistan and Angola, as well as a ceasefire in Nicaragua between the Sandinistas and the Contra forces. There was no progress on superpower arms control negotiations during the year. Instead, the Moscow summit from 29 May to 1 June placed priority on the issue of human rights and of democratization, and Reagan met a group of Soviet political dissidents.[88] Otherwise, the summit became more of a social occasion for Ronald and Nancy Reagan and they strolled around Red Square. The summit was also remembered for Reagan's remark about his 1983 'evil empire' speech. Asked in Moscow whether the President still regarded the Soviet Union as an 'evil empire', he answered that 'No. I was talking about another time, another era.' This comment was not unanimously welcomed in the White House: Reagan's Vice-President and would-be successor, George Bush, maintained on the following day that 'the Cold War is not over'.[89] During the Moscow summit, Gorbachev hoped to secure America's agreement on providing the Soviet Union with most favoured nation (MNF) status, but the subject was tied to the improvement of the Soviet emigration system.[90] However, on a personal level at least, Reagan felt that the relationship with Gorbachev had become relatively close and in his farewell speech in Moscow, Reagan referred to Gorbachev as his 'friend'. Such a display of warmth was of help to the Soviet leader on the eve of the opening of the party conference in the summer.[91]

Gorbachev's last visit to New York came in December of that year, when he made an important speech to the UN General Assembly. His speech was to mark, in his words, 'the watershed', inaugurating Perestroika (restructuring) of the international order. He called for the renunciation of the use of force in resolving international conflicts, 'freedom of choice' and the importance of human rights. It was also his farewell to the international class struggle, which the Kremlin had long upheld, as Gorbachev stated that ideological differences would no longer be regarded as a factor in the conduct of international politics. Taken together, the speech was Gorbachev's declaration of the end of the Cold War and his vision for a new world order.

In a series of unilateral initiatives, which began with the moratorium on Soviet nuclear testing in July 1985, Gorbachev also modified the traditional concept of 'equal security', which meant 'matching not only US capabilities but also those of China and US allies in NATO'. Scholars compared Gorbachev's unilateral arms reductions initiative to 'graduated and reciprocated initiatives in tension reduction', or (GRIT), shifting from an 'armament race' to a 'disarmament race'.[92] After the mid 1980s, the superpowers began to see the merit of reducing the nuclear threat by actually withdrawing nuclear weapons from their respective regional spheres of influence, instead of deploying more nuclear weapons in an effort to strengthen deterrence through modernization, as had taken place in the 1970s.

The American public was delighted with Gorbachev's speech at the UN, with the majority now rejecting the idea that the Soviet Union was a major threat to the USA.[93] If Gorbachev believed that democracy meant that the government would follow the lead given by public opinion, he was mistaken. Reagan, in his final radio address, pointed out that Gorbachev's pledged reductions (about 10–12 per cent of the Soviet armed forces) would still give the Warsaw Pact 'a large conventional advantage'. After Gorbachev's UN speech, Bush, now President-elect, asked the Soviet leader whether his Perestroika could ever succeed, and whether American investors could safely put money into the precarious Soviet economy.[94] On the day of Gorbachev's speech, the UN General Assembly passed a Soviet resolution calling for 'international dialogue' on a comprehensive security system. The USA opposed the resolution, while other NATO countries abstained.[95] Superpower relations were entering into the final stage of the Cold War, mainly because the Soviet Union came closer to the position of the USA, and was prepared to adopt Western values. However, the USA and the West still remained cautious and uncertain about the implications of Gorbachev's new thinking for the future of international relations. Reagan had achieved a rapprochement with Gorbachev, but not yet with the Soviet Union, which remained a huge military power.

6

The Demise of the Superpower Arms Race

THE BUSH ADMINISTRATION AND GORBACHEV

The Bush administration is often described as being more cautious and hesitant about reacting to Gorbachev's new thinking than its predecessor. However, we have seen in the previous chapter that this was not quite true: behind the personal rapport between Reagan and Gorbachev there existed a degree of strong and persistent conservatism in the White House's Soviet policy. Bush's judgement was, therefore, to take stock of Gorbachev's new thinking in foreign policy during the President's initial months, as he was in no hurry to negotiate more nuclear arms reductions for the sake of making public relations points. Gorbachev's Perestroika was seen to be in the interest of the USA, but the prospects of its being successful were increasingly suspect. The US National Intelligence Estimate (NIE) in December 1988 claimed that the current reforms would not improve the Soviet economy. There was even 'some chance' that Gorbachev's reform would fail, which would strengthen the hands of the conservatives in Moscow. In addition, the increasing separatist movements and the nationality questions in the USSR might force Gorbachev into a 'major retreat'.[1] The American leadership also believed that Gorbachev's anxiety to secure arms reductions was motivated not only by the economic factor, but also by a political interest in undermining the resolve of NATO to 'modernize' conventional and tactical nuclear weapons. It judged that the Soviet Union was eager to benefit from 'a non-confrontational international environment' through its weakness. Under the circumstances, the CIA believed that the USA and its allies were provided with 'considerable leverage in bargaining with the Soviets over the terms of that environment' in the field of arms control or regional conflicts. Overall, Gorbachev's conciliatory approach was seen to be a device to secure a respite from the Cold War, in order to revive the USSR as a 'more competitive superpower'.[2]

The USA was, therefore, confronted with two plausible cases. Case 1 – if Gorbachev's reforms continued and his country's civil economy revived, the USA might find itself confronted with a more competitive Soviet Union. Case 2 – if the conservatives took over from Gorbachev and reversed Glasnost and Perestroika, then the Cold War would return in earnest. Either way, it was likely that the Soviet Union would remain a major rival, or worse a major enemy. These scenarios haunted the Bush administration from its inception. The new American leadership, therefore, sought to test the sincerity of Gorbachev's new thinking in regional conflicts and on other bilateral issues, while the arms control issue should be dealt with as an integral part of the overall improvement of superpower relations.[3] Bush, for one, did not believe in the Reaganite utopian ideal of total nuclear disarmament, but wanted to uphold the traditional validity of nuclear deterrence as the best protection for the USA, a view which was shared by his National Security Adviser, Brent Scowcroft. There was also a division in the White House as to how to approach START, which was fundamentally a more important and more substantial arms reductions treaty than INF. All this meant slowing down START negotiations, as Bush did not want to feel obliged to participate in Gorbachev's 'disarmament race'. Nevertheless, if the Soviets wanted to make unilateral concessions, Baker thought (as did his predecessor), 'why not let them do so again now?'[4] Gorbachev's tendency to appeal to a wider audience in Western Europe, China and the rest of the Western world over the head of the USA displeased Washington.[5] Nor was the USA enthused with Moscow's apparent eagerness to obtain credit for disarming the Soviet Union, which made the USA look both conservative and traditionalist. The Bush administration, therefore, observed Gorbachev's popularity in the international arena with considerable suspicion and jealousy.

In fact, Gorbachev was not in an enviable position. His hands were tied by the increasing internal troubles at home, while the Kremlin viewed the reforms in Poland and Hungary with growing concern. The General Secretary was even more in a hurry than he had been during the Reagan years to establish a peaceful partnership with the USA, in order to strengthen his position at home. Based on his well-received UN speech in December 1988, the Soviet leadership also wanted to develop his 'messianic' idea of disseminating Perestroika worldwide. Accordingly, he was hugely frustrated by the Bush administration's 'pause'. Just as Washington was concerned about Gorbachev's possible retreat into a more conservative policy, the Soviet leadership, too, was worried lest the momentum created by Gorbachev and Reagan should be lost in favour of 'obsolete stereotypes'.[6]

In March 1989, the Soviet Union announced a major reduction of the Red Army in Mongolia, and in May Gorbachev surprised Baker during a meeting in Moscow, by offering large unilateral cuts in Soviet tactical nuclear weapons in Europe. Furthermore, Gorbachev was well aware that the Warsaw Pact's superiority in conventional weaponry in Europe had been seen as the main threat to Western Europe. Therefore, in March NATO and the Warsaw Pact formally began the negotiations on Conventional Armed Forces in Europe (CFE), in Vienna. CFE would replace the previously long and futile talks on Mutual

Balanced Force Reductions (MBFR), which had begun in 1973. The issue of reducing conventional forces had been raised on numerous occasions by Gorbachev, and discussed within NATO. Now in 1989, 23 member countries were assembled in Vienna to eliminate 'disparities in major conventional arms from the Atlantic to the Urals', and to achieve 'conventional forces stability at lower levels'. This was by no means a small achievement for the security of Europe and due credit went to Gorbachev.[7]

It was now the Bush administration's turn to show that they could play Gorbachev's 'game equally skilfully'.[8] The USA needed to respond to two problems – the question of the short-range (with a range less than 500 kilometres) nuclear forces in Europe (SNF), and the issue of conventional forces. The conclusion of the INF Treaty in 1987 had left NATO powers with the fear of the denuclearization of Europe. The Reagan administration had promised to keep American tactical nuclear weapons there and also to modernize the US Lance missiles currently based in West Germany.[9] Britain, France and other NATO powers accepted the American proposal as a reassurance, but West Germany did not. Now, with signs of the reduction of the conventional military threat in Europe, the Kohl government was vehemently opposed to the modernization of SNF missiles, as if they were used, they would hit both East and West Germany. Even if the current 88 Lance missiles were replaced with new ones, Bonn would still confront some 1400 similar weapons stationed in the Eastern bloc. Kohl instead demanded the elimination of all short-range tactical nuclear weapons from Europe.[10]

The Soviet Union was desperate to prevent NATO's modernization programme and the arrival of new missiles in Western Germany, and Gorbachev's May offer to reduce Soviet SNF divided NATO further. The timing was also awkward, with the NATO summit to celebrate its 40th anniversary only three weeks away. Thatcher was resolved to go ahead with the modernization, while Kohl adamantly rejected it. Mitterrand was concerned that Britain and the USA were 'risking a debacle in Brussels'.[11] Meanwhile, the US media was becoming more critical of the Bush administration's 'pause' with no apparent initiative forthcoming. Bush's speech on 12 May on moving 'beyond the Cold War' did not contain any new concrete proposals, except for reviving Eisenhower's 'Open Sky proposal', and the media remained unimpressed. Bush complained to Scowcroft that he was 'sick and tired of getting beat up day after day for having no vision and letting Gorbachev run the show'.[12] Clearly the USA now needed to engage in some serious thinking to avert a major row at the forthcoming NATO summit.

The USA decided to revamp the CFE proposal, quickening the process of completing the reductions to five years earlier than Gorbachev proposed. At the NATO summit, Bush called for a cut of 15 per cent in the conventional arms of NATO and the Warsaw Pact and, more importantly, for a 20 per cent reduction of American and Soviet military personnel in Europe. This would require Moscow to withdraw nearly 325,000 troops from Eastern Europe, as opposed to America's 30,000.[13] The Bush peace initiative was designed to achieve a number of practical objectives. First, the reduction of American troops in Europe would meet a long-standing Congressional demand, as Bush himself felt that the USA

had carried 'a disproportionate responsibility for peace in Europe'.[14] Both
Reagan's rapid rearmament programme and Bush's pledge not to increase taxes
compelled the new Republican administration to reduce accumulating government deficits by other means. Any peace dividend arising from East–West
détente could be used to reduce US defence expenditure.[15] Bush and Baker also
calculated that a rapid implementation of the CFE process would help to minimize the dispute over SNF. NATO's nuclear weapons were intended to compensate for the inequalities in the levels of conventional force; if the latter was
reduced to equally low levels between the two blocs, the urgency accorded to the
SNF modernization should lessen accordingly. Thatcher was persuaded to postpone the subject.[16] At the NATO summit meeting, Bush secured a 'Solomon-like'
compromise, whereby both the decision on the SNF modernization and negotiations on SNF reductions would be postponed until the CFE negotiations had
been agreed and implemented.[17]

THE MALTA SUMMIT IN DECEMBER 1989

By the middle of 1989, with Poland and Hungary embarking on their own
reforms, the Soviet Union's retreat from Eastern Europe was becoming more discernible. The timing coincided with America's more serious engagement with
Gorbachev's new thinking. Even earlier than Bush, Baker had established an
excellent rapport with his counterpart, Shevardnadze, at a meeting in July in
Paris during the G-7 conference, at a bilateral meeting in September in
Washington, and at Baker's ranch in Wyoming in the same month. The Soviet
Union was prepared to make further concessions in an effort to reach agreement
on START. During the September meeting with Baker, the Soviet Foreign
Minister made it clear that SDI was no longer linked to progress with the START
Treaty. He also hinted that the Krasnoyarsk radar station was illegal and would
be dismantled. The US Senate had made the resolution of this subject an essential condition for agreement on START. On 23 October Shevardnadze publicly
admitted before the Supreme Soviet that the Soviet radar near Krasnoyarsk was
'frankly' a violation of the ABM Treaty.[18]

These meetings proved to be a breakthrough for Baker, who felt that 'we had
turned a corner . . . from confrontation to dialogue, to cooperation'.[19]
Convinced that the new thinking was not phoney, Baker began, in the autumn of
1989, to speak about the need for the USA to work closely with Gorbachev's
Soviet Union and to support his Perestroika. Bush also sought an informal dialogue with Gorbachev, and both agreed to have an interim summit meeting in
Malta in December 1989, with a formal summit scheduled in Washington in
1990. Prior to the Malta summit, the Berlin Wall was breached and Eastern
Europe began to unravel, with far-reaching consequences for the future of
Communism in that part of the world. Not all of the Bush administration offi-
cials were convinced that Gorbachev's new thinking was worth serious consider-
ation by the USA. The conservatives, including Vice-President Dan Quayle, Dick
Cheney, the Defense Secretary, and Robert Gates, deputy National Security
Adviser, continued to believe that the Soviet Union was still 'our potential

adversary'. In Quayle's view Gorbachev was a 'Stalinist'.[20] The otherwise level-headed General Scowcroft viewed Baker's new-found enthusiasm with some concern, as 'we can't tie our policy to Gorbachev'.[21] In mid November 1989, the NIE predicted that the current Soviet domestic crisis was likely to continue for the next two years, which 'threatened the system's viability'.[22] Bush occupied a middle position between the conservatives and the revisionists. If the Kremlin sought to use the Malta meeting to give the US President 'a greater sense of his country's stake in the success of Perestroika and in Gorbachev's own survival', Bush was clear that he would not give him such an assurance, as if he did, 'it would have a lasting historical, political, and moral price'. Understandably, the USA could not be implicated by entering into a mutual 'understanding' of Gorbachev's situation or 'the measures he might take to crack down'.[23]

The Malta summit (2–3 December) began on the Soviet cruise ship *Maxim Gorky*, anchored at the dockside in Valletta harbour. The two leaders were greeted by stormy Mediterranean weather, which resulted in the cancellation of one of the scheduled meetings. Neither side planned to make substantive agreements at Malta, although they agreed to continue the negotiations on the START Treaty and also on the reduction of superpower chemical weapons (which was first raised by Baker when he met Shevardnadze at Wyoming in September). Bush and Gorbachev also agreed to press ahead with the conclusion of the CFE Treaty in 1990. Bush brought up Central America, urging Gorbachev to stop supporting Castro's Cuba, which, in Bush's view, remained 'the most contentious issue' between the two countries.[24]

The President encouraged the Soviet leader to continue with his reforms at home, stating firmly that 'the world would be better off for Perestroika's success'.[25] Gorbachev showed keen interest in a number of Bush's proposals (subject to Congressional agreement) to normalize economic relations between the two countries. Bush also supported the conferment of observer status to the Soviet Union in the General Agreement on Tariffs and Trade (GATT).[26] Gorbachev took these concessions as evidence of America's economic support for his policy and, to Bush's relief, he did not ask for US financial assistance to bail out the Soviet Union. The Bush administration responded to the turbulent events after the fall of the Berlin Wall in Eastern Europe with 'remarkable reserve'. Critics wanted Bush to 'exult in the West's triumph' and to celebrate the West's victory loudly.[27] However, the President was aware that doing so might harm the position of Gorbachev at home, which might 'tear the Soviet Union apart'. At Malta, the Soviet leadership felt assured that the US was not trying to undermine Gorbachev's Perestroika in relation to the events in the Baltic states or in Eastern Europe.[28]

The Americans were impressed by Gorbachev on two counts. The first was his statement that the Soviet Union was ready to 'no longer consider the US as its enemy', and the second was Gorbachev's affirmation of the importance of the USA's role in Europe. America's deeper commitment to Europe, first with the Marshall Plan and then with NATO, had been the main source of Soviet hostility towards the West. Now, given that the Soviet Union was no longer willing or able to impose law and order in its former European sphere of influence,

Gorbachev wanted the USA to remain in Europe and help him with the reordering of the whole of Europe.[29]

Despite the atrocious weather, the Malta summit went well. The end of the Malta summit was marked by a joint press conference held in the *Maxim Gorky's* discothèque, the first such undertaking in the entire history of US–Soviet summitry. It was a symbolic gesture to show that superpower relations had moved on to a new plain or, as Gorbachev put it, 'we had finally crossed the Rubicon'. For Bush, the Malta summit humanized his relationship with the Soviet leader and helped to build mutual trust and confidence.[30]

BALTIC CLOUDS

The Malta summit opened up a new, but still uncertain, final phase of the superpower relationship. Based on the informal understanding that had been established in Malta, both sides could now enter into serious arms control agreements. Timing, however, became an important factor. Given the increasing turbulence in domestic Soviet politics, Washington wondered 'how long the window of opportunity would remain open'. The Bush administration, therefore, intended to secure firmly the changes in the international environment favourable to the USA and the West, which now existed while Gorbachev remained in power. Under this timetable, the White House expected the two sides to strike a START deal by mid 1990.[31]

We now know that this plan proved over-optimistic, for it was not until July 1991 that the START Treaty was finally signed at the Moscow summit. The growing problems facing Gorbachev's leadership invariably affected the overall development of Soviet–American relations. In other words, the Bush administration was no longer dealing with a stable and progressive Soviet Union under the firm control of Gorbachev and Shevardnadze. The Foreign Minister, in particular, was highly regarded by American policy makers. He was seen as a Kremlin politician firmly committed to the peaceful transformation of the Soviet Union into a democratic country, but, conversely, he was distrusted and criticized by Soviet conservative officials, civilian and military alike, in Moscow.[32] At the end of 1990, Shevardnadze resigned from his post as Foreign Minister, while after 1988 General Akhromeyev was no longer Deputy Defence Minister and Chief of the General Staff. This situation meant that Gorbachev now found it more difficult to make unilateral concessions to the USA, since he was compelled to take into account the Soviet military's objections to various aspects of the arms control negotiations. This, in turn, resulted in sudden changes in the Soviet Union's position on the subject, often leaning towards more conservative policies, thereby widening the differences between Washington and Moscow.[33]

More importantly, the Malta accord between Bush and Gorbachev was by no means unconditional, since it was based on the US assumption that Gorbachev would continue with Perestroika and the democratization of the country. Once the country began to disintegrate, with the Baltic states seeking independence from the Union, Perestroika was caught in a dilemma. Gorbachev stated on a number of occasions, most recently at Malta, his conviction that if the Soviets resorted to the use of force to maintain the Union's unity, this would destroy Perestroika. However, in the same breath, he stated that he could not tolerate the unilateral independence of the Baltic states from the Soviet Union.[34] The Bush administration was, however, clear that if Moscow exercised coercion in an effort to resolve the separatist question, US–Soviet relations would severely deteriorate. Simply, the Americans could not do 'business with Gorbachev if he doesn't get out of the Baltic dilemma'.[35]

The first signs of strain in superpower relations after Malta came during the early months of 1990. When Lithuania declared UDI (unilateral declaration of independence) on 12 March 1990, Gorbachev in retaliation sent Soviet para-troopers to occupy the Communist Party buildings in Vilnius and placed Soviet tanks around the capital. At the end of March, the Soviet military arrested Lithuanians who were resisting conscription, and on 17 April, despite a private warning from the Bush administration of the possible adverse consequences for American–Soviet relations, Gorbachev resorted to the use of an economic embargo against Lithuania until the latter withdraw UDI. The crisis in the Baltic placed the Bush administration in a difficult position. The USA had never rec-ognized Moscow's forceful incorporation of the Baltic states into the Soviet Union. Historically, there was no doubt about America's attachment to the prin-ciples of self-determination, liberal democracy and freedom of choice. However, how could Washington extend unqualified support for Lithuania's UDI without humiliating or weakening Gorbachev's leadership in the Kremlin? Gorbachev was still the best leader so far, with whom the USA could work, and the Baltic crisis had to be weighed against America's wider national interests. As the crisis deepened, Baltic Americans and the press increased pressure on the Bush administration and Congress to support actively Lithuanian independence, in opposition to Gorbachev.[36]

The Bush administration kept its responses measured and neutral. The President avoided publicly criticizing Gorbachev, while encouraging the Lithuanians to enter into peaceful negotiations with the Soviet Union. None of the US allies wanted to impose punitive sanctions on the Soviet Union. However, the US Senate restricted American trade relations with the Soviet Union until Gorbachev's economic embargo against Lithuania was abandoned. Meanwhile, Bush approved a joint letter, produced by Kohl and Mitterrand, which was sent to the Lithuanian leadership, urging them to begin negotiations with Moscow and suspend its UDI. Gorbachev also promised the Baltics that their independence from the Union could be negotiated with the introduction of a new Union Treaty. The crisis was eventually defused by the end of June, when the Lithuanian parliament voted for the suspension of their declared independence.[37]

THE WASHINGTON SUMMIT, 30 MAY–3 JUNE 1990

The Washington summit, which was nearly cancelled at the height of the Baltic crisis, was held between 30 May and 3 June in 1990. No major breakthrough on arms control was expected, but it is important to note that Gorbachev and Bush agreed to cut substantially (by 80 per cent) chemical weapons, without awaiting the outcome of the multilateral negotiations on the comprehensive ban on chemical weapons. Bush felt particularly strongly about banning chemical weapons, as he had witnessed the use of such weapons by Saddam Hussein against Iraq's Kurdish minority, and also against Iran.[38] As has been shown in chapter 4, the Washington summit was also important, in that Gorbachev was persuaded to agree to the West's plan to include a united Germany in NATO. Bush also made sure that the Soviet leader would not return home empty handed, by signing trade and grain agreements with Moscow.[39] While the Lithuanian crisis still hung over Washington, Bush, nevertheless, felt that the personal rapport with Gorbachev established earlier in Malta had been strengthened in Washington. Towards the end of 1990, the USA softened its earlier opposition to the Soviet Union's associate membership of the International Monetary Fund and the World Bank, and Bush also promised to waive the Jackson–Vanik amendments to allow the USSR to secure improved trading relations with the USA. In his January 1991 State of the Union address, the President stressed that the continuing working relationship with the Soviet Union was 'important not only to us but to the world'.[40]

Against these positive steps was the deepening chaos within the Soviet Union. The political, social and economic problems of the Soviet Union were multiplying by the beginning of 1991. Gorbachev, now more concerned to restore law and order in his country, turned to the right and strengthened the power of the KGB. In the Baltic, the Soviet military resorted to the use of force again in January 1991 (see chapter 2). These developments once more threatened the superpower relationship during the Gulf War and affected the pace of the START negotiations. By March 1991 the Soviet Union appeared to be in a 'pre-revolutionary condition'. America's doubts about Gorbachev's leadership increased, and Bush wrote in his diary on 17 March 1991, 'I'm wondering, where do we go and how do we get there'.[41]

THE RED ARMY'S RETREAT FROM EUROPE, 1990–1

It was only during the early summer of 1991, when Gorbachev reverted to his reformist policy, forged an alliance with Yeltsin, and entered negotiations with the other republics to reach an agreement over a new Union Treaty, that the Soviet leader managed to reassert his dominance over arms control issues. There were disputes arising from the conclusion of the CFE Treaty in November 1990 (see chapter 4) and the conclusion of the START Treaty. The latter progressed intentionally slowly, as the Americans wished to resolve the problem of conventional forces before embarking on a major agreement on nuclear weapons.

On the basis of the Malta accord in December 1989, the USA was anxious to eliminate the Red Army from Central Europe. Throughout the Cold War, the existence of a large Red Army stationed in Eastern Europe, which could advance into Western Europe at short notice, remained the 'heart of the West European perception of the Soviet threat'.[42] In February 1990, the Soviet Union agreed to

Bush's proposal for deep cuts in American and Soviet troops in Central Europe to 195,000, but the USA would keep an additional 30,000 troops stationed in Western Europe where the Soviets had no troops. The proposal required the Soviet Union to reduce its forces by 370,000 men, nearly five times more than the number of American troops withdrawing from Europe.[43] Moreover, the CFE Treaty concluded in November 1990 clearly favoured NATO at the expense of the Soviets, since it ended the Eastern superiority in conventional forces in Europe. The treaty endeavoured to reduce armed forces in Central Europe by dispersing the remaining forces elsewhere towards the rear of the region stretching from the Atlantic to the Urals (ATTU). Accordingly, the treaty imposed limits on military hardware (battle tanks, armoured vehicles, aircraft and helicopters), rather than on the size of military manpower. Under the treaty, each side was allowed 20,000 tanks, 30,000 armoured combat vehicles, 6800 air planes and 2000 helicopters. NATO was required to destroy 2100 tanks, as opposed to 12,000 Soviet tanks.[44] However, soon after the signature of the CFE Treaty, the Soviet military raised objections to it.

The Soviet military now claimed that the treaty amounted to Moscow's 'overall surrender to the West', and they tried to use loopholes in the text to sabotage the November 1990 agreement. In anticipation of the conclusion of the CFE Treaty, the Soviet Union had begun to move military equipment, including 17,000 tanks, away from Central Europe. Moscow now claimed that they were not, therefore, subject to the restrictions of the treaty and would not be destroyed. This action, though not illegal, was seen in the West as a sign of Soviet reluctance to destroy military equipment, and was criticized for 'breaching the spirit of the CFE Treaty'.[45] Secondly, after the treaty was signed, the Soviet Union informed the West that it had redeployed three motorized infantry divisions, comprising nearly 3000 pieces of equipment, to the newly formed 'shore defence units', which, they insisted, were exempted from destruction under the CFE Treaty. The USA, supported by the rest of the signatory states, including the former Warsaw Pact countries, protested against this Soviet back-door attempt to violate the treaty. The Soviet Foreign Ministry officials admitted privately to the Americans that they were under strong pressure from the Soviet Defence Ministry, and Shevardnadze himself was mortified by the military's refusal to approve the treaty, which he had himself negotiated with the West in good faith. His successor after December 1990 was Aleksandr Bessmertnykh, then First Deputy Foreign Minister, but he found himself in no better position to resolve the CFE dispute with the Soviet Defence Ministry.[46] The Soviet Union explained that the need for the redeployment of equipment was because of the precarious Soviet security situation and without the armoured combat vehicles (ACVs), the Union would be unable to control the population.[47] The Americans suggested that the ACVs be converted to 'look-alikes' – the emasculated version of the ACVs – by reducing or eliminating their war-fighting capability, which was allowed under the CFE Treaty. On 1 June this compromise solution was finally accepted and in mid June the CFE Treaty was formally ratified at 'an extraordinary conference' of CFE ambassadors in Vienna.[48]

THE CONCLUSION OF THE START TREATY, 1991

As soon as the CFE dispute was resolved, the Bush administration turned its attention to START. Because of the Soviet repression of the Baltic states, and also the First Gulf War, the fourth summit in Moscow (30 July–1 August 1991) was delayed until July 1991. The last technical hitch was settled on 17 July when Gorbachev and Bush met at the G-7 economic summit in London and the treaty was signed during the Moscow summit.[49] This is not the place to discuss in detail the lengthy treaty, which consisted of 47 pages plus 700-page protocols, but it is sufficient to point out that, despite the earlier pledge on nuclear disarmament during the Reagan–Gorbachev summit at Reykjavik in 1986, the START I Treaty was essentially modelled on 'some of the old logic of arms control', and was based on the assumption that 'two antagonistic powers' sought to 'limit and control their confrontation'.[50] Although the framework of the START I Treaty had been agreed by both parties during 1986–7, it took an additional few years to resolve the remaining differences over Cruise missiles, mobile ICBMs, and America's continued interest in SDI.

The START I made a significant step towards banning MIRVs (multiple independently targettable re-entry vehicles), which would 'substantially reduce the vulnerability of land-based systems on both sides as long as there was more or less parity in the number of launchers'.[51] However, 'de-MIRVing' proved to be an expensive and cumbersome task. In the end, it was agreed that both sides would remove the existing warheads, instead of producing new de-MIRVed missiles. For instance, the Reagan administration had reduced the triple-warhead Minuteman ICBM to a single-warhead missile. However, when the Soviet Union claimed that it was de-MIRVing their counterparts, the USA was not convinced. The US Intelligence Community believed that the Soviet SS-25 mobile ICBM was in fact able to carry three warheads, and not one, as stated by Moscow.[52] The last hurdle was America's concern about the modernization of the remaining SS-18 heavy missiles, which were regarded as the most deadly element of the Soviet nuclear force (half of which were to be destroyed under START I). On the other hand, the Soviet Union was worried that by increasing US–UK nuclear cooperation the existing strategic balance might be altered in the West's favour. More provisions were added to allay each superpower's fears of undermining strategic stability at each other's expense, before they could safely sign the treaty in Moscow.

Thus, despite the fact that a majority of the Soviet and American people no longer regarded each other as enemies by the end of 1989, the strategic arms control negotiations were still affected by the residue of scepticism inherent in superpower arms control negotiations over the decades, in that the other party might cheat or exploit the loopholes in the treaties dealing with arms control. Under the START I agreement, the USA was asked to cut its nuclear strategic nuclear weapons by 25 per cent, and the Soviet Union by 35 per cent, bringing the total size of nuclear weapons down to the level they had been in 1982, when Reagan proposed START negotiations. The treaty still allowed both parties to maintain considerable nuclear destructive power spread evenly within the triad system (ICBM, SLBM and strategic bombers).[53] Nevertheless, it was, in Scowcroft's words, 'a large step on the road to rationalizing strategic nuclear forces in a new era'.[54] More importantly, the treaty was accompanied by a mutual agreement on a comprehensive on-site verification system to oversee the implementation of the treaty.

By the time the Moscow summit took place in July 1991, the superpower nuclear arms control negotiations, which had preoccupied the world only a few years before, came to be regarded as insignificant. After all, given the relaxed East–West climate by then, there was less anxiety about nuclear weapons, while there were more opportunities for the two parties to make agreements on the subject. At the summit in Moscow, the media seemed to have lost interest in reporting what had now become the routine business of conducting amicable talks between the superpowers.[55] Instead, a more immediate concern for the media after the August coup was how much the West could afford to assist a faltering Soviet Union under Gorbachev. In the end, there was to be no massive aid package coming from the Bush administration on the scale of the Marshall Plan to help former socialist countries or the newly independent Soviet successor states.

Congress and the administration were divided over the issue of economic assistance to the former enemy.[56] Any expression of America's goodwill was hampered by various other factors. The Kremlin's repressive measures to prevent the Baltics from seceding from the Union, and the Soviet military's objections to the CFE and START treaties, demonstrated that Gorbachev's reforms still rested on shaky ground. The CIA continually pointed out that the Soviet Union was still spending large sums of money on defence, as well as on the leftist regimes in the Third World, such as Cuba, Afghanistan, and Vietnam. Western money might help to resolve temporary economic shortfalls, but it was feared that they might dampen Soviet incentives to reform the economic system.[57] All this indicated to Washington that there was no imperative for the West to provide the Soviet Union with immediate assistance, although Washington took several steps to normalize economic relations between the two countries in 1991, such as the granting of MFN status to Moscow.[58]

It should also be pointed out that the Soviet Union only began to press publicly for economic assistance from the West in 1991. Shevardnadze once told Bush in the autumn of 1989 'we don't seek unilateral assistance. We want economic cooperation.' In ending the Cold War, Gorbachev did not want 'losers and winners', and probably expected a simultaneous acknowledgement of the end of the Cold War by both sides. Nor did Bush wish to appear to 'downgrade the position the Soviet Union rightly occupied' as a great power.[59] In any case, by 1991 too much damage had been inflicted on the Soviet economy to allow for any quick recovery, even if the USA had poured a lot of money into the system. The USA was, in any case, convinced by 1988 that the economic crisis in the Soviet Union was largely created by Gorbachev's lukewarm and disorganized reforms.[60]

THE ARMS REDUCTION RACE CONTINUES AFTER THE AUGUST COUP – THE AUTUMN OF 1991

The August coup further weakened Gorbachev's leadership. This placed the US administration in a quandary about what to do next. The US Intelligence

Community stated in September 1991 that 'the USSR and its Communist systems are dead', but confessed that 'what ultimately replaces them will not be known within the next year'.[61] Within the administration, Defense Secretary Cheney felt that the USA 'ought to lead and shape the events' in the collapsing Soviet empire, but the State Department sought a non-committal attitude and hoped to see the 'peaceful break up' of the Soviet Union. Nor did the President believe that the USA could, or should, play a big role in 'determining the outcome of what was transpiring in the Soviet Union'.[62] On his return from the Moscow summit, Bush visited Kiev in Ukraine, where the decision of whether or not to remain in the Soviet Union was an important factor in causing the final collapse of the Soviet Union (see chapter 2). In Kiev, Bush extended his full support to freedom and democracy proclaimed by the Ukrainian Republic, while at the same time commending Gorbachev's efforts to secure the conclusion of a new Union Treaty. The speech was regarded by Ukrainians as lukewarm and indecisive, especially when the American President stated that 'Freedom is not the same as independence.' It was quickly dubbed the 'Chicken Kiev' speech. After the August coup, separatist movements intensified and the Russian Republic under Yeltsin began to determine the fate of Gorbachev's Perestroika. While the Moscow coup was collapsing on 20/21 August, the Baltic states declared their bona fide independence from the Soviet Union. Despite media pressure, the Bush administration did not immediately recognize their independence. The White House first sought to persuade Gorbachev to offer a 'voluntary Soviet recognition' of Baltic independence, which came on 1 September, before the USA recognized the independence of Latvia, Estonia and Lithuania – which it did on the following day.[63]

As soon as the USA concluded the START Treaty with the Soviet Union in July, there emerged new anxieties about the diffusion of nuclear weapons between the several republics within the Union. In early August 1991 (and before the August coup), the US NIE had pointed out that, given the decline of the Soviet Union, its leaders were now more concerned to preserve nuclear strategic power as the only source of the Soviet's national security as well as its 'superpower status'. The NIE report forecast that the Soviet Union would continue to modernize their nuclear arsenals 'throughout the next decade', given the recent evidence that it was developing five new strategic ballistic missiles.[64] During the autumn of 1991, the Bush administration began to negotiate with the key republics individually and agreed to provide them with emergency humanitarian aid packages. However, this did not preclude the need to deal with the centre. The Soviet Union's cooperation still remained important for the USA in convening the peace talks on the Middle East in October, in settling outstanding regional issues (Cuba and Afghanistan) and, most importantly for the purpose of this chapter, in resolving nuclear problems.

In the event of the break up of the Soviet Union, the Bush administration agreed with both Gorbachev and Yeltsin that nuclear weapons (which were now divided between the four republics) should be in the hands of 'one entity', which was then presumed to be the Union. It was also judged that, given a unified Germany, short-range tactical nuclear weapons were no longer desirable or useful.[65] At the end of September 1991, the Bush administration announced a host of nuclear disarmament initiatives, including the elimination of most ground- and sea-launched tactical nuclear weapons (some being destroyed with the rest being stored safely), the decision not to go ahead with certain new US weapons programmes (including mobile ICBMs), and the removal of all strategic bombers and many missiles from alert status. On 5 October, Gorbachev reciprocated with a more ambitious proposal for reductions than Bush had called for; as Raymond Garthoff stated, 'he seemed to enjoy an "arms race downhill" in reverse'.[66] Gorbachev suggested the planned reduction of 700,000 military personnel, in response to Bush's proposed figure of 500,000.

Of more importance, Moscow was prepared to reduce further the number of nuclear warheads recently agreed under START I, and called for new arms control negotiations, leading to START II, which would halve the number of the remaining strategic offensive weapons.[67] In November 1991, the US Congress provided $400 million to help Moscow dismantle Soviet nuclear and chemical weapons.[68] In the same month, the CIA predicted the 'most significant civil disorder in the former USSR since the Bolsheviks consolidated power'; but the demise of the Soviet Union came quickly and peacefully.[69] On Christmas Day Bush was phoned by Gorbachev, who reported that the command and control of the former Soviet nuclear weapons was to be transferred to the President of the Russian Republic, and that there would be no 'disconnection'. Gorbachev also asked Bush to continue America's collaborative relationship with Moscow, from now on with Yeltsin's Russian Republic. The American President promised to do just that.

Arms control negotiations were an important confidence-building measure in changing the shape of the superpower relationship over the decades. Weapons were a 'symptom', rather than the 'basic causes of hostility' between the two sides.[70] This reflected the classical dilemma inherent in arms control negotiations: parties who need arms control often mistrust each other, while the success of arms control negotiations requires a level of mutual confidence which is so often lacking. Throughout Gorbachev's era, arms control negotiations helped to humanise Cold War politics and gradually led to a workable partnership backed by a degree of mutual confidence. Gorbachev was the first Soviet leader to acknowledge the source of the Soviet military threat to the West, and to embark on eliminating it through arms 'de-racing'. It was he who had conceded that the Soviet Union was no longer capable of competing with the West in the field of nuclear weapons, and it was only on this basis that the USA was able to enter the arms reductions negotiations with Moscow.

Arms reductions do not necessarily make the world a safer place, and in the case of nuclear weapons their reduction in numbers would make little difference to the devastation that would be caused if the remaining missiles were used. In the political climate of the 1980s, the accumulation of nuclear weapons in the hands of the two superpowers was no longer seen to be morally correct. This scepticism was supported by the fact that, despite the ongoing arms control negotiations, the superpowers' arms race continued. An extensive survey showed that neither Moscow nor Washington was able to reduce their defence expenditures as a result of the arms negotiations. In other words, superpower arms control negotiations no longer provided 'reassurances' to the general public of both sides.[71] Reagan seemed to be aware of this and it was he who first sought to turn the tables on Moscow by calling for substantial reductions in, and not merely the controlling of, the superpowers' nuclear arsenal. In the process, trust and confidence building played an important part, thanks to the emergence of Gorbachev, in making such reduction agreements possible between Moscow and Washington. President Bush was moved by Gorbachev's last phone call as the President of the Soviet Union, and in his diary Bush recorded that 'it was the voice of a good friend; it was the voice of a man to whom history will give enormous credit'.[72]

MANAGING THE END OF THE COLD WAR

With the end of the Soviet Union in December 1991 arms control negotiators on both sides were left with the daunting task of how to adapt to the new situation. It is, therefore, worth noting briefly in this last section what happened to the CFE and the START negotiations and other arms control agreements. More importantly, we need to ask whether the Soviet/Russian strategic threat, the main cause of the Cold War, had disappeared after the collapse of the Soviet Union. What is the role of nuclear weapons in the post-Cold War world?

The CFE Treaty of November 1990 had not come into effect by the time of the collapse of the Soviet Union. Thereafter, the Red Army became 'an army without a state'. A working group (formed at the first meeting of the North Atlantic Cooperation Council in December 1991) was assigned to deal with the implementation of the CFE Treaty. The group, which first met in January 1992, quickly established a consensus that the CFE Treaty should be implemented without the need to renegotiate with the former Soviet Union, and that the new successor states should take over collectively the position of the Soviet Union.[73] The Russian Republic initially sought to preserve 'the former Soviet military space intact' and to acquire a large portion of the remaining military equipment. Ukraine, on the other hand, refused to hand over to Russia the equipment it held in its territory. It soon became clear that it was impossible to preserve the integrity of the former Soviet military forces, as some of the republics, notably the Baltic states, had left the Union altogether.

By mid 1992, however, there were three notable achievements. Firstly, eight former Soviet republics agreed in May about the distribution of the former Soviet military equipment. The Russian Republic received nearly half of the major items: tanks, helicopters and artillery. The May agreement paved the way for the implementation of the CFE Treaty in November 1992. Secondly, the Open Sky Treaty, proposed by President Bush three years before, was also signed in May 1992 by the NATO powers, the former Warsaw Pact states, together with Belarus, Georgia, Russia and Ukraine.[74] When Republican President, Dwight D. Eisenhower, first presented the Open Skies Proposal to the Soviet Union during the 1955 Geneva summit, no agreement could be reached between the two sides on the subject; but the end of the Cold War facilitated the idea of peer surveillance of each other's territory from the air to ensure the observance of the arms control treaties.[75] Finally, the elimination of tactical nuclear weapons proposed just before the collapse of the Soviet Union began to take shape, as the new Soviet successor states supported the idea. In May 1992, such weapons held by the new states were moved to the Russian Republic for dismantling, which helped to allay the fears of a residual Russian military threat to Europe.[76] By 2003, some 60,000 pieces of Soviet/Russian military equipment had been demolished in the area covered by the treaty.[77] Altogether, the Soviet conventional and nuclear threat to *Europe* had much diminished.

The subsequent story of the American–Soviet bilateral nuclear arms reductions negotiations after 1991 is important, not least because the role of nuclear weapons in the post-Cold War era has changed. When the Soviet Union began to disintegrate, US concerns were shifted to the potential lack of control over the vast Soviet arsenal of nuclear weapons.[78] During Gorbachev's final years, the Bush administration was not ready to give a favourable verdict on Yeltsin, who had first met the President and Baker in September 1989 in Washington. 'What a flake!' was Baker's initial impression. His view on Yeltsin in March 1991 had not changed since 1989, as the Secretary of State considered the rising Russian politician as 'a man prone to larger-than-life gestures'.[79] While Cheney, Gates and the CIA estimates were more positive about the effectiveness of Yeltsin's leadership, most Bush administration officials remained sceptical about the Russian President. Especially after the August coup, Yeltsin looked like a man who 'worked assiduously to complete the dismantling of the USSR', and Scowcroft felt that it was 'painful to watch Yeltsin rip the Soviet Union brick by brick away from Gorbachev'.[80]

The collapse of the Soviet Union led to the creation of new unstable states. The Russian Republic was supposed to take over the control of nuclear weapons from the former Union, but some Soviet strategic nuclear weapons were based in other Soviet successor states (Belarus, Ukraine and Kazakhstan). This unsatisfactory situation prompted Bush to press on with the arms reductions negotiations with the Russian Federation. While conservative elements in the Russian military still tended to see post-1991 relations with the USA in terms of continuing 'strategic competition', the truth was that Moscow, in economic chaos, found it difficult to keep pace with the modernization of many obsolete strategic weapons, and even to maintain the reduced force levels agreed under the proposed START II. It was, therefore, important for Yeltsin to maintain cooperation with the West, to secure Western economic help in arresting the economic collapse of his country, and to manage the expensive process of dismantling many unwanted weapons systems in cooperation with the West.[81]

After the Bush–Yeltsin summit in February 1992, START II was swiftly negotiated and was signed in January 1993, just before Bush left office. START II provided for much deeper cuts (by about two thirds) in the number of strategic nuclear weapons than START I and it represented the most far reaching bilateral arms control agreement between Washington and Moscow. Significantly, both parties agreed to eliminate multi-warhead (MIRVed) land-based missiles, a key objective which had been sought since the beginning of the strategic arms control negotiations in 1969. The number of nuclear strategic weapons would within a decade be reduced to some 3000–3500 on each side, including a ceiling of 1750 submarine-launched ballistic missiles. For a time, the proliferation of former Soviet strategic nuclear weapons in the four republics raised much concern, but Belarus and Kazakhstan in 1993, and eventually Ukraine in January 1994, decided to transfer all their strategic nuclear weapons to Russia and adhere to the Nuclear Non-Proliferation Treaty (NPT) as non-nuclear states.[82]

START II was welcomed in the West as the first stage of a 'cooperative de-nuclearization'. The treaty constituted a second stage of 'nuclear settlement' after the Cold War, on the basis of the 'traditionalist one of reducing the military resources of defeated states' and as an attempt to end the proliferation of nuclear weapons in the former Soviet Union.[83] In March 1997, Yeltsin moved his nuclear disarmament programme forward at the Helsinki summit, where it was agreed to plan further reductions of American and Russian strategic forces under the framework of START III. Altogether, compared with the pre-START levels, the former superpower nuclear arsenals would be reduced from 20,000 to 2000–2500 by 2007. Meanwhile, in January 1993 a conference in Paris of 130 nations signed the Chemical Weapons Convention (CWC), negotiations for which had been underway since the early 1970s.[84]

After the end of the Cold War the salience of bilateral arms control had been lost. The two powers were no longer adversarial, and the USA clearly came out of the Cold War victorious, and was now extending a helping hand to its old enemy. The bipolar system collapsed and, as a result, the political utility of nuclear deterrence lessened. The post-Cold War world began to witness more localized conflicts, and the rise of nationalism and other separatist movements, such as the disintegration of the former Yugoslavia, where nuclear deterrence was irrelevant. The concentration of nuclear weapons was no longer seen to be the major security problem it had appeared a decade before, but their proliferation in the Third World loomed larger in the post-Cold War security environment. In the case of the former Soviet Union, America's top agenda throughout the 1990s remained that of a decade long 'under funding for the management of the [Soviet/Russian] nuclear weapons infrastructure', and the aging of Russia's nuclear arsenal in a fragmented society struggling with painful reforms. In the eyes of the Western world, these factors increased the risk of accidental nuclear explosions, mismanagement of nuclear material and the 'prospects of a black-market flow of nuclear materials, technology and human talent to countries of proliferation concern'.[85]

All these issues were linked to the notion that nuclear weapons were dangerous to the future development of international security. Although the anti-nuclear movement was not a new phenomenon, the end of the Cold War raised hopes of eliminating nuclear weapons altogether. In December 1995 the Oslo Nobel Institute awarded the Nobel prize for peace to the International Pugwash Movement and its president, in order to place the 'abolitionist message high on the international agenda'. The Canberra Commission on the Elimination of Nuclear Weapons produced a report in 1996, calling for an 'immediate and determined effort' to abolish nuclear weapons.[86] The same year saw the signature of a

Comprehensive Test Ban Treaty (CTBT) by more than 160 countries. The CTBT is designed to reduce both 'the spread of nuclear weapons to non-nuclear states and improvements of existing weapons by nuclear states', but it would not come into effect until 44 countries with nuclear capabilities listed in the treaty signed

TABLE 3 – STRATEGIC NUCLEAR WEAPONS: THE USA AND THE USSR/RUSSIA, 1990–2004

| | USA | | | | USSR/Russia | | | | |
| | Strategic Nuclear Delivery Vehicles | | Strategic Nuclear Warheads | | Strategic Nuclear Delivery Vehicles | | Strategic Nuclear Warheads | | |
	Sept. 1990	Jan. 2004	Sept. 1990	Jan. 2004	Sept. 1990	Jan. 2004	Sept. 1990	Jan. 2004	
Intercontinental Ballistic Missiles (ICBMs)									**Intercontinental Ballistic Missiles (ICBMs)**
MX/Peacekeeper	50	50	500	500	326	0	326	0	SS-11
Minuteman III	500	500	1500	1200	40	0	40	0	SS-13
Minuteman II	450	0	450	0	47	0	188	0	SS-17
					308	126	3080	1260	SS-18
					300	144	1800	864	SS-19
					56	0	560	0	SS-24 (silo)
					33	15	330	150	SS-24 (rail)
					288	312	288	312	SS-25
					0	36	0	36	SS-27 (silo)
ICBM subtotal	**1000**	**550**	**2450**	**1700**	**1398**	**633**	**6612**	**2622**	**ICBM subtotal**
Submarine-Launched Ballistic Missiles (SLBMs)									**Submarine-Launched Ballistic Missiles (SLBMs)**
Poseidon (C3)	192	0	1920	0	192	0	192	0	SS-N-6
Trident I (C-4)	384	144	3072	864	280	12	280	12	SS-N-8
Trident II (D-5)	96	288	768	2304	12	0	12	0	SS-N-17
					224	112	672	336	SS-N-18
					120	100	1200	1000	SS-N-20
					112	96	448	384	SS-N-23
SLBM subtotal	**672**	**432**	**5760**	**3168**	**940**	**320**	**2804**	**1732**	**SLBM subtotal**
Bombers									**Bombers**
B-52 (Air-Launched Cruise Missile)	189	95	1968	950	84	64	672	512	Bear (ALCM)
B-52 (Non ALCM)	290	47	290	47	63	0	63	0	Bear (Non-ALCM)
B-1	95	83	95	83	15	14	120	112	Blackjack
B-2	0	20	0	20					
Bomber subtotal	**574**	**245**	**2353**	**1100**	**162**	**78**	**855**	**624**	**Bomber subtotal**
Total	**2246**	**1227**	**10,563**	**5968**	**2500**	**1031**	**10,271**	**4978**	**Total**

Source: START Memorandum of Understanding (MOU) of 1 September 1990 and the MOU of 31 January 2004. The Arms Control Association.

the treaty. Pakistan, India and North Korea are not signatory members.[87] In 1995 the non-proliferation treaty was extended for an indefinite period. Despite growing pressures to reduce and eliminate Weapons of Mass Destruction (WMD), the case for maintaining nuclear capabilities remains resilient in the post-Cold War world. Neo-realist scholars like Kenneth Waltz and John Mearsheimer suggested in the mid 1990s that the retention of nuclear power would outweigh the potential danger of the proliferation of nuclear weapons. Mearsheimer claims that the role that nuclear weapons played in the bipolar world could be extended to the multipolar environment of post-Cold War Europe, for nuclear and conventional forces of the USA and Western Europe should serve to 'compensate for an apparent Russian inability to function as a Great Power' against a possible threat to the region.[88]

Compared with 7000 American nuclear weapons at the height of the Cold War, it is estimated that the USA now has some 500–700 nuclear weapons in Europe.[89] The massive reduction during and after the end of the Cold War again led to differences between the European allies and the USA. France, determined to remain a nuclear power, conducted a series of nuclear tests in 1995 in defiance of anti-nuclear world opinion. Paris feared that the USA might remove its nuclear weapons from Europe and proposed the creation of a European nuclear capability. Two nuclear states, Britain and France, also began nuclear cooperation. Germany, a non-nuclear state, had never relied on Anglo-French nuclear protection and the end of the Cold War increased its dilemma as to whether to cling to the remaining American nuclear forces or, as Mearsheimer suggested, to become a nuclear power in its own right. So far, NATO has used the instability of Russia, still a big nuclear power, as the main motive for its reliance on US extended deterrence. Then, the decision to enlarge NATO has provided Western Europe with another reason for the continuing US protection of that region. China, a nuclear state, supports the ultimate goal of world nuclear disarmament, but is not prepared to enter into negotiations to reduce China's nuclear arsenal unless other nuclear states are prepared to reduce their capabilities to China's levels, or unless the USA enters into negotiations about the limited military use of space.[90]

The existing nuclear powers are likely to continue to retain their nuclear capability for reasons of prestige, deterrence, bargaining, and as weapons of last resort, and at least until the threat of proliferation of WMD is overcome. The first post-Cold War administration, led by Bill Clinton, identified the so-called 'rogue states' (Iran, Iraq, North Korea and Libya) as the West's enemies. They were branded as 'outlaw' states who 'refuse to accept and abide by some of the most important norms and practices of the international system', and whose rulers were 'aggressive and defiant', pursued WMD and remained on 'the wrong side of history'.[91] In 1998, India and Pakistan conducted nuclear tests, as did Iran and North Korea. By the end of the 1990s, proliferation outside NATO had produced a further justification for the retention of US nuclear weapons in NATO, since this 'might deter the acquisition or use of WMD'.[92]

Nuclear weapons remain an important pillar of Russian security policy. Despite the follow-up negotiations with Yeltsin's Russia, START II has never been implemented. Russian critics pointed out that START II was a one-sided treaty negotiated at Russia's expense, as it required Moscow to make large cuts in land-based ballistic missiles (SS-18s), which they felt were still the mainstay of their strategic nuclear forces. Then, the renewed debates in the USA over missile defence in the mid 1990s added a further obstacle to Moscow's ratification of START II. It was only in April 2001 that Russia ratified the treaty, nearly four and half years later than the US Senate, but for the new Russian President, Vladmir Putin, the implementation of the treaty was dependent upon continued US observation of the ABM Treaty.[93]

Russia, as had been the case for the Soviet Union before it, found it difficult to reconcile itself to America's intention to create a defensive system. The Bush Senior administration did not share the same degree of enthusiasm Reagan had attached to the SDI, and considerably reduced the cost of developing it. However, during the First Gulf War (1990–1) the US-led coalition forces and Israeli forces were subjected to attack by Iraq's Russian-made SCUD missiles. These were 'lousy' weapons, cheap, crude and with poor target accuracy, but, despite the use of American Patriot missiles, the SCUDs were still able to harass Tel Aviv and allied barracks in Saudi Arabia. This episode had significant psychological and political impacts on Washington's nuclear policy.[94]

The Clinton administration put the idea of constructing a controversial national defence system on hold, but began to develop the Theatre Missile Defence (TMD) system. The growing proliferation of WMD in the 1990s convinced the USA that non-proliferation efforts through multilateral treaties were ineffective. The apocalyptic warning from the Rumsfeld Commission's report that the USA would be under a missile threat from the 'rogue' states sooner than it had anticipated, combined with North Korea's surprise launch of the Tepodong I in 1998, galvanized a Republican Congress into demanding the development of a national defence system, if necessary at the cost of withdrawing from the ABM Treaty.[95]

The incoming 43rd President, George W. Bush, was determined to do just that. Given the sympathetic attitude expressed by Putin's Russia in the aftermath of 11 September 2001, the USA publicly announced its intention of withdrawing from the ABM Treaty. Unlike the previous Democratic administration, the new Republican administration had a clear vision of America's unilateral nuclear posture, and put no faith in multilateral efforts to prevent WMD proliferation, such as through the CTBT. The USA would retain the freedom to structure its nuclear strategic forces as it wished, might resort to the use of nuclear weapons against those countries who possess WMD capability, and was willing to develop a national missile defence system. The events of 11 September multiplied the White House's determination to do whatever they could to defend the USA from 'super' terrorism.[96]

Now that the USA had turned its back on the ABM Treaty, Russia was not going to implement the START II Treaty and it was allowed to lapse. Despite or because of its much weakened conventional strength, and the need to reduce defence spending, Russia's reliance on the remaining nuclear weapons in the post-Cold War era was stronger than ever before. Moscow's professed fears of

'Western encirclement', which were increased by the latest NATO and EU enlargements, further reinforced the arguments for 'heightened emphasis on nuclear weapons in its military doctrine'. After all, nuclear weapons were all that were left to the Russian Federation to uphold 'its superpower status'.[97] During the May 2002 American–Russian summit talks in Moscow, the Kremlin accepted America's offer to cooperate with the National Missile Defence (NMD) project. Putin and Bush signed the Strategic Offensive Reductions Treaty (SORT) or the Moscow Treaty, an agreement that committed the two sides to reducing their operationally deployed warheads to 1700 to 2200, by 2012. The figure 2200 was certainly lower than the ceiling agreed under START II (which limited US strategic warheads to 3500 and Russian ones to 3000), but large enough to lead critics to suspect that a lingering Cold War mentality was still in operation. SORT replaced START II and, as a result, the two welcome features contained in START II, 'the ban on MIRVed ICBM and the commitment to destroy the SS-18s', were pigeonholed. The Russians now decided to extend the shelf life of the SS-18s until 2015.[98] In February 2004, Moscow, in response to America's decision to build NMD in Alaska, proudly announced that the Russians were developing a new generation of warheads, which could overcome the 'most sophisticated defence systems'.[99]

Compared with the heyday of superpower arms control negotiations, the Russian nuclear/military threat posed a much less serious threat to the world. However, despite their learning experiences with nuclear weapons, both superpowers, one former and one existing, failed to set the stage for freeing the world from the menace of WMD in the post-Cold War era. On the contrary, nuclear states still cling to the retention of their nuclear capabilities (although most of them claim to be agreeable to the eventual elimination of nuclear weapons), while nuclear weapons have proliferated with the impetus of globalization. The degree of predictability and regulation that existed during the Cold War has become a thing of the past. Still, we can congratulate ourselves that we are at least free from the nightmare of gigantic nuclear standoffs between the two superpowers. On the other hand, we are still faced with possible unexpected nuclear or other WMD accidents, or the mismanagement of WMD material in the hands of terrorists, dictators or criminals. During the Cold War era, the superpower strategic arms control negotiations had wider ramifications for world politics in general, and for Moscow–Washington bilateral relations in particular. This, too, has gone. Yet, with the introduction of the national military defence programme and given the evermore complex weapons systems in the information age, any serious attempt to regulate multilateral or American–Russian strategic nuclear weapons is becoming a near impossible task. The Soviet threat has gone, but the threat of nuclear and other weapons of mass destruction still very much remains with us.

7

Ideology and Great Power Politics in the Third World

The superpower rivalry in the Third World was the major source of international instability that demonstrated the limitations of the 1970s East–West détente. A determined Kremlin leader, Leonid Brezhnev, now used détente as a smokescreen behind which to increase Soviet incursions into the Third World. In appearance at least, the Soviet empire during the 1970s reached the height of its prestige and power. It had no intention of accepting Henry Kissinger's 'linkage' concept, whereby the USA would buy Soviet goodwill through dialogue, trade and arms control negotiations. A post-Vietnam USA (Britain had also decided to withdraw from East of Suez in 1967) was too discredited politically and weakened economically to be able to develop a coherent policy to contain the Soviet Union in the Third World. The 1972 détente did not have any impact on the Yom Kippur War in 1973 in the Middle East, and in 1979 any residue of détente completely disappeared when the Soviet Union invaded Afghanistan.

The geographical area of regional conflict was often loosely termed as the Third World during the Cold War to identify a group of developing countries (but including some oil-rich countries in the Middle East) outside Europe and North America, which neither belonged to the First World (the industrialized and capitalist West), nor the Second World (the Communist socialist bloc). Many Third World countries emerged from the yoke of Western imperialism after 1947, and they were often ill disposed towards the former Western colonial powers, but found themselves in need of economic development assistance from more advanced industrial countries.[1] In the USA, the term, 'developing' world was used more frequently and it adopted a policy of 'development' as a means of obtaining 'long-term immunity against the contagion of communism'.[2]

We have seen in the previous chapter how strategic nuclear arms control had lost its importance in the final stage of the Cold War, thereby removing the deadly element which shaped that war. The USA had, however, long regarded the Soviet efforts to 'promote Marxism Leninist revolution in other countries' as signs of aggression.[3] Although Gorbachev was keen to modify the Soviet approach to arms control negotiations, the USA would not be convinced that there were genuine changes in Soviet policy unless it demonstrated that it had ceased supporting anti-Western socialist leaders in the Third World. Indeed, American–Soviet disputes over numerous regional conflicts in the 1980s in Afghanistan, Angola and Nicaragua remained the most persistent, if not the most important, factors in the final stage of the Cold War. This chapter will focus on the superpowers' engagement in the Third World, examine the role of ideology in driving them into the often unstable, divided, and economically stricken states in the Third World, and investigate the rise of the Soviet–US confrontation over regional conflicts in the late 1970s and early 1980s.

PATTERNS OF SOVIET POLICY IN THE COLONIAL AND THIRD WORLD

There is no need to remind the reader that the Soviet Union, born out of the October 1917 Bolshevik revolution, was ideologically driven to weaken its capitalist competitors, and to promote socialist revolutions elsewhere in the world. To this end, the Soviet Union publicly supported 'national liberation and social revolution throughout the Third World'.[4] In practice, however, from time to time the Soviet Union circumscribed its ideological zeal and did not play a major role in helping or creating revolutionary movements in the Third World, since often 'the Marxist revolutions stemmed primarily from problems in the countries where the revolutions had taken place – problems that the existing governments were unable or unwilling to solve'. Similarly, the idea of exporting the Soviet style of socialism encountered some difficulties: China, Yugoslavia and Albania had decided to go their own separate ways from Moscow's traditional Marxist orthodoxy.[5]

Throughout the entire history of the Soviet Union, ideological factors had to be weighed against other considerations, such as Soviet national interests, their geopolitical concerns, the growing competition with China for prestige and influence, the deep-rooted fear of an open military confrontation with the capitalist West, Soviet economic and military conditions, and the nature and scope of the demands on the Soviet Union from revolutionary Marxist regimes. The question of how to reconcile the drive for ideology with the quest for Soviet power and influence had haunted the Soviet Union since its revolutionary beginnings. Lenin founded the notion of allying Communism with nationalism in the hope that nationalist liberation, even if 'those forces were nationalist and bourgeois', would eventually lead to the emergence of socialism in the 'liberated' countries.[6] Overall, Soviet policy for the Third World was never a primary consideration in Soviet external policy. It received varying degrees of priority at particular times for a specific set of strategic reasons.

This apparent lack of coherence drew the attention of scholars to the ideological factors in Soviet foreign policy.[7] For example, Fukuyama employed a more ideologically focused method of differentiating the numerous shifts between 'right' and 'left'. During the 'left' periods the Soviet Union was more conscious of promoting Marxist-Leninist regimes, as was seen during Stalin's early years (when 'hopes for instability in the capitalist world and imminent communist revolutions were high') and during Brezhnev's leadership in the 1970s with the upsurge of socialist revolutions in the Third World. On the other hand, there were periods of shifting to the 'right' when ideology was subordinated to the need to maintain the Soviet Union's security interests and further its aspirations to extend its power and influence well beyond its borders.[8] Another school of thought explained Moscow's alternating attitudes to Marxist revolutions in terms of the Soviet leadership's 'optimism' and 'pessimism' about the eventual goal of achieving a Communist world under Soviet leadership.[9] Others looked at Soviet Third World policy in terms of its geopolitical competition with the USA, and the latter's 'assertiveness' was interspersed with that of the Soviet Union, creating an 'action and reaction' dynamism, as in the superpower nuclear arms race.[10] However, a Russian scholar, Constantine Pleshakov, asserts that while Stalin combined Soviet geopolitical interests with its ideological drive in equal measure, the ideological factor faded away after Stalin's death and, indeed, Soviet ideology was 'best before 1939', but ended in that year when the Soviet Union decided to ally with Hitler's Nazi Germany. He and Zubok further argue that ideology was merged with other Soviet considerations and it is, therefore, difficult to deal with ideology in isolation.[11] Neil MacFarlane sets out a comprehensive analysis of Soviet Third World policy and explains that Soviet security interests tended to take precedence over their hopes of exporting the Soviet style of socialism worldwide, while recent scholarship (Arne Odd Westad and Robert Patman) draws a close parallel between ideology and the conduct of Soviet foreign policy.[12]

It can be argued that an ideological undercurrent constituted an important factor in explaining Soviet behaviour towards the Third World as a means of legitimizing its influence and power in the region. Moreover, Soviet ambitions were, in no small part, aided by their anti-imperialist principles and their prejudice against the ills of the capitalist system. During the post-Second World War years, the Soviet Union had an overall advantage over the Western industrialized (and former imperialist) countries in attracting revolutionary leaders from the developing world. These Third World leaders sought to stabilize and strengthen their countries quickly and thoroughly, and Stalinist socialism seemed to offer a much needed methodology to achieve these objectives. Gorbachev was, after all, one who, until the end of his regime, believed in the potential strength and virtues of socialism, and aimed at revitalizing it through Perestroika. Viewed thus, the ideological factor remained resilient in the last years of the Soviet Union, although the notion of supporting the international class struggle soon became too heavy a burden for the Soviet Union to carry, and Gorbachev eventually discarded it in favour of collaboration with the capitalist West.

Promoting Marxist revolutions in the developing world was by no means an easy task, as the theory may have suggested. During the Stalin years (1928–53), attention to geopolitics and security became equally important in his calculations and, indeed, the Soviet leadership appeared to show little interest in providing support and financial assistance to the vanguard socialist parties in the colonial and Third Worlds. Stalin rejected the Lenin dictum of collaboration with nation-alist liberation movements and turned to a theme, 'socialism in one country', which encouraged local Communist Parties to take their own revolutionary paths against their indigenous opposition, but with little direct involvement by Moscow. In the dark years of the 1930s, Stalin concentrated his efforts on consolidating his power at home, and was preoccupied with new threats from Germany and Japan. After 1941, with Germany's invasion of the Soviet Union, Moscow insisted on Communist collaboration with 'the national bourgeoisie' or 'their colonial masters', in order to defeat the Axis powers.

After the Second World War, Stalin was intent on consolidating his gains in the Soviet Union's 'national security zones' in Europe and Asia, and avoided hostilities with the West. With the onset of the Cold War after 1947, Andrei Zhdanov, Stalin's aide in charge of relations with external Communists, set out a new bipolar view of the world. The Third World Communist movements were now to be very much in the vanguard of the struggle against the imperialist Western capitalist world.[13] The results of this theory produced little in the way of increased Communist power in the Third World. For instance, the Soviet Union denounced those nationalist independence movements that sought non-Communist revolutions in India, Pakistan, Ceylon and the Philippines as 'stooges of imperialism', whereas Communist revolutionaries were often suppressed by the nationalist elites, or by the colonial powers, as in India, Burma and the Philippines. The bulk of the Malayan population was hostile to the Chinese-led Communist Party in Malaya, and the government, together with the British military, helped to destroy the Communist threat to that country.[14]

By the middle of the 1950s, there were only three independent Communist countries under Soviet influence in the Third World: Mongolia, Communist China and North Korea. All these countries had fallen into the Soviet 'national security zone' by virtue of their proximity and their strategic importance to the Soviet Union, with Mongolia after 1921 becoming Moscow's oldest and most dependable satellite state.[15] China was where Lenin's notion of a Communist–Nationalist fusion did not succeed in the late 1920s and, since then, Moscow lost much of its control over the political situation there. However, Stalin still held onto the faint hope of seeing a 'political' agreement between the Chinese Nationalist Party and Chinese Communist Party (CCP), which would help Moscow to secure its strategic and economic interests in Manchuria. The success of Communist revolution in China in 1949 was the consequence of the rise of Mao Zedong's CCP and the failures of the corrupt and feeble Chinese Nationalist Party led by Chiang Kai Shek. Moscow's role in supporting the CCP remained minimal. Stalin did not sever his ties with the Nationalist government until 1949, when the Soviet Union recognized the People's Republic of China.[16]

Stalin's cautious optimism did not serve him very well in Korea either. While the Soviet leader focused his attention on his former enemy, Germany, in the post-war security situation in Europe, Stalin was also concerned about a possible resurgence of Japan's military threat to the Soviet Far East. The Korean penin-sular was regarded as an important security buffer zone for the Soviet Union. After the Second World War, the former Japanese colony was divided at the

38th parallel, initially for occupation purposes, between the USA in the south and the Soviet Union in the north, but it soon became clear that there could be no superpower agreement on the unification of Korea. By the end of 1948, two independent states were formed: the Republic of Korea (ROK) organized by the anti-Communist Syngman Rhee in the south, and the Democratic People's Republic of Korea (DPRK) in the north led by Stalin's protégé, Kim Il Sung.

Stalin was eventually persuaded by Kim's fervent pressure to agree to the military unification of Korea. The Soviet leadership calculated that the USA, having withdrawn its troops from South Korea in 1949, would be most unlikely to return to the peninsular. Stalin's opportunism was also reinforced by the fact that Donald McLean, a Cambridge-educated British spy in the Foreign Office, assured Moscow that US defence policy for Asia (adopted in December 1949) did not include the Asian mainland. Moscow also noted that the USA had not intervened to prevent Mao's unification of China. Moreover, in the early months of 1950, Soviet influence over Asia was expanding with the conclusion of an alliance with Mao's China, and Moscow's recognition of Ho Chi Minh's government in Vietnam. Although Stalin continued to dread the possibility of an American intervention if Kim went ahead with his military adventure, he took a gamble, in the belief that there was now a security vacuum created by America's apparent retreat from the Asian mainland. In the spring of 1950, Stalin finally gave Kim the green light to invade the South, which led to the escalation of the Cold War in Asia.[17] The Korean War confirmed the West's suspicions that Stalin was now embarking on a new Cold War offensive. It galvanized Washington and the European NATO powers into launching rearmament programmes, and it moulded America's mindset firmly into what now appeared to have become a lengthy struggle to resist Communist world domination.

With the rise of Khrushchev as Soviet leader by the mid 1950s, there was a significant shift in Soviet policy in the Third World. By then, Europe had achieved relative stability with a divided Germany at its core, while the growing nuclear capabilities accumulated by both superpowers made superpower war extremely dangerous and almost unthinkable. The new Soviet leader thus changed the Stalinist idea of confrontation with the West into the concept of 'peaceful coexistence'. The situation in the Third World was now fluid, with rising numbers of newly independent states, as a result of the first wave of post-war decolonizations in the Middle East, Africa and Asia. In 1955, Khrushchev identified the Third World as an area of new competition between the capitalist and the Communist blocs, and reverted to the Lenin dictum of increasing contacts with nationalist elites, who were now regarded as taking a 'progressive role' in eventually leading their countries to socialism. As Pleshakov contends, Khrushchev was probably more convinced than Stalin had been of the ultimate victory of socialism over capitalism.[18] Supported by this optimism, but anxious not to upset superpower relations unduly, the Soviet Union expanded significantly its contact with those major Third World countries that were largely outside the USA's sphere of influence – Algeria, Egypt, Iraq, Syria, Afghanistan, Indonesia and India. Under the banner of Khrushchev's 1961 declaration of 'wars of national liberation', the Soviets at first supported the Pathet Lao, but

Khrushchev later reached agreement with US President, John F. Kennedy, for a neutral Laos.[19] The Soviets were initially hesitant about providing outright support to Fidel Castro's Cuba in the USA's back yard, regarding Castro as an 'authentic leader of the leftist bourgeoisie'. Moscow's relations with Havana only took off when US–Cuban relations had deteriorated significantly in the late 1950s, with Castro's increasing anti-Americanism, his fear of an American invasion, and Khrushchev's desire to help his Latin American comrade in achieving a socialist revolution.[20] After the Cuban Missile Crisis, however, the Kremlin was anxious to remove all nuclear weapons, including tactical ones, from the island. This strained the relationship with Castro, who wanted a solid security guarantee from Moscow against the USA. Soviet aid to Cuba steadily increased in subsequent years, but Soviet leaders often found Castro too independent, too emotional and too 'unreliable'.[21]

Khrushchev sought to make the Soviet Union a major player in the Third World, but the results were rather mixed. It did expand its influence over left wing regimes and increased its financial support, but very few of them actually moved towards socialism in this period. On top of this, China enhanced its prestige and power by its role in the Korean War and became more confident about dealing with the Soviet Union as an equal partner. Convinced that the Western capitalist world was now weaker than the Communist camp, Mao took an assertive approach towards achieving China's security concerns, resulting in Beijing's attack on the Taiwan offshore islands in 1958, the suppression of the separatist Tibetan rebels, and growing tensions with India. The Soviet Union found an increasingly militant and independent China difficult to deal with, and the relationship between the two powers irrevocably broke down in the early 1960s.[22] The Sino–Soviet rivalry increased regional competitiveness between the two capitals, notably in South-east Asia. Moscow had to increase its economic and military help to the Vietnamese Communists (which might otherwise have been designated as China's responsibility), but in return only secured a modest influence in Hanoi.[23] North Vietnam, Indonesia, India and Egypt were all willing to receive Soviet material assistance, but they were reluctant to accept Soviet intervention in their local affairs and, except for North Vietnam, had little incentive to adopt socialism in their own countries. Meanwhile, Khrushchev's forward policy was back-pedalled by his successors, in favour of the expansion of Soviet conventional capabilities in response to NATO's adoption of flexible response. Moscow's domestic economic problems also compelled the Kremlin to emphasize the 'construction of socialism and Communism at home'. This moderation in Soviet activities in the Third World was also made possible by China's retreat into the Cultural Revolution at home.[24]

The resurgence of Soviet activities in the Third World came in the mid to late 1970s. During this period, Moscow enhanced its relations with pro-Soviet powers in the Third World, as well as with important but non-Marxist countries, like Nigeria and Argentina. Moreover, the Soviet Union stepped up its support for weak but revolutionary anti-Western regimes, including Angola, Ethiopia, Afghanistan, Nicaragua and Grenada. The main form of Soviet support in previous decades had been advice and financial assistance, but now the Soviet Union appeared willing to adopt a militant strategy and, in the case of Africa, it took advantage of Cuba's readiness to send troops to help its revolutionary comrades.[25] Moscow supported North Vietnam's military attack on the South to achieve the unification of Vietnam in 1975, and also supported Vietnam's invasion of Cambodia in 1978.

Why this apparent turn took place will be explained later, but it is important to note that despite the ups and downs in Soviet policy in the Third World, Soviet activities were often underpinned by opportunism and cautious optimism, based on their assumptions about the West's likely reactions and responses. We shall now turn to US policy in the Third World to explain American ideology that drove the USA into the Third World.

THE EVOLUTION OF AMERICAN IDEAS TOWARDS THE THIRD WORLD

The USA occupied a unique position in the history of great powers because of its historical origins, geopolitics, capabilities and political beliefs. Born out of revolution and war, the USA obtained its independence, with sheer determination and resolve, from Britain. Hence, the USA regarded itself (like the Soviet Union) as an anti-colonial and an anti-imperialist power; it remained conscious of the limits of its power and retained a deep sense of 'vulnerability to external pressures in a world of scheming nations'.[26] These, combined with the USA's earlier experiences with the European imperial powers, codified its mental map in the form of isolationism, which was expressed in the early part of the 20th century as preferring neutrality and avoiding close entanglement with European powers. The other side of isolationism was the rejection of foreign intervention in American affairs, and this mindset was epitomized in the Monroe Doctrine of 1823, which amounted to a declaration of the USA's legitimate right to determine its own destiny on the American continent, as demonstrated by the USA's frequent military interventions in Latin America in the 20th century. From this, a school of thought suggests that American isolationism could in fact be more suitably termed as 'unilateralist'.[27]

The sense of vulnerability to external threats and the rejection of European interventionism further cultivated America's incentive to pursue bona fide independence and to achieve 'national greatness'. The USA looked towards a 'continental republic rather than a maritime state dependent on the British navy and economy'.[28] Starting with the original 13 colonies, by the mid 19th century, the USA had purchased Louisiana from France, Florida from Spain, and had annexed Texas. It had also, as a result of Mexico's defeat, obtained the southwestern part of Mexico (California, San Francisco and New Mexico) and, in 1846, secured from Britain the Oregon country (Oregon, Idaho and Washington). By the beginning of the 20th century, the USA emerged as an expansive, dynamic and industrial power to be reckoned with in the world community. As the country became stronger and more united, it increased its impulse to disseminate its values to the outside world and to 'intervene in order to guide revolutions'.[29] Captain Alfred Thayer Mahan and Theodore Roosevelt were both leading enthusiasts for the Americanization of the world. The Spanish–American war of 1898 was the catalyst for Mahan's imperial view of naval strategy, and resulted in the annexation of the Hawaiian Islands and part of Samoa, and the seizure of the Philippine islands and Guam from Spain. The war led to the strengthening of American power in the Asia-Pacific region and over the Latin American states. The completion of the Panama Canal in 1914 enabled the USA to exert a much wider control of sea communications from the Pacific through to the Caribbean area. In September 1899, Secretary of State John Hay launched the 'open door' policy, an unsuccessful attempt to stem the monopolization of the Chinese economy by other great powers, and to provide the USA with the opportunity to exploit the Chinese market.[30]

The imperial thrust was replaced in the 1920s by an isolationist upsurge, although this did not constrain the expansion of the US economy worldwide. Between 1890 and 1928 its industrial potential increased by ten times, and the USA had become an economic superpower, with the size of its industrial potential almost equivalent to the combined economic and industrial strengths of Britain, Germany, France, Russia and Japan.[31] President Woodrow Wilson developed his idealistic views about the world order based on Jeffersonian values. Wilson's 'deep faith in the ultimate triumph of liberty' meant that he could be tolerant about foreign revolutions, in the hope that the revolutionaries would eventually learn 'to preserve their self-control and the orderly processes of their governments'. On the other hand, the same enthusiasm led the President to think ambitiously about remaking the world in America's image, based on 'ordered liberty, free-trade, and international progress and stability'.[32] However, the end of the First World War saw the emergence of a confusing and disorderly world. The second Russian revolution and the survival of Bolshevism, whose values were antithetical to those of the USA, was a great disappointment to Washington. The Moscow-led Third Communist International, or 'Comintern', actively propagated Communist ideology in Europe, Asia and even in Latin America: it encouraged working class unrest and fostered anti-colonial nationalist movements in countries like India and China and elsewhere. Within the USA there was an increase in labour unrest and race riots, while immigrants were arriving in the country in ever increasing numbers. The majority of the American public regarded these trends as the uncomfortable ripple effects of the Bolshevik revolution, which led to the 'Red Scare', the promotion of anti-Communist witch hunts, and severe curbs on immigration. American political elites, whether Republican or Democrat, regarded Bolshevism as a sort of 'disease', and tried to keep the country from 'revolutionary contagion'.[33]

In the Pacific, Japan was initially regarded by Washington (as London had thought when it signed an alliance with Tokyo in 1902) as a useful counterpoise to Russian expansionism in Asia, but with Japan's victory in the Russo-Japanese war of 1904–5 and its imperial activities in China, the US leadership began to regard the 'rising sun' with an increasing sense of foreboding. In Latin America, the fragility of democracy kept the region restless, engulfed in a series of crises, revolutions and wars, which required US intervention from time to time. In the 1930s, the USA found itself facing a potentially more expansive and dangerous menace than the short-lived Red Scare after the First World War – the rise of Fascism, led by a resurgent Germany with its Axis allies, Italy and Japan. The magnitude of the world crisis meant that neither the Atlantic nor the Pacific constituted the security buffer zones on which the USA had previously relied to preserve its national independence. The Democrat President, Franklin D. Roosevelt, was convinced of the need to 'return to a policy of active greatness'. We will never know whether Roosevelt could have taken the country into war on two fronts, Europe and the Pacific, without the shock of Pearl Harbor. Japan's decision to challenge the Western imperial powers and the USA in December 1941 helped to kill the 'dissenting Jeffersonian tradition'.[34] The Asian–Pacific war could be said to be the first American involvement in war in the Third World on a large scale.

Thus, the USA had become a fully fledged world economic power with specific interests in the Third World, before the Cold War began in earnest in 1947. Scholars have long debated whether the USA became the key global player mainly in response to the growing menace from Moscow (as John Lewis Gaddis argued), or whether it was already on the road to pursuing global hegemony after the Second World War (as Melvyn Leffler suggests).[35] A number of interrelated factors are worth noting. As explained above, the USA was already acquainted with the Third World well before the onset of the Cold War. The USA came out of the Second World War even stronger than before. Economically, the world was its oyster. In military terms, the USA was now an atomic power. The Second World War also pushed the USA towards becoming a more outward looking power with global responsibilities, although it appeared uncertain as to how long the USA would remain a global power after the war ended and its occupation duties were completed. By contrast, the recent war had exhausted Britain economically, and the European continent was in ruins. A stronger USA, the weakened European imperial powers, and the spread of Communist challenges beyond Europe after 1949 were all responsible for America's continuing determination to resist Communist threats elsewhere in the Third World, although that determination was sometimes expressed out of all proportion, as in the case of Vietnam.

With the shock of the Korean War, America's concern over its peripheries grew. America's long interest in 'the raw materials and markets of the developing world' was brought home with renewed consciousness after having witnessed 'how important Third World resources had been in the German–Japanese drive for world hegemony'.[36] In response, the American leadership adopted a policy of 'development', which could be applied to the problems of many Third World countries as a means of reducing their vulnerability to the threat of Soviet or Chinese Communism. Michael Hunt aptly terms America's policy of development as 'the younger sibling of containment', to be distinguished from US containment policy in Europe.[37]

There were, however, two related obstacles which the USA had to overcome in dealing with the Third World in the 1950s. First, was the appreciation that, unlike Stalin, Khrushchev was engaging in a 'new cold war offensive' by providing economic aid and technical assistance to many Third World countries.

Secondly, the US leadership was often bewildered by the fact that, despite the West's alleged superiority of values and wealth over the Communist world, the USA was not effectively competing with the Soviet Union and China in winning the 'hearts and minds' campaigns in the Third World. In the mid 1950s, the number of trade agreements the Communist bloc entered into with the 'free world' expanded rapidly, and more than half of such agreements were with Third World countries. Not only the Soviet Union, but also China and Eastern European countries became active in Africa, the Middle East and Asia. In fact, of course, the expanding influence of the USA in the post-war world was equally impressive. Within the decade after the Second World War, the USA had some 400,000 officers and men stationed in 73 foreign countries, engaged in training foreign armies or on active duty, and had enlisted 42 allies through collective and bilateral security arrangements, albeit that most of these allies were in Europe. However, Washington noted that Moscow, despite the meagre assistance it provided, by comparison with the USA, was often received more warmly by its prospective client states. For instance, the Soviet Union had built major roads in Kabul, which had 'won considerable applause' from the Afghan people, while Burma, rejecting Washington's offer of economic assistance, was making 'economic googoo [gu gu] eyes at Moscow'.[38]

The US policy in the developing world was intended to counter the infiltration of Communism. Thus, the USA, in a similar fashion to the Soviet Union under Khrushchev and later Brezhnev, avowedly took a globalist approach to the Third World. Globalists tend to separate the Third World between pro-Western and pro-Communist camps, and gauge the outcome in terms of gains and losses for each respective bloc. In the process, the role of the superpowers in Third World conflicts was exaggerated, while less attention was devoted to indigenous conditions or the role of regional players.[39] The Cold War was a relatively new phenomenon in the 1950s, but the notion of development was not. It came from the 'old American vision of appropriate or legitimate processes of social change and an abiding sense of superiority over the dark-skinned peoples of the Third World'. Allen Dulles, the Director of the CIA, warned the Eisenhower administration that if the USA wished to outdo 'diabolical Soviet cleverness', it should not be using words like 'backward' and 'underdeveloped', in referring to the Third World. Dulles also pointed out that regional leaders were quite adept at playing off 'Soviet and US assistance against one another'.[40]

The Republican administration's policy was further undermined by its simplistic approach to the Third World and by the lack of fully fledged support from Congress to underwrite America's Third World policy. With its long-held anti-imperialist and isolationist traditions, and given the conscious effort to conserve American power during the Eisenhower years, the USA wanted to avoid, if possible, a long-term engagement to specific countries. Instead, the USA employed covert operations in Iran and Guatemala, resorted to a short and less controversial military intervention in Lebanon, and managed to defuse two Taiwan offshore crises in Asia. In the end the USA was compelled in the mid 1950s to enter a formal defence treaty with South Korea and with Taiwan, as well as to establish the South East Asian Treaty Organization (SEATO), which were all part of US containment strategies in Asia. The Eisenhower administration was agreeable to the notion of cooperating with Britain in the Middle East in 1953, but their policy differences over Egypt continued. The State Department was clear that, while the USA 'would in fact be little interested in a situation there (the Middle East) but for the perilous state of affairs arising from East–West tensions', it was US policy to support the British in the Middle East wherever feasible, so long as this did not interfere with 'United States global security interests'. Thus, Washington decided to support the defence of the 'northern tier' of the Middle Eastern countries bordering the Soviet Union, but it agreed only to establish a 'military liaison' with the Baghdad pact organization, which was formed in 1955.[41]

However, Eisenhower was opposed to the 'concept of line drawing', because this might give 'the initiative to the enemy to seize whatever falls short of the defensive line'. Instead, he preferred foreign assistance programmes as the 'the cheapest insurance in the world', since, he argued, the 'want of a few million bucks had put the United States into a war in Korea'. Taking on new commitments in the Third World had to be weighed carefully, since 'if we get our prestige involved anywhere then we can't get out'.[42] Congress remained suspicious of giving away taxpayers' money to the increasing number of regional countries, in the absence of a clear guarantee that these would serve US national interests. Usually, various plans for advice and support agreed at the highest levels were not 'translated into institutional support further down in the national security bureaucracy'.[43] The frustration in Washington with this situation had increased, as had America's stake in the Third World, by the time John F. Kennedy came to the Oval Office.

During the presidential election campaign, Kennedy accused Eisenhower of failing to 'prosecute vigorously the Cold War' and, when in office, the new President sent thousands of young Americans as aid workers to many countries in the Third World to overcome 'the efforts of Mr Khrushchev's missionaries'.[44] As the new Democrat President, he had the additional baggage to carry from Truman's legacy in the Third World, namely the loss of China and the unresolved war in Korea. The immediate fiasco of the Bay of Pigs operation, which exposed his inexperience, further increased his determination to 'bear any burden' and 'meet any hardship', to counter Khrushchev's assertion that 'communism was forcing capitalism into retreat'.[45] Kennedy realized that there was no possibility of the USA winning a clear victory in Berlin or Cuba, and that Vietnam had become the test case of America's 'credibility'. Returning from the Vienna summit with Khrushchev, Kennedy felt that 'Now we have a problem in making our power credible, and Vietnam looks the place'.[46]

After the departure of the French from Indo-China in 1956, South Vietnam, Cambodia and Laos were provided with increasing US mutual security aid. In 1961, South Vietnam became the fifth major recipient of American foreign aid, while more than 1500 Americans were there to provide technical, military and political advice to the Ngo Dinh Diem government. Kennedy intensified American efforts to strengthen South Vietnam: in November 1963, nearly 16,000 American advisers were engaged in patrolling the jungles in South

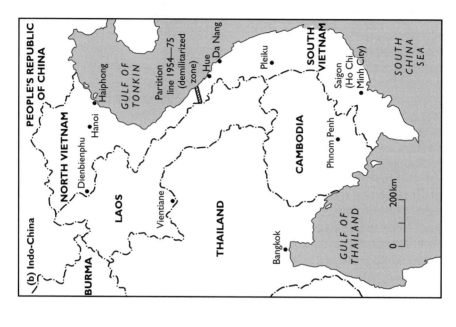

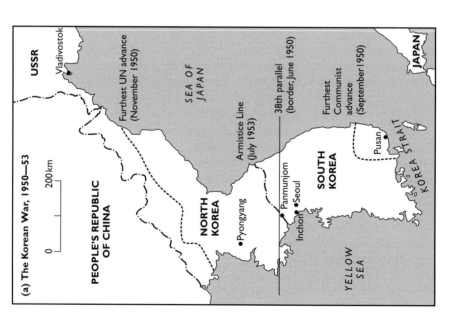

3. Cold War in the Far East (Korea and Vietnam)

Vietnam, but without producing enhanced security in the country.[47] Kennedy did not instinctively believe that the USA should become involved in a war against Communism in Vietnam, and insisted that it was the task of South Vietnam to defeat the Communists. Kennedy's increased help and commitment to South Vietnam was intended to open the way for America's eventual withdrawal from the region, but by 1963 the situation was deteriorating, which compelled Kennedy to encourage a coup against the Diem leadership, the erstwhile American ally. However, the assassinations of Diem and his brother did not produce the stability and order that the USA had expected.[48]

Vice-President Lyndon Johnson, who became President after Kennedy's tragic death in November 1963, inherited the same American objective in Vietnam: that is, the formation of a politically strong and anti-Communist South Vietnam. While Kennedy had been brought up in Boston and was educated at Harvard, Johnson was a self-made man from a humble Texas family background. Johnson was committed to domestic reforms under his Great Society programme. As for Vietnam, Johnson, more hawkish than Kennedy, initially thought it sufficient to do more of the same but do it more efficiently, but he became increasingly alarmed by the precarious situation in South Vietnam. This eventually led, by the spring of 1965, to a step by step escalation of the military conflict in Vietnam. With the beginning of America's aerial bombing campaign (Rolling Thunder) in early March 1965, the USA decided to increase the number of US troops in South Vietnam, in order to fight the Viet Cong and infiltrators from the North. However, these decisions were seen more as 'an exercise in crisis management than the war it had become'.[49]

Johnson imposed a number of limitations on the scale and the goal of America's military commitment to Vietnam, as he did not want to encourage Communist China and/or the Soviet Union to intervene in the conflict, as in Korea, nor to invite adverse public repercussions at home and abroad. In the process, the USA put a further premium on winning the war in Vietnam: by 1967, the USA had committed more than half a million troops to Vietnam. The air force was dropping more bombs than had been dropped in all Second World War theatres, and the price of this effort was costing the USA $2 billion per month. In the summer of 1965, opinion polls indicated that a large section of the public approved Johnson's handling of the Vietnam conflict, but his popularity fell to an all-time low after the 1968 Tet Offensive, which persuaded him not to seek re-election in that year. Vietnam had become a huge credibility test for America's leadership, and the key to America's determination to win the Cold War. This mindset was clearly summarized by Johnson himself:

> I knew from the start that I was bound to be crucified either way I moved. If I left the woman I really loved – the Great Society – in order to get involved with that bitch of a war on the other side of the world, then I would lose everything at home . . . But if I left that war and let the Communists take over South Vietnam then, I would be seen as a coward and my nation would be seen as an appeaser, and we would both find it impossible to accomplish anything for anybody anywhere on the entire globe.[50]

In January 1969, the new Republican President, Richard Nixon, found himself in a similar position to that of his Republican predecessor, Eisenhower, whose first credibility test was to end the war in Korea in 1953. For Nixon, how to extricate the USA from the unpopular war in Vietnam had become the test of his credibility and that of his country. This implied that 'Vietnam' would be downgraded in America's political agenda and would become, in Kissinger's words, 'a little fourth rate power'. Eisenhower's Massive Retaliation strategy became, under Nixon, the so-called Madman theory – 'I want the North Vietnamese to believe I've reached the point where I might do anything to stop the war.'[51] Nixon also reverted to a vigorous policy of 'support and advice', which had been adopted by Eisenhower in the 1950s: that is, the Vietnamese should take the chief responsibility for defending their own country. Under Nixon, this concept became known as 'Vietnamization'. Thus, Nixon's notion of 'Peace with Honour' precluded a quick end to the war, since time was needed to allow South Vietnam to become stronger, and Nixon's initiative in East–West détente, first with China and then the Soviet Union, helped to divert public attention from the Vietnam quagmire. By mid 1971, a majority of the American public (71 per cent) regarded the war in Indochina as a mistake.[52] The Paris Accords were signed in January 1973, which allowed the USA to extricate itself from Indochina. At the war's end, America's first objective in South Vietnam still remained unresolved: South Vietnam did not become a strong, united and anti-Communist country, and it succumbed to Hanoi's military onslaught in 1975, which was followed by the Communization of Laos and Cambodia. In retrospect, America's fear of the domino theory in Indochina seemed to be justified, but, by the mid 1970s, following the withdrawal of American troops from Vietnam and after Nixon's overtures to Beijing, the strategic importance the USA attached to the region had waned considerably.

Even if one took a global stance, it was clear that there was initially no serious competition between the superpowers over Vietnam. Stalin and Khrushchev in the 1950s assumed that China would be responsible for encouraging successful revolutionary movements in Asia, as the Soviet Union was busy dealing with global (by implication superior) problems, the German question and East–West détente.[53] China, after the end of the Korean War, sought to concentrate on its domestic agenda, and it encouraged Hanoi to solidify its revolutionary gains in the North. It was only in 1962 that China, given the deeper American commitment to South Vietnam, was compelled to increase its support for Hanoi, and this was followed by the decision in Moscow in October 1964 (immediately after Khrushchev's dismissal) to supply offensive weapons to enhance the North's fighting capabilities.[54] Thus, superpower competition in Vietnam was largely the result of USA action and not the other way around. Neither the Soviet Union nor China, however, exerted any significant degree of control over the direction of the war itself, but massive external support to the Vietnamese civil war eventually contributed to a shift in the nature of the war from insurgency to conventional fighting in urban areas, intensified the scale of the military conflict, and thus made the war bloodier and more costly in human and economic terms on both sides.

THE VIETNAM SYNDROME AND MOSCOW'S 'WHEEL OF FORTUNE' IN THE THIRD WORLD

What brought the USA into the Vietnam quagmire has been the subject of considerable debate. Was this 'the single blunder' and an 'aberration', or does the Vietnam War reflect 'a logical culmination of well-entrenched national tendencies'?[55] For the USA, the Vietnam War was a disaster on a large scale, with far-reaching implications for its foreign and national security policy during and beyond the 1970s. Vietnam allowed the Soviet Union to close the nuclear gap with the USA, weakened NATO (with de Gaulle's decision to withdraw France from NATO's military command), undermined the cohesion of American society, aroused international criticism against America's conduct in the war in Vietnam (Johnson's massive troops commitment, Nixon's incursion into Cambodia, and his Christmas bombing of the North), challenged the supremacy of the dollar, and destroyed two American presidencies (Johnson and Nixon).

The Vietnam War was not directly responsible for all of the above outcomes, but the defeat of the USA in Vietnam led to a considerable degree of frustration and incomprehension in the formulation of US policy towards the Third World. The successive South Vietnamese governments had never been capable of controlling their country. In addition, the USA sought only to help the South Vietnamese 'liberate' South Vietnam from Communism, not to 'conquer' it. The British concept of 'clear and hold' to win the hearts and minds campaign was somewhat incongruous to the mindset of American officials at the time of the US involvement in Vietnam, and the USA chose a 'search and destroy' mission instead. It was more about America's traditional tendency to disseminate their 'greatness' and liberate the world from 'evil', whether it be Communism, terrorism or dictatorship, than about defeating the enemy and holding on to South Vietnam, with whom the USA had had little historical association.

American public disillusion with the Vietnam War was also accompanied by several social and economic changes during the late 1960s. If the decade of the 1950s can be characterized by the 'unquestionable respect for authority', the code of behaviour, the rule of law, 'repressed attitudes to sex', prejudices against the weaker members of the population (women, ethnic minorities, youngsters), the opposite trends dominated the cultural and social agenda of the early 1970s in the USA.[56] There was a sense of the 'fragmentation' of American society, 'the drift of power away from the traditional institutions', concerns for civil and human rights, presentation of individual rights rather than representation by the elites and, overall, a lack of confidence in traditional values and beliefs.[57]

The pre-eminence of the dollar, which initially shaped the post-war economic order, had ended in 1971 with the devaluation of the dollar and the end of the Breton Woods system. The international market became more competitive, with the result that the American share of world trade suffered and more goods were imported into the USA. The federal government's overseas expenditures grew with an increasing amount of economic and military assistance to the Third World since the 1950s and with the war in Vietnam. There was also the growth of multinational corporations in Western Europe (some owned by Western

Europeans and the others by Americans), which tended to use dollars for their transactions, leading to the rise of the Eurodollar market. This led to speculation against the dollar and in 1971, Nixon ended dollar–gold convertibility and let the dollar float.[58] The war in the Middle East and the consequent oil embargo by the oil producers in the Arab world created further serious economic problems for many industrial countries. The USA's economic growth had peaked by 1973, with a decline of GNP starting in 1974. This downturn was accompanied by a rise in inflation parallel with the growth of the rate of unemployment, creating a curious economic situation called 'stagflation'.

The long, wearing and, ultimately, unsuccessful war in Vietnam contributed to the polarization of US society, but the decline of the American economy and the fragmentation of cultural and social values added to the magnitude of the so-called 'Vietnam syndrome'. At the highest official level, this was reflected in the reduction of the 'imperial presidency' vis-à-vis Congress. The credibility of authority was further tarnished by the Watergate scandal. In 1973, Congress passed the War Powers Act constraining presidential power to despatch American troops overseas, imposing controls over the activities of the CIA, and terminating funding for America's military activities in Indochina. The White House was restricted in money and power in the conduct of foreign affairs; the public was becoming inward looking and generally 'disenchanted' with higher politics.[59]

All these tumultuous changes in the West provided lucrative opportunities for the Soviet Union to catch up with, and equal, the USA in arms and influence in the world. As with Stalin, the Brezhnev regime was willing to exploit strategic changes occurring in the West, to Moscow's advantage. With Great Britain's announcement of its decision to withdraw from East of Suez in July 1967, the Soviet Union quickly projected its naval power into the Indian Ocean. Prior to that date, there had been no *permanent* Soviet naval presence recorded in the Indian Ocean and between 1964 and 1966 no Soviet warships had entered the Indian Ocean. However, things started to change after 1967, when the Soviet naval presence there became a permanent feature. Moscow initially deployed 200 ships in 1967, but the number rose to 10,500 by 1974, declined to 7000–8000 between 1975 and 1979, and increased again after 1979 to over 10,000 between 1980 and 1983. This new-found naval expansion into the Indian Ocean was intended to serve the Kremlin's growing interest in the Horn of Africa and in the Arabian peninsula, and especially Aden, in the aftermath of Great Britain's decision to abandon its military base there after its 128-year presence. It was also intended to check America's military intervention in the region, as the USA began to establish a new strategic base on Diego Garcia in the British Indian Ocean Territory, which was loaned to the USA by Great Britain in 1966.[60] The Soviet naval expansion was not just about competing with the capitalist world. With the Moscow-led Warsaw Pact invasion of Czechoslovakia in 1968, relations with China took a sharp turn for the worse. The growing hostility between the two countries was reflected in the 1969 border clash in the Ussuri river region. Beijing now branded the Soviet Union as a 'socialist-imperialist country', which had replaced the USA as China's number one enemy. Moscow, in turn, saw

China's increasingly competitive role in Africa and the rest of the Third World as undermining the Kremlin's influence there. The Soviet naval presence in the Indian Ocean was regarded as an important strategic instrument to challenge and outdo China's ambitions in Africa, the Middle East and South Asia.[61]

The Soviet Union's determination to exploit the weaknesses of its enemies (which now included China), was no doubt boosted by the remarkable growth in its naval and air fighting capabilities, as a result of Moscow's rearmament efforts in the latter half of the 1960s. With the Soviet sphere of influence in Europe now guaranteed by détente, the Party leadership in the International Department in the Central Committee (led by Boris Nikolaevich Ponomarev) appreciated that the Cold War battlefield had now shifted to the Third World. Yuri Andropov, then the chairman of the KGB, had predicted in 1965 that the Soviet Union 'will compete for every piece of land, for every country'.[62] The Kremlin optimistically saw the fragmentation of American society after Vietnam as a sign of the failure of the Western capitalist system.[63] There was rising confidence in Moscow that the Soviet Union, and not the USA, was 'becoming the dominant actor' in the world.[64]

The outcome was the assertion of Soviet influence in Africa, the Middle East, South East Asia and Central America in the latter half of the 1970s. In Angola, the civil war had worsened in 1975, in the wake of the Portuguese decision to grant independence to its colony. Three factions were fighting to rule the country: the National Front for the Liberation of Angola (FNLA), the Popular Movement for the Liberation of Angola (MPLA), and the Union for the Total Independence of Angola (UNITA). FNLA was initially supported by the USA, and also briefly by China; UNITA by South Africa; and MPLA (the main left wing faction) by the Soviet Union. After Angola's independence in the autumn of 1975, FNLA joined UNITA in opposition to the Moscow-sponsored MPLA, and the civil war intensified. South Africa increased its military involvement with the USA, providing limited economic backing, while Cuba (with Castro taking the initiative in intervening militarily in support of MPLA without first telling Moscow) and the Soviet Union (who had become concerned about a possible Sino–US collaboration in helping the anti-Soviet factions), together mounted a military operation involving more than 10,000 Cuban troops, which helped MPLA to defeat their enemies. In the spring of 1976, the Kremlin congratulated itself on winning the Angolan war, and the Cubans and Angolans were also careful to show their loyalty and devotion to the Kremlin's supreme leadership.[65]

This apparent easy victory in Angola increased the Soviet Union's confidence in its leadership in Africa and other developing countries. Moscow's credibility was also enhanced in the eyes of aspiring African socialist leaders. Mozambique was moving towards the Soviet bloc, as was Zimbabwe. The Soviet Union won Ethiopian friendship (a treaty with Addis Ababa was signed in November 1978), at the cost of upsetting its recent ally, Somalia. In the southern Arabian peninsula, South Yemen became a Marxist country, supporting Soviet activities in the Horn of Africa, and concluding a treaty of friendship and cooperation with the Soviet Union in October 1979, with North Yemen, against America's expectations, also tilting towards the Soviet bloc.[66]

The developments in Angola concerned Washington. Henry Kissinger, now President Gerald Ford's National Security Adviser, as well as Secretary of State, thought that if Angola fell to Communism, 'other African dominoes would start to fall'. Ford secretly sent a green signal to the CIA to launch covert operations in Angola, codenamed IAFEATURE, which proved to be 'too small to achieve victory' against an MPLA backed by the Soviet Union and Cuban troops. Congress was still suffering from strong anti-interventionist sentiments and was determined to ensure that the 'culture of the Cold War Congress' should not lead once again to the US involvement in civil wars'. As a result, it passed the Clark Amendment, banning American aid to Angola.[67] Ford's successor, Jimmy Carter, downgraded the Cold War, in favour of promoting human rights in Latin America and of resolving the disparity of economic wealth between the South and the North. Carter, following in the footsteps of Woodrow Wilson, wanted to revert to upholding the morality of individuals and nations. Thus, foreign policy, in Carter's view, became 'the external manifestation of American ideas and the continuation of US domestic politics'.[68] The White House sought both to maintain the remnants of détente with Moscow and to contain the growing Soviet influence in the Third World, but the outcome was rather confused and lacked consistency.

Carter's efforts to resolve the problems in the Middle East with the Soviet Union floundered. By 1975, the Soviet Union's relations with its erstwhile ally, Egypt, had collapsed and Moscow had lost its extensive naval and air reconnaissance facilities in that country. In 1977, Carter and Brezhnev publicly announced their intention of making a joint effort to bring about peace in the Middle East, but this proved to be untenable in the face of opposition from Israel, Egypt, and Washington's pro-Israeli lobby. The Egyptian leader, Anwar Sadat, made a solo trip to Tel Aviv to negotiate peace with Israel, ignoring the planned peace conference in Cairo. Egypt and Israel, however, allowed the USA to sponsor a peace settlement at Camp David, which Carter organized successfully. Carter's 'finest hour' in the Middle Eastern settlement effectively excluded Moscow from the Middle East, prompting the angry Soviet leadership to rearm friendly states in the region, especially Egypt's arch rival, Syria.[69]

Carter's 'China' card (the initiative leading to the normalization of relations between Beijing and Washington in January 1979) proved to be a fatal blow to Moscow's strategic calculations. Moreover, Carter's hardline National Security Adviser, Zbigniew Brzezinski, skilfully fed Moscow's fears by arranging for the announcement of Deng Xiaoping's visit to the USA in January 1979 on the eve of the planned superpower meeting over SALT II, which, as a result, had to be postponed for several months. Moreover, after the Chinese leader's visit to Washington, Beijing invaded Vietnam, thereby creating the impression in Moscow that the USA was behind China's military adventure. Carter's China card did not end the Cold War in East Asia conclusively either (Vietnam remained closely allied to the Soviet Union, while Japan had a long-standing territorial dispute with the USSR over the northern islands off Hokkaido), but the formal restoration of Sino–US relations increased suspicions in Soviet minds about Carter's sincerity in continuing with détente with the Soviet Union.[70]

The divisions within the Carter administration added to the incoherence of America's foreign policy. Brzezinski wanted to adopt a confrontational stance against Moscow's activism in the Third World, and urged Carter to establish a linkage between Soviet Third World policies and superpower arms control negotiations over SALT II. For example, he wanted to give solid backing to Somalia, but the latter's invasion of the Ogaden in Ethiopia reduced the Carter administration's confidence in an aggressor who was now fighting Soviet-backed Ethiopia. Secretary of State Cyrus Vance, on the other hand, appreciated that East–West détente was not a perfect mechanism, and did not want to undermine the SALT process because of problems in the Third World.[71] Carter's position was somewhat ambiguous, but during the summer of 1979, SALT II was finally signed by the USA and the USSR. While Moscow quickly ratified it, many in the US Senate suspected that the treaty favoured the Soviet Union at the USA's expense. A crisis over Cuba further undermined the prospect of US ratification of the treaty. In late August, the US intelligence community had belatedly found out that there was a Soviet combat brigade in Cuba (which had been deployed even before the Cuban Missile Crisis broke out) and Congress and the US media demanded the immediate withdrawal of the Soviet force from Cuba. After intense negotiations between Washington and Moscow, the crisis was defused in October, but, in consequence, preparations for Senate ratification of SALT II were considerably delayed. Moscow viewed the Cuban saga as part of a US anti-Soviet campaign to destroy détente, or, more cynically, an attempt to improve Carter's image as a strong President.[72]

The delicate balance between détente and confrontation finally collapsed as a result of the Iranian hostage crisis, and by the Soviet invasion of Afghanistan in the winter of 1979. President Nixon, after the Vietnam debacle, had been keen to strengthen the Shah of Iran, through massive arms sales to Iran, so that it could become a 'stabiliser' in the Middle East. However, the Shah's dictatorial government alienated the Muslim masses, who had not benefited from Iran's oil revenues, and increased the opposition to the regime by radical religious leaders led by Ayatollah Khomeini. The resurgence of anti-modernism and anti-Western sentiments culminated in February 1979, when the Shah was ousted and his regime replaced by a fundamental Islamic government controlled by Khomeini. Carter's human rights crusade had not been applied to China or to the Shah of Iran. In October 1979, Carter agreed that the ailing Shah should be admitted into the USA for medical treatment. This led angry Iranians, encouraged by Khomeini, to attack the US Embassy in Tehran, taking 69 American hostages, who were not released (given Carter's failed rescue operation in 1980) until 1981 when Reagan came to power.[73]

While the Iranian revolution humiliated the Americans, it also strengthened Moscow's resolve to use force in Afghanistan in December 1979. The Kremlin leadership was concerned about the spread of Muslim fundamentalism into a neighbouring Muslim country, and into the southern borders of the USSR where there were many Muslim populations. It was also feared that a humiliated USA might resort to an aggressive policy in Iran, with adverse effects on the Soviet position in Afghanistan.[74] In any case, the Iranian revolution and the subsequent

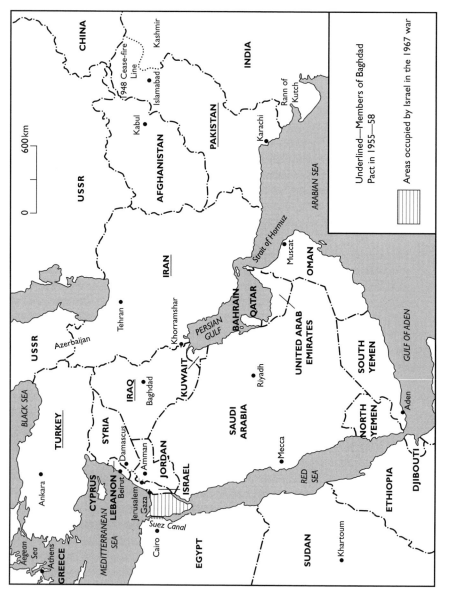

4. Cold War in the Middle East and Central Asia

Underlined—Members of Baghdad Pact in 1955—58

Areas occupied by Israel in the 1967 war

instability in the region reinforced the need to strengthen the Afghan Communist government. Afghanistan was within the Soviet security zone and Kabul had a friendship treaty with Moscow dating back to 1920. The Soviet Secret Service (which after 1954 became the KGB) and its counterpart Afghan agency made sure that Afghanistan would not succumb to the influence of other anti-Soviet countries. The Communist Party of the Soviet Union (CPSU) also provided financial support to the Afghan Communists, and helped to create the People's Democratic Party of Afghanistan (a Communist Party, PDPA) in 1965.[75]

In April 1978, a small group of Communists in the Afghan army (without first consulting Moscow) brought the PDPA into power. The coup took the Kremlin by surprise. Moscow hoped initially that the new socialist government would stabilize the country, which would in turn help the Soviet Union to consolidate its position in that part of the world. Moscow concluded a fresh friendship treaty with Kabul's new government in December 1978, and increased the number of Soviet advisers from 350 to 4000. The successful coup was an isolated incident and was not backed by the majority of the Afghan public.[76] Moreover, the PDPA was hardly a unified organization, but embraced two rival factions: the Khalq (hardliners) and the Parcham (moderates). It was the Khalq which formed the new Marxist government led by Hafizullah Amin (the Prime Minister) and Nur Mohammed Taraki (the President). The new government launched a series of radical reforms that were incompatible with Muslim religious practices, while Amin used terror to overcome his opponents. As a result, the Afghan population became swiftly disenchanted with the new Communist government, and soon civil war broke out in Afghanistan between the government and Muslim rebels. The credibility of the Amin government was increasingly called into question. The KGB was suspicious of Amin's links with Washington and, in September 1979, when Taraki visited Moscow, the Kremlin ordered him to eliminate Amin. However, Taraki was outmanoeuvred by Amin, who had the President executed in prison in October 1979.[77]

The Politburo had begun serious discussions in March 1979 about whether or not to intervene in Afghanistan. Amin's execution of Taraki 'hurt the pride of the Kremlin elders and the KGB'. Andropov (then the KGB chief) and Ustinov (the Defence Minister) presented the case for intervention to the ailing Brezhnev, who approved it on 8 December and, four days later, the Politburo ratified the decision to intervene. Soviet motives were numerous: the need to contain Islamic fundamentalism by keeping Iran and Pakistan at bay; the fear of the domino effect on other Communist revolutionary movements if the Soviet Union were unable to sustain Afghanistan; concern about the alleged connection between Amin and the USA and his possible shift to the West; and the need to bolster the Afghan army, whose morale was reported to be low.[78] On 27 December, the Red Army stormed into Kabul. The number of Soviet troops quickly reached 100,000. The intervention was meant to be decisive and short, but for the following ten years the Afghan rebels pinned down the bulk of the Red Army.

Moscow's invasion of Afghanistan was seen in the West as 'the extension of the Brezhnev doctrine beyond Europe', and put an end to the already declining détente.[79] Carter boycotted the Moscow Olympics of 1980, suspended the ratification of SALT II and, in the same year, announced the Carter Doctrine, a pledge to intervene in the Persian Gulf if the Soviet Union expanded into the region. By then, however, Carter's policy was no more sustainable than it had been a year before: he was attacked both from the left (who wanted détente to continue) and from the right (who blamed Carter for letting détente continue so long, despite Moscow's aggressive policy elsewhere in the Third World).[80]

THE RETURN OF AMERICAN ASSERTIVENESS: THE REAGAN DOCTRINE

Reagan's victory led to revival of the globalist stance in US policy towards the Third World. The new President was convinced that the Soviet Union was responsible for all the ills of, and instability in, the world. The Reagan administration was particularly concerned about Soviet meddling in Central America: Nicaragua, El Salvador and Grenada all experienced revolutionary movements against existing regimes in 1979.

Initially, the Soviet Union's attitude towards the revolutions in the Caribbean was a cautious one and showed some political sensitivity about interfering in America's backyard. Nonetheless, the Kremlin believed that the revolutionary movements were 'morally right', as they were based on Marx's theory of the inevitability of anti-capitalist revolution. The Kremlin was hopeful about possible progressive change in El Salvador, but was less certain about Grenada's 'New Jewel Movement', which was part of Castro's ambition to turn Central America into a Communist sphere of influence. In large measure, Moscow's penetration into the Caribbean was facilitated by Cuban efforts, which helped Moscow to minimize the risk of deeper and more expensive commitments to the region.[81]

Nicaragua was central to the subsequent revolutions in Central America. The Sandinista National Liberation Front (FSLN) ousted the autocratic and corrupt Somoza dynasty, Washington's long-term ally in Nicaragua. The victory of the Sandinistas, after 20 years of fighting Somoza's national guards, was warmly received by the bulk of the international community, including its neighbouring countries, Panama, Costa Rica, Venezuela and Mexico. Moscow gave its blessing to the new revolutionary power in Central America and increased its assistance to the Sandinistas, who in turn supported the revolutionary forces in neighbouring El Salvador.

Unlike the Carter administration, the neo-Conservative Republican leadership was determined to respond to Soviet adventurism in the Third World and, to this end, Central America was described as 'the place for the United States firmly to "draw the line" against the spread of international Communism'.[82] The idea of turning the Third World once again into the Cold War battleground – as it had been in the 1960s and early 1970s – meant that the USA would support non-democratic and authoritarian states like Guatemala and Honduras, so long as they were anti-Communist and friendly to the USA. For example, the Chilean socialist leader, Salvador Allende, had been overthrown by a military coup in

1973. Nixon and Kissinger had both been anxious to get rid of Allende, a friend of Castro, and the CIA organized covert operations to undermine Allende's regime and encouraged the anti-Allende group to take action against the President. After the coup, Allende was replaced by Augusto Pinochet, the most brutal dictator in Chile's recent history, who imposed a reign of terror on the Chilean population until 1989.[83]

America's determination to de-legitimize Communist regimes was, therefore, not new. In the late 1970s, Jean Kirkpatrick, then Professor of Political Science at Georgetown University in Washington DC, was a vocal critic of Carter's policy of promoting human rights and democratic reforms in the Third World, dismissing it as 'ineffectual' and 'downright dangerous'. Carter's policy, she claimed, allowed anti-government revolutionaries to put in place regimes which were hostile to the USA. Kirkpatrick distinguished between authoritarians and totalitarians: the former upheld traditional societies and clung to the capitalist system, with the prospect of accommodation with the West, while the latter had no such policies and were exemplified by Hitler and Stalin.[84] Kirkpatrick's thesis had many contemporary critics, but Reagan and Haig used it as the intellectual justification for their policy in the Third World. Kirkpatrick was appointed US ambassador to the UN and, together with Haig, presided over US foreign policy making. In their opinion, the USA should have no moral qualms about assisting rightist, militant and undemocratic dictators or other terrorist groups (like the anti-Sandinista groups or Afghan rebels), provided that they were anti-Communist and friendly to the West.

Reagan authorized the use of force in Lebanon in 1982 and Grenada in 1983. The USA as part of a Multinational Force (MNF) (together with French and Italian formations) intervened militarily in Lebanon after Israeli's invasion of the country in June 1982. Lebanon was a strategic pawn between Israel and pro-Soviet Syria, and the Israeli–Syrian rivalry intensified internal hostility between Christian and Muslim populations in Lebanon, resulting in civil war. Israel's declared war aim was to secure a Palestinian Liberation Organization (PLO) free zone in the south of Lebanon, but while bloody fighting continued, it became clear that Israeli troops also sought to expel the Syrian forces from Lebanon, and destroy the PLO army in Beirut. Haig tended to see the conflict in purely Cold War terms, that is between pro-American Israel and pro-Soviet Syria. He calculated that Israel's victory over Syria would be a success for US policy. Casper Weinberger and Vice-President George Bush were more concerned about the implications of Israel's victory for the stability of the Middle East, and about Tel Aviv's isolation in the world, given the staggering number of Palestinian and Lebanese casualties at the hands of the Israeli troops.[85] The MNF was soon embroiled in the Lebanese civil war. After a terrorist attack, which killed 239 American soldiers in October 1983, the Reagan administration decided to withdraw from what had turned out be an unpopular military intervention in the Middle East.[86]

In the same month, however, Reagan and the new US Secretary of State, George Shultz, sent 1900 US troops to destroy a pro-Cuban left wing regime in Grenada. The Pentagon had some reservations about intervention and, indeed, the USA managed to overcome the opposition forces, which included 784 Cubans, only after reinforcements of 4000 troops arrived on the island. The American pretext was to rescue 500 American medical students trapped by the left wing coup, and after six days of fighting, they were safely brought back home.[87] The British Prime Minister was distressed by America's hurried intervention in a former British colony now in the Commonwealth, and the timing was unfortunate, as the intervention took place the day after the British Foreign Secretary stated in the House of Commons that the UK had no knowledge of any American plan to intervene in Grenada. Nonetheless, a majority of the US public was pleased by Reagan's decisive military action, which in effect compensated for America's recent disaster in Lebanon.[88]

Reagan's assertive policy in the Third World was not, however, universally accepted. Despite his call for the Vietnam War to be recognized as a 'noble cause', the Lebanon imbroglio once again brought home to Congress and the American public the fear of a repetition of the Vietnam experience. This preoccupation with Vietnam was also reflected in the executive branch. Secretary of Defense Casper Weinberger set out the conditions that would have to be met if the USA again decided to resort to the use of force, known as the Weinberger Doctrine of November 1984. The use of force, asserted Weinberger, should be considered 'only as a last resort', when 'truly vital interests are at stake', and when the government secured the 'support of the American people and Congress'. If a decision to intervene with combat forces was made, they must be deployed in 'sufficient numbers to win' and given 'clearly defined political and military objectives', which in the case of the Lebanon invasion and in the Vietnam War had been clearly lacking. Instead, Weinberger and the Pentagon preferred advice and support (economic and military assistance) and the greater use of covert operations, in order to achieve American political objectives in regional conflicts. George Shultz, however, contended that 'power and diplomacy always go together', and took the view that diplomacy not backed by the threat of, or actual use of, military force, was not likely to be successful.[89] This division between the Pentagon and the State Department provided the background to the Grenada invasion. Shultz supported the invasion, backed by Reagan. The Secretary of State was more pragmatic than Weinberger and was willing to negotiate with the Soviet Union, while Weinberger and the other hardliners rejected negotiations and sought to keep 'an atmosphere of threat alive', in order also to secure Congressional votes for large funds for the Pentagon.[90] Reagan upheld Kirkpartrick's thesis, went along with Weinberger's covert operations, and adopted Shultz's determined, pragmatic and interventionist approach.

These Cold War warriors were initially hampered by the reluctance of Congress to support an assertive Republican foreign policy. In key battlegrounds, like Angola and Nicaragua, Congress restricted funds to the executive branch and a frustrated Reagan increasingly resorted to covert operations to achieve his goals. In November 1981, Reagan signed the secret National Security directive (NSDD-17), which enabled the CIA to train and equip Nicaraguan exiles in the southern USA – the so-called Contras. The Contras would then be transported via Honduras to Nicaragua to fight the Sandinistas. A similar covert operation was also used in Afghanistan and in Angola, where the CIA asked Saudi Arabia to fund the Angolan rebels in return for America's agreement to sell Airborne Warning and Control System (AWACS) planes to Saudi Arabia (see chapter 8). Nevertheless, buoyed by the successful intervention in Grenada, Reagan's determination to resist Soviet expansionism in the Third World increased. His State of the Union address in February 1985 hit a high moral tone, openly calling for a crusade to liberate the world from the 'evil' Soviet empire, and urging Congress to roll back Soviet-sponsored regimes in Afghanistan, Angola, Nicaragua and other countries. In Reagan's terms, those resisting 'totalitarianism' were 'freedom fighters', and the USA, as the leader of the free world, had an obligation to support them in the 'interests of national security'.[91] Strengthened by Reagan's rearmament programme, the USA in 1985 was confident that it could deal with the Soviet Union from a position of strength.

Both the USA and the Soviet Union possessed the ideological impulse to disseminate their ideals and remake the Third Word in their own respective images. Neither of these countries pretended to be imperialist, but both had a streak of interventionism when circumstances so demanded. However, the Soviet Union was still in the process of discovering whether Marxist-Leninist theory would work in practice, and tended to react optimistically to signs of weakness in the capitalist world and/or successful revolutionary movements in the Third World. The USA, exhausted by Vietnam, took a more cautious attitude towards the problems of the Third World. By the early 1980s, when the USA re-established itself, it was determined to project a firm front against what it considered to be Soviet attempts to change the regimes of many Third World countries. The American message was clear: it was the Soviet Union that had to abandon its support for socialist regimes, before superpower rivalry in the Third World could be ended.

8

The End of Superpower Competition in the Third World

GORBACHEV'S 'NEW THINKING' AND REGIONAL CONFLICT

Soon after coming to power, Gorbachev emphasized détente with the West and cooperation with the rest of the world. He wanted to reduce the cost of supporting Soviet clients in the Third World, and encouraged Third World revolutionary regimes to improve their economies 'mainly through their own efforts'.[1] By the end of 1991, the two superpowers had agreed to end the supply of arms to the warring factions in Afghanistan and had negotiated settlements over Nicaragua, Angola and Cambodia, and in January 1992, over El Salvador. From this sequence of events it would be tempting to conclude that Gorbachev was now prepared to disengage from the Third World, thereby admitting the limits of Soviet power – that he had finally bowed to the inevitable. This chapter explains that this was not really the case.

Prior to Gorbachev, the Kremlin leadership had already begun to reconsider its Third World activism of the 1970s and, as a result, the issue had been downgraded in the list of the Kremlin's priorities. Indeed, what appeared to have been the prosperity of the Soviet Union in the 1970s was, by the beginning of the 1980s, seen as only a qualified success. Brezhnev, in a speech in 1981, hinted that Soviet assistance to aspiring socialist countries might not be as generous as hitherto, owing to 'other demands on Soviet resources'.[2] The 1970s saw a rapidly rising number of self-declared socialist states, but few of these new Soviet clients were able to consolidate themselves in power after the revolutions. Most of them were small, underdeveloped and vulnerable to counter-revolutionary forces. Vietnam was now regarded as a socialist state (which was in the upper echelon of the list of Soviet priorities, separating it from the group who merely had 'socialist orientations'),[3] but the Hanoi-backed Cambodian regime was unable to control the whole of Cambodia. Nor was the Communist government in Kabul able to cope with the activities of anti-Communist guerrilla units supported by the USA and Pakistan.

Despite significantly increased Soviet assistance, Mozambique and South Yemen remained poverty stricken and, in the case of Ethiopia, the Soviet Union was no longer able or willing to feed its starving population, which forced Addis Ababa to ask for Western humanitarian aid instead.[4] Soviet academic experts were increasingly critical of the Kremlin's underestimation of the scope of the regional problems confronting pro-Soviet regimes in the Third World, such as Afghanistan.[5]

Overall, the cost of supporting Soviet Third World clients militarily had more than doubled since the late 1970s. The number of Soviet advisers had grown steadily in Africa and the Middle East to over 16,000 in 1981. However, Soviet assistance was not necessarily translated into Soviet control over these client states, for their rulers tended to take an independent approach to local problems.[6] Nonetheless, these weak regimes had to rely on Soviet military might and/or Cuban or Vietnamese troops to support their efforts to counter indigenous anti-Communist guerrillas (as in Afghanistan, Cambodia, Nicaragua and Angola), but this made the Soviet Union look like an imperialist power, rather than as the leader of Socialist revolutionary forces. In particular, the Soviet invasion of Afghanistan in 1979 damaged the former's image 'far worse than the Kremlin feared'. It was the use of Soviet, not surrogate, troops in Afghanistan that drew severe criticism not only from Western capitalist countries, but also from India, China and other regional powers close to Afghanistan. The Soviet public was not fully behind the invasion. That the UN General Assembly condemned the Soviet Union with 104 votes to 18 clearly indicated how unpopular the Soviet Union had become.[7]

Of course, the Kremlin was well aware that its support for revolutionary regimes in the 1970s had contributed to the worsening of Soviet relations with the West. The optimum conditions (East–West détente accompanied by a reduction of American activities in the Third World after Vietnam) in the 1970s had given way to a series of undesirable trends in the 1980s – the breakdown of the East–West détente, the un-ratified SALT II agreement, the deployment of new American missiles in Europe, and the Polish crisis, all of which compelled the Soviet Union under Andropov to rethink its policy towards the Third World. Andropov now accepted that Soviet active support for the Third World was 'vastly more risky and less feasible', than in the 1970s, and he now paid more attention to Europe, East–West relations, and the deterioration of economic and social conditions at home. The Soviet leadership signalled more qualified Soviet support towards the Third World and Andropov defined Moscow's primary role there as propagating the Soviet Union's economic well-being as a 'model for the rest of the world', and not through 'direct economic assistance'.[8]

Nicaragua and Cuba were both informed that future Soviet commitments to the defence of their countries would be reduced, which angered the Cuban leader, Castro, who refused to attend the funeral of Chernenko in March 1985. America's invasion in Grenada in 1983 led to greater restraint in Cuba, which now informed the Sandinista government that it could not defend Nicaragua if it were attacked, and withdrew nearly 1000 personnel from the country. The Soviet Union, too, cancelled an arms sales agreement with Nicaragua in the same year.[9] Cuba also withdrew the bulk of its troops from Ethiopia in 1984–5, partly because neither Ethiopia nor the Soviet Union was able or willing to fund Cuban troops. In some cases, however, Moscow increased its arms sales to the Third World, thereby seeking to maintain Moscow's interests there.[10] Much of Andropov's policy was reflected in Gorbachev's strategy towards the Third World. This can be explained under the following five points:

Guiding Themes

Regional conflicts continued to receive a lower priority during the Gorbachev years. The USA wanted the Soviet Union to abandon competition with the USA and to withdraw Moscow's current military and economic support from the Third World. Gorbachev could accept all these demands, on condition that the USA did the same. Gorbachev's new thinking – disarmament, negotiations, mutual respect for the differences between reformed socialism and capitalism, and the right to defend each other's individual national interests – also guided his policy towards the Third World (see chapter 2). Accordingly, the Soviet Union increased its effort to settle regional conflicts, advising Cuba and Vietnam to withdraw their military forces from their client countries and encouraging pro-Soviet regimes, such as Afghanistan and Nicaragua, to seek negotiations with their adversaries and achieve 'national reconciliation'.[11]

Pragmatism and Rationalization: the Cost of Maintaining Soviet Allies in the Third World

With Gorbachev's first aim of reinvigorating the Soviet economy in mind, it was hardly surprising that the spiralling costs of defending Soviet client states overseas was a severe dilemma for the new Kremlin. Since the late 1970s, the Soviet Union had become the world's leading arms supplier to the Third World, accounting for nearly 37 per cent of the international armaments market. Nearly 40 per cent of these arms went to Marxist or Marxist orientated states. These were usually bought on credit and the debts incurred were usually written off. Moreover, in the 1970s the pro-Soviet Third World states received nearly 20 per cent of the total amount of Soviet overseas assistance. This figure rose to 28 per cent between 1978 and 1982, and to a further 50 per cent in the latter half of the 1980s. The largest aid recipients (more than one half of the total aid) were Cuba and Vietnam. They were both officially classified by Moscow as socialist states and were the only two countries in the Third World that were made full members of the Council for Mutual Economic Assistance (CMEA, or COMECON). Shevardnadze publicly stated in 1988 that the Soviet Union could not maintain its 'current levels' of assistance to the Third World and, in 1989, that 'good policy costs less'.[12]

In the atmosphere of the relaxation in East–West tensions after 1986, these client states were extracting valuable resources from the Soviet Union at the cost of upsetting Washington. In the context of Moscow's geopolitical considerations, the allies, however, did bring some strategic gains to Moscow. Cuba and Vietnam sent troops to Indochina, Central America and Africa, which helped to increase Soviet power and influence in these regions. At the same time, the Kremlin was often compelled to react to unilateral actions by Cuba and Vietnam. For instance, Moscow was not consulted by Hanoi in advance about its decision to invade Cambodia in 1978. The Russians regarded the Vietnamese as secretive, obsessed with 'their narrow national interests', not sufficiently 'sincere' and not 'truly brotherly'. The conclusion of the June 1978 treaty of friendship and cooperation between the USSR and Vietnam was regarded by Hanoi as securing Moscow's 'protective shield' over Hanoi, while Moscow understood that the treaty required 'consultation' and not immediate Soviet military intervention in the event of 'any military attack' on Vietnam.[13] After Vietnam's invasion of Cambodia, the Soviet Union increased its military and naval presence in Indochina and in the South China Sea. One big strategic bonus was the use by the Soviet navy of the former American base, Cam Ranh Bay, which served also as a useful information and intelligence centre.[14]

Cuban–Soviet relations had been neither smooth nor consistent throughout their alliance. Although the Cubans depended upon Moscow's financial and military support, they fiercely maintained their independence from Soviet interference. Havana's propensity to resort to arms and to encourage violent revolutions elsewhere (one of these attempts failed in Bolivia in 1968, upsetting Moscow's plans to improve relations with Latin America) often left Moscow perplexed by the unpredictability of its Cuban ally. The relationship became closer in the 1970s, as Cuban surrogate troops were useful to the Soviet Union's efforts to advance its influence in Africa and later in Central America (Nicaragua, El Salvador and Grenada), although none of the revolutionary movements in these regions were 'of Moscow's making'.[15] In turn, these Cuban activities overseas necessitated increasing Soviet assistance to Havana and, by 1980, Moscow was spending annually $3 billion on Cuba, an amount which more than doubled by 1989. In the climate of Glasnost, Soviet officials, commentators and intellectuals increasingly criticized both the size and the utility of Soviet assistance to Cuba, Vietnam and other radical regimes in the Third World.[16]

Gorbachev's strategy was to apply pragmatism in maintaining alliance relationships, which, in his view, should be mutually beneficial. The Vietnamese were bitterly criticized in 1986 for their mismanagement of Soviet financial assistance, which amounted to $1–2 billion in that year alone. The relationship between the two became strained, as Gorbachev improved Moscow's relations with China. According to Chernyaev, the Soviet leadership did not approve, or understand, Vietnam's expansionist and anti-Chinese policies in Indochina.[17]

With Gorbachev in power, Castro launched his own version of Perestroika, but this was the reverse of Moscow's vision, since it resulted in increased control over (instead of liberating) Cuban society. The economy, which once enjoyed an annual 10 per cent growth, stagnated in the 1980s. The country, ill governed and stifled with regulations, had become 'a sadly disconsolate state'.[18] After 1986, the Soviet Union began to reduce oil exports to Cuba, adjusted the cost of Cuban sugar it purchased to the world price (instead of paying extra for it), and decreased Soviet–Cuban trade substantially. The KGB noted in early 1989 that Castro remained resolute in clinging to his Marxist-Leninist dogmas and that he dismissed Gorbachev's Perestroika as a 'betrayal of Marxism-Leninism'.[19]

Globalism

In fact, there was no cut and dried Soviet policy for the Third World. Most of Gorbachev's ideas derived from his global policy, which he applied to the problems of the Third World. Gorbachev and Shevardnadze publicly emphasized the need to tackle global problems (ecological and environmental issues, as well as poverty and economic underdevelopment), which should transcend ideological differences. For this purpose, the Soviet leadership called for the creation of a 'comprehensive international system of common security', designed to resolve regional conflicts, with the greater use of UN peacekeeping forces.[20] The issue of 'development', as Gorbachev told the UN General Assembly in December 1988, was now 'a truly universal human problem', as 'the conditions in which tens of millions of people live in a number of Third World regions are becoming a real threat to all mankind'. The implications were that, as Andropov had admitted earlier, the economic problems of the pro-Soviet regimes in the Third World were no longer 'Moscow's responsibility'.[21] By 1990, Moscow introduced more strident conditions for maintaining economic relations with Third World countries, which should in future be governed by 'the principles of mutual benefit and mutual interests'.[22]

Thus, Gorbachev's globalization of Third World problems was geared to reducing the ideological factor in the Cold War in the Third World and, in so doing, reducing the heavy burdens such conflicts imposed on the Soviet Union. Instead of admitting the limits of Soviet economic and political ability to support the poor countries in the Third World, Gorbachev resorted to a method similar to that which he employed in Europe under the concept of creating a 'common European home'. As Gorbachev encouraged East Germany to obtain more financial help from Bonn, he advised other pro-Soviet Third World countries not to sever their economic and trade ties with the West. For some Western commentators, this was designed to disguise the economic difficulties facing the Soviet Union, which the West could exploit for its own purposes. This could also be regarded as a convenient method of keeping Moscow's political influence (while the Soviet economy was being revitalized) intact, while 'allowing the West to pick up the economic bills' for the problems of the socialist bloc.[23]

Comprehensive Détente with a Nixonian Flavour

In addition to globalism, Gorbachev also resorted to the diplomacy of détente with many countries outside Europe. This policy can be seen as an attempt to reduce tensions from the top down, bearing some resemblance to Nixon's détente policy towards Beijing and Moscow in the early 1970s. Gorbachev's approach was visionary and was driven by his rather altruistic belief that the international community should cooperate closely to achieve peace, rather than to fight each other on the basis of narrowly based geopolitical or ideological considerations. In the Asia-Pacific region, Gorbachev's immediate attention turned to India, the leader of the Non-Aligned group in the Third World, which had drawn closer to the Soviet Union since the mid 1960s. After two months in the Kremlin, Gorbachev increased trade between the two countries and concluded a series of trade and arms sales agreements with India. The Soviet Union was also expanding its economic relations with the ASEAN countries (Singapore, Malaysia, Indonesia, Philippines, Thailand and, from 1985, Brunei), which were afraid of an over-mighty China and wary of Vietnamese ambitions in South-east Asia. Soviet activities did not end here, since Gorbachev made overtures to Australia, China, Japan and South Korea in order to improve Soviet relations with virtually all the major countries in the region.

Moscow's attempts to improve its relations with China predated the Gorbachev era. The new leadership pursued Soviet détente policy towards China with renewed vigour and persistence in an effort to reduce China's grievances against the Soviet Union. The Kremlin abandoned its anti-Chinese broadcast propaganda and also stopped jamming Chinese broadcasts. In 1986, at Vladivostok, Gorbachev pledged a negotiated settlement in Afghanistan, a reduction of Soviet troops along its borders with China, and support for the normalization of relations between China and Vietnam, while in 1988, at Kranovarsk in Siberia, he spoke of deepening cooperation in the Asia–Pacific region and called for tripartite talks between Beijing, Moscow and Washington.[24]

These promises were in line with China's three conditions for the normalization of relations between the two countries: Soviet withdrawal from Afghanistan, Vietnam's withdrawal from Cambodia, and the end of the Soviet military threat on the Chinese border. Gorbachev's efforts culminated in May 1989 in a summit meeting between Deng Xiaoping and Gorbachev (on the eve of the Tiananmen Square massacre), and in April 1990 the Chinese Prime Minister, Le Peng, made a return visit to Moscow.[25] The improved relationship with Moscow helped China to reduce its feeling of insecurity vis-à-vis the USSR, ended the strategic cooperation between the USA and China against 'the common Soviet problem', and removed the relative strategic importance accorded to Vietnam from the equation.[26] Gorbachev's efforts to improve Japanese–Russian relations foundered on the long-standing dispute between the two countries over the northern islands, but because of the end of the Cold War in Asia, this was now likely to become (although Japan often urged its Western partners and especially the USA to put pressure on the Soviet Union to soften its stance on the issue) a bilateral issue between Moscow and Tokyo. Similarly, Gorbachev's efforts to improve relations with China diminished North Korea's strategic leverage vis-à-vis the two Communist powers on the Korean peninsula. China and the Soviet Union further undermined the importance of North Korea by balancing their influence between South and North Korea. In 1990, the Soviet Union established diplomatic relations with South Korea, and China followed suit two years later.[27] In Latin America, the Soviet Union increased its contacts with Mexico, Brazil and Argentina to improve Moscow's position in that region.[28]

The Middle East continued to receive Moscow's attention, an area in which the Soviet Union felt it had lost strategic leverage after the Camp David Accords in the late 1970s. Here, also, Gorbachev began to loosen the Soviet Union's ties with formally pro-Soviet radical but weak regimes, and entered into broader relations with the other major regional powers. The Soviet Union restored diplomatic relations with Egypt in 1984. Gorbachev quickly re-scheduled Egyptian debts to the Soviet

Union at a time when Western creditors were demanding Egyptian domestic reforms prior to the cancellation of Cairo's debts.[29] The Soviet Union also endeavoured to reduce the fears of the Persian Gulf states about Soviet ambitions there. In 1985, Moscow established diplomatic relations with Oman and the United Arab Emirates (UAE). During the Iran–Iraq war in 1987, the Soviet Union leased three oil tankers to Kuwait at the latter's request. Since 1984, Kuwait and Jordan (recognized by the Soviet Union in 1963 and 1964, respectively) had purchased Soviet arms. The Soviet Union promised to cooperate with the Organization of Petroleum Exporting Countries (OPEC), and it re-established diplomatic relations with Saudi Arabia – a state visit took place between Moscow and Riyadh in 1987.[30]

Elsewhere in the Middle East, Gorbachev's diplomacy for peace was paying Moscow some dividends. While the Soviet Union had had a friendship treaty with Iraq since 1972, the relationship was not an easy one. Iraq was unhappy with the growing Communist influence in the country and also complained about the Soviet Union's inability to meet Iraq's increasing military and economic requirements.[31] However, relations with Iran were improving with the result that Moscow began to import Iranian crude oil in return for sending light oil products and machinery to Tehran. In the autumn of 1987, Aeroflot flights between Moscow and Tehran were resumed. This balancing act between Iraq and Iran, which had been fighting each other since 1981, was reflected by the support, for the first time, by the two superpowers for a UN resolution calling for Iran and Iraq to accept a ceasefire. Another significant action was Moscow's attempt after 1986 to re-open a dialogue with Israel, relations between the two having broken down during the 1967 Six-Day War. Between 1987 and 1988, nearly 9000 Soviet Jews were allowed to leave the Soviet Union. These developments suggested that the Soviet Union would now be unlikely to support the radical Arab states, like Syria, by providing the latter with military assistance to defeat Israel. During a state visit by President Asad to Moscow in 1987, Gorbachev pointed out to him that 'the absence of diplomatic relations between the Soviet Union and Israel "cannot be considered normal"', and in the autumn of 1991, the Soviet Union recognized Israel.[32]

Sensitivities of great power concerns

Gorbachev's emphasis on both globalism and wider détente was one way of indicating to the Soviet Union's clients that their importance had now lessened in his 'new thinking' about Soviet foreign policy. The Soviet Union had long since discovered that it possessed 'virtually no control over the sometimes unpredictable actions' of the radical regimes in Yemen, Syria and Libya. Moscow's attempts to help to resolve the infighting in Yemen (Moscow's 1979 friendship treaty with South Yemen was followed in 1984 by a similar treaty with North Yemen) was rewarded only by the eruption of civil war in 1986, which caught the Soviet Union by surprise. Yemen had been riven with terrorism and factional internal fighting for many years, which had compelled Great Britain to abandon its protectorate of Aden, an important strategic base. It was, therefore, not surprising that Gorbachev actually welcomed the unification of Yemen, which came two years after the outbreak of the civil war, and which resulted in the collapse of the Yemen Socialist

Party. This indicated that the Soviet Union was now giving less importance to those states with 'socialist orientations', in favour of trying to pacify the entire region. Gorbachev cautioned Libya for its militant actions, which, according to the Soviet leadership, merely invited American reprisals, and encouraged Syria to soften its longstanding hostility towards Yasser Arafat's PLO.[33]

However, all this did not mean that Gorbachev was abandoning the Marxist regimes out of hand. As shown earlier, the size of the Soviet Union's arms sales to the Third World was rising when Gorbachev came to power. Under Gorbachev Angola, Cuba Libya, Syria, Iraq, Vietnam and Nicaragua received fresh military supplies. Similarly, Hanoi received increased subsidies from Moscow. Syria's debts were generously re-scheduled in 1987. The Soviet Union, in cooperation with Cuba, organized a major offensive against UNITA in Angola, while Soviet military activities were also intensifying in Afghanistan in 1985 and 1986. Even minor countries like Ethiopia succeeded in getting new supplies of arms from Gorbachev in 1988, and Soviet assistance to Addis Ababa was apparently increasing well into 1989.[34]

What can we make of Gorbachev's policy towards the Third World? On the one hand, the Kremlin was clear about according a lower priority to regional conflicts. On the other hand, Moscow was expanding or strengthening its ties with almost all the major countries outside Europe. Gorbachev was advising the Soviet Union's Third World clients to strive for 'national reconciliation', but he was still providing them with arms and subsidies. This all seemed confusing and contradictory, as his personal adviser, Chernyaev, complained at the time. He lamented Gorbachev's 'vacillation between tactics and strategy', and soon after a new arms deal with Ethiopia (in April 1988), Chernyaev reminded the Soviet leader that 'Both at Politburo meetings and in public you're always urging people to make real political decisions. And here we have the same old routine: a friend asks, and we immediately give. Our arms will not change anything . . .'[35]

In the late 1980s scholars and analysts also believed that the Soviet Union was 'not abandoning' the Third World and that the old agenda still remained alive and well. While some appreciated that Gorbachev were making some new changes to Soviet policy towards the Third World, they still agreed that these were not 'necessarily signalling a retreat' from the Third World.[36] One school of thought contended that Gorbachev was 'trying to stake out a more combative position in the Third World . . . despite a desire to reduce costs over the long term'. Overall, the impression that the Soviet Union 'remained ready to advance its own interests wherever it could' echoed the views of many policy makers in Washington in the latter part of the 1980s.[37]

The Soviet Union's detached, but still active, policy in the Third World can be explained by several factors. The first factor was that the costs of sustaining its clients were not as exorbitant as was claimed by Gorbachev and Shevardnadze. Even during the height of the Soviet commitment to Afghanistan, the total amount of assistance towards the Third World accounted for only 1–2 per cent of the country's total defence expenditure. Although Gorbachev was anxious to revive the civilian economy, it could be argued that Soviet expenditure in the Third World was still of manageable proportions. It could thus be concluded that there was no urgent imperative to discard Soviet clients for purely economic reasons.[38]

Secondly, the time it took the Soviet Union to disengage from regional conflicts indicated the difficulties that Gorbachev experienced with local leaders, who were either recalcitrant (like Castro), or too weak to stabilize the situation without the help of Soviet assistance (like the PDPA in Afghanistan). Gorbachev also needed to carry the conservative wing of the Politburo with him. Moreover, the Soviet leadership did not want to be seen as imposing Kremlin decisions on pro-Soviet Third World leaders and so he took a roundabout way of achieving his aims. His approach was top-down – to create overall détente with the West and to use this to make East–West rivalries in the Third World redundant. This also required Washington to abandon competition, but this was not easy to secure. As has been discussed in previous chapters, Washington had long held a sceptical view of Gorbachev's reforms and it was still felt in spring 1989 that the Soviet Union 'aspired to become a more competitive power'.[39] All this suggested it would take time to end the East–West competition in the Third World.

Thirdly, it is important to remember that while Gorbachev's approach to the Third World was less confrontational and less expensive than that of his predecessor, there was no prescription for a total 'retreat' from the Third World. On the contrary, as in the case of his domestic policy, or his concept of a 'common European home', Gorbachev was very much interested in reviving the Soviet Union as a country commensurate with the status of a great power in modern times, and which could work with, and not against, the USA and other Western powers. In fact, it was likely that he wanted to maintain as much Soviet power and influence as possible in the developing world. He believed 'undoubtedly' that 'the Soviet Union and the United States are two powerful states with vast interests', who were, therefore, 'especially responsible for the future of the world'.[40]

Thus, the Soviet Union did not want to relinquish a degree of 'political leverage' over its client states. Arms sales in particular constituted a lucrative source of income comprising 15–20 per cent of the Soviet Union's total earnings of hard currency.[41] These implicit and explicit benefits had served, in the past, to nurture Soviet prestige and influence (if not control) over regional politics and these were most difficult to abandon even if the Soviet Union found it had to sustain the increasing demands of its client states, even if Gorbachev preferred peaceful compromise and sought to press ahead with reconciliation with the West.

By the end of 1988, the volume of arms sales had decreased substantially by 47 per cent. The continuation of Moscow's supply of arms to its clients, like Nicaragua and Afghanistan, unnerved Washington, and Gorbachev was, in any case, morally against 'any armed conflict' which 'can poison the atmosphere of the entire region'.[42] There were also other problems with Soviet arms transfers. Many – former or regular – clients (Egypt, Algeria, Syria, Iraq and South Yemen) complained about the poor quality of Soviet arms, services and technical support, and became disenchanted with the 'intrusive and overbearing manner of Soviet advisers'. After the mid 1980s, a sharp decline in the price of oil in many oil producing states in the Middle East, the largest purchasers of Soviet arms, reduced the volume of Soviet military exports. At the same time, the market for arms sales became competitive, as many Western and other Third World arms suppliers (including India, Brazil and Libya) were also looking for buyers. Moreover, Third World states often preferred 'offset trade' to save the cost of actually buying arms, including barter trade (Libya's oil for Soviet arms) or reciprocal investment. Alternatively, they wanted the Soviet Union to grant 'direct' offsets, meaning that the Soviet Union would transfer 'manufacturing technology' to the recipient states to produce weapons locally, at the risk of 'compromising key Soviet military technology', or sometimes turning the purchasers of Soviet arms into competitors (like China).[43] All this indicated that successful arms providers had to have sophisticated and modern production facilities, capable of meeting the increasingly diverse demands from prospective purchasers. Thus, the Soviet Union was increasingly finding it difficult to translate arms sales into influence over its client states, let alone securing large amounts of hard currency.

Overall, behind the new thinking, Gorbachev's dealing with Third World countries exhibited 'a profound sensitivity to the traditional concerns of great powers'.[44] As in Europe, Gorbachev employed a pan-Third World policy, which eventually helped to produce international cooperation, especially cooperation with the USA, to pave the way for Soviet disengagement from the key major regional conflicts. The demise of East–West rivalries in the Third World came slowly but steadily, and this was no less painful a process than the end of the Cold War in Europe, or the end of the superpower arms race.

AFGHANISTAN

The Outbreak of the Soviet–Afghan War

There was nothing clearer than the case of the Soviet war in Afghanistan to demonstrate how the leaders of a great power easily assumed that its military intervention could resolve a crisis quickly, but soon realized its mistake. By then, however, the situation would have deteriorated to such an extent that it would have been impossible to obtain terms of disengagement which would have been acceptable to all the parties involved. The outcome would be a long drawn out military intervention without any clear prospect of victory. These are, perhaps, the main reasons why the Soviet war in Afghanistan has often been compared to the American war in Vietnam. In the early 1980s, a KGB general privately expressed his concern: 'Afghanistan is our Vietnam . . . We are bogged down in a war we cannot win and cannot abandon.'[45] From the outset, Gorbachev was sceptical about Brezhnev's 'hopeless military adventure' in Afghanistan and objected to the stepping up of Soviet military commitments there. Coming to power as General Secretary, Gorbachev decided to end the war in Afghanistan as quickly as possible, but Soviet disengagement from that country did not materialize until January 1992.[46] Meanwhile, the war had become international, involving not only the two superpowers, but also Pakistan, China, Saudi Arabia and other states.

At the time of the Soviet invasion in December 1979, Brezhnev assumed that 'it would be over in a few weeks' time'. The main objective was to overthrow a corrupt and unpopular leader, Amin, and install a moderate socialist government led by

Babrak Karmal, who had been a KGB operative since the 1950s. The new government could then, it was hoped, stabilize the country and allow the Red Army to withdraw.[47] These initial assumptions went badly wrong. The Afghan people did not take kindly to the introduction of Soviet forces, viewing the new Afghan leader, Karmal, as a Soviet 'protégé'. As a result, the Karmal government became even more unpopular than its notorious predecessor. Afghan resistance soon spread across the country, where the Red Army soon encountered the Mujahidin, or 'the combat formations of the government's opposition'.[48] Prior to the invasion, Moscow had expected that the Afghan army would undertake most of the fighting, but Karmal almost immediately requested that the Red Army engage with the Mujahidin, as he doubted the loyalty of his army. The number of regular Afghan troops dwindled rapidly as a result of high desertion rates and, by the end of 1980, it had only 35,000 personnel, compared with 150,000 in 1979. The initial fighting was conventional in nature, but the Mujahidin then changed their tactics to guerrilla warfare to conserve their resources and maximize their strength in the face of large Soviet conventional formations. This irregular warfare put the Red Army at a disadvantage, as the Soviets were unprepared to deal with small and 'exceedingly mobile groups of Mujahidin using manoeuvre tactics'.[49]

This outcome spoke volumes about Moscow's underestimation of the scale and intensity of the anti-Soviet Islamic forces. It can be argued that the potential base for a socialist state had already become too tenuous to be realistic in Afghanistan by the summer of 1979, and even before the Soviet invasion of Afghanistan.[50] In late January 1980, the gravity of the situation led the Kremlin's inner circle to discuss the prospect of an early withdrawal from Afghanistan. Moreover, the ruling circle in the Kremlin (Gorbachev included), who were excluded from the Afghan decision and had only heard about it on the radio, were critical about the Soviet invasion.[51] In early 1981, the Soviet Union agreed to seek a peace settlement under UN auspices, and talks began in Geneva in June 1982. However, a number of factors contributed to the prolongation of the Soviet–Afghan war, prior to the thaw in superpower relations between Reagan and Gorbachev.

The Internationalization of the Soviet–Afghan War

First of all, the Mujahidin or Afghan resistance groups were by no means a unified organization. They consisted of numerous factions, with often different ideological, religious and ethnic orientations. The peculiarities and complexities of the Mujahidin presented the Soviet Union with an enormous challenge, described by the Soviet military leadership as an 'unusual enemy for the Soviets'.[52] Part of this difficulty was rooted in the history of Afghanistan, a predominantly Muslim and multiethnic country. The dominant minorities were the Pushtuns (42 per cent of the Afghan population before 1979), who lived in the south and east of Afghanistan and who had links with their fellow Pushtuns in Pakistan. The Pushtuns had been divided by the Durand Line set up by the British in the 19th century. The Pushtun-led Afghan nationalism, in turn, fed Pakistan's hostility towards Kabul and, as a result, Afghanistan became closer to India, an arch enemy of Pakistan. The minorities in Afghanistan included

Tajiks, Uzbeks, Hazaras and Turkmen. The majority of Afghans followed the orthodox Sunni form of Islam, while the Hazaras of the central mountain areas belonged to the minority Shiite Islam.[53]

The Mujahidin were anti-Soviet and anti-Karmal, but were divided about the future of Afghanistan: some moderate Mujahidin wanted to build an Islamic state with the restoration of the Afghan monarchy, while others envisaged a state based on more radical and fundamentalist concepts. The Afghan fundamentalists, invariably influenced by the pan-Islamic ideology, which had originated in Egypt or had been imported from other radical Muslim groups in Saudi Arabia, were small in number in the early 1970s. Most of them escaped to Pakistan where they began to forge links with Pakistani fundamentalists and Pakistani intelligence agencies, both of whom were hostile to the then Pushtun-dominated Kabul regime. The rise of Communism in Afghanistan after 1978 and the success of the pan-Islamic revolution in Iran in 1979, provided these exiled Afghan fundamentalist groups with a 'golden opportunity' to expand their organizations within the Afghan refugee camps in the border region of Pakistan, with the help of Pakistan, Saudi Arabia, Iran and other fundamentalist groups in the Middle East. Since 1978, the Carter administration also began to support the Afghan resistance movement, in an effort to contain the Communization of Afghanistan.[54]

With the Soviet invasion of Afghanistan, the USA sought unsuccessfully to fuse the Afghan resistance groups into a coherent organization. In June 1981, the Mujahidin formed the Islamic Union of Afghan Mujahidin (IUAM), but within a year IUAM had split into two unions, one consisting of seven groups of Muslim fundamentalists (IUAM-7) and the other made up of three traditionalist Muslim groups (IUAM-3). In May 1985, these two unions joined together within the IUAM framework and became an organization called the 'Peshawar Seven', consisting of seven different quasi-political parties, each with its own headquarters and secretariat.[55] The Mujahidin leadership directed military operations inside Afghanistan from their headquarters in Pakistan, with the Islamic committee as a link between the parties and the local populations. Despite the name, Islamic Union, these resistance organizations, divided by internal wrangling and ideological differences, often resorted to armed conflict against each other. Moreover, the leaders of these organizations carved out their own spheres of influence in Afghanistan 'sharing nothing in common but hatred and lack of trust'.[56]

US intervention also contributed to the intensification of the Afghan–Soviet war. Washington organized multinational assistance for the Mujahidin, which was channelled through the Pakistan army, acting as the key 'conduit of external aid'. During the last days of the Carter administration, the CIA began to transfer small arms to the Mujahidin. By the summer of 1980, these transfers included 'all manner of weapons and military support'. During the pre-Reagan years, the CIA's operations were somewhat restrained, as its director, Stansfield Turner, had moral qualms about covert operations in Afghanistan. At that time, Saudi Arabia (which was then providing more funds than the USA to the Afghan rebels), Egypt, Pakistan, Iran and China were also supporting anti-Communist Afghan resistance groups.[57] President Reagan brought into his administration energetic, focused and hardline individuals, such as William Casey, the new CIA director, and Alexander Haig, who wanted to raise the stakes on the Soviet forces fighting in Afghanistan. Casey had come to the agency determined to 'wage war against the Soviet Union' and, as a result, he was intent on upgrading the Afghan covert assistance programme.[58]

Not quite foreseen at the time, the Soviet invasion of Afghanistan helped to turn the USA into the major benefactor of the Islamic fundamentalists and of those countries which offered safe havens for the Mujahidin. A controversial deal with Saudi Arabia for the purchase of US Airborne Warning and Control System planes was finally struck in April 1981, at the cost of Israel's security interests, in return for Saudi Arabia's agreement to expand its assistance to help anti-Communist insurgents in Afghanistan and Nicaragua.[59] Pakistan had been an international pariah since 1977 when its army, headed by a notorious general, Muhammad Zia ul-Haq, took over the government. Nearly two years later in 1979, the general executed a former Pakistani Prime Minister, Zulfiqar Ali Bhutto. The general was also known for his fanatical support of the 'relatively unpopular intolerant fringe of Muslim fundamentalism', although he did not take the same road as Khomeini did in Iran, by turning the country into a fundamentalist state ruled by Islamic law.[60] All this was changed as a result of the Soviet invasion of Afghanistan. In the eyes of Washington's policy makers, Pakistan's standing as the Mujahidin's front line state was enhanced, while Zia also needed American help to protect Pakistan's security against the Soviet Union and India. However, when the Carter administration offered $400 million in aid, the general dismissed it as too small. Zia's fortunes improved significantly with the change of the administration in the USA. Reagan generously rewarded Pakistan with a $3.2 billion aid programme, in return for Islamabad's steadfast support of the Mujahidin.[61]

During the initial years, however, despite Casey's lobbying, the CIA did not obtain much funding from Congress. There were mixed signals in Washington as to how far the USA should push the Soviet Union in Afghanistan. General Zia was concerned about provoking the Soviet Union too much, fearing Soviet retaliation against Pakistan, and he was reluctant to increase the current level of arms supplies to the Mujahidin, that is, 'to keep the pot boiling, but not boil over'.[62] The CIA continued to observe 'plausible deniability' in transferring arms to the Mujahidin, and the bulk of American-funded weapons was provided by Egypt. In 1980, the CIA gave funds to Cairo to produce Soviet-type weapons for the Mujahidin's use. China was also providing the Afghan rebels with Soviet-type weapons, for which the USA was paying about $100 million per year.[63]

However, after 1983, the Soviet Union began to mount effective offensive campaigns with the use of helicopters.[64] This renewed Soviet aggression helped to galvanize the US administration and Congress into providing more support to the Mujahidin. A group of influential Senators – Republicans and Democrats – became stanch critics of the Reagan administration's inability to provide enough assistance to the Afghan rebels 'to win' the war. The driving force among them was Representative Charles Wilson from East Texas, who hated the Soviets. Wilson, a senior Democrat on the Defence Appropriations Subcommittee of the House Appropriation Committee, was ideally positioned to secure favourable votes for bigger funding for the CIA, which now received $120 million, a sharp rise from its usual $50 million per year. This increased amount, however, appeared insignificant compared with the massive aid Moscow was providing to the Kabul regime – about $1 billion or more annually. For Congress, Afghanistan (unlike 'the moral ambiguities of Nicaragua') offered 'a model case for anti-Communist action'.[65] After 1984, Congress generously funded America's Afghan programme, which rose to $600 million by 1987.[66]

As more money poured into the CIA, American clandestine assistance to the Mujahidin became more ambitious. Pakistan was persuaded to open up a 'delivery route' for more weapons and supplies, much-needed and effective anti-aircraft weapons were sought from Britain, France and Switzerland, and in 1986 came the decision to send US-made 'Stingers'. The USA orchestrated an international coalition of the willing, to share intelligence activities with the UK, Pakistan, Saudi Arabia, Egypt and China. With the help of the Pakistan Inter-services Intelligence Directorate (ISI), the CIA set up Radio Free Afghanistan, which broadcast from Pakistan, recruiting foreign volunteers to the Mujahidin and also training them in urban sabotage and terrorist operations, mainly in Pakistan, but also in Iran, Egypt and China.[67] Casey's CIA also persuaded the ISI to launch propaganda activities, such as the distribution of copies of the Koran inside the Soviet Union across the Afghan borders of Central Asia, to incite unrest among Islamic fundamentalists in Uzbekistan and Tajikistan.

As for the distribution of American aid, the ISI was given broad responsibility, which allowed Islamabad to give preferential treatment to the radical fundamentalist groups at the cost of more moderate local tribal leaders. Moreover, the Pakistani army allegedly kept some of the weapons for itself, instead of distributing them to the Mujahidin. Not surprisingly, the ISI and the CIA often suffered from 'endless bickering . . . vying for influence as to the distribution of the aid'. The ISI's treasury 'began to swell with CIA and Saudi Arabian subsidies', which encouraged 'pervasive corruption and smuggling in the aid pipeline'.[68]

By 1991, the USA on its own spent more than $2 billion on the Mujahidin, while the Saudis spent nearly half of that amount, most of which was funnelled to the radical fundamentalists.[69] Weinberger recalled, 'they were not very nice people . . . but we had this terrible problem of making choices'.[70] In the climate of fighting the Soviet 'evil' empire, it was important for the USA to encourage the Soviet Union to 'stay and bleed' in Afghanistan by financing and strengthening the Afghan 'freedom fighters'. In March 1985, when Gorbachev was elected General Secretary, the USA made the decision to step up its covert operations to defeat the Soviet Union in Afghanistan. Washington's goal had now shifted away from 'increasing the costs to the Soviets to trying to win'.[71]

The American decision to escalate the war in Afghanistan was hardly likely to further the UN-backed peace negotiations (led by Diego Cordovez, UN Under-Secretary General for Special Political Affairs) between the Kabul government and Pakistan. Moreover, the two delegations did not want to meet face to face, and the negotiations had to be carried out with the UN mediators shuttling between the two capitals, Kabul and Islamabad or (after August 1984) between the rooms occupied by the two parties at the UN Headquarters in Geneva.[72] Andropov wanted to secure peace in Afghanistan, but not unconditionally.

In the spring of 1983, the Politburo assessed the Afghan situation based on a recent fact-finding trip to Kabul by high ranking party officials. Andrei Gromyko, the Foreign Minister, admitted gloomily that the situation in Afghanistan continued to be 'difficult': the number of Afghan resistance fighters was 'not decreasing' and, despite a recent increase in the size of the Afghan army, the existing Communist regime was unable to control the countryside. Andropov responded that the Soviet Union 'cannot back off' as '[w]e are fighting against American imperialism'. The Politburo agreed that the Soviet Union would, therefore, continue to assist the Karmal government financially, to help it to negotiate with Pakistan from a position of strength.[73]

In fact, the Pakistani leadership wanted to destroy the Communist regime in Kabul and install a regime friendly to Pakistan. As a result, Pakistan was easily persuaded by the Reagan administration to increase further its help to the Afghan insurgents. In Kabul, President Karmal was by no means a mere 'puppet' of the Kremlin and he was unwilling to accept all the concessions demanded by 'his own diplomats under Soviet pressure', such as including non-Communists in his government. Here, too, was an obstacle to any early political settlement.[74]

The situation in Afghanistan was now bleak. The Kabul government, installed by Moscow in December 1979, remained fragile, and was vulnerable to urban guerrilla warfare through sporadic assassinations of high ranking Communist officials and the bombing of government buildings. Despite Moscow's pressure for the Party to remain united, the regime was constantly being undermined by internal factional fighting. KGB officers working in Afghanistan 'slept with pistols and machine-guns by their beds' to deal with 'rebels' night-time attacks'.[75] In the cities the anti-government resistance groups formed 'a diverse network of very clandestine cells' and, to counter their activities, the Afghanistan intelligence services (KHAD), the KGB's offspring, was established in June 1980 as 'a department within the Prime Minister's office'. The KHAD, trained and organized by KGB officers, 'revived the horrors of its Stalinist past'. The agency became notorious, as the findings of Amnesty International and Human Rights Watch demonstrated, for torturing prisoners, often in the 'presence of Soviet officers directing interrogations'.[76] The number of KHAD operatives increased substantially from 800 in 1980 to 16,650 in 1982, more than half of its staff coming from the PDPA. Apart from torturing its prisoners, its activities ranged from armed struggle against the insurgents, covert operations (such as hijacking a Pakistani airliner in March 1980), the formation of various underground organizations to uproot the anti-government groups, foreign intelligence activities against Pakistan, Iran and other countries, and the collection of 'preemptive information' on the Afghan émigrés from CIA's operatives, other informants in China and the Islamic countries.[77]

From the Soviet perspective, the war on the ground made little headway, but between 1983 and 1985 (before the advent of Gorbachev) the Soviet Union mounted a series of fierce offensive campaigns against the Mujahidin. By then, the number of Red Army troops in Afghanistan had risen from an initial 50,000 to 108,000. The Red Army introduced a heliborne special (Spetsnaz) counterinsurgency force and adopted a Soviet version of 'search and destroy' missions to find, and destroy, the Mujahidin's regional hideouts and to clear and hold the border areas adjacent to Afghanistan, to cut off the Mujahidin's supply routes to and from Pakistan. Despite efforts to prevent the exodus of Afghan refugees (who were the main source of Mujahidin recruitment), nearly 5 million Afghans left the country during the six years of Soviet intervention and by 1985 the Red Army was encountering greater numbers of Mujahidin guerrillas.[78]

Gorbachev's Plan for Disengagement

By the time Gorbachev came to power, the stakes in Afghanistan were high for both sides (the Soviet Union and the US–Pakistan coalition), thus ensuring that an early settlement was most unlikely. Gorbachev initially escalated the war by mounting the largest offensive operation so far against Mujahidin resistance bases close to the Pakistani border. Moscow also provided ever increasing amounts of weapons to the Afghan army. The military escalation reflected the fact that the Politburo remained divided on the issue,[79] but in October 1985 Gorbachev persuaded his officials to agree, in principle, to the Soviet Union's disengagement from Afghanistan when it had secured 'an independent, neutral, and non-aligned government' in Kabul. At the 27th Party Congress, he described the Afghan war as 'a bleeding wound', and expressed his intention of withdrawing Soviet troops in the 'near future', thereby placing the new Soviet policy for Afghanistan on the domestic as well as on the international agenda.[80] In July 1986, in a speech at Vladivostok, Gorbachev announced Moscow's willingness to reduce Soviet troops in the Far East, Afghanistan and Mongolia. Behind the scenes, Gorbachev also pressed the Karmal regime to create a broader based coalition government, but when this failed to materialize, he replaced Karmal with Mohammed Najibullah (or Comrade Najib) as General Party Secretary in May 1986. Najib, more energetic and forceful, was a former head of the notorious KHAD, and was distrusted even by his own Parcham faction of the Afghan Communist Party. However, Najib was protected by KGB agents in Afghanistan and was prepared to go along with Gorbachev's peace plans. Not surprisingly, however, Najib's attempts to achieve national reconciliation with the non-Communist factions faced formidable odds. Moreover, Gorbachev told the Kabul regime that in future it would have to take more responsibility for fighting the Afghan rebels as a means of reducing Moscow's burdens – so-called Afghanization. In 1987, Najib announced a new constitution and plans for a coalition government, but the Kremlin was becoming increasingly impatient with his slow progress towards achieving these goals.[81]

Between 1985 and 1987, Washington continued to doubt the seriousness of Gorbachev's intention to leave Afghanistan. While the USA was aware that the Afghan war had not been Gorbachev's responsibility, the recent Soviet deployment of air assault helicopters increased pressures in Washington to provide the Mujahidin with more effective weapons on the ground. In March 1986, the Reagan administration decided to equip the Mujahidin with the Stinger, an American-made shoulder-held anti-aircraft missile. The Stinger decision was controversial: the Pentagon feared that America's latest military technology must be compromised if the Soviet Union obtained it, while the CIA warned Reagan that it would lose its 'plausible deniability' if a Stinger was captured, thus making the war seem to be one between the two superpowers, rather than one between 'Moscow and the Afghan people'. Officials in the State Department were worried that the introduction of the Stinger might provoke Moscow too much and undermine efforts to improve East–West relations. However, Casey and Shultz had other ideas. Both believed that 'the only way to bring about a Soviet withdrawal' was to 'increase the military pressure against Soviet troops and the Kabul regime they were supporting'.[82]

Scholars continue to debate whether the Stingers contributed to the Soviet decision to withdraw from Afghanistan. The simple answer to this is no, as we now know that Gorbachev had already secured the Politburo's agreement to withdraw in the autumn of 1985, well before America's decision to introduce the Stingers into the Afghan battlefield. We also know that the military impact of Stinger missiles was rather mixed: a Soviet commander claimed that heavy Chinese anti-aircraft guns had more deadly effects on Soviet aircraft than the Stinger missiles, although Soviet pilots had frequently to change their altitudes to avoid the Stingers, thus reducing somewhat their military effectiveness.[83] In psychological and political terms, one may find a more nuanced answer in Moscow. Gorbachev felt that, despite his hints about Moscow's forthcoming disengagement from Afghanistan, the USA had increased its military interference (the Stingers were part of this) there. It appeared to the Soviet leader that the USA had decided upon the 'goal of obstructing a settlement in the Afghanistan war'. Referring to the Stingers, Gorbachev bluntly told Shultz at a meeting in April 1987 that US policy now was to 'put sticks in the spokes'.[84] Thus, the Stingers did have an indirect impact on the delay in the formulation of Gorbachev's withdrawal plans from Afghanistan.

What were the implications of Gorbachev's disengagement plan? The decision to disengage was closely connected with Moscow's vision of a post-Soviet Afghanistan. Given that it shared 2000 km of its borders with Afghanistan, Gorbachev wanted the USA to recognize that Afghanistan was a special case, in terms of Moscow's security concerns. He was also mindful of the hatred of the Mujahidin for the Soviet Union – he told the Politburo in May 1987 that they 'will long remember how we were killing them'.[85] The issue of credibility concerned Moscow as well. The USSR's disengagement should not appear to be scuttling from Afghanistan, as 'the United States did from Vietnam'. Nor should a Soviet withdrawal turn Afghanistan into a 'slaughterhouse' if the Najib regime there disintegrated. Finally, Moscow obviously did not want to see Najib replaced by an American-led government in Afghanistan.[86]

It was one thing for Gorbachev to lecture Najib about how he should handle the situation, but it was another to achieve Moscow's political objectives in Afghanistan, as the country had no 'sense of a homeland'. However, there appeared to be no one but Najib with whom the Soviet Union could work, and Gorbachev wondered whether the Mujahidin should be 'more aggressively' invited to share 'power' with the current Kabul government. There was no simple solution, but Gorbachev told the Politburo in May 1987 that 'it would be a mistake if we simply cleared out of there'. The Soviet Union wanted to see Afghanistan stabilized under a pro-Soviet government, since it was 'impossible to continue this war endlessly'.[87]

Just like the American dilemma in Vietnam, the Soviet Union exhibited a 'profound sensibility to the traditional concerns of great powers', who wanted to extricate themselves from commitments without appearing to be conceding defeat. The end of superpower rivalry in the Third World should be, in Gorbachev's view, a joint task shared by both superpowers. In Afghanistan, Gorbachev, therefore, insisted that Soviet Union's withdrawal would require the discontinuation of external assistance (led by the USA) to the Mujahidin – a step that the USA was not prepared to take. Gorbachev soon found that his new thinking proved to be rather naive.

Why should the USA help the Soviet Union to exit Afghanistan with honour? Why should the USA agree with Moscow that its support for the Mujahidin was the 'core of the problem'? Shultz dismissed these assumptions as 'nonsense', as the USA was 'responding to' the Soviet invasion of, and armed presence in, Afghanistan.[88] True, in December 1985 the US Deputy Secretary of State inadvertently gave his blessing to the Geneva peace talks, agreeing with Moscow that US aid would cease 'at the beginning of Soviet military withdrawal'. At that time, Washington did not give much weight to the UN peace negotiations and there appeared to be no serious discussion on the subject at the highest level.[89] What the Reagan administration first wanted from Moscow was that it translated into reality its pledges (oft-promised) to withdraw from Afghanistan. As it turned out, the Soviet Union did not make any clear public announcement on this until February 1988. Even at the time of the Washington summit in December 1987, Gorbachev appeared to raise his conditions for a Soviet withdrawal: 'from the very start', asserted the Soviet leader, 'the process should be tied to national reconciliation and the creation of a coalition government'. This might take years to achieve and Washington, therefore, believed that the Soviet Union was determined to continue to assist the current Kabul regime.[90]

The Settlement, 1988–91

Once the Soviet Union was definitely committed to its withdrawal plan in the early months of 1988, the USA insisted unequivocally that the end of American assistance to the Afghan rebels must coincide with the end of Moscow's assistance to the Kabul regime, and not just with the withdrawal of the Red Army from Afghanistan. Shultz correctly calculated that Moscow was in 'no position to resist the US demand for symmetry on arms supply'.[91] The Soviet Union felt 'betrayed' by the USA, but there was no going back on its withdrawal plan, as the continuing occupation of Afghanistan had become a huge obstacle to the Kremlin's credibility at home, and to the acceptance of Gorbachev's new thinking abroad.[92] On 14 April 1988, the peace accords on Afghanistan were signed in Geneva between Afghanistan and Pakistan, and guaranteed by the USA and the USSR. These paved the way for a Soviet troop withdrawal, which began on 15 May 1988 and was completed by the deadline, 15 February 1989.

The 1988 accords did not bring peace to troubled Afghanistan. Nor did it end supplies of superpower armaments to the various warring factions until January 1992. Against both the CIA's and the KGB's estimates, the Najib regime survived the withdrawal of the Red Army until April 1992, but, by then, the Soviet Union had collapsed.[93] After 1988, the Kabul government hoped to take advantage of the divisions within the Mujahidin by appealing to the Afghan public using the rhetoric of Afghan nationalism, by abandoning Marxist socialist doctrine, and by including non-Party members in the government. The key to Najib's survival was for the Soviet Union to continue its supplies to Kabul. Although Gorbachev rejected Najib's request in January 1989 for the despatch of a Soviet brigade to Kandahar, the Soviet Union kept up deliveries of some 700 tonnes of supplies a day – by installing an 'air-bridge unrivalled since the days of the Berlin blockade'. Moscow also supplied air defence capabilities, including SCUD missiles, to the Afghan government, and altogether the total amount of aid increased to some $3.6 billion a year, a considerable expenditure for a country which was struggling to feed the Soviet population during the deepening economic crisis.[94] When the Bush administration came to power, Afghanistan was no longer an issue. Washington's attention had shifted to the First Gulf War and the fall of the Berlin Wall, while superpower relations had steadily improved after the Malta summit in December 1989. By the autumn of 1991, Moscow and Washington were able to agree that both sides should halt assistance to Afghanistan and support the UN's attempts to install a transitional broad-based government. This superpower agreement came into effect in January 1992 and Yeltsin, as one of his first actions as Russian President, stopped all aid to Afghanistan. It ended the superpowers' 'great game' in Afghanistan, but the civil war there continued.

ANGOLA AND AFRICA

Eight months after the conclusion of the Afghanistan accords in December 1988, the world witnessed the signature of the Brazzaville protocol on Angola and Namibia. The protocol marked an important step towards ending the ongoing Angolan civil war (see chapter 7). As with the war in Afghanistan, the Brazzaville protocol did not settle the Angolan conflict immediately, and it was not until May 1991 that the superpowers agreed to cease all assistance to the respective warring factions: the MPLA under the leadership of Jose Eduardo Dos Santos, backed by Cubans and Soviets, opposed to UNITA led by Dr Jonas Savimbi and supported by South Africa and the USA. While in Afghanistan the Soviet Union was directly militarily involved, in Angola the main fighting units were Cubans and South Africans. The US Congress found it easy to justify the appropriation of funds for Afghanistan on the grounds that the USA was fighting Soviet imperialism, but the administration had little success in extracting funds from Congress to support its protégés in Angola and Nicaragua.[95] In the Soviet–Afghan war, the USA was supported by international opinion, but in the Angolan conflict, the USA and South Africa were the only main supporters of Savimbi's UNITA, while the African National Congress (which the USA regarded as pro-Communist), the

United Nations, and most of America's Western European allies all backed the Angolan government set up by the MPLA. Indeed, Africa always remained low on America's international agenda, except in the Cold War context, as in the case of US involvement in the crisis in Congo in the early 1960s. In the 1970s, Congress's interest in Africa, despite the outbreak of the Angolan civil war, was almost 'non existent'. Even in the reinvigorated Cold War atmosphere of the 1980s, the Reagan administration's association with South Africa in Angola, given Pretoria's policy of apartheid, was not easily accepted, either by the international community or by Congress. In December 1984, the Anglican Bishop Desmond Tutu branded the USA's lukewarm policy towards South Africa as 'immoral, evil, and un-Christian'.[96]

Within Africa, Angola occupied a prominent place in the Reagan Doctrine, as opposed to Mozambique or Ethiopia. In Mozambique there were no Cuban troops, although Cuba provided some economic and military assistance. The Reagan administration sought to persuade Mozambique, through diplomacy, to loosen its ties with Moscow/Cuba, and in this it was encouraged by Mrs Thatcher's Britain. To Shultz's annoyance, the CIA was pursuing its own agenda in rolling back the Soviet surrogate states in Africa, and was encouraging South Africa to provide covert assistance to the Mozambique National Resistance (RENAMO).[97] In September 1985, President Samora Machel of Mozambique visited the White House, where Machel impressed Reagan with his jokes about the Soviet Union and Communism. Reagan 'loved nothing better', and this strengthened Shultz's confidence in making Mozambique an American friend and to 'take him [Machel] away from the Soviets'.[98] By the mid 1980s, the Cuban troops had withdrawn from Ethiopia and the country kept a low profile in the Reagan Doctrine.

Angola was different, partly because of the sheer numbers of Cuban troops involved (some 40,000 in the mid 1980s). Moreover, the Angolan civil war became entangled with the Namibian issue. Namibia, the former German colony of South West Africa and Angola's neighbour in the south, was governed by South Africa. However, South Africa's mandate over Namibia had been in dispute since the end of the Second World War and, in 1971, the International Court of Justice and the UN both upheld the verdict that South Africa's occupation of Namibia was illegal. South Africa was asked to leave Namibia.[99] This sparked off a liberation movement in Namibia, led by the South West Africa People's Organization (SWAPO), and the Ovambo people 'who straddled the border between Namibia and Angola' and who supported SWAPO. Before Angola's independence in 1975, Portugal and South Africa had cooperated in undertaking 'search and destroy' missions against SWAPO insurgents operating from south-eastern Angola. After Angola's independence in 1975, South Africa became friendly with Savimbi's UNITA; UNITA helped South Africa by preventing SWAPO from entering Namibia from Angola, in return for Pretoria's military assistance to UNITA's cause in Angola. All this pushed SWAPO into siding with the Cubans and the MPLA government in Luanda, Angola. The two conflicts in Angola and Namibia thus became fused in the early 1980s.[100]

In the early part of the 1980s, the UN sought, unsuccessfully, to achieve peace in southern Africa. The 1975 Congressional ban on assisting anti-Communist

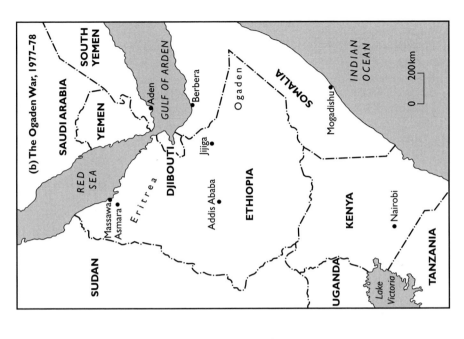

(b) The Ogaden War, 1977–78

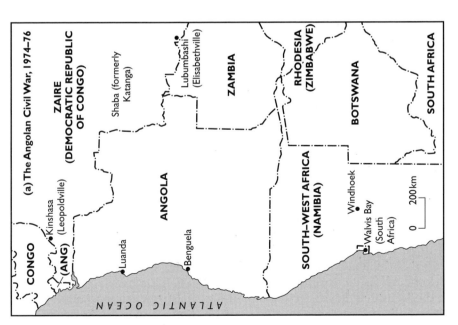

(a) The Angolan Civil War, 1974–76

5. Cold War in Africa

forces in Angola still remained in force at this stage and, as a result, the USA became involved in finding a diplomatic solution to the Angola–Namibia–South Africa imbroglio. Assistant Secretary of State, Chet Crocker, was charged with this task. The US approach was to link the Cuban withdrawal from Angola to the independence of Namibia. By 1984, the South African government had agreed to withdraw its troops from Angola, if the Cubans and MPLA ceased to support SWAPO's attacks on Namibia.[101]

When Gorbachev came to power in 1985, the issue became even more divisive. The new Soviet leader encouraged the African warring factions to seek national reconciliation, while at the same time the Soviet Union appeared to intensify its military role in the Angolan civil war against UNITA. In the summer of 1985, MPLA went on the offensive, forcing UNITA to retreat. It was reported that Soviet advisers were closely monitoring the operation with 40,000 Cuban troops (the number had risen from 17,000 in the early 1980s) supporting the MPLA's campaign.[102] Gorbachev's strategy of negotiating while fighting (as in Afghanistan and also in Nicaragua) had one crucial outcome in Angola – a closer US engagement. In August 1985, Congress finally agreed to repeal the Clark Amendments (which the Reagan administration had been urging since 1981), thereby transferring the USA from a 'bystander' to a major military supplier in the Angolan civil war.[103] Although the amount of US assistance was much smaller (about $250 million) than that being provided to the Mujahidin ($2 billion in total by 1991), the USA began to send Stinger missiles and other weapons to UNITA. South Africa was also sending more troops to support UNITA's efforts. Shultz and the CIA both believed that Stinger missiles played a significant role in reversing the tide of war in favour of UNITA.[104]

In 1986, Reagan's policy of constructive engagement with South Africa was called into question when, in August, Congress passed bills imposing comprehensive economic sanctions against South Africa, as a result of its continuing apartheid. Reagan vetoed the bill. However, Congress overrode this veto, for the first time since it had overridden Nixon's veto against the 1973 War Powers Resolution. Meanwhile, MPLA and the Cubans mounted another offensive in August 1987, but UNITA, helped by South African troops and American weapons, defeated their enemies in the autumn in the 'largest battle of the 12-year conflict'.[105]

The escalation of the Angolan civil war was becoming intolerable to all the parties involved: South African's lengthy intervention was taking a severe toll, with rising numbers of 'white casualties'; Angola's defence expenditure and debts were also increasing, while its dependence on Cuban/Soviet military tutelage isolated Angola from 'Western economies and financial institutions'. Despite Cuba's heavy investment in Angola, the war was increasingly seen in Havana to be a 'quagmire'.[106] Meanwhile, Shultz was pushing Moscow to exert pressure on the Cubans to withdraw. The Kremlin now admitted that there seemed to be no military solution in Angola, but Cuba attributed the defeat in 1987 to the failure of Soviet strategic planning. Castro was apparently opposed to another military campaign in 1987, but he thought that the Soviet military wanted a new offensive, which in the end cost Cuba well over 60,000 lives.

Castro's bitterness against the Soviet Union suggested to the US negotiator, Croker, that there existed room for an accommodation if the Cubans could be persuaded to agree to it.[107]

In January 1988, the Cubans decided to withdraw their troops from Angola, if South Africa granted independence to Namibia. By the summer of that year, the basic framework for the Angola–Namibia accords were agreed. However, Cuba's slow pace of withdrawal became a 'stubborn' obstacle, while MPLA had expected, incorrectly, that the USA would cut off military supplies to UNITA as a result of the recent Moscow–Washington agreement. Behind the scenes, Britain and West Germany were pressing South Africa to expedite the peace process. By the beginning of September, all South African forces had been withdrawn from Angola, while Cuban forces on the Angola–Namibia border also stopped offensive attacks.[108] These favourable indications eventually led to the signature of the Brazzaville protocol between Angola, Cuba and South Africa at the UN Headquarters in New York on 22 December 1988. The US Secretary of State presided over the ceremony, while a Soviet Deputy Foreign Minister 'looked on approvingly'. The protocol bound South Africa to grant Namibia independence by November 1989 and Cuba to withdraw its troops in stages by May 1991.[109]

Namibia finally became independent in March 1990, but peace in Angola continued to elude the superpowers. In December 1989, MPLA launched another offensive, in an effort to destroy UNITA once and for all and, in response, Washington increased its military supplies to Savimbi's forces.[110] The Angolan civil war had never been a major priority for the superpowers, but by December 1990 Baker persuaded the Soviet Foreign Minister to cooperate with the USA to find a formula which would end the fighting between UNITA and MPLA. The result was a ceasefire agreement in May 1991, with the help of Portuguese mediation. The accords at Bicesse in Portugal also called for the discontinuation of the superpowers' military supplies to the warring factions. The Bicesse accords also asked UNITA to respect the governing MPLA party as Angola's legitimate government until free elections were held.

The 1991 ceasefire held for a time, at least until September 1992 when Angola's first general elections took place, with a high turn-out exceeding 90 per cent. In the presidential election 49.6 per cent of the vote went to Dos Santos (of MPLA), as opposed to 40.7 per cent to Savimbi (of UNITA). In the parliamentary vote, the MPLA party secured 54 per cent, with UNITA 34 per cent. Savimbi denounced the elections as 'fraudulent', and UNITA mobilized for war. In October 1992, fierce fighting started in the capital, Luanda, and the Angolan civil war now re-opened in earnest, continuing, with a four-week ceasefire in December 1991, until 1994, during which time a further 300,000 Angolans were killed.[111]

In retrospect, after 1988, Gorbachev seemed to have given up any hope of securing military victories for pro-Moscow revolutionary forces in Africa. The Soviet Union gradually began to reduce, and eventually terminated, its military commitments to its client states there. After the ceasefire between Ethiopia and Somalia in July 1988, Cuba began to withdraw its remaining troops, while Soviet advisers had already left the combat area in 1990. In 1991, the Soviet Union evacuated its military base at the Dahlak Islands, and President Mengistu Haile Mariam left the country. In June 1989, the Soviet Union gave 18-months notice to the government of Mozambique of the termination of its military assistance. About the same time, South Africa also agreed to withdraw its support to RENAMO. After lengthy and difficult peace negotiations between the Mozambique government and the rebels, between 1990 and 1992, a ceasefire was finally put into effect in October 1992. In Angola, however, civil war continued and was only finally terminated after the death of Savimbi in 2002. Baker recalled that the continuing civil war in Angola was no longer a 'proxy war' and that 'the Cold War had ended in Africa'.[112] The Angolan civil war, once regarded as a highly politically charged Cold War battleground, showed that superpower patronage increased the determination of each respective warring party to overcome the other. The Cold War made the conflict hotter, bloodier and more intensive, but in the final analysis, Africa did not sustain much superpower enthusiasm, and it was a region which proved the easiest to discard once East–West relations improved elsewhere. The USA did not renew its base agreement with its erstwhile ally, Somalia, in 1990, and American military and economic assistance to that country was also terminated.[113]

NICARAGUA, CENTRAL AMERICA AND BEYOND

Among all the other regional conflicts, Nicaragua became the focal point of the Reagan Doctrine, and the most controversial. With the support of the Cubans, the Sandinistas, who replaced the unpopular Somoza regime in the 1979 revolution, were supplying arms to the leftist rebels in El Salvador. By the summer of 1980, the CIA became concerned about the growing number of Cuban advisers (3400–4000) in Nicaragua and also in El Salvador.[114] In his last years in office, Carter sought to contain the spread of Communism in Central America: he suspended aid to Nicaragua and provided American advisers and considerable aid to the El Salvador government, which was fighting against the leftist rebels. At that time, there was no direct Soviet involvement, but Washington believed that the Soviets were 'letting the Cubans take the lead' in extending Havana's support to revolutionary movements in Central America.[115]

The Reagan administration revitalized and expanded Carter's containment policy by creating the Contra force to counter the Sandinista government in Nicaragua (see chapter 7). Nicaragua was the largest of the five former Spanish colonies in Central America (together with Guatemala, Honduras, El Salvador and Costa Rica). Costa Rica was the only democratic country in the region.

During the initial years of his presidency, El Salvador became a 'test case' to 'establish Reagan's tough foreign policy'. The White House believed the spread of the pro-Cuban Nicaraguan revolution to El Salvador, a country which was dominated by an elite landowning class, with the support of the military, must be stopped.[116] The revolution in October 1979 ousted General Romero's repressive government in El Salvador, replacing it with American-backed José Napoleón Duarte (the leader of the Christian Democratic Party) as the president of El Salvador. It soon became clear, however, that the new Salvadorian government

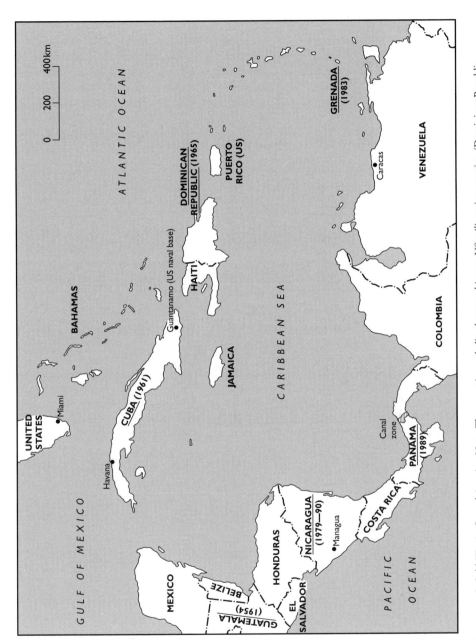

6. Cold War in Central America. Note: The countries underlined were subject to US military intervention (Dominican Republic, Grenada, Panama), CIA-backed invasions (Guatemala, Cuba), and diplomatic and economic pressure (Nicaragua).

could not control the country, which was subjected to increasing violence by both leftist and rightist extremists. In October 1980, the leftist insurgents were able to unite and form a national liberation front (FMLN), but the extreme right wing was also mobilizing to take over the country. Rightist 'death-squads' were now killing 300–400 civilians monthly on average, while more than 40 Christian Democratic Party officials were murdered by the end of April 1981. Before Reagan came to power in January 1981, a major offensive by the FMLN had failed, but the Salvadorian army, trained and supplied by the USA, were unable to defeat them decisively.[117]

If the Reagan administration looked at the Salvadoran civil war through the prism of the Cold War, there was evidence that the Cubans, the Soviets and Nicaraguan Sandinistas were actively supplying arms to the Salvador leftist insurgents, while the USA was providing substantially increased amounts of military aid (from $6 million in 1980 to $35.5 million in 1981, to $82 million in 1982) to the Salvadorian army. Indeed, Reagan used his presidential emergency powers to send the bulk of the initial American funds directly to El Salvador, without seeking Congressional approval. One scholar argues that this was 'indicative of the administration's penchant for resorting to unilateral actions to circumvent congressional opponents'.[118] The situation became murkier still, when in March 1982 elections were won by an extreme right wing party, ARENA, which took over the government from the Christian Democrats. This happened despite American financial assistance to Duarte prior to the elections.[119] Washington's subsequent efforts to 'undo' the election results, in order to keep Duarte in power only increased anti-American sentiments in El Salvador. Meanwhile, the leftist revolutionaries had become divided between moderate and hardline Marxist elements, which delayed any early prospect of an FMLN victory in the Salvadorian civil war.[120]

While the situation in El Salvador became stalemated, the CIA and right wingers in the White House were becoming increasingly concerned about the growing power of the Sandinista government in Nicaragua. Following a number of bilateral (cultural, economic and scientific) agreements with Moscow in March 1980, the Nicaraguan government and the Soviet Union signed a five-year aid agreement in May 1982. Now publicly allied to Cuba, as well as to the Soviet Union, the Sandinistas appeared determined to promote revolutions in El Salvador and elsewhere in Central America. The domino theory re-emerged as a factor in Washington's thinking, this time in relation to America's backyard.[121]

William Casey, the director of the CIA, was as 'obsessed with Central America' as Alexander Haig (US Secretary of State), but the two men saw the problem differently. Haig's idea was to go to the 'source', namely, to purge Cuba of its revolutionary regime once and for all. He once insisted that 'I'll turn the . . . island into a parking lot', but his 'bellicosity' scared even the most conservative elements in the NSC. Haig was keen to impose a naval blockade on Cuba to 'interdict the flow of arms' to Nicaragua and El Salvador, but no senior official accepted Haig's plan as feasible. Baker (then White House Chief of Staff) thought that 'if we give Al Haig his way, . . . the next thing you know, we'll be carpet-bombing Central America'. Reagan was sympathetic to Haig's blockade proposal, since the President had stated frequently during the election campaign that the USA would blockade Cuba 'in return for the Soviet invasion of Afghanistan'. The President was, however, dissuaded from pursuing the Haig plan and settled instead for Casey's equally bellicose, but covert operations.[122]

Casey believed that the Soviet Union was the cause of all these problems in Central America, and in this he had the support of Casper Weinberger's Pentagon. The formation of the Contra force was presented to the Congress as a modest effort to put pressure on the Sandinista government to stop aiding the Salvadoran rebels, but, in reality, Casey's idea was bolder and more ambitious. He wanted to make the Contras a 'third force', able to defeat the Sandinista army. His plan was accepted by the NSC and by the President in December 1981. As in Afghanistan, American covert operations in Nicaragua were supplemented by international cooperation: Honduras was providing surplus weapons and bases, and Argentina (until the USA sided with Britain in the Falklands war) was training the Contras. It was proposed that the Contras should be limited to 500 personnel, but as a result of the CIA's vigorous recruitment campaign, the number rose to 10,000 men by July 1983.[123]

The CIA believed that Nicaragua's aim, 'with active Soviet and Cuban support', was the 'overthrow of democratic governments in the region', and wanted to avert this by Christmas 1983. The agency mounted the first offensive into Nicaragua in March 1983, attacking a town near the Honduras border. The Contras (made up mostly of former members of the Nicaraguan National Guard) soon displayed the brutality and terror they had acquired when they worked for the former dictator, Somoza. The Contras resorted to violence, sabotage, kidnapping and the assassination of civilian officials, but they remained militarily inefficient. Congress became increasingly restive about these CIA-led Contra campaigns, while 80 per cent of the US public was opposed to America's involvement in military action in Central America.[124]

Undaunted, however, the CIA organized the mining of Nicaragua's harbours (approved by Reagan and the NSC in late 1983), in order to reinforce the Contras' operations and prevent supplies reaching the Sandinistas. From September 1983, the agency mounted 19 attacks targeted on Nicaragua's three oil refineries until April 1984, when these attacks were revealed in the media. The USA refused to accept responsibility for placing the mines, but the Contras were 'anxious to take the credit'. In order to avoid criticism from other countries, the CIA used specially made 'firecracker' mines which were 'not big enough to sink a vessel or kill anyone', but several merchant ships from Europe, Latin America, Japan and the Soviet Union were damaged by the mines.[125] This caused a domestic and international uproar against the CIA's actions. Nicaragua took the case to the International Court of Justice in the Hague, which concluded in November 1984 that the USA was 'guilty of supporting terrorism in Nicaragua'. Even the Republican-dominated Senate, as well as the majority of the American public, condemned the mining.[126] In October 1984, Congress passed a resolution banning funds to the CIA, the Pentagon, or 'any other agency or entity . . . involved in intelligence activities . . . directly or indirectly, military or paramilitary operations in Nicaragua' during the fiscal year 1985. Reagan, believing that he could override it if he so wished, signed this resolution into law.[127]

The Nicaraguan economy was by then in ruins. The US government had terminated aid to Nicaragua in April 1981, and persuaded the World Bank to stop its economic aid to Managua in 1982. Mexico, fearing American domination of Latin America, and West Germany and France (who were sympathetic to the Sandinistas' cause), provided some aid to Nicaragua. Nevertheless, by 1985 Nicaragua was almost completely cut off from the major international lending agencies. Added to this was the scarcity of oil. Two main oil providers cut off their oil supplies to Nicaragua – Venezuela in September 1982 and Mexico in 1984 – while Nicaragua's oil facilities were damaged by the CIA's mining operations in 1984. The severity of Nicaragua's economic and energy crisis compelled Managua to tilt further towards Moscow in order to obtain Soviet military support and oil.[128] By 1985 the Soviet Union had supplied arms worth $250 million, which enabled the Sandinista army to increase its size by three times. Initially, arms were delivered from Eastern Europe and Algeria, but after November 1984, with Reagan's re-election, the Soviet Union began to send shipments direct to Managua, and its assistance further increased during Gorbachev's initial years.[129]

Despite the lack of Congress's enthusiasm for the war in Nicaragua, that country remained the White House's priority when Reagan began his second term. The President claimed that the Soviet Union had 'violated the Monroe Doctrine and gotten away with it twice, first in Cuba, then in Nicaragua'.[130] The NSC was tasked to undertake 'public diplomacy' – an illicit propaganda programme – to sell the Nicaraguan issue to the Congress, to the public and to the media. For example, a March 1985 NSC document stated that the Nicaraguan 'Freedom Fighters are fighters for freedom in the American tradition' and the Sandinistas 'are evil'.[131]

Despite this NSC-funded public diplomacy, the limitation and eventual withdrawal of funds by Congress in November 1984 to fight the Contra war ultimately compelled the White House to look for alternative sources, which led to the Iran–Contra affair. Since the spring of 1984, the NSC and the CIA had been discussing other possible foreign sources.[132] Casey was particularly keen to secure donations from overseas, and the administration obtained financial help from Israel (although that country became increasingly doubtful about supporting the administration, given Congressional opposition to such funding), Saudi Arabia (who agreed to provide monthly payments of $1 million to the Contras until the end of 1984), Taiwan, and assistance in kind from Honduras, Guatemala and El Salvador. However, these were not enough to sustain the Contras.[133] At one of the NSC meetings in June 1984, Shultz voiced his concern about soliciting external funding for the Contras, but he was in the minority. The President was determined that some covert measures must continue in order to 'keep the Contras together "body and soul"'.[134] His determination never waned – indeed Congressional opposition merely reinforced it. In the summer of 1984, the control of the Contra war was moved to the NSC in the White House, to circumvent Congressional pressure against CIA covert activities. Oliver North, an ex-Marine on the NSC staff, was chosen to manage the Contra war.

In early 1986, North came up with a 'neat idea' of illegally transferring money to the Contra forces, raised by arms sales to Iran (which was still fighting Iraq), ostensibly in return for Tehran's help in securing the release of American hostages held by Hizballah, a pro-Iranian party in Lebanon.[135] The USA had initially sought to contain Iran by supplying arms to Iraq. However, the White House became increasing concerned about the possible adverse impact of the hostage issue on Reagan's second term presidential election, and also about Moscow's ambitions in Iran as a result of the conflict in Afghanistan. The CIA and the NSC, therefore, became attracted to the idea of maximizing Khomeini's anti-Communist sentiments to the benefit of Washington. The CIA's secret arms sales to Iran via Israel began in November 1985 and the profits raised from these sales were diverted into funding the Contra forces.

Meanwhile, President Reagan continued to press Congress to resume funding for the Contras. The escalation of the Soviet/Cuban engagement in Nicaragua helped to persuade Congress to release $100 million from October 1986, to support the CIA's efforts to prop up the Contras.[136] In the same month, however, the convoluted Iran–Contra operations became public knowledge, when a cargo plane carrying military supplies to the Contras was shot down over Nicaragua. One crew member, who turned out to be a CIA operative, was captured by the Sandinistas. Subsequently, a Lebanese magazine disclosed a visit by MacFarlane (Reagan's former National Security Adviser) to Iran in May 1986, as part of the arms-for-hostage negotiations. Realizing that his cover-up was about to unravel, Oliver North began to shred hundreds of incriminating documents, while his secretary hid some of them in 'her boots and clothing'. Reagan agreed that Attorney General Edwin Meese should review the Iran–Contra affair. Meese soon discovered that some $4 million raised in arms sales to Iran had gone to the Contras.[137] Reagan insisted that he did not know about the diversion of these funds to the Contras (despite 'considerable evidence that he knew a great deal about the Contra support operation') and managed to avoid impeachment. However, his credibility and popularity suffered considerably as a result.[138]

Not surprisingly Congress, after the Iran–Contra affair, lost interest in funding the Contra war, but Reagan, in his State of the Union speech in early 1987, asserted that he would continue to maintain his support for the Contras as one of 'his main foreign policy priorities' during his remaining two years. The President could not understand why the American people and the Congress underestimated the 'seriousness of the threat in Central America',[139] but the Iran–Contra scandal effectively ended recourse to the covert use of American power. Accordingly, there was renewed pressure by the Latin Americans to achieve peace by negotiations.

In 1983, Mexico, Panama, Colombia and Venezuela had called for a ceasefire between the Contras and the Sandinistas. The Reagan administration often publicly complimented peace initiatives of this kind, while it destroyed them behind the scenes. The USA believed that a ceasefire could only be brought about when a democratic (and by implication non-Communist) Nicaraguan government, when it was established, approached the Contras to end the war. In January 1987, Oscar Arias, the anti-Communist President of Costa Rica, pursued another peace initiative, based on the 1983 peace proposal. He called on Nicaragua to introduce democratic reforms, agree to a ceasefire and free elections, and to an amnesty for the Contras, while asking the superpowers to halt assistance to the rival parties. Shultz was tempted to go along with this initiative, but the NSC disagreed. Nevertheless, in August 1987, the Central American Presidents, including Nicaraguan President Ortega (who was under pressure from Gorbachev to support the peace initiative) signed the peace documents, known as Esquipulas II. Arias was awarded the Nobel Peace Prize in that year, as his plan produced the long awaited peace in Central America.[140]

Nicaragua began to take Glasnost to heart, but the deterioration of its society was beyond repair. Owing to the militarization of the Nicaraguan conflict, the government had spent more than half of its revenue in fighting the Contras, lost 40,000 lives in the recent war, and 350,000 people had left the country. The effect of America's total economic embargo was keenly felt on the streets – falling wages, the lack of essential commodities, rising unemployment – while the rate of inflation in 1989 reached an astonishing 3300 per cent.[141] The fortunes of the Contras were also declining rapidly. Despite fresh funding from Congress, as well as private funding collected by Washington during the Iran–Contra scandal in 1986, the Contras' army had never become more than a 'cross-border raiding party'. The CIA's attempts to prop up the Contras finally ceased at the end of February 1988, as there were no more funds available. This compelled the Contras to accept a ceasefire with the Sandinistas in February 1988.[142]

The Bush–Baker team never attached the same degree of importance to Central America as their predecessors did and only wanted to take Central America off the US domestic political agenda. To this end, Baker concentrated his efforts on re-establishing a bipartisan US foreign policy, as well as restoring trust for the administration within the legislative branch. Baker was determined to seek a diplomatic settlement and regarded Arias' proposal as an 'opportune vehicle' to drive the peace settlement forward, and he valued it even more because the initiative came from the Central Americans themselves (and was not imposed by Washington).[143] The USA was also informed by Arias that the Sandinistas had agreed to hold a free and fair presidential election in February 1990.[144]

Baker, however, upheld the Reagan Doctrine and was determined to roll back 'Soviet beachheads around the globe' by using free elections to 'dislodge them'.[145] In May 1989, Baker told Shevardnadze that the USA would honour the outcome of the Nicaraguan election and asked whether the Soviet Union would do the same. The Soviet Foreign Minister agreed. This was the first, and (as it turned out) the last time, as Baker recalled, that the USA offered the Soviet Union a legitimate role in America's backyard, but on this occasion the USA had to secure Moscow's cooperation to end the Nicaraguan conflict.[146]

Another and more emotional issue was that, despite Gorbachev's denials, arms shipments from the Eastern bloc continued to arrive in Central America. The Soviet Union provided Managua with military and economic aid, including much needed oil, in the region of $700–800 million per year. Gorbachev claimed in May 1989 that Moscow had ceased to supply arms to Nicaragua at the end of 1988. However, the Cubans stepped in and increased their supplies to the Sandinistas, who, in turn, were helping the rebels in El Salvador. Prior to the Malta summit in December 1989, the White House was informed of a Nicaraguan plane packed with Soviet–made ground-to-air missiles making a crash landing in El Salvador, as well as of Soviet shipments of MIG-29 fighters to Havana.

At Malta, Bush told Gorbachev in no uncertain terms that Soviet and Cuban inter-ference in Central America was 'the single most disruptive element' standing in the way of improving superpower relations, although Bush was convinced that Gorbachev was unable to control Castro and Ortega, who, despite Moscow's admonitions, continued to support their 'Socialist brothers'.[147]

The election in Nicaragua was held in February 1990. Washington had encouraged and supported a broad anti-Sandinista coalition (the National Opposition Union, UNO) led by an ex-Sandinistan minister, Violeta Chamorro. The result was a UNO victory over the Sandinistas, which, to Baker, 'represented a stunning ideological defeat for communism'.[148] The Contras were to be dis-banded, while Chamorro's new government sought national reconciliation with the Sandinistas (with Ortega and other Sandinista leaders retaining key posts in the new government). The USA subsequently lifted its trade embargo and pro-vided the new Nicaraguan government with a $230 million economic aid package to help restore the war-torn Nicaraguan economy.

Peace through diplomacy was also paying dividends in El Salvador, where the USA was supporting the government, whose forces had been fighting the anti-government Marxist guerrillas (FMLN) since 1979. The year 1989 brought a right wing government to power, but the elected President was keen to achieve a negotiated settlement with the rebels. The FMLN's last offensive in November 1989 ended in failure and opened up an opportunity for peace. Multinational pressure was applied to El Salvador – the USA was now cooperating with Mexico, Venezuela, Spain and Colombia, as well as with the Soviet Union – to declare a ceasefire. Together they pushed forward the peace accords, which were signed in January 1992 in Mexico City between the president of El Salvador and the leader of the FMLN, with the latter agreeing to disband his forces. The collapse of Communism in the Soviet Union and Eastern Europe reinforced the cause of liberal democracy and capitalism in Central America, and its leaders found it 'even less easy . . . to resist the economic and ideological domination of the North'.[149] However, in the mid 1990s, tension was rising again in the region: in Nicaragua, the Sandinista-led Nicaraguan army was fending off attacks from both ex-Sandinista and ex-Contra armed units. El Salvador saw an increase in death squad activities. Regional and domestic problems remained, but the only difference from the Cold War period may have been that the perception of these issues had changed. Central America had been removed from the global security agenda and had become the subject of 'less academic enquiry'.[150]

Across the Pacific Ocean, Vietnam had agreed, under Moscow's prodding, to wind down its military commitment in Cambodia and, in April 1989, Hanoi promised to withdraw all its remaining troops from Cambodia (which it did by the end of September 1989). The USA subsequently terminated its assistance to the non-Communist insurgents. Finally, in October 1991, the Cambodian peace set-tlement was signed in Paris under the auspices of the UN by all parties concerned. The USA also lifted its trade embargo on Cambodia and was prepared to restore normal diplomatic relations with Phnom Penh. By then, the Soviet Union had largely withdrawn from the region and Vietnam had restored full diplomatic relations with Beijing. The new Cambodian government shed Marxist ideology and sought to open up society and embrace the market economy. Sadly, however, the Khmer Rouge (China's former client faction) reneged on the 1991 Peace Accords and the country sank into another bloody civil war.[151]

FROM RIVALRY TO COOPERATION IN THE THIRD WORLD?: THE FIRST GULF WAR, 1990–1

The Reagan Doctrine represented America's determination to challenge the Soviet Union's expansionism in the Third World. The most frequent questions asked by scholars are whether the Reagan Doctrine squeezed the Soviet Union out of the Third World. Alternatively, even without the Reagan Doctrine and without the Republicans' assertiveness, one wonders whether Gorbachev's new thinking would have prevailed in the end, and the strategic importance of regional conflicts in the Cold War would have, in any case, declined, as East–West relations improved elsewhere.[152] There are no easy answers to these questions, but one way of looking at them is to examine what sort of environment the Reagan administration created in Cold War terms, and how this may have affected Gorbachev's policy options when he became General Secretary.

We must first remember that America's policy in the Third World during the late 1970s reacted slowly to the growing Soviet (and Cuban, in the case of Angola and Nicaragua) expansionism in the Third World. Moreover, the USA was severely embarrassed by the Iranian hostage issue, while Congress and the general public were still suffering from 'the Vietnam syndrome' and, as a result, they were reluctant to intervene overtly in the Third World. The Republican right wing led by Reagan was determined to change this attitude. To this end, the ideas underlying the Reagan Doctrine were important for our discussion in this section. The policy epitomized in the Reagan Doctrine had three key elements – initiative, legitimacy and security. The USA would no longer 'wait passively for free institutions to evolve', nor would it 'confine itself to resisting direct threats to its security'.[153] Instead, the USA would take the initiative in 'defying Soviet aggression' with whatever it might take to demonstrate that the free world was 'capable of' fighting Soviet expansionism in the Third World. In other words, the Reagan Doctrine was intended to counter the Brezhnev Doctrine for the Third World. At the same time, Reagan boosted Carter's final rearmament programme, doggedly pursued his SDI project, and revived confidence in America's power at home and abroad. The Communist threat to Central America was the foremost concern of the Republican right and the Reagan Doctrine, in essence, revolved around America's fear of the domino effect in that region. As Reagan put it, there was no time to be 'passive when freedom is under siege'.[154] In order to achieve America's security, and that of the Free World, the Republican right adopted a policy of 'exclusiveness' and 'punishment' to those who were aligned either to the Soviet Union or Cuba, while those who were not became, under this formula, almost automatically 'freedom fighters', that is, 'One of Us'.

The support of freedom fighters was, in fact, the other side of the coin of Reagan's effort to de-legitimize Communism and the Soviet Union, the 'evil' empire.[155] The doctrine was not just about sending the Red Army or Soviet advisers one-way tickets from the Third World back to Moscow, but it also aspired to change the Soviet system itself. Reaganite neo-conservatives were not enthused with the ideas of peaceful coexistence, or détente, or friendly negotiations with Moscow, unless the Soviets changed their system at home, and until that happened, the Soviet Union and its protégés were to be denied legitimacy in the American-led capitalist world. Witness America's total trade and economic embargo against Nicaragua, which resulted in Managua's almost complete isolation from the Western world. Reagan believed in democratically elected, but imperial, presidential power, and the strength of his leadership was reinforced by the phenomenon of 'group think'. Those who embraced Reagan's simplistic, but tough and exclusive approach to the Soviet Union remained at the centre of policy making until the Iran–Contra affair discredited them, and those who harboured scepticism over certain policy decisions were ignored and, ultimately, excluded from the inner policy making group. For instance, when the NSC discussed soliciting private or foreign donations to support the Contra forces against Sandinistas, Shultz objected to the proposal as 'an impeachable offence', but Kirkpatrick, Casey and Weinberger endorsed it. Reagan, in any case, was drawn to right wing ideas. In the end, Shultz's reservations were ignored and the hardline approach was adopted.[156] Reagan conservatives thus thrived and shaped the Cold War as it had become by the first half of the 1980s.

The Reagan Doctrine and its support for 'freedom fighters' have long been criticized by scholars and commentators, because of its lack of concern with human rights abuses and anti-democratic dictators so long as they were fighting against pro-Soviet warring factions. Congress and a large section of the American public remained reluctant to give all-out support for the CIA's covert operations in Central America. A critic also pointed out that the Reagan administration intensified the Third World conflict, which in turn made a pro-Soviet regime like Nicaragua more dependent on Cuba and the Soviet Union – 'exactly the kind of dependency the Reagan policies supposedly sought to prevent'.[157]

When Gorbachev came to power, superpower competition in the Third World had intensified and the USA was now very much engaged in Afghanistan, Nicaragua and Angola. In view of the fact that pro-reformist thinking like that of Gorbachev had been underway in the Soviet establishment for some time, it is difficult to refute the argument that Gorbachev, without the Reagan Doctrine, would probably have sought peace with Washington over regional conflicts. Some even argued that America's power did not force the Soviet Union to seek the end of rivalry in the Third World.[158] However, whatever the reasons may have been, one cannot dispute the fact that the Cold War situation Gorbachev found in the mid 1980s was highly unsatisfactory. Gorbachev's new thinking ultimately sought to legitimize the Soviet Union's position in the global community, while Reagan was making real (in the case of covert operations and military supplies) and declaratory (in the case of the 'Evil Empire' speech) efforts to de-legitimize Moscow's sphere of influence in the Third World.

Many regional conflicts were escalating and pro-Soviet regimes were finding it difficult to consolidate their power in their respective territories; as a result, they demanded more Soviet arms and support. All this meant that Gorbachev's aim of reducing Cold War tensions became more urgent and exacting. Obviously, Gorbachev was not the first Soviet leader to realize that Soviet activism in the Third World was, in fact, affecting overall East–West relations and that a more cautious approach was in order. Gorbachev, however, inherited that approach from his predecessors, an approach which was in itself, in part, a response to the Reagan administration's serious, if covert, engagement in Afghanistan, Angola and Central America by the mid 1980s. Fortunately for Gorbachev, Reagan was ready to talk to the Soviet leader, if only on American terms, and was interested in establishing a cordial relationship with the Soviet Union if the latter was prepared to change its system. Coming to power, Gorbachev had allowed no time to pass in seeking engagement with the USA, Western Europe and the Third World, in an effort to secure a new legitimate role for the USSR in the Western-led global order, as otherwise he could have done more to improve the Soviet economy and society if the world surrounding the Soviet Union had not so been mobilized against it. Thus, Reagan's hardline policy did help to engage Gorbachev much earlier, and more intensively, in the problems of the Third World.

Gorbachev had three goals in the Third World: firstly he sought to make more powerful friends in the Third World, regardless of their ideology, which would not only reduce the sources of the regional conflicts in which the existing pro-Soviet regimes were currently fighting, but would also lead to the legitimacy of the Soviet Union in the wider world. This, of course, was based on Gorbachev's realization that if the Soviet Union relied solely on socialist liberation movements in the Third World to maintain its influence, the Soviet Union, given the poor showing of its economy and its outdated technology, would be eventually discounted or isolated in the Third World. Secondly, Gorbachev was willing to involve the USA in resolving regional conflicts, especially in Afghanistan, in an effort to disarm America's hostility towards both the Soviet Union and pro-Soviet regimes. More importantly, however, this served Gorbachev's interest in searching for a 'balance of interests' between the USA and the Soviet Union.[159] The Soviet Union maintained its arms shipments to its client states as a leverage not just over them, but also over the USA. Finally, Gorbachev often tried to make deals with the USA over the terms of Soviet disengagement. During a meeting with Reagan in December 1987, Gorbachev insisted that 'the issue of American aid' to the Afghan rebels must be tied to 'the day of' the Soviet military withdrawal from Afghanistan.[160] When these goals were achieved, the Soviet Union could legitimately claim a key role in resolving regional conflicts in the Third World, possibly as an equal to the USA. During a meeting with Shultz in February 1988, Gorbachev spoke of the role of the USA and the Soviet Union in showing 'the world an example of cooperation' in the Third World. 'If we establish such cooperation', said Gorbachev, 'then it's possible to hope that conflicts will be resolved considering the interests of all involved countries.' Gorbachev's plans to move the Soviet Union from a rival to a global partner with the USA were neat, but whether the USA could or would accept the Soviet Union's terms was an entirely different matter.

The Secretary of State, James Baker, recalled that 3 August 1990 was the day when the Cold War really ended. On that day, Baker and Shevardnadze stood shoulder to shoulder before a joint press conference held in the Vnukovo II Airport lobby outside Moscow. At that conference, both condemned Iraq's invasion of Kuwait. The timing of the First Gulf War could not have been more opportune, since it was after the Malta summit had established mutual trust between Moscow and Washington, and before Gorbachev's leadership finally collapsed.[161] It was, of course, in Shevardnadze's words, 'a rather difficult decision . . . because of the long-standing relations that we have had with Iraq'. However, Moscow decided to work with Washington over the Gulf War because 'this aggression is inconsistent with the principles of new political thinking and, in fact, with the civilized relations between nations'.[162] The Gulf War epitomized a number of key factors characterizing the Cold War endgame. Gorbachev's overestimation of the power and influence of the Soviet Union coexisted with Moscow's growing dependence (financially and politically) on the USA. Washington, backed by right wing conservative leaders in the West, took a firm and determined approach to ending the Cold War with Moscow. In the case of the Gulf War, the Soviet Union, which had been cultivating Iraq, was taken by surprise by Saddam Hussein's invasion of Kuwait. Soviet intelligence failed to alert Moscow about its imminence and, when Baker presented Shevardnadze with the very 'disturbing' news about the movement of Iraq's troops towards Kuwait, just two days before the invasion, the Soviet Foreign Minister denied it, insisting that 'it would be completely irrational for Saddam Hussein to do this. It's not going to happen, don't worry about it.' Then, of course, it happened. Gorbachev, who was spending his summer holidays in the Crimea, was infuriated by the news, denouncing Saddam as a 'paranoid man'.[163] Moscow helped to rally international support against Saddam's aggression. The Americans appreciated Moscow's decision to join the USA in standing up to Iraq, as otherwise the Bush administration would have found it more difficult to secure Congressional approval of the war against Iraq in 1990.

However, Gorbachev, partly because of his desire to salvage his declining credibility at home, and because of his ambition to become a global peacemaker on a par with the USA, made the new-found superpower cooperation over the Gulf War a rather less than smooth operation. From the start, the Bush administration, strongly supported by the Thatcher government (Bush and Thatcher were meeting in Aspen on the very day of Saddam's invasion of Kuwait), was determined to eject Iraq from Kuwait with the use of force; as Thatcher put it, 'this is no time to go wobbly'.[164] The USA was, accordingly, resolute in demanding Iraq's unconditional acceptance of the UN resolution, rejected any negotiations with Iraq, and had no inclination to broaden the Iraq problem by linking it to other political issues. Washington's message to Saddam was simply, in Baker's words, 'You get out, and you get out unconditionally.'[165]

What Gorbachev tried to do was to unravel the above. He wanted to persuade Saddam to withdraw from Kuwait, link the Iraq issue with the wider problems of the Middle East, such as Lebanon and the Arab–Israeli conflict, to resurrect the Middle East peace process (which had been neglected after the Camp David Accords), to play a key role in the Middle East settlement, and, more than anything else, to seek a political, and not a military, solution to the Iraq–Kuwait crisis, avoiding a US-led ground war. Gorbachev even provided Saddam with an 'escape route', as Moscow was afraid that Saddam, if provoked by the USA, might end up risking 'the destruction of his country'.[166] However, from the outset, Gorbachev's efforts failed: his meeting with Iraqi Foreign Minister, Tariq Aziz, on 5 September 1990 was just one example. Aziz asserted that the Iraq leadership was 'not afraid of confrontation', and continued that 'the potential of hatred and anger that has accumulated for many years in Iraq and in the entire Arab world against the United States, against the pro-Israeli policy of the United States, is at a boiling point'. Finally, he accused Gorbachev of 'speaking in an American language about the Persian Gulf'.[167]

Undaunted, Gorbachev continued, until the beginning of the Desert Storm operation in February 1991, to press Bush to give Moscow more time to persuade Iraq to withdraw from Kuwait. However, the Iraq concessions that Gorbachev apparently extracted from Saddam did not specify unconditional and immediate withdrawal. On the contrary, at the very moment in which Gorbachev was speaking to Bush of Iraq's readiness to withdraw, Iraq was destroying the Kuwait oil refineries. The USA probably felt at the beginning of the conflict that Moscow might retain enough influence over Baghdad to persuade Saddam to withdraw from Kuwait, but by February it was clear that 'the Soviets had still been unable to persuade the Iraqis to agree to anything more than a bare minimum'.[168] The White House was irritated and frustrated by Gorbachev's vain and persistent attempts to delay the UN ground operation, but as Scowcroft recalled, 'Our efforts to discourage him were more in sorrow than in anger, and we tried hard to say no as gently as possible without causing him difficulty.' The American leadership appreciated just how rapid Gorbachev's fortunes at home and abroad were declining (Gorbachev was soon compelled to agree to German unification on Western terms), and that he needed a 'major foreign policy coup to burnish his reputation'. However, there was no way that the USA would let Gorbachev 'interfere with' US diplomacy and operations in the Gulf. Of course, if the Gulf War had taken place at the height of the Cold War, and if there had been no Gorbachev in the Kremlin, the Bush administration would have had 'far fewer options'.[169] However, if Gorbachev was looking for an opportunity to reach a 'balance of interests' between the Soviet Union and the USA, or even further to play a global peace-making role, he was to be disappointed. In Europe, and in the arms control negotiations, Gorbachev was a visionary leader. In the Third World he was also far-sighted in his thinking about keeping Moscow's influence there at less cost, and courageous enough to remove Soviet troops from Afghanistan. However, once the period of rivalry had passed, the USA had much less cause to concern itself with the role of the Soviet Union/Russia in the Third World. The shift from rivalry to cooperation did not come overnight, or in the way Gorbachev had wished, as Moscow soon discovered during the Gulf War crisis.

The demise of the competition in the Third World did not lead to the resolution of the regional conflicts there either. In Angola, Afghanistan, Nicaragua and Cambodia, fighting continued, but by the end of the 1991, argues Herrmann, 'few leaders in either Washington or Moscow saw these conflicts as central to national security'.[170]

9

The End of the Cold War and the Road to the War on Terror

The end of the Cold War in 1989–91 and the 11 September terrorist attack have been two defining events in the recent history of international relations. The former event witnessed the collapse of the West's long-term enemy, which left the USA to enjoy the position of being the world's largest hegemonic power. The events of 11 September, however, exposed the vulnerability of that hegemony to the international community. Hence, the two superpowers that shaped the post-1945 international system had undergone, to a different degree, a dramatic experience: one in 1991 and the other in 2001. This chapter will first summarize the perspectives of the end of the Cold War, as seen from the Soviet Union, Europe and the USA. After some reflections on the legacy of the Cold War and its limitations in relation to other global trends, such as globalization, the chapter will discuss the development of international relations after the end of the Cold War, and the changes to US national security policy from the Bill Clinton and George W. Bush years.

THE END OF THE COLD WAR

The realist school has found Gorbachev's apparent acquiescence in the peaceful transformation of Europe incongruous with its theoretical framework, which assumes that states normally uphold, and not give up, power and national interests.[1] More baffling, perhaps, is the fact that the manner in which the Cold War ended was different from what Gorbachev had sought to achieve. He was not, of course, seeking to abandon Eastern Europe or destroy his own country, let alone concede the Soviet Union's defeat in the Cold War.

This, in turn, suggests that there were a number of options that the Soviet leader could have taken: however, the path he chose, or was sometimes compelled to take, led to the collapse of the Soviet empire in Europe, Moscow's withdrawal of support from its Third World clients, and deep cuts in Soviet nuclear and conventional arms. He also abandoned the international class struggle and resigned as General Secretary of the Communist Party of the Soviet Union in August 1991. Overall, he removed the very foundations on which the Soviet Union had exerted its power and influence in the world, and this resulted in the end of the Cold War.

The Cold War was a lengthy period of living with the fear arising from the concentration of nearly 50,000 nuclear weapons in the hands of the Soviet Union and the USA. These superpowers could have destroyed the world in a few seconds. The Cold War was extraordinary, for although the enemy was identified, open military conflict with that enemy was avoided for nearly half a century. Instead, it was waged by other means, in an effort to counter and contract (roll back) the expansion of each other's strategic zones. These included the competition of ideas and ideology, intelligence gathering, covert operations, and proxy battles in the Third World. After the death of Stalin in 1953, NATO believed that the prospect of a Third World War was unlikely, except by accident or miscalculation. Nevertheless, there was still a great degree of uncertainty in the West surrounding Soviet military intentions. Michael Herman states that 'On a medical analogy, the West by the 1980s had become well informed about Soviet anatomy and physiology; but the windows to the antagonist's mind remained largely opaque.'[2]

Similarly, the Soviet Union and the Eastern bloc were aware that NATO's strategy was defensive, but this did not dispel the fear that NATO strategy could be a 'cover up for a possible surprise nuclear strike'. This also explained why the Kremlin's suspicions of a NATO pre-emptive attack increased in the aftermath of the November 1983 Able Archer exercise. Just as the West viewed the Soviet Union as the main threat to Western civilization, the Soviet Union saw the East–West contest as an 'irreconcilable' struggle. Just as Washington often interpreted American gains as Soviet losses, Moscow interpreted pro-Americanism as meaning anti-Soviet Union.[3]

The image of bipolarity masked the differences between these two blocs. The Soviet Union had never been on an equal level with the USA. Here we are not merely talking about the disparities of economic and military power between the two, but their two different ideologies and historical backgrounds created two totally different states, each of which led two blocs – one consisting of mostly liberal democratic capitalist societies and the other of authoritarian state socialist regimes. In the Communist bloc, their leaders imposed their own rules on their citizens and the stability of the bloc depended upon the elimination of actual or potential anti-establishment individuals. There was no rule of law, since the Communist party was above the law. While the dissolution of the Warsaw Pact surprised the world, the continuation of NATO puzzled many observers. This, too, was the result of seeing the Cold War purely through the prism of a bipolar system. As has been discussed in this book, the Warsaw Pact was intended to keep Eastern Europe together under the sole leadership of the USSR. Its unity owed much to the Brezhnev Doctrine, and to ideological cohesion under the slogans of 'proletarian solidarity' and 'socialist internationalism'. When Gorbachev reduced the role of ideology and made deep cuts in Soviet military might, and when 'popular resentment' against Soviet imperialism 'outweighed the lingering public concerns about Germany', the *raison d'être* for the Warsaw Pact no longer existed.[4] NATO, on the other hand, vindicated its role, in Geir Lundestad's phrase, as 'an American empire by invitation'. In contrast with the coercive alliance of the Warsaw Pact, NATO developed as a means of preserving and promoting Western democratic values.

For Moscow, the Cold War became an endless race to catch up with, and then equal, the USA in global power and influence. It was remarkable how quickly the Soviet Union exploited power vacuums created by the West – whether it was in the Korean peninsula (after the USA excluded it from its defence perimeter in late 1949), in the Indian Ocean or the Arabian peninsula (after Britain decided to withdraw from east of Suez in the late 1960s), or in the Third World (where the USA became much less willing to intervene in the aftermath of the Vietnam War). Moscow's pursuit of equality lasted to the end of the Gorbachev era. During the Brezhnev years, the Soviet Union endeavoured to become a global military power equal to that of the USA. Gorbachev chose instead to adopt a non-military and diplomatic alternative, but he, too, was intent on maintaining Moscow's global influence on a par with that of the USA. In an important respect, the Cold War was, therefore, a 'credible but ultimately failed Soviet challenge to US hegemony' or, to be more precise, a challenge by Communism to Western values and systems.[5] The end of the Cold War inevitably entailed the disappearance of the Soviet challenge to the West.

DIFFERENT VISIONS OF THE END OF THE COLD WAR

Gorbachev, the USSR and Russia

Gorbachev sought to make the Soviet Union efficient and competitive, albeit friendly to the West. For a while the Soviet leader was confident that he was succeeding in these aims and he thought that he was regarded by the West as an influential global statesman, especially when he was informed that the West relied on his agreement on matters concerning German unification or nuclear arms negotiations. The other side of the coin was that the end of the Cold War largely depended upon whether the Soviet Union would accept the Western position on key issues; that is, whether Moscow would (tacitly) concede defeat in the Cold War. Understandably, this was a situation that Gorbachev wanted to avoid and the West was sometimes sympathetic towards his dilemma. Instead, the Soviet Union stressed the bipolar nature of the international system and wanted to change the mood of hostility (i.e. the Cold War) to that of cooperation. In this way, he sought to avoid producing 'winners and losers'.[6] The West's position was clear: if the Soviet Union wanted reconciliation, it was the Soviet Union which must change its ways. As far as the West was concerned, there was no mutual ground to be found between the two blocs. The West, therefore, was indeed thinking of the end of the Cold War in terms of defeat and victory. The Soviet Union wanted a negotiated settlement through mutual concessions and sought equality with the USA after the Cold War. How could these totally different positions be reconciled?

To Gorbachev the key problem of the Soviet system was that it was corrupt, inefficient and undemocratic. In examining Gorbachev's ideas, we must also remember that he made significant changes to the running of the Soviet Union and to Soviet foreign policy, which could not have been achieved in a democratic country. He was not a popularly elected leader and he was able to make many important decisions 'with remarkably few constraints'.[7] As General Secretary, Gorbachev possessed enormous power, which was not available to any democratic leader in the West. We must, therefore, be grateful in a sense that the Soviet system was undemocratic, since this made the birth of Gorbachev's Glasnost and Perestroika possible.

The paradox continued. Gorbachev's inclination towards openness, Western democratic values, and his affinity with Western leaders and peoples sat uneasily with his traditional attitude towards the Soviet Union's allies in Europe and the Third World. Some writers have compared Soviet relations with their allies in the developing world to the 'roles of King and his vassals in medieval natural law'. So long as the vassals (whether they were Cubans, Vietnamese or Afghans) observed the proper code of behaviour in approaching the 'King', they retained relative freedom of action and received material assistance.[8] The Eastern European allies were treated like a group of young siblings, who always asked for help and advice. Moscow thought they would never grow up. Gorbachev did not regard Moscow's relations with these allies as important as those with the West. He somehow believed that Soviet democratization would gain the respect of the Eastern Europeans and, as a result, they would voluntarily reform themselves and remain in the Warsaw Pact. Similarly, he paid scant attention to the importance of keeping the Soviet Union republics together when he embarked on Perestroika.

While he was certainly pro-Western in his thinking, he clung to Leninism for its theoretical wealth and political sagacity. Despite his enthusiastic speech calling for the revitalization of UN institutions, he believed that the world would continue to be governed by the USA and the Soviet Union, now working together to maintain global peace. He resented nuclear weapons and regarded them as the cause, rather than the consequence, of the East–West confrontation. In particular, the Chernobyl disaster in 1986 had huge implications for Gorbachev's drive for Glasnost and Perestroika. The incident was an important reminder to the General Secretary that his country must open up and regenerate itself.[9] He was strongly anti-Stalinist, and this was reflected in his vision of future Soviet security. Gorbachev regarded Stalin's erection of a security buffer zone in Eastern Europe as outdated and an obstacle to the successful achievement of his own new thinking. He believed that if he managed to establish a genuine détente with the West, Moscow would reap security and economic benefits beyond its current security borders.

In retrospect, the end of the Cold War started with Gorbachev's Glasnost and Perestroika, but the many paradoxical ideas contained in his reform programme increased the Soviet dilemma. Meanwhile, the changes Gorbachev encouraged in

Eastern Europe created chain reactions, which occurred so quickly that the Kremlin simply could not cope with them. By then, Gorbachev's goal had become one of overcoming the deepening crisis at home, and to do this it was important to maintain close cooperation with the West and especially with the USA. This meant that it was imperative for him to keep up the momentum of Glasnost and Perestroika. Ironically, Gorbachev, a student of Lenin, did exactly what Lenin had cautioned against: 'Collapse, revolution, occur when the rulers can no longer rule in the old way, and the people no longer obey in the old way.'[10] Gorbachev felt he had to rule the Soviet Union and its empire in a new way, and the people should obey in a new way, simply because he ardently believed that the old way no longer worked.

If the last decade of the Soviet Union had been bad enough in terms of its rapidly declining economic and social condition, the situation further deteriorated in the years following the breakup of the Soviet Union. Its former Soviet successor states were riven by ethnic tensions and border disputes of various kinds, and the crisis in Ukraine in the autumn of 2004 demonstrates that the ideological differences between pro-Western and pro-Russian elements remains an obstacle to peace and stability in that region. Despite more than a decade of effort by the Russian leadership, the Russian economy is still in the doldrums. Russia, however, continues to assert its national interests and is resolved to maintain the unity of the country. Yeltsin resorted fitfully to the use of military force in an effort to destroy Chechnya's separatist ambitions in the mid 1990s, but the lack of any semblance of agreement between the two sides led to renewed conflict in 1999. Vladimir Putin (President 2000–), a former KGB officer, was less hesitant about deploying military force against Chechnya's separatism, and after the 11 September terrorist attack Moscow interpreted the Russian struggle against Chechnya's independence as part of the broader war on terror. Putin, re-elected as President in March 2004 for four more years, demonstrated his firm resolve to crush the Chechens, as was shown by his brutal and clumsy reaction to the Chechen seizure of a school in Beslan, resulting in the deaths of 335 hostages. In this and other ways, Russia's road to a prosperous democratic country remains a long way off; as one critic has pointed out, 'the country's experiment with democracy is all but dead'.[11] History may not repeat itself, but the USA will need to keep a wary eye on future developments in Russia. Condoleezza Rice, a Russian expert and Bush's Secretary of State in 2005, believes in the importance of dealing firmly with great powers which are not fully democratic and, therefore, untrustworthy, like Russia and China. The events of 9:11 distracted the USA's attention from them, but this might change during the second Bush administration.[12]

Western European Perspectives

At the outbreak of the Cold War, France and Britain entertained the notion of creating an independent Western Europe as a 'third force', by utilizing the resources of Europe's colonial possessions in Africa, in the Middle East and Far East. They hoped that such a power bloc might become strong enough to withstand the Soviet monolith, but this concept was soon overtaken by the magnitude of the perceived Soviet threat, and by the USA's willingness to become involved in the defence of Western Europe. Geographical proximity meant that the fear of the Red Army and of a Soviet nuclear onslaught was stronger in Europe than in the USA. In this situation, if the Soviet Union attacked Western Europe there always existed uncertainty in the minds of Europeans as to whether the USA would come to their rescue, at the cost of its own security and even survival. This led to the assumption that Western Europe needed the USA more than the latter needed Europe. Throughout the history of the Cold War and after, it has never been easy for Europeans to accept this sense of dependency (in the 1960s de Gaulle demonstrated his resentment against this directly, when he withdrew France from NATO's integrated command), as Europe has become more economically and politically assertive in recent years. However, history shows that the Atlantic Alliance has worked quite well so far, despite occasional feelings of 'unhappiness' which clouded many observers' judgements on the success of the Atlantic marriage, and it has helped to keep European nationalism under control, with the USA as a 'counterweight to ascendant German power'.[13]

Within Western Europe, there were different visions of how the Cold War could be ended and, as a result, Western Europe on the whole never tried to open a Pandora's Box by discussing how they saw a future Europe *sans* the Cold War. The Federal Republic of Germany felt that its European allies and the Soviet Union had long denied Bonn the option of unifying its country. The FRG wanted a proper post-war settlement, full independence, and the eventual unification of Germany in a climate of deep détente with the East, although by the 1980s this possibility was regarded as too remote to contemplate.

France wanted a Europe governed by Europeans and led by the French, and free of any single or combined hegemonic control, either by the Soviet Union, Germany, or the USA. When the Cold War intensified, the USA took a more heavy-handed interventionist approach towards Europe, which the French resented. On the other hand, when East–West relations relaxed, as in the early 1970s, there was the possibility that the Germans might start thinking about unifying their country, a prospect which the French regarded with trepidation. Britain, on the other hand, consistently pursued a leading role both in Europe and in the World, through cooperation with the USA, with or without the Cold War. However, France and Britain shared with the majority of Western Europeans the view that a slow and almost unremarkable progress with détente with the East over the years would be the best strategy for the benefit of their national interests.[14]

Moreover, within the confines of the Cold War framework, Western Europe had carved out a prominent position in the international community, through trial and error. In 1945, the Western European countries had been in ruins, but by the end of the Cold War and beyond, the European Union became a group of predominantly democratic and advanced industrialized societies with a combined economic strength equal to that of the USA. The FRG has built up its power and influence, despite the restraints imposed on it by its fellow Europeans in the form of West Germany's inclusion in the European Community and in the

Atlantic Alliance. Germany's Ostpolitik was the best that the Germans could come up with, as an alternative to the end of the Cold War. As it turned out, Ostpolitik provided the FRG with an opportunity of reaping commercial and economic benefits, and it soon became 'the most important Western trading partner' for Eastern Europe.[15] In the process, the Germans learnt to work with other Europeans, in order to advance their national goals. Thus, the Western Europeans devised NATO and the EU as two important mechanisms which served, and are likely to continue to serve, a number of common interests, which Europe could share jointly during the Cold War and after. The EU has been a device to gain some independence from the USA, but also to maintain Europe as an efficient global economic player. The deepening of EU integration in the 1980s was not only intended to keep the Germans under control, as Bonn suspected, but it also helped Europe to compete more effectively with the East Asian economic powers.[16]

Within this wider framework, one needs to examine how Western Europe constructed its détente policy in the 1970s. Western Europeans pursued détente with the Soviet Union mainly as an alternative to the end of the Cold War. European détente entailed a degree of cooperation within the framework of the Cold War, and this was partially secured by the German Ostpolitik in the 1970s. Whether détente delayed the peaceful end of the Cold War or precipitated it is still difficult to answer conclusively. However, we now know that the exercise of détente in the 1970s helped to soften the rigidity of the state socialist systems in Eastern Europe, while détente also encouraged pro-Western Soviet thinkers to promote reforms at home. Furthermore, the relaxation of East–West tension reduced mutual fears of a 'surprise attack', and the breakdown of détente did contribute to the 1983 war scare in Moscow. On the eve of the Gorbachev era, Soviet satellite countries in Europe began to resemble long-term hospital patients, who needed delicate treatment, but Gorbachev's radical reforms were only likely to make their condition worse.[17]

Western Europe could encourage Gorbachev's peaceful overtures to the West, as long as this helped to restore détente in Europe. However, what Western Europeans did not realize was that Gorbachev could have been reconciled to the idea of abandoning the Soviet empire in Eastern Europe peacefully. The West remained convinced that Eastern Europe was the prize Stalin had wanted most, in return for the Soviet Union's huge sacrifices during the Great Patriotic War, and it was assumed in the West that his successors felt the same.[18] After all, most Western European powers were imperial powers. They knew how hard it had been to relinquish their empires and their natural instinct had been to keep their empires intact for as long as they could, and they believed that this applied equally to the Soviet empire.

Historically, empires progress from the centre to the periphery, but they could not grow indefinitely. They eventually draw borders, as in the case of the 'Princes' Wall, built by the Middle Egyptian Empire across the Sinai in about 2000 BC. Imperial China had also built the Wall which became the Great Wall by the 14th century. The Soviet empire was, of course, different from previous European empires. Eastern European countries were supposedly independent sovereign states, but in the important fields of their economies and their foreign and defence policies, the Warsaw Pact countries were controlled more or less directly from Moscow. When an empire begins to define its borders, this often means that it has tacitly admitted that it has reached the limit of its capacity to expand further.[19] The Berlin Wall symbolized the division of Europe, and the media gave considerable attention to it when it was breached in the autumn of 1989. However, the Brezhnev Doctrine was equally important. In fact, the doctrine meant 'what we have, we hold' and, as such, was the recognition of the limits of Soviet expansionism.[20] Gorbachev renounced the doctrine in public at the UN General Assembly in December 1988, but this was taken by the West as a welcome sign of a forthcoming relaxation of East–West tensions, not as an ominous indication of the impending instability and chaos in Eastern Europe, which Western Europe wanted to avoid. On the other hand, Eastern European leaders read between the lines and were afraid of the consequences of Gorbachev's statement at the UN for the future stability of their countries. Even Gorbachev himself did not fully appreciate the implications of his speech for the future of his country. He was pleased with the West's favourable response, as he was preoccupied with his campaign to win the hearts and minds of the Western public.

However, as recent history shows, when an empire collapses, however weakened it had become, as in the case of the Ottoman Empire at the end of the First World War, or the French Union in Indochina after the Second World War, it rarely escapes a period of turmoil, while its collapse also imposes extra burdens on other great powers. Britain, despite the fact that its own empire was already being weakened by nationalist pressures, took on additional responsibilities by taking Mesopotamia and Palestine from the former Ottoman Empire in 1919–20. As this book has shown, the USA suffered severely after it replaced France in Vietnam in 1954. It was not a coincidence that when the Western European leaders and their American counterparts realized that they were facing the collapse of the Soviet empire in Eastern Europe, their initial reactions were of apprehension, not of rejoicing. Not only that, but Western Europeans also had to confront the question of German unification much earlier than they had previously thought possible or desirable. The West Germans themselves were stunned by the sudden development of the situation leading to the unification of Germany, which 'most no longer wished to come true'.[21] Indeed, if there was a choice between Soviet domination of Eastern Europe and German domination of the whole of Europe, the majority of Western Europeans (and not just Mrs Thatcher) would have chosen the former.[22] However, the Western Europeans did in the end agree to a unified Germany, without causing the collapse of the key security and economic structures of Western Europe. There has been, therefore, a considerable degree of continuity in the Western European order in the years since the end of the Cold War.

Of course, West Germans as well as East Germans, after what proved to be a brief period of euphoria over the unification of their country, had to face the difficult problems of putting the two states together at enormous financial cost to the Bonn Republic. In the months after unification, the FRG was exposed to considerable external uneasiness about, and latent hostility to, a possible resurgence of German hegemony in the middle of Europe. For example, Germany's unilateral recognition of Slovenia and Croatia in December 1991 was taken as evidence for such a tendency, although in fact this came about as a result of a series of mishaps, and was not an indication of a new German foreign policy. Kohl carefully allayed France's fears of a unified Germany by becoming deeply involved in the strengthening of the EC, and he pursued a multilateral foreign policy. Given the continuing instability in Central and Eastern Europe across Germany's borders, Bonn was compelled to play a key role in providing generous financial assistance to the region and supported, in cooperation with the USA, the widening of NATO and the EU eastwards. In return, Germany has now become the predominant power in Europe.[23] Together with America's recent re-deployment of troops to the former Communist Eastern European countries, the centre of gravity in Europe seems to have shifted to Central Europe, with Germany at the top of the European league.[24]

The USA and the End of the Cold War and After

As in the Second World War (when the USA fought in two main theatres, Europe and Asia), the USA was not fighting the Cold War solely in Europe, but on a variety of fronts. As far as the USA was concerned, there were four conditions to be met if the Cold War was to be regarded as at an end: the Soviet Union must withdraw from Eastern Europe (self-determination); it must agree to nuclear control agreements, which would substantially diminish America's fear of a surprise nuclear attack from Moscow; Soviet expansionism in the Third World must end; and, finally, the Soviet Union must demonstrate that it was changing its political and economic system and was prepared to adopt Western democratic values. For Gorbachev this was a tall order. Nuclear weapons and regime change in the Soviet Union constituted the most important part of the exercise of the end of the Cold War. This explains why the USA did not want to conclude the START Treaty prematurely with the Soviet Union, despite intensive pressure from Gorbachev. After all, there would be no point in taking the risk of reducing the size of American nuclear weapons as part of the START agreement, unless Washington was convinced that the Soviet Union would no longer harbour thoughts of challenging the USA and the Western world.

By the time Reagan came to power, nuclear offensive weaponry – the major method of managing security during the Cold War – was becoming increasingly diversified, and added a further complexity to superpower arms negotiations. In the condition of strategic parity, superpower deterrence based on offensive strategic nuclear weapons increasingly contributed to instability in their political relationship. Reagan's SDI proposal reflected America's frustration over the efficacy of offensive nuclear weapons, which no longer appeared to do justice to American security requirements in the 1980s.[25] The SDI was, therefore, presented as a master plan to address American fears of a surprise nuclear or missile attack, whether from the Soviet Union or from other sources.

When one examines the series of US–Soviet negotiations in the late 1980s (over Europe, nuclear weapons and the Third World), one is struck by Washington's sheer determination to 'impose American terms' on the Soviet Union.[26] Its determination was reinforced by Republican scepticism about Gorbachev's reforms and about the ulterior motives he might be harbouring about the future role of the Soviet Union in the world. While Reagan's friendly posing with Gorbachev in front of the world media was not entirely a charade, it did not reveal the whole story of the US attitude towards the Soviet Union. During the negotiations, the USA skilfully extracted as many concessions as they could from the Soviet Union. If the Soviet Union rejected the American terms, there would no longer be any point in the USA pursuing negotiations with Moscow. Under the circumstances, the USA could afford to continue with the Cold War. As it turned out, Gorbachev's new thinking proved to be much harder to sell to policy makers in the West than he might have expected.

Bush's statement about 'moving beyond containment' in May 1989 in no way reflected the true feelings and anxieties inside the White House. It was only when the USA became convinced about the critical domestic situation Gorbachev was facing that the Bush administration began to exhibit a more sympathetic attitude towards Gorbachev's leadership; but this was often tarnished by a growing concern that Soviet right-wingers might take over the Kremlin, who might then revert to confrontation with the West. The collapse of the Soviet Union was received with 'feelings of numbness and disbelief' in America, showing that this possibility had not previously entered into Washington's thinking.[27]

The Cold War had been a lengthy struggle preoccupying nine post-war Presidents from Truman to George Bush and in the process the USA had built up a formidable Cold War infrastructure, with huge resources dedicated to its upkeep. Partly because of institutional inertia, the USA had not seriously thought that it could win the Cold War by extracting 'unconditional surrender' from the USSR without going to actual war. Both Europe and the USA rejected the idea of militarily defeating the Soviet Union and, partly because of this, the differences between the two (Europe and the USA) were less obvious than they became after the end of the Cold War. Nevertheless, during the Cold War, the growing difference in the strategic culture between both sides of the Atlantic Ocean was already apparent: Western Europe emphasized diplomacy, negotiations, economic ties, compromise and evolved changes, while the USA could be more confrontational, coercive, thorough, determined and decisive in ensuring that the USSR clearly abandoned its ambitions to compete with, and to defeat, the West, and that Moscow accept the Western terms unconditionally.[28]

ENTERING THE POST-COLD WAR ERA

The end of the Cold War unleashed a set of competing but sometimes interrelated visions of the post-Cold War world. They ranged from euphoria to alarmism, expressed in such phrases as the 'triumph of liberalism', 'the new world order', 'the warless society', 'globalization', the 'fragmentation of societies', 'the disappearance of the state', 'clash of civilisations', 'back to the future', 'the coming anarchy' and 'the world disorder'. Those who depicted the new post-Cold War order as one of chaos and instability tended to see the Cold War era as a peaceful interlude. Mearsheimer predicted that, once the bipolar Cold War system was over, there would be a return of the violence in Europe which had characterized the first half of the 20th century. This was certainly true of the spread of civil war in Yugoslavia, but in large measure, Western Europe maintained the peace by deepening integration and was ready, by the mid 1990s, to accept the former state socialist countries from Central and Eastern Europe into their Western organizations.[29]

Similar alarmist concerns about instability were also raised about the Asia-Pacific region, where two major Cold War proxy wars had been fought. The prediction here was that old territorial disputes, schisms and nationalisms, which had been suppressed during the Cold War, would re-emerge. There was some evidence to support this prognosis. Given its increase in military and economic power, Beijing could become the dominant superpower in the region, and thus become a threat to the USA. While this still may happen during this century, China's threatening behaviour over a disputed island in the South China Sea, and its military pressure to prevent a possible Taiwanese move towards independence in the mid 1990s, seemed to indicate that the region was facing serious turmoil. While Western Europeans were enjoying the peace dividend after the end of the Cold War, their Asian counterparts increased defence spending and modernized their armed forces, partly to cope with the rise of China. However, the growth of Asian economic power, the greater availability of Western advanced weapons and technology as a result of the end of the Cold War in Europe, and the initial uncertainties surrounding the future role of the USA in the region after the Cold War, were also responsible for this phenomenon. In any case, the Cold War had become a declining influence in the region for some time before the actual end of that war, and this also explains why the end itself, with the exception of Vietnam and North Korea, did not cause instability in the region.[30]

Peace on the Eurasian and African continents at the end of the Cold War was, however, abruptly disrupted by Saddam Hussein's attack on Kuwait (the Gulf War), Yeltsin's military clampdown on Chechnya, and numerous regional conflicts such as in Somalia, Rwanda, Bosnia and Kosovo. These tragic events culminated in the 11 September terrorist attack on the USA, the Operation Freedom campaign in Afghanistan, and the recent war against Iraq. The only few bright spots seemed to be Nelson Mandela's release from prison and the end of apartheid in South Africa, and the recent abandonment by Libya of its nuclear ambitions. The post-Cold War era reminds us of the *Punch* cartoon about a breakfast between a Bishop and a young English curate: the Bishop, as host, points out that 'I'm afraid you've got a bad egg' and the curate replies 'Oh no, my lord, I assure you! Parts of it are excellent!'[31]

BEYOND THE COLD WAR

As has been shown above, many things happened during the period between 1991 and 9:11, but these were ill-organized and not particularly focused. Part of the reason is the misperception of the Cold War. In fact, what followed after its end was to reveal, paradoxically, the limits of the bipolar structure which was supposed to have governed the Cold War. Just as the Second World War had been devoted to the fight against fascism and, as a result, submerged the conflict between the capitalist democratic system and the authoritarian socialist system, the devotion to Cold War thinking ignored the interconnections between that war and other long-term trends which ran concurrently with the Cold War. Economic globalization, especially after the 1970s, continuously expanded, almost 'leading a life of its own'.[32] The USA, and other industrialized countries in the West, were the leaders of the 'information revolution' in the 1980s. George Shultz, a former professor of economics, once delivered a short lecture to Gorbachev about 'big changes going on in the world economy' and explained to him how some of the nations were taking on an 'influential world role in a particular field, such as computers, weapons, finance'. Gorbachev showed keen interest in Shultz' message: 'Many extremely important things going on had little to do with the East–West confrontation, but would go far to determine the future of every country.'[33]

The post-1945 world witnessed the increasing globalization of almost every level of human activity. By the time Gorbachev came to power in 1982, the number of intergovernmental organizations had increased from 123 in 1951 to about 400. Perhaps more importantly, world contacts are no longer confined to inter-state relations, but transactional actors (multinational companies, terrorist groups and non-governmental organizations) have substantially increased in number during and after the Cold War.[34] It is true that the number of states has increased over time: from around 50 in 1945 to over 200 at present. During the industrial revolution in the late 18th century and the 19th century, communication improvements and transport technology increased the power of the state beyond its borders, and helped to advance its territorial ambitions beyond its boundaries. Modern globalization has made the boundaries between domestic and external issues rather obscure, resulting in the erosion of the sovereignty of states. Integration, multilateralism, interdependence and 'openness', are all the result of globalization.[35]

If globalization is an attempt to create the 'net work' at the centre, which would regulate the flow of information or concerns about certain issues (e.g. epidemics, natural disasters or organized crime), thereby creating a semblance of order and stability, from the opposite direction come efforts of fragmentation by groups who assert their differences in order to protect their interests as minorities. This fragmentation could take the form of unilateralism, separatism, regionalism, devolution and nationalism, which could lead to revolutionary turmoil or, even worse, to anarchy.[36] In the late 1960s and 1970s, many societies experienced fragmentation in the form of women's liberation, the rise of political Islam, the distrust of authority, and the breakdown of traditional codes of behaviour and beliefs.

Thus, globalization and fragmentation are two sides of the same coin; each works to develop society in a push–pull fashion. These trends also have gradually demolished the Westphalian values of modern statehood. Indeed, state sovereignty is now regarded as neither absolute, nor completely autonomous.

The Cold War coincided with the erosion of state sovereignty, and the collapse of the Soviet Union, if anything, accentuated the notion that state sovereignty was indeed becoming a 'negotiable value'.[37] In the field of international relations, the Cold War increased the pressure for globalization or concentration at the top. Most of the arrows shaping the Cold War pointed in a vertical direction. Consider the Hungarian uprising, where 200,000 Red Army soldiers and 4000 Soviet tanks were roaming about the streets of Budapest. The mass display of military might has sustained the fabric of the Soviet Union's empire. Similarly, America's concern lay in the concentration of nuclear weapons in the hands of the Soviet Union. With the end of the Soviet nuclear threat, the drive for fragmentation increased, and horizontal proliferation of WMD has become American's foremost security fear in the post-Cold War world.

Gorbachev was aware of the pressure for globalization and his Glasnost and Perestroika were intended to integrate the Soviet Union into the mainstream of economic and technological globalization. However, he paid much less attention to the forces for fragmentation, which existed within both Soviet society and the rest of the Eastern bloc. It soon became clear to many Eastern European elites that the practice of state socialism, as adopted in Eastern Europe and the Soviet Union, proved to be much less tenable once Moscow adopted globalization and abandoned the ideology of Communism (another important drive for globalization). As Václav Havel states: 'Communism as a system went against life, against man's fundamental needs; against the need for freedom; the need to be enterprising, to associate freely, against the will of the nation. It suppressed national identity. Something that goes against life may last a long time, but sooner or later, it will collapse.'[38]

Détente as conceived especially by Western Europeans was a double-edged sword – involving both an urge to globalize Europe, as well as an urge to fragment it by asserting the importance of human rights. The USA and Western Europe in the last years of the Cold War both encouraged the Soviet Union to globalize, but they were oblivious to the underlying forces of fragmentation. The Western powers preferred stability and respected the sovereignty of the Soviet Union, although they were keen to see Eastern European countries breaking their ties with the Soviet Union in favour of self-determination. As a result of all this, the rulers both in the Soviet Union and its Eastern European satellites were squeezed between two opposing pressures, globalization and fragmentation, and in the end they were unable to sustain the balance and had to give in.

The end of the Cold War appears to have produced many states which are unable to deal with internal threats (economic mismanagement, religious and ethnic differences), but those did not simply emerge because of the end of the bipolar system. These fragile states are not limited to those directly affected by the Cold War, but include other developing states, which are also incapable of conducting themselves as responsible members of the international community.[39] There are two reasons for this phenomenon. Firstly, both globalization and fragmentation challenged the exclusive power of state sovereignty, and newer and weaker states found these pressures too great to sustain. More industrialized and democratic countries have become accustomed to balancing these two opposing forces to maintain domestic stability. In the case of Europe, its answer to globalization has been partially met by deepening European integration, and it has also coped with the force for fragmentation in the form of devolution or localization.

Secondly, the bipolar system during the Cold War often overlooked and neglected the problems arising from the decolonization process, which took place concurrently with the ongoing Cold War. The end of European empires left many newly independent countries still vulnerable to external and internal threats, and most of them were struggling to improve their economies. The superpowers' engagement in the Third World was selective and undertaken mainly for the sake of credibility and prestige. As it turned out, neither power mastered counter-insurgency warfare effectively. As the British and French had already discovered, modern insurgency warfare was neither primitive (in the sense that more technologically advanced armed forces could easily defeat the insurgents), nor simplistic (in the sense that gun boat diplomacy would prevail over the insurgents). Without the fabric of the so-called imperial-colonial structure which had been built up over the years between mother country and its colony, nation building (in the form of providing advice and support without much knowledge of regional and local problems) in the post-imperial age proved to be a much harder task to apply to a country where its indigenous populations were often bitterly divided by different ethnic, tribal, racial and religious orientations. Some of the Third World rulers brought the Cold War to their countries by playing the West off against the East, in order to advance their political goals at home, and, in the process, the military conflict intensified, in terms of human and material losses, and became prolonged struggles, as in Vietnam, Afghanistan and Angola.

That the superpowers were not really concerned about stability and order in the Third World was demonstrated by the fact that during the Cold War and after, the North–South gap continued to widen. While people in the West complain about new computer software, nearly 3 billion people live on less than $60 per month and the same number live without clean water.[40] The 'triumph of capitalism' has not been translated into an improvement in the lives of these people and, if anything, the situation has become worse with the quickened tempo of globalization in recent years.

THE WEST BECOMES ASSERTIVE

The post-Cold War world witnessed the emergence of the previously neglected problems of developing countries, together with the new instability created in parts of Europe as a result of the Soviet Union's abrupt disengagement from its former Eastern European empire. All these led to the broadening of the concept of security.

The concept of security now goes well beyond national security and implies 'freedom from threats' to core values upheld by individuals or groups. Security includes protection against traditional military threats, terrorist attacks, epidemic diseases, environmental hazards and domestic violence, as well as stalking.[41] Industrialized nations, in particular, have become sensitive to the need for security against terrorist groups, which are often involved in organized crime, drug smuggling and arms trading, and this is reflected in the growing number of employees working for private or official security firms to provide protection against unexpected violence or terror for celebrities, high ranking officials, executive corporate members, and other individuals. Already by the middle of the 1990s, American citizens were paying 'more for private security than for their country's armed forces'. Terrorist attacks on the World Trade Center in New York in 1992 and on the federal building in Oklahoma City in 1995, reminded Washington that additional protection against terrorism was a sine qua non for the security of the country. Accordingly, the 1996 Atlanta Olympic Games saw twice as many security officers working as the number of athletes participating.[42]

Moreover, as a result of the globalization and fragmentation, the post-Cold War world has generally become more critical of the 'parameters of state sovereignty'.[43] The West has also strong reason to believe that the sacrifices made to wage the lengthy Cold War have paid off. Elsewhere, in former socialist countries, there are signs of the decline of authoritarianism, and incentives to democratize their societies. With the USA concerned about its economy in the immediate aftermath of the Cold War, it was no wonder that the UN and other intergovernmental Western organizations became more active in dealing with the new or ongoing regional conflicts left over from the Cold War years.

Between 1991 and 1999, the UN made major interventions in Somalia, Cambodia, Bosnia (with NATO), Haiti, Rwanda, Sierra Leone and East Timor, while NATO intervened in Kosovo. Behind this surge of interventions, the concept of sovereignty was reviewed by the UN in relation to growing concerns about violations of human rights. Within the two decades between 1975 and 1995, the number of refugees grew substantially, from 2.4 million to 14.5 million. The number of internally displaced persons arising from military conflict increased from an estimated 1.2 million in 1982 to 20 million in over 30 countries in 1997. The greater penetration of the media into all corners of the world added a further incentive to correct abuses of human rights in many internal conflicts. Kofi Annan, the UN Secretary-General, noted in 1998 that, while the UN charter 'protects the sovereign of peoples, it was never meant as a license for governments to trample on human rights and human dignity'. He concluded that sovereignty means 'responsibility, not just power'.[44]

These sentiments have been translated into an expansion of the meaning of the 'threat to international peace and security' under the UN charter, at the cost of degrading the sovereignty of states.[45] This has resulted in lowering the threshold of military intervention in other states on humanitarian grounds. However, the rationale for humanitarian interventions has raised a complex set of questions about morality, choice and national interests. Some argue that external groups or states have no legal right to intervene in other states. Meanwhile, realists have raised concerns about legitimizing the use of force on humanitarian grounds, which might lead to the abuse of the principle of the 'non-use of force', other than for reasons of self-defence. How far should the intervening powers be aware of the limits of interventions in resolving inter-state problems, or should they go farther when 'suffering and human rights violations' occur 'on a scale offending the "moral conscience of mankind"', as in the case of Bosnia, Somalia or Kosovo?[46] If so, who should decide when to intervene and what measures should they impose on a country in which they are intervening? Moreover, do humanitarian issues justify the use of force, even though the values attached to humanitarianism are mainly those which are upheld by the West? Some writers have, therefore, attacked the concept of intervention as merely a cover to achieve Western imperialism.[47] There is also the realization that the UN has become much too unwieldy to reach quick decisions, leaving open the option to the powers involved to decide whether or not to intervene. However compelling the appalling images of violence and torture transmitted by the media may be, it does not follow that the West can afford to intervene in every conflict, as there are still many 'oppressive states' in the world.[48] The question of whether or not to intervene in a particular conflict – witness the differences in terms of the scale and timing of the West's interventions in Bosnia and Kosovo, or in Somalia and Rwanda – comes down to a matter of choice for individual states, to be considered alongside its respective national interests.

There is no space here to discuss more nuanced arguments for and against humanitarian interventions, but for the purpose of this chapter it is important to note the following: if the great powers regarded military power, or the threat to use it, as an important ingredient in fighting the Cold War, then the post-Cold War world, for different reasons, has increasingly appreciated the validity of the use of military force on humanitarian or other security grounds. Moreover, the Cold War victory has been taken (perhaps wrongly) to mean that Western values are now universal, and this belief has led the West to take a more universalist and, at times, idealist approach to global and regional security issues. A scholar characterized the post-Cold War world as one in which 'the urge to assert national identity – to bring nation state boundaries into line with ethnic identities – has never been stronger'.[49]

POST-COLD WAR AMERICAN GRAND STRATEGY – SETTING THE AGENDA FOR THE FUTURE

The Cold War was the single most important factor that shaped US foreign policy throughout that period. With the end of the Cold War, it is argued that the USA had lost its vision of its world role. However, there appeared to be no indication that the USA might revert to isolationism. Between 1974 and 1994, a significant section of the American public continued to favour the USA playing an active role in the world. During the same period, the majority of the American population consistently put the promotion of American economic interests worldwide as a top priority. The continuing instability of Russia and the Soviet successor states has also suggested the need for America to keep a vigilant watch on its former enemy.[50] The White House did not alter the fundamental US foreign policy objective either: the USA would continue to create an environment where American democratic and capitalist values would thrive in a world in which the USA would 'remain a dominant actor'.[51] However, there has been a gradual but steady shift in attitudes taking place in American society. In the middle of the 1990s, nearly half the population believed that the USA 'should mind its own business'. Opinion polls indicated in 1997 that only a quarter of the respondents took any interest in the Yeltsin–Clinton summit talks, whereas in 1990, nearly 80 per cent had paid close attention to the international summit meetings.[52] With the disappearance of the Soviet strategic threat after the end of the Cold War, and in response to the consequent pressure for fragmentation (indicated by the debates in Europe about nationalism or about European, French and German distinctiveness), the Americans felt that it was 'possible for American foreign policy to "return to normal"'. In the process, the concept of the 'West' – which at one time signified the bloc led by the USA against the Communist bloc – has become obscure. The West means for Robert Kagan the transatlantic alliance or NATO, but neither the EU nor the UN, in his view, is accepted as the 'West'.[53]

The Cold War also managed to gloss over an important shift that took place within the USA. The President traditionally commands the pre-eminent role in making US foreign policy, but since the 1970s, with the pressure for fragmentation, the relationship between the President, Congress and other societal factors influencing US foreign policy making (public opinion, interest groups and the media) has been shifting, to the detriment of presidential power.[54] After Vietnam, the US public and Congress alike had no 'stomach for foreign adventures' (which also affected the nature and scale of the implementation of the Reagan Doctrine), and it has created a situation where the White House '*may* dominate [the making of US foreign policy], but it does not *necessarily* dominate'. During the Cold War, the President was, after all, the only person who had privileged access to nuclear information, and who wielded the single most important authority to decide whether or not the USA should launch 'a pre-emptive or retaliatory nuclear attack against the USSR'. Congress and the public trusted the President's judgement of threat perceptions and supported a huge national security programme throughout the Cold War. In other words, the Cold War not only 'simplified' the making of US foreign policy, but it also allowed the President to retain leverage over Congress and also over the American public, by virtue of 'the Cold War consensus'.[55] In the 1990s (the first decade after the Cold War), the interaction between these three parameters (the President, Congress and other societal factors) was no longer a 'series of concentric circles beginning with the president and expanding outward' into Congress and other influential opinion makers. Instead, the three parameters were all becoming separate actors, who would respond separately or collectively to other domestic and international factors.[56] Altogether, the post-Cold War era created a difficult climate, in which the President tried to formulate the nation's foreign policy.

Throughout his election campaign, Bill Clinton, the first post-Cold War President, emphasized domestic and not foreign affairs, and the revitalization of the American economy, not America's global role, points which the Republican party 'stupidly' missed. As soon as he came to power, Clinton set up the National Economic Council, headed by a Wall Street financier, on a par with the National Security Council. Trading with the Asia-Pacific region provided buoyant economic opportunities for the USA in the 1990s. In 1996, the amount of the USA's trade with Asia came to $579 billion, 50 per cent more than that with Europe.[57]

In terms of US foreign policy, Clinton sought to develop a liberal internationalist approach and tried to link foreign policy goals to US economic security. Washington initially appeared to support the renewed role of the UN, multilateralism, and a universalist approach to international security problems. Following in the footsteps of Carter, Clinton placed human rights at the centre of his foreign policy and promoted the concept of the 'enlargement of democracy' to replace the containment of Communism, which opened the way for NATO and later EU enlargement.[58] However, the problem remained as to the extent and limits of American interventions in numerous world trouble spots. This in itself was not surprising. Even during the height of the Cold War, the USA never asserted the role of world policeman, but insisted on a division of labour and on sharing the burdens of fighting the Cold War with its allies. After the Cold War this tendency, of course, increased, as did where to engage. If the President could not decide whether the USA should intervene in an international crisis, the media might. During the crisis in Somalia, it was the media that first raised alarm bells, which triggered the public cry for US intervention to deal with what appeared to be the most appalling human rights conditions of late. However, after the loss of 18 American soldiers when the USA had moved on to the uncertain task of nation building, the media reversed their opinion and forced the President to withdraw US troops from Somalia. In the aftermath of the crisis, Clinton apparently stated that 'Gosh, I miss the Cold War.' Nor did post-Somalia USA feel able to intervene when faced with the genocide in Rwanda in 1994–5.[59] There were, of course, deeper reasons for the conflicting US attitudes towards humanitarian intervention. The American public was, in general, not convinced that the USA should commit itself to intervention, at the risk of losing American lives in a country where no national security interests were directly involved. The Vietnam factor still played an important role in the USA. Moreover, American historical origins and cultural outlook also suggest that purely humanitarian interventions have never appealed to the wider American public.[60]

If the public mood remained somewhat volatile and difficult to judge, dealing with Congress was an even tougher proposition for the President. With considerable skill, Clinton extracted $2.5 billion from Congress to help to integrate the former Soviet states into the European community. After 1994, he had to face an even more hostile environment in Congress, which was now controlled by the Republicans. The isolationist neo-conservative wing was particularly vocal in asserting anti-internationalism (anti-UN, anti-multilateralism, anti-humanitarian interventions and anti-foreign assistance bills).[61] Their views were somewhat extreme, in the sense that a large majority of the US public still believed in a multipolar world, and supported NATO and increasing world economic interdependence. However, generally speaking, American society was shifting to the right, and the message was clear – the USA should act only for the sake of its 'national interest' and should be less concerned with its allies and international public opinion. As the US Secretary of State, Madeleine Albright, put it, 'multilateral when you can, unilateral when you must' symbolized the spirit of US foreign policy in the post-Cold War era. Although this attitude was discernible throughout the Cold War and, in retrospect, there were very few things that the USA felt it had had to do at the expense of its national interests because of the Cold War, it is true that the slogan became more compelling after the Cold War.

Although transatlantic relations survived the end of the Cold War, cracks, real or imagined, began to appear more distinctly in the latter half of the 1990s. Europe sought its own methods of managing international crises through supranational institutions, such as the UN, the EU and NATO. On the other hand, the Americans had their own method of dealing with international crises, if necessary with the decisive use of advanced military technology. NATO's intervention in Kosovo in 1999 demonstrated how difficult it had become for NATO to produce a unified military strategy and agreed tactics, and how hard it was to distribute a fair share of the burden of fighting among its member states. The USA, as in the case of dealing with the Soviet Union during the Cold War, wanted to strike hard at the source of the problem, that is Milošević and his regime, while the Europeans wanted only to punish the Serb forces conducting 'the ethnic cleansing' in Kosovo.[62] In general, the Europeans were irritated by America's dominant role and criticized Washington's heavy reliance on information technology and its over-protection of its armed forces. On the other hand, the USA (especially the military) remembered the Kosovo campaign as one of excessive 'European meddling'. Kosovo also revealed the Europeans' general lack of military resources and technological competence, which prevented them from influencing the US-led campaign.[63]

Thus, the end of the Cold War revealed, and accentuated, the evolving changes (in US public opinion, Congress, presidential power, US–alliance relationships, and pressures for fragmentation in the domestic and international environment), which had already been taking place. Added to these, was the increased sense of freedom of action, which was felt not only by the USA, but also by its European allies. Clinton did not have to focus his attention on the national security agenda or foreign policy, as there was no imperative to do so during his years in office. However, US foreign policy is strong and united when it is able to focus on a few targets, or preferably a single target, rather than outlining illusive objectives. Clinton responded to this by concentrating on a few selective states, and he combined this with ongoing security concerns which had engaged America's attention since the 1980s: the proliferation of WMD and, to a lesser extent, international terrorism. In September 1993 Anthony Lake, Clinton's National Security Adviser, in a major speech, addressed a range of determinants which would define future American foreign policy. They included whether the rate of the proliferation of WMD would go over the current number of suspected or confirmed states, or whether the 'next quarter century will see terrorism, which injured or killed more than 2000 Americans during the last quarter century, expand or recede as a threat'.[64]

Given these criteria, the Clinton administration named Iraq, Iran, North Korea and Libya as 'backlash' or 'rogue' states, which refused to move to a democratic system and a market-oriented economy, were not afraid of using terrorism as an 'instrument of state policy', and who all pursued WMD. North

Korea and Iran tested their long-range missiles in 1998. However, Iraq had become the most important target after the First Gulf War of 1990–1. The experience of this war led the Clinton administration to adopt the Theatre Missile Defence system, by abandoning the idea of a multilateral approach to the issue of the proliferation of WMD. During the post-Gulf War years, Washington sought to remove the threat from Iraq. However, neither the strategy of 'roll back to change the Baghdad regime', nor 'to keep Saddam Hussein in his box' worked, and Saddam remained in power.[65]

Meanwhile, in Afghanistan, the Pakistan-backed Taliban regime (Taliban is a faction of the Mujahidin groups, which represents the anti-modernization movement) came to power in 1994. After the withdrawal of the Soviet Union, Russia tried to keep a foothold in the northern part of that country by supporting the formation of the Northern Alliance, while Iran supported the minority group called Hazaras, to prevent the 'Sunni variant of political Islam movement' from becoming 'predominant' in Afghanistan. This meant that the civil war continued until the autumn of 2001, when the Taliban regime was destroyed by the US-led coalition.[66] In the mid-1990s, Osama Bin Laden (a Saudi Islamic extremist, and the leader of a loosely organized group, Al-Qaida) found a safe haven in Afghanistan protected by Taliban. This did not go unnoticed in the USA and, in August 1998, Osama Bin Laden became a major US security concern: US embassies in Kenya and Tanzania were targeted by suicide car bombers, and it was evident that Bin Laden was behind these atrocities. In the same month, the Clinton administration made a reprisal attack on Bin Laden's hideout in Afghanistan with Tomahawk cruise missiles, but Bin Laden escaped.[67]

The Clinton administration set the agenda for the future, but there was still something missing which would force the USA to declare total war on international terrorism.

9:11 – THE RETURN OF THE HEGEMONY TO THE GLOBAL SECURITY AGENDA

On 11 September 2001, the weather on the East Coast was pleasant, mild and sunny, when the Al-Qaida terrorist group attacked the World Trade Center in New York, and the Pentagon, and killed over 3000 people. How would the new President, George W. Bush, respond to this shocking tragedy? In a very narrow sense, 11 September could be compared to Pearl Harbor. Despite its concern about Japanese ambitions, prior to the attack, the Franklin Roosevelt administration did not have sufficient evidence to go to Congress to request a declaration of war on Japan. Japan's attack on Pearl Harbor tipped that balance in Roosevelt's favour.[68] The events of 11 September were however, quite different from Pearl Harbor in most respects: 9:11 occurred when the USA felt so proud of its strength that it 'needs to worry very little about what the rest of the world does'. Having witnessed various terrorist actions occurring outside the USA in the past, it was felt that 'it cannot happen here', but it did.[69] Even worse, 9:11 attacked the central nerve of the USA, and not a remote state in the Pacific Ocean. Unlike Pearl Harbor, the initial target for US retaliation against the

Taliban seemed clear enough, but the whole implication of removing the cause of that terror remains less clear-cut and broader than defeating Japan and Nazi Germany in conventional war.

The Bush government, however, skilfully put the ongoing security concerns into the one single box of *national security*, containing the 'trinity of evil'[70] – terrorism, the WMD threat and the rogue states (the last of which came to be called after January 2002 'the axis of evil'). The 9:11 tragedy served to change the balance of power between the President, Congress (which was, in any case, controlled by the Republicans) and other opinion and interest groups, since the 'politics of U.S. national security is always a reflection of the sense of national danger'.[71] The Cold War fighting was sustainable because of the sense of national danger from Soviet or other Communist nuclear attack. After 9:11, national security was back on the global agenda of the USA, under the firm control of the White House.

Bush was also surrounded by a group of neo-conservatives, who had been flexing their muscles since the mid 1990s. The 1990s witnessed the opening of a unipolar world dominated by the USA. US defence expenditure has fallen much more slowly than the defence expenditures of other major powers, resulting in 'greater relative US military capabilities' by the beginning of the millennium. Between 1990 and 1998, the US economy grew by 27 per cent, compared with 15 per cent in the European Union and 9 per cent in Japan. 9:11 allowed the White House to request the 'biggest military increase' in US defence spending of the previous 20 years. In 2002, the USA spent over $350 billion, about a 15 per cent increase on their previous estimate, an amount which was more than double the total defence expenditure of all the EU countries combined.[72] The 1990s also became the age of Americanization – American fast food, popular culture and fashion all poured into the world's capitals. As the USA became such a superpower, the world became suspicious of the possible uses of that power, and concerned about the 'style of its leadership'.[73] The pre-9:11 Bush administration was already clear about how to reply to these suspicions.

TABLE 4 – US PUBLIC OPINION, 1993 – POST-SEPTEMBER 2001

Top Priority US Foreign Policy Goals	Sept. 1993	June 1995	Sept. 1997	Early Sept. 2001	Post-11 Sept. 2001
Taking measures to protect USA from terrorist attacks	N/A	N/A	N/A	80	93
Preventing the spread of weapons of mass destruction	69	68	70	78	81
Insuring adequate energy supplies for the USA	60	59	58	74	69
Promoting democracy in other nations	22	16	22	29	24
Promoting US business and economic interests abroad	27	26	16	37	30
Strengthening the United Nations	41	36	30	42	46
Protecting the jobs of American workers	85	80	77	77	74
Dealing with global warming	56	56	50	44	31
Combating international drug trafficking	N/A	N/A	67	64	55

Percentages polled who agree with the foreign policy goals listed becoming top priority.
Source: *America's New Internationalist Point of View*, The PEW Research Center in association with the Council on Foreign Relations, 24 October 2001.

Bush and his advisers at the Oval Office were deeply suspicious of globalization, which was, in their view, 'undercutting the authority of individual states'.[74] They regarded multilateralism, transnational actors, multinational corporations, and inter-governmental organizations as devices to erode sovereignty and American power. While the Clinton administration also exhibited qualms about multilateralism, unilateralism is more closely associated with the George W. Bush administration. A series of unilateral actions – the rejection of the Kyoto protocol, the Rome Statute of the International Criminal Court, the ABM Treaty, and the decision to go ahead with the National Missile Defence – before and after 9:11 – raised international concerns about the new hardline stance in Washington. Bush and his 'Vulcans' (a group of Republican advisers) or 'sovereignists' take an almost classical realist view of the world. Instead of targeting a group of terrorists who could get access to WMD, they would target the axis of evil, on the assumption that without the protection and support from such states, international terrorists would not survive. Bush takes power seriously and believes in 'military might' in dealing with the rogue states, and especially Iraq, whose leader could only understand the 'language of military power', not Clinton's 'smiles and scowls' of diplomacy.[75]

Within a month of 9:11, the Bush administration mounted 'Operation Enduring Freedom' in Afghanistan, initially a modest air campaign, but within the next two months, on 7 December, Kandahar, the Taliban's key base, fell surprisingly quickly. By early January 2002, the Taliban regime was destroyed and an interim government installed in Afghanistan. The USA was able to build up 'the multinational coalition force' in Afghanistan fairly quickly, drawing more than 16,500 personnel from more than 17 countries. The next target was Iraq.

On 21 November 2001 Bush asked his Secretary of Defense, Donald Rumsfeld, to begin planning for war against Iraq. Saddam Hussein was long regarded as the major threat to peace in the Middle East, but after 9:11, his potential as the supplier of WMD to terrorist groups like Al-Qaida strengthened Washington's anxiety to change his regime and remove WMD from Iraq. After 9:11, Bush thought that Clinton's previous containment policy had become 'less and less feasible' and Saddam's capacity to 'create harm' must be punished before harm was done.[76] The decision was supported by the US Congress and the public alike, but the USA (partly on account of Britain's interest in securing international legitimacy) was irritated by having to go through the lengthy and ultimately divisive discussions in the UN Security Council during the autumn of 2002. In Britain, which also put Iraq high on its security agenda, Prime Minister Tony Blair and his close associates had held intensive discussions with the Clinton and Bush administrations over Iraq for some time. In other words, Iraq had long been on the Anglo–American security agenda prior to 9:11. Britain, however, attached greater importance to the UN sanction on the use of force than the USA, and it was only after a further, and ultimately unsuccessful, round of attempts by the UN inspection team to find and destroy Iraq's WMD, that both the USA and UK leaders agreed that the use of force was now their only option, if the Iraqi regime was to be changed and the WMD threat was to be removed.[77]

On the evening of 19 March 2003, the US-led coalition force began Campaign 'Shock and Awe', massive air strikes on key strategic targets in Iraq. Along with 250,000 US troops, Britain contributed 45,000 personnel, who took over control of the south-eastern area of Iraq, after having secured Basra. Altogether, nearly 40 countries supported, to varying degrees, the Second Gulf War, including 7000 Australian and 200 Polish troops.[78] On 9 April 2003, Baghdad was liberated, a statue of Saddam pulled down by the liberated Iraqi people, and Saddam himself was captured in December of that year. In his January 2004 State of the Union address, Bush called for the 'rapid democratisation of the Middle East', possibly in accordance with the 1975 Helsinki Accords, which emphasized human rights and freedom for individuals. At the time of writing, the bulk of the intervention force still remains in Iraq, struggling to overcome resistance from tenacious insurgents in a country riven by various warring factions and political infighting. The short-term result of the military intervention in Iraq has not been promising – it appears to have increased the hostility of Islamic and other anti-Western extremists towards the USA, UK and other countries that were involved in the war in Iraq. The failure to find WMD in Iraq has cast a gloom over the accuracy of intelligence information about the nature and scope of the threat Iraq posed, and has made Anglo–US intervention 'look all the more like a war of choice'.[79] In Washington and London, the credibility of the leadership now depends on whether Iraq will eventually move towards unity and democratization, and whether the regime change has contributed to peace in the region.

How far this Iraq type of intervention would become a normative case remains to be seen. We have already discussed how the West has become more active in recent years in using military force for humanitarian reasons, or for enforcing or making peace in various troubled countries. The larger issue with the Iraq invasion is that of a pre-emptive attack. The USA claimed in the 2002 National Security Strategy Document that the USA would in future employ pre-emptive attacks, if necessary unilaterally. 'The great danger our Nation faces', Bush wrote in the introduction, 'lies at the crossroads of radicalism and technology.' The USA identifies new security problems coming from 'rogue states *and* terrorists' and it intends to '*defeat these threats* to our Nation, allies, and friends', and to prevent 'our enemies from *threatening* us, our allies, and our friends, with weapons of mass destruction'.[80] Bush believes that it is 'a matter of common sense and self-defense' that 'America will act against such emerging threats before they are fully formed'. While the USA will 'work with our allies' and will endeavour to 'enlist the support of the international community', the USA, the document continues, 'will not hesitate to act alone, if necessary, to exercise our right of self defense by acting *pre-emptively* against such terrorists, to prevent them from doing harm against our people and our country'.[81]

The adoption of pre-emptive attack is often seen as 'a major departure for American foreign policy'.[82] The USA has always maintained an element of unilateralism in its national security policy in the past. During the Reagan years, terrorism was already regarded as an issue in US national security, and Shultz stated that 'there is no question about our ability to use force where and when it is needed to counter terrorism', and added that 'the public must understand before the fact that occasions will come when their government must act before each and every fact is known'.[83] More importantly, the UN is also working on similar lines about a pre-emptive attack. It presupposes that intervention would occur when 'waves of refugees', as a result of a humanitarian crisis '*could* overcome, the infrastructure of neighbouring host states and *could* destabilise their internal policies by altering ethnic balances'. The timing of, or even the decision for, humanitarian interventions entails the problem of pre-judging the situation before it becomes too late to act successfully. Similarly, the EU has also admitted that 'threats such as terrorism and weapons of mass destruction may require action even before crises arise'.[84] However, the issue of pre-emptive attack remains controversial: to some it appears to be deeply disconcerting when it is exercised by the single hegemonic superpower, as though it wanted 'single-handedly to rewrite the rule book'.[85]

At the moment, it seems clear that the US–UK intervention in Iraq has had multiple effects on the transatlantic relationship. The current rift goes beyond the matter of a difference of opinion about whether Saddam posed a threat which required the use of force. The USA reasons that Europe no longer regards US world leadership as legitimate, as it was during the Cold War because of the lack of a common threat in the absence of a common ideological enemy. Moreover, Europe no longer requires the protection of America's military might, the only instrument which was able to deter the Soviet military threat during the Cold War.[86] While France and Germany were opposed, Britain, Spain, Italy, Poland and most of the other new Eastern European members of NATO went along with America's active and moralistic approach to the Middle East. Europe's pacific and inclusive approach to the Soviet Union during the Cold War continues today, when it applies to the EU's dealing with super-terrorism. Similarly, America's determined and tenacious, and ultimately successful, Cold War fighting is also expressed in the way the Bush administration is handling the war against terror.

The USA has now found *the* single cause to overcome, as a result of the tragic circumstance of 9:11, just as the Cold War absorbed Washington's attention and resources. During the Cold War, the USA employed numerous methods of containing and reducing the threat from the enemy (intelligence, psychological warfare, public diplomacy, alliances, nuclear deterrence and limited war). The current war on terror is also likely to be a lengthy struggle, as the National Security Strategy Document concluded in September 2002 – global terrorism would be 'fought on many fronts against a particularly elusive enemy over an extended period of time'.[87] In fact, the USA thinks the current issue is not merely about 'war between the West and Islam', but more about a long-range global struggle about 'ideas', arising from different cultures, religions, races and historical backgrounds. It is about how the USA can communicate with different audiences (and not just states, but also a group of individuals) in the world about the value of democracy and freedom, and how the USA could change their ideas so as to make them more favourable to American beliefs and values. In doing so, the USA aims at mobilizing all sources of communication: official, semi-official, non-profit private organizations, commercial media, the Internet and other Cold

War propaganda agencies (Voice of America, Radio Free Europe, Radio Liberty).[88] The defeat of Communist ideology took the USA more than 40 years to achieve, and this new struggle about ideas might take longer.

A strong section of the international community was concerned about the continuation of the Bush administration for 'four more years'. At the moment, other rogue states are being dealt with differently. A potentially more frightening, if regionally confined crisis, is North Korea's nuclear threat. Washington's preoccupation with Iraq meant that the Bush administration agreed to deal with Kim Jong Il through multilateral talks with other north-east Asian powers. This suggests that Washington is waiting for a collapse of North Korea through internal contradictions, or a diplomatic solution led by powers other than the USA. The USA continues to be suspicious about Iranian intentions, but the crisis there is less acute than North Korea's nuclear stand-off. A pre-emptive attack would be premature, as Iran is not yet regarded as capable of manufacturing nuclear weapons. For the last decade, the EU has differed from the USA about the Iranian nuclear issue, and Europe has tasked itself to diffuse the crisis through diplomacy and engagement, in cooperation with the USA and Russia. This may change, as current signs in Washington are that the White House and the Pentagon are anxious to pay more serious attention to the combination of Iranian nuclear ambitions and their support for international terrorism.[89] If neo-conservatives, led by Rumsfeld, Dick Cheney (the Vice-President), and Paul Wolfowitz, continue to push their policy for the Middle East in the belief that, once the USA succeeded in democratizing Iraq 'with its tradition of secular leadership', democratization would spread across the region and transform 'the entire Muslim Middle East', the second Bush administration is likely to continue to give first priority to the security of the Middle East.[90]

However, elsewhere in the world, the UN, its credibility somewhat reduced by the Iraq war, has increased the number of its humanitarian missions during 2003–4 to restore stability and peace to many countries in Africa, while the EU has taken more interest in adopting a constructive approach to the region.[91] Moreover, while 9:11 reminds us of the crucial importance of dealing with international terrorism, there are of course other global problems with which we must concern ourselves. As the international community has become more globalized, so its values and beliefs have become fragmented or diversified. Even in the West (where the USA and Europe supposedly share more or less common values and beliefs), there are different perceptions of the current threat from international terrorism and of the danger of WMD proliferation. Accordingly, different responses are prescribed on both sides of the Atlantic Ocean. In the 21st century, it will become more difficult to unite our responses at an international, or even national, level over how to respond to challenges thrust upon us, unless they threaten unequivocally the survival of a state, a region, or the world.

If the USA wishes to sustain a respectable global leadership, it will be difficult for it to continue to resort to the use of massive military power, as it did against Iraq, without securing a kind of legitimacy from the international community.

How this could be obtained remains debatable. For example, revitalizing NATO, or securing European support (such as from France or Germany) may not be sufficient if the element of hostility remains anti-American or anti-Western. Without the perceived legitimacy, which must also come from the non-Western world, the USA will be seen to be acting on its own in a lawless world.[92] This will be even more true as Britain's previous role east of Suez is increasingly falling to the USA.

Notes

Preface

1 For instance, Philip Zelikow and Condoleezza Rice, *Germany United and Europe Transformed: A Study in Statecraft* (Cambridge, MA: Harvard University Press, 1995); Don Oberdorfer, *From the Cold War to a New Era: The United States and the Soviet Union, 1983–1991* (Baltimore: The Johns Hopkins University Press, 1991); Timothy Garton Ash, *In Europe's Name: Germany and the Divided Continent* (London: Jonathan Cape, 1993); Michael R. Beschloss and Strobe Talbott, *At the Highest Levels: The Inside Story of the End of the Cold War* (London: Warner Books, 1993); Raymond Garthoff, *The Great Transition: American-Soviet Relations and the End of the Cold War* (Washington, DC: The Brookings Institution, 1994); Anatoly Chernyaev, *My Six Years with Gorbachev* (Pennsylvania: The Pennsylvania State University Press, 2000); Hans Jürgen Küsters and Daniel Hofmann (eds), *Dokumente zur Deutschlandpolitik: Deutsche Einheit Sonderedition aus den Akten des Bundeskanzleramtes, 1989–90* (München: Oldenbourg, 1998); Christopher Simpson, *National Security Directives of the Reagan and Bush Administrations: The Declassified History of U.S. Political and Military Policy, 1981–1991* (Boulder: Westview Press, 1995). See also 'New Evidence on the End of the Cold War', *Cold War International History Project Bulletin* (hereafter cited as CWIHP), #12/13 (fall/winter 2001) by the Woodrow Wilson International Centre for Scholars, Washington, DC; and Jonathan Haslam, 'Collecting and Assembling Pieces of the Jigsaw: Copying with Cold War Archives', *Cold War History*, 4:3 (April 2004), pp. 140–52.

2 Cold War International History Project, Woodrow Wilson International Centre for Scholars, Washington, DC at <http://cwihp.si.edu>. The Parallel History Project (PHP), organized by the Centre for Security Studies and Conflict Research in Zurich, Switzerland, can be found at <http://www.isn.ethz.ch/php>.

3 Two main journals are *Cold War Studies* (Harvard University Press) and *Cold War History* (T&F Informa). Stanford University Press, North Carolina University Press, Palgrave Macmillan, and Frank Cass have published numerous books in series dedicated to the Cold War.

4 See the select bibliography at the end of this book.

5 Thomas Donnelly, 'Rebasing, Revisited', *National Security Outlook* (December 2004).

6 Eisenhower's meeting with Herter, Dillon, et al., 22 April 1960, *Diaries of Dwight D. Eisenhower, 1953–61*, A Micro Film Project of University of Publications of America Inc., Washington, DC, housed at the Liddell Hart Centre for Military Archives, King's College London. See also Saki Dockrill, *Eisenhower's New Look National Security Policy, 1953–1961* (Basingstoke: Macmillan, 1996), p. 273.

Chapter 1

1 John Young, *America, Russia and the Cold War, 1941–1998* (London: Longman, 1999) pp. 243–2.

2 John Lewis Gaddis, *Russia, the Soviet Union and the United States: An Interpretive History* (New York: McGraw-Hill, 1990) p. xv. Stephen White, *After Gorbachev* (Cambridge: Cambridge University Press, 1993) pp. 186–7.

3 Alan Bullock, *Hitler and Stalin: Parallel Lives* (London: HarperCollins, 1991) p. 867.

4 Vladislav Zubok and Constantine Pleshakov, *Inside the Kremlin's Cold War: From Stalin to Khrushchev* (Cambridge, MA: Harvard University Press, 1996) pp. 104–8; Mikhail M. Narinskii,

'The Soviet Union and the Marshall Plan', in Antonio Varsori and Elena Calandri (eds), *The Failure of Peace in Europe, 1943–1948* (Basingstoke: Palgrave Macmillan, 2002) pp. 275–86.

5   Saki Dockrill, 'Britain's Strategy for Europe: Must West Germany be Rearmed?', in Richard Aldrich (ed.), *British Intelligence, Strategy and the Cold War, 1945–1951* (London: Routledge, 1992) pp. 193–214; N. I. Egorova, 'Soviet Leaders' Perceptions of NATO and the Decision-Making Process', in Saki Dockrill, Robert Frank, Georges-Henri Soutou and Antonio Varsori (eds), *L'Europe: d'Est et d'Ouest dans la Guerre froide, 1948–1953* (Paris: Pressess de L'Université Paris-Sorbonne, 2002) pp. 217–26.

6   Fredrik Logevall, 'A Critique of Containment', *Diplomatic History*, 28:4 (September 2004) pp. 473–99.

7   See for example, Wilfried Loth, *Stalin's Unwanted Child: The Soviet Union, the German Question and the Founding of the GDR* (Basingstoke: Macmillan, 1998); Gerhard Wettig, 'Stalin's Note of 10 March 1952: Historical Context', in *L'Europe: d'Est et d'Ouest dans la Guerre froide, 1948–1953*, pp. 137–149; Charles S. Maier, *Dissolution: The Crisis of Communism and the End of East Germany* (Princeton: Princeton University Press, 1997) p. 16; John Lewis Gaddis, *We Now Know: Rethinking Cold War History* (Oxford: Oxford University Press, 1997), p. 127.

8   Vladislav Zubok, 'Soviet Policy Aims at the Geneva Conference, 1955', in Günter Bischof and Saki Dockrill (ed.), *Cold War Respite: The Geneva Summit of 1955* (Baton Rouge: Louisiana State University Press, 2000) pp. 55–74; Saki Dockrill, 'The Eden Plan and European Security' in *ibid.*, pp. 161–89.

9   Robert English, 'The Road(s) Not Taken: Causality and Contingency in Analysis of the Cold War's End', in William C. Wohlforth (ed.), *Cold War Endgame* (Pennsylvania: The Pennsylvania State University Press, 2003) p. 251; Vojtech Mastny, 'The New History of Cold War Alliances', *Journal of Cold War Studies* 4:2 (spring 2002) p. 79; Jussi Hanhimäki, 'Ironies and Turning Points: Détente in Perspective', in Odd Arne Westad (ed.), *Reviewing the Cold War: Approaches, Interpretations, Theory* (London: Frank Cass, 2000) pp. 326–38.

10 Sophie Arie, 'Out in the Cold', *The Guardian* G2, 8 March 2005, pp. 4–5.

11 John W. Young and John Kent, *International Relations Since 1945: A Global History* (Oxford: Oxford University Press, 2004) p. 496.

12 Michael Alexander, *Managing the Cold War: A View from the Front Line* (London: The Royal United Services Institute for Defence and Security Studies (RUSI), 2005) p. 103.

13 Fraser J. Harbutt, *The Cold War Era* (Oxford: Blackwell, 2002) pp. 270–1; Richard Crockatt, *The Fifty Years War: The United States and the Soviet Union in World Politics, 1941–1991* (London: Routledge, 1995) p. 305.

14 Harbutt, *The Cold War Era*, p. 270.

15 Philip Odeen, 'Domestic Factors in US Defence Policy', *Adelphi Paper* no. 173 (London: International Institute for Strategic Studies, 1982) p. 28.

16 Thomas L. Hughes, 'Up From Reaganism', *Foreign Policy* no.44 (fall, 1981) p. 6.

17 Harbutt, *The Cold War Era*, p. 274.

18 Anatoly Dobrynin, *In Confidence: Moscow's Ambassador to America's Six Cold War Presidents* (New York: Random House, 1995) pp. 528–30; Aleksandr' G. Savel'yev and Nikolay N. Detinov (trans. by Dmitriy Trenin and ed. by Grefoy Varhall), *The Big Five: Arms Control Decision-Making in the Soviet Union* (Westport: Praeger, 1995) pp. 163–5; 'East German spy reports reveal NATO war plans', 6 November 2003, ISN Security Watch http://www.isn.ethz.ch, accessed 18 Nov. 2003.

19 John W. Young, *Cold War Europe, 1945–1991: A Political History* (London: Arnold, 1996) p. 36.

20 Alexander, *Managing the Cold War*, p. 105.

21 Alexander, *Managing the Cold War*, p. 106.

22 Michael R. Beschloss and Strobe Talbott, *At the Highest Levels: The Inside Story of the End of the Cold War* (London: Warner Books, 1994) p. 106.

23 While superpower cooperation is not a new subject, Roger Kanet and Edward Kolodziej have edited a volume on this particular aspect of the superpower relationship. See Roger E. Kanet and Edward A. Kolodziej (ed.) *The Cold War as Cooperation* (Basingstoke: Macmillan, 1991). See also chapter 7 'Aspirations for Atomic Peace', in Saki Dockrill, *Eisenhower's New National Security Policy*, pp. 116–48.

24 Michael Mandelbaum, 'Ending the Cold War', *Foreign Affairs* 68:2 (spring 1989) p. 21.

25 John Mueller, 'Quiet Cataclysm: Some Afterthoughts about World War III', *Diplomatic History* 16:1 (winter 1992) pp. 67–8.

26 Vladislav M. Zubok, 'New Evidence on the End of the Cold War: New Evidence on the "Soviet Factor" in the Peaceful Revolutions in 1989', *CWIHP Bulletin*, #12/13, p. 9.

27 Zelikow and Rice, *Germany Unified*, p. 19; George P. Shultz, *Turmoil and Triumph: My Years as Secretary of State* (New York: Charles Scribner's Sons, 1993) p. 1131.

28 Beschloss and Talbott, *At the Highest Levels*, p. 25.

29 Mark Mazower, *Dark Continent: Europe's Twentieth Century* (New York: Vintage Books, 2000) p. 388.

30 As for the role of Gorbachev, see Jacques Lévesque, *The Enigma of 1989: The USSR and the Liberation of Eastern Europe* (California: University of California Press, 1997); Archie Brown, *The Gorbachev Factor* (Oxford: Oxford University Press, 1996); Robert English, *Russia and the Idea of the West: Gorbachev, Intellectuals, and the End of the Cold War* (New York: Columbia University Press, 2000) p. 76. For a recent and informative study of the Soviet Union/Russia, see Adam B. Ulam, *Understanding the Cold War* (New Brunswick: Transaction Publishers, 2002).

31 For instance, Reagan's role was emphasized in Peter Schweizer, *Victory: The Reagan Administration's Secret Strategy that Hastened the Collapse of the Soviet Union* (New York: The Atlantic Monthly Press, 1994). Beth A. Fischer maintains that Reagan's efforts to change superpower relations came earlier than Gorbachev's rise to power in 1985; see her *The Reagan Reversal: Foreign Policy and the End of the Cold* War (Columbia: University of Missouri Press, 1997). Overdorfer points out in his *From the Cold War to a New Era*, that Reagan was willing to improve relations with Moscow as early as February 1983; see pp. 15–21. Kenneth A. Oye argues that Reagan's military build-up was not directly responsible for the USSR's retrenchment, and that Moscow did not respond to the US build-up during the Reagan years; see Kenneth A. Oye, 'Explaining the End of the Cold War: Morphological and Behavioural Adaptations to the Nuclear Peace?', in Richard Ned Lebow and Thomas Risse-Kappen (ed.), *International Relations Theory and the End of the Cold War* (New York: Columbia University Press, 1995) pp. 57–8.

32 For a recent analysis of this subject, see Wallander, 'Western Policy and the Demise of the Soviet Union', pp. 137–77. See also John Lewis Gaddis, *The United States and the End of the Cold War: Implications, Reconsiderations, Provocations* (Oxford: Oxford University Press, 1992) pp. 119–32; *idem*, 'Hanging Tough Paid Off', *Bulletin of the Atomic Scientists* 45:1 (January, 1989) pp. 11–14.

33 F. Fukuyama, *The End of History and the Last Man* (London: Hamish Hamilton, 1992).

34 Robert D. Schulzinger, 'The End of the Old World Order', *Diplomatic History* 20:4 (fall 1996) p. 690; John Lewis Gaddis, 'The Cold War, the Long Peace, and the Future', in Michael J. Hogan (ed.), *The End of the Cold War: Its Meaning and Implications* (New York: Cambridge University Press, 1994) p. 38.

35 Crockatt, *The Fifty Years War*, p. 371.

36 Author's italics. Alexei Filitov, 'Victory in the Postwar Era: Despite the Cold War or Because of It?', *Diplomatic History* 16:1 (winter 1992) p. 54.

37 Walter LaFeber, *America, Russia and the Cold War, 1945–1996* (8th edn) (New York: McGraw-Hill, 1997) pp. 314–15; Geir Lundestad, 'The End of the Cold War, the New Role for Europe, and the Decline of the United States', *Diplomatic History* 16:2 (spring 1992) pp. 247–55. For a concise analysis of the Clinton administration policies, see Michael Cox, *US Foreign Policy after the Cold War: Superpower Without a Mission?* (London: The Royal Institute of International Affairs, 1995) esp. chapter 3.

38 See for example, Zubok, 'New Evidence on the End of the Cold War', p. 10.

39 Thomas Donnelly, 'Rebasing, Revisited', *National Security Outlook* (December 2004).

Chapter 2

1 The Politburo had 14 full and 6 candidate members in 1987, most of whom were Russian. See the glossary by Martin McCauley in Mikhail Gorbachev, *Memoirs* (London: Bantam Books, 1995) p. 932.

2 Stephen White, *After Gorbachev* (Cambridge: Cambridge University Press, 1993) p. 2.

3 Mark Galeotti, *Gorbachev and his Revolution* (Basingstoke: Macmillan, 1997) pp. 1–18 ff.

4 Richard Sakwa, *Gorbachev and His Reforms, 1985–1990* (New Jersey: Prentice Hall, 1991) pp. 270–1; Paul M. Kennedy, *The Rise and Fall of the Great Powers* (New York: Random House, 1987) p. 436.

5 Galeotti, *Gorbachev and his Revolution*, pp. 22–6 ff.; Brown, *The Gorbachev Factor*, pp. 4, 49–50, 64–5; Mark Kramer, 'Ideology and the Cold War', *Review of International Studies* 25:4 (October 1999) pp. 566–7.

6 White, *After Gorbachev*, p. 6.

7 English, *Russia and the Idea of the West*, pp. 188–9; Ben Fischer, 'More Dangerous than We Thought? New Evidence on the Soviet War Scare', *Nobel Institute Research Seminar Paper* (May 2002), Norwegian Nobel Institute, Oslo.

8 Rachel Walker, *Six Years that Shook the World: Perestroika – The Impossible Project* (Manchester: Manchester University Press, 1993) pp. 57, 73.

9 English, *Russia and the Idea of the West*, pp. 197–8; Gromyko's remarks quoted in Sakwa, *Gorbachev and his Reforms*, p. 1.

10 English, *Russia and the Idea of the West*, pp. 197–8.

11 Author's italics. Gorbachev, *Memoirs*, p. 212.

12 *Ibid.*, p. 219.

13 Walker, *Six Years that Shook the World*, pp. 19–39 ff.; 'pre-crisis' mentioned on p. 19. Gorbachev, *Memoirs*, p. 278.

14 Sakwa, *Gorbachev and His Reforms*, p. 26; Walker, *Six Years that Shook the World*, p. 22.

15 Lévesque, *The Enigma of 1989*, pp. 39, 49; English, *Russia and the Idea of the West*, pp. 208–10.

16 Brown, *The Gorbachev Factor*, pp. 101–2.

17 *Ibid.*, p. 98.

18 English, *Russia and the Idea of the West*, pp. 208–9; Brown, *The Gorbachev Factor*, pp. 98–102 ff.

19 Gorbachev, *Memoirs*, p. 222.

20 Walker, *Six Years that Shook the World*, p. 102.

21 Galeotti, *Gorbachev and his Revolution*, pp. 55–6, 62.

22 Galeotti, *Gorbachev and his Revolution*, pp. 57–9; Brown, *The Gorbachev Factor*, pp. 141–2.

23 Sakwa, *Gorbachev and His Reforms*, p. 8.

24 Sakwa, *Gorbachev and His Reforms*, p. 65.

25 Walker, *Six Years that Shook the World*, p. 110; Sakwa, *Gorbachev and His Reforms*, p. 65; McCauley in Gorbachev, *Memoirs*, p. 931.

26 Galeotti, *Gorbachev and his Revolution*, pp. 71–2; Brown, *The Gorbachev Factor*, p. 163; English, *Russia and the Idea of the West*, pp. 215–18.

27 White, *After Gorbachev*, pp. 83–94 ff.; Sakwa, *Gorbachev and His Reforms*, pp. 66–77 ff.

28 White, *After Gorbachev*, p. 79.

29 White, *After Gorbachev*, pp. 77–83.

30 The Central Committee of the Communist Party included the leading Party officials, government ministers, high-ranking diplomats and military officers, and top academics. They were elected at each Party Congress. Meetings of the Central Committee were to be held at least twice a year. McCauley in Gorbachev, *Memoirs*, p. 921.

31 Brown, *The Gorbachev Factor*, pp. 119–21; Gorbachev's speech, see Document 10.7 in Richard Sakwa, *The Rise and Fall of the Soviet Union 1917–1991* (London: Routledge, 2002) pp. 429, 430.

32 Sakwa, *Gorbachev and his Reforms*, pp. 71–2.

33 White, *After Gorbachev*, p. 95.

34 Galeotti, *Gorbachev and his Revolution*, p. 76–7; White, *After Gorbachev*, pp. 109–12.

35 Walker, *Six Years that Shook the World*, p. 194; Brown, *The Gorbachev Factor*, p. 132.

36 John W. Young, *Cold War Europe, 1945–1991: A Political History* (London: Arnold, 1996) p. 228.

37 Marc Zlotnik, 'Yeltsin and Gorbachev: The Politics of Confrontation', *Cold War Studies* 5:1 (winter 2003) pp. 128–33 ff.

38 Gorbachev made sure that Yeltsin resigned from the Politburo formally in February 1988, although Yeltsin remained as a member of the Central Committee until he resigned from the Communist Party of the Soviet Union (CPSU) in 1990.

39 Boris Yeltsin, *Against the Grain* (New York: Summit Books, 1990) pp. 128–9.

40 Gorbachev, *Memoirs*, p. 318; Yeltsin, *Against the Grain*, p. 199; Zlotnik, 'Yeltsin and Gorbachev', pp. 137–8.

41 Yeltsin, *Against the Grain*, pp. 200–2.

42 Wilfried Loth, *Overcoming the Cold War* (Basingstoke: Palgrave Macmillan, 2001) pp. 194–202 ff.; Brown, *The Gorbachev Factor*, p. 234.

43 Brown, *The Gorbachev Factor*, pp. 237–8; Gorbachev, *Memoirs*, p. 307.

44 Sakwa, Document 10.7, in *The Rise and Fall of the Soviet Union*, p. 428; White, *After Gorbachev*, pp. 29–33 ff.

45 Galeotti, *Gorbachev and his Revolution*, p. 82.

46 White, *After Gorbachev*, p. 143.

47 White, *After Gorbachev*, p. 83; Sakwa, *Gorbachev and his Reforms*, p. 233.

48 Galeotti, *Gorbachev and his Revolution*, p. 85.

49 Sakwa, Document 10.7, in *The Rise and Fall of the Soviet Union*, p. 431.

50 Sakwa, *Gorbachev and his Reforms*, pp. 247–8.

51 Peter Calvocoressi, *World Politics 1945–2000* (Harlow: Pearson Education Ltd, 2001) pp. 77–8; White, *After Gorbachev*, pp. 156–7, 162–4; Sakwa, *Gorbachev and his Reforms*, pp. 243–4.

52 Galeotti, *Gorbachev and his Revolution*, p. 89; Christoph Bluth, *The Two Germanies and Military Security in Europe* (Basingstoke: Palgrave Macmillan, 2002) pp. 199–204 ff.

53 Sakwa, Documents 10.10 'Nina Andreeva, "I Cannot Forgo Principles"', in *The Rise and Fall of the Soviet Union*, pp. 440–6; White, *After Gorbachev*, pp. 237–8; Gorbachev, *Memoirs*, p. 326.

54 Chernyaev, *My Six Years with Gorbachev*, p. 135; Sakwa, Documents 10.12 'The Nineteenth Party Conference', in *The Rise and Fall of the Soviet Union*, p. 447; White, *After Gorbachev*, pp. 225–6.

55 Walker, *Six Years that Shook the World*, pp. 118–39 ff.; Sakwa, *Gorbachev and his Reforms*, pp. 128–31.

56 Galeotti, pp. 90–1.

57 White, *After Gorbachev*, pp. 38–41; Sakwa, *Gorbachev and his Reforms*, p. 173.

58 *Ibid.*, pp. 12–17.

59 White, *After Gorbachev*, p. 51; Galeotti, *Gorbachev and his Revolution*, p. 92.

60 Quote from Sakwa, *Gorbachev and his Reforms*, p. 138; see also Walker, *Six Years that Shook the World*, p. 152; White, *After Gorbachev*, pp. 52–3.

61 Galeotti, *Gorbachev and his Revolution*, p. 95; White, *After Gorbachev*, pp. 68–71.

62 White, *After Gorbachev*, p. 54; Walker, *Six Years that Shook the World*, pp. 144–5.

63 Galeotti, *Gorbachev and his Revolution*, p. 98; Sakwa, *Gorbachev and his Reforms*, pp. 144–5.

64 White, *After Gorbachev*, pp. 56–64 ff.; Walker, *Six Years that Shook the World*, pp. 149–53.

65 White, *After Gorbachev*, p. 41.

66 White, *After Gorbachev*, pp. 64–8 ff.; Galeotti, *Gorbachev and his Revolution*, p. 102.

67 Walker, *Six Years that Shook the World*, pp. 133–6.

68 Sakwa, *Gorbachev and his Reforms*, p. 273.

69 Galeotti, *Gorbachev and his Revolution*, p. 102.

70 White, *After Gorbachev*, pp. 136–8.

71 *Ibid.*, pp. 136–7; Walker, *Six Years that Shook the World*, pp. 191–2.

72 Walker, *Six Years that Shook the World*, p. 203; White, *After Gorbachev*, pp. 138–9; Sakwa, *Gorbachev and his Reforms*, pp. 273–4.

73 White, *After Gorbachev*, p. 117; Walker, *Six Years that Shook the World*, pp. 198–202.

74 Galeotti, *Gorbachev and his Revolution*, p. 102; Walker, *Six Years that Shook the World*, p. 204.

75 Christoph Bluth, *New Thinking in Soviet Military Policy* (London: The Royal Institute of International Affairs/Pinter Publishers, 1990) p. 33; David A. Dyker, *Restructuring the Soviet Economy* (London: Routledge, 1997) p. 194.

76 Sakwa, *Gorbachev and his Reforms*, pp. 282–3.

77 White, *After Gorbachev*, pp. 118–9. Sakwa, *Gorbachev and his Reforms*, p. 275.

78 The Presidential Council or USSR Council of the President was established in March 1990, and was replaced in early 1991 by the USSR Security Council.

79 White, *After Gorbachev*, p. 132.

80 Walker, *Six Years that Shook the World*, pp. 197, 205; White, *After Gorbachev*, p. 138.
81 White, *After Gorbachev*, pp. 121, 135–8; Sakwa, *Gorbachev and his Reforms*, p. 296; Walker, *Six Years that Shook the World*, pp. 205–6.
82 White, *After Gorbachev*, p. 254; Walker, *Six Years that Shook the World*, pp. 154–5.
83 Brown, *The Gorbachev Factor*, p. 6.
84 Chernyaev, *My Six Years with Gorbachev*, p. 244.
85 'The Tbilisi Massacre, April 1989: Documents', *CWIHP Bulletin*, #12113 (fall/winter 2001) p. 31.
86 Walker, *Six Years that Shook the World*, pp. 177–80.
87 Sakwa, *Gorbachev and his Reforms*, p. 263.
88 Walker, *Six Years that Shook the World*, pp. 173–8 ff.
89 White, *After Gorbachev*, p. 68; Walker, *Six Years that Shook the World*, pp. 181–2.
90 Walker, *Six Years that Shook the World*, p. 173.
91 White, *After Gorbachev*, p. 253.
92 White, *After Gorbachev*, p. 177; Walker, *Six Years that Shook the World*, pp. 183–4.
93 Galeotti, *Gorbachev and His Revolution*, p. 108.
94 Brian D. Taylor, 'The Soviet Military and the Disintegration of the USSR', *Cold War Studies* 5:1 (winter 2003) pp. 40–2; Brown, *The Gorbachev Factor*, p. 280; George Bush and Brent Scowcroft, *A World Transformed* (New York: Alfred A Knopf, 1998) pp. 257, 329.
95 Brown, *The Gorbachev Factor*, p. 256; Galeotti, *Gorbachev and His Revolution*, pp. 110–13.
96 Walker, *Six Years that Shook the World*, p. 223; White, *After Gorbachev*, p. 179.
97 White, *After Gorbachev*, p. 23.
98 Brown, *The Gorbachev Factor*, pp. 294–300.
99 Walker, *Six Years that Shook the World*, pp. 226–33 ff.; Chernyaev, *My Six Years with Gorbachev*, p. 352.
100 Oberdorfer, *From the Cold War to a New Era*, pp. 456, 461; Zlotnik, 'Yeltsin and Gorbachev', p. 155.
101 Galeotti, *Gorbachev and His Revolution*, p. 119; White, *After Gorbachev*, p. 25.
102 Walker, *Six Years that Shook the World*, pp. 231–2.
103 Quoted in Brown, *The Gorbachev Factor*, p. 130.
104 Zlotnik, 'Yeltsin and Gorbachev', p. 161.
105 Walker, *Six Years that Shook the World*, pp. 238–42; Zlotnik, 'Yeltsin and Gorbachev', pp. 155–6.
106 White, *After Gorbachev*, p. 180.
107 Gorbachev, *Memoirs*, p. 846.
108 Brown, *The Gorbachev Factor*, pp. 303–5; Galeotti, *Gorbachev and His Revolution*, p. 120.
109 Walker, *Six Years that Shook the World*, p. 244.
110 White, *After Gorbachev*, pp. 218, 249, 255.
111 English, *Russia and the Idea of the West*, pp. 180–92 ff.
112 Sakwa, *Gorbachev and his Revolution*, pp. 192–3.
113 Mikhail Gorbachev, *Perestroika: New Thinking for Our Country and the World* (London: Fontana/Collins, 1987) p. 221.
114 Sakwa, *Gorbachev and his Revolution*, pp. 319–20; Brown, *The Gorbachev Factor*, pp. 221–3.
115 Sakwa, *Gorbachev and his Revolution*, p. 321.
116 English, *Russia and the Idea of the West*, pp. 195, 205, 215–17; Zubok, 'New Evidence on the Soviet Factor', p. 9.
117 White, *After Gorbachev*, pp. 224–5.
118 Brown, *The Gorbachev Factor*, p. 222.
119 Gorbachev, *Perestroika*, pp. 140, 218.
120 Sakwa, *Gorbachev and his Revolution*, pp. 324–5.
121 Bluth, *New Thinking in Soviet Military Policy*, pp. 17–18; White, *After Gorbachev*, p. 196; Sakwa, *Gorbachev and his Revolution*, pp. 323–4.
122 Gorbachev, *Memoirs*, pp. 191–2.
123 Sakwa, *Gorbachev and his Revolution*, p. 327.
124 Gorbachev, *Memoirs*, pp. 655–7.

125 Brown, *The Gorbachev Factor*, p. 232.
126 Dobrynin, *In Confidence*, p. 633; Walker, *Six Years that Shook the World*, p. 219.
127 Walker, *Six Years that Shook the World*, p. 220.
128 White, *After Gorbachev*, pp. 218–220.
129 Documents on the December 1989 Malta summit, *CWIHP Bulletin*, #12/13, pp. 232–3.
130 Robert M. Gates, *From the Shadows: The Ultimate Insider's Story of five Presidents and how they won the Cold War* (New York: Touchstone, 1996) p. 505; Chernyaev, *My Six Years with Gorbachev*, pp. 364–6, 383–9.
131 Mikhail Gorbachev, *Gorbachev on my Country and the World* (New York: Columbia University Press, 1999) pp. 158–61.
132 Chernyaev, *My Six Years with Gorbachev*, pp. 387–8.
133 Brown, *The Gorbachev Factor*, pp. 90–1.
134 Gorbachev, *Memoirs*, pp. 638–9.

Chapter 3

1 Ben Fowkes, *The Rise and Fall of Communism in Eastern Europe* (Basingstoke: Macmillan, 1995) p. 172.
2 R. J. Crampton, *Eastern Europe in the Twentieth Century and After* (London: Routledge, 1997) pp. 308–13; Geoffrey Swain and Nigel Swain, *Eastern Europe since 1945* (Basingstoke: Macmillan, 1993) p. 141.
3 Vladislav Zubok, 'The Brezhnev Factor in Détente, 1968–1972', in N. I. Yegorova (ed.), *Cold War and the Policy of Détente: Problems and Discussions* (Moscow: Russian Academy of Sciences, Institute of Universal History, 2003) p. 291.
4 Fowkes, *The Rise and Fall of Communism in Eastern Europe*, pp. 106–7; G. Swain and N. Swain, *Eastern Europe*, pp. 127–30.
5 Fowkes, *The Rise and Fall of Communism in Eastern Europe*, pp. 121–2; Crampton, *Eastern Europe*, pp. 315–19.
6 Crampton, *Eastern Europe*, pp. 326–40.
7 Wilfried Loth, 'Moscow, Prague and Warsaw: Overcoming the Brezhnev Doctrine', *Cold War History* 1:2 (January 2001) pp. 105–6.
8 Vojtech Mastny, ' "We are in a Bind" Polish and Czechoslovak Attempts at Reforming the Warsaw Pact, 1956–1969', *CWIHP Bulletin #11* (winter 1998) pp. 234–5.
9 Zubok, 'The Brezhnev Factor in Détente, 1968–1972', pp. 291–2; Andrei Gromyko, *Memories* (London: Hutchinson, 1989) pp. 232–3; Kramer, 'Ideology and the Cold War' (1999) p. 545.
10 Crampton, *Eastern Europe*, pp. 336–40.
11 Loth, 'Moscow, Prague and Warsaw: Overcoming the Brezhnev Doctrine', p. 108; Arne Odd Westad, 'Introduction', in Westad, Sven Holtsmark and Iver B. Neumann (ed.), *The Soviet Union in Eastern Europe 1945–89* (Basingstoke: Macmillan, 1994) p. 5.
12 Garthoff, *Détente and Confrontation*, pp. 40, 41–57 ff.
13 Vojtech Mastny, *Helsinki, Human Rights, and European Security: Analysis and Documentation* (Durham: Duke University Press, 1986) p. 7–8, 11; Crampton, *Eastern Europe*, pp. 347–8.
14 Mazower, *Dark Continent*, p. 367; Crampton, *Eastern Europe*, p. 345.
15 Crampton, *Eastern Europe*, pp. 345–6; Mazower, *Dark Continent*, p. 367; Young, *Cold War Europe*, p. 256; Fowkes, *The Rise and Fall of Communism in Eastern Europe*, pp. 174–5.
16 Fowkes, *The Rise and Fall of Communism in Eastern Europe*, p. 143; Crampton, *Eastern Europe*, pp. 350–1; G. Swain and N. Swain, *Eastern Europe*, pp. 176–80.
17 Crampton, *Eastern Europe*, pp. 359–66; Mazower, *Dark Continent*, pp. 364–8 ff.
18 Crampton, *Eastern Europe*, pp. 367–8.
19 Vojtech Mastny, 'The Soviet Non-invasion of Poland in 1980/81 and the End of the Cold War', *CWIHP Working paper* no. 23 (September 1998) pp. 9–10; Loth, *Overcoming the Brezhnev Doctrine*, p. 110.
20 Mastny, 'The Soviet Non-invasion of Poland in 1980/81', p. 8.
21 Mastny, 'The Soviet Non-invasion of Poland in 1980/81', p. 9; William E. Pemberton, *Exist with Honor: the Life and Presidency of Ronald Reagan* (London: M. E. Sharpe, 1998), p. 157.

22 Crampton, *Eastern Europe*, pp. 370, 374; Fowkes, *The Rise and Fall of Communism*, p. 166.

23 Loth, *Overcoming the Brezhnev Doctrine*, p. 113.

24 Mastny, 'The Soviet Non-invasion of Poland in 1980/81', p. 18; Mark Kramer, 'Jaruzelski, the Soviet Union, and the Imposition of Martial Law in Poland: New Light on the Mystery of December 1981', *CWIHP Bulletin*, # 11 (winter 1998) pp. 5–11.

25 Ann Lane, *Yugoslavia: When Ideals Collide* (Basingstoke: Palgrave Macmillan, 2004) pp. 129-58 ff.; G. Swain and N. Swain, *Eastern Europe*, pp. 169–70.

26 A. James. McAdams, *Germany Divided: From the Wall to Reunification* (Princeton: Princeton University Press, 1993) pp. 97–105 ff.

27 McAdams, *Germany Divided*, p. 100.

28 G. Swain and N. Swain, *Eastern Europe*, pp. 174–5; Crampton, *Eastern Europe*, p. 358.

29 Mazower, *Dark Continent*, p. 368; Crampton, *Eastern Europe*, pp. 358-9.

30 Loth, *Overcoming the Brezhnev Doctrine*, pp. 113-4; Mastny, 'The Soviet Non-invasion of Poland in 1980/81', pp. 18–19.

31 Christopher Andrew, *For the President's Eyes Only: Secret Intelligence and the American Presidency from Washington to Bush* (London: HarperCollins, 1996) pp. 462, 466; Helene Sjursen, *The United States, Western Europe and the Polish Crisis* (Basingstoke: Palgrave Macmillan, 2003) p. 41.

32 Mastny, 'The Soviet Non-invasion of Poland in 1980/81', p. 21.

33 Geir Lundestad, *The United States and Western Europe since 1945: From "Empire" by Invitation to Transatlantic Drift* (Oxford: Oxford University Press, 2003) pp. 216-17; Sjursen, *The United States, Western Europe and the Polish Crisis*, pp. 71–89 ff.

34 Pemberton, *Exist with Honour*, pp. 156-7.

35 Lévesque, *The Enigma of 1989*, p. 39.

36 Brown, *The Gorbachev Factor*, pp. 243-4.

37 Lévesque, *The Enigma of 1989*, p. 46; Brown, *The Gorbachev Factor*, p. 242.

38 Lévesque, *The Enigma of 1989*, p. 46.

39 Brown, *The Gorbachev Factor*, p. 243-9 ff.; Chernyaev, *Gorbachev*, p. 105; Lévesque, *The Enigma of 1989*, p. 40.

40 For this argument, see Lévesque, *The Enigma of 1989*, pp. 40-5.

41 Oberdorfer, *From the Cold War to a New Era*, pp. 189-207; Marie-Pierre Rey, 'Europe is our Common Home: Gorbachevian USSR and Western Europe, 1985-1991', *Nobel Institute Research Seminar Paper* (May 2002), Norwegian Nobel Institute, Oslo, p. 25.

42 Gorbachev, *Memoirs*, pp. 557-8.

43 Lévesque, *The Enigma of 1989*, pp. 40-1; Gorbachev, *Memoirs*, p. 564.

44 Janusz Bugajski, *Nations in Turmoil: Conflict and Cooperation in Eastern Europe* (Boulder: Westview Press, 1993) p. 187; Lévesque, *The Enigma of 1989*, pp. 42-3.

45 Lévesque, *The Enigma of 1989*, p. 42.

46 Lévesque, *The Enigma of 1989*, pp. 47-8.

47 Oberdorfer, *From the Cold War to a New Era*, p. 382.

48 See Bischof and Dockrill, *Cold War Respite*, pp. 1-20, 161-89; Gorbachev, *Perestroika*, p. 195.

49 Gorbachev, *Perestroika*, pp. 207-8.

50 Marie-Pierre Rey, 'Europe is our Common Home', p. 6.

51 Lévesque, *The Enigma of 1989*, pp. 50-1.

52 Zubok, 'New Evidence on the Soviet Factor in the Peaceful Revolutions of 1989', pp. 7-8.

53 Zubok, *ibid.*, pp. 8-9; Lévesque, *The Enigma of 1989*, pp. 52-3.

54 Zubok, 'New Evidence on the Soviet Factor in the Peaceful Revolutions of 1989', p. 8.

55 Vojtech Mastny, 'Did NATO Win the Cold War?: Looking over the Wall', *Foreign Affairs* 78:3 (May/June 1999) pp. 181-2; Mastny, 'The Soviet Non-invasion of Poland in 1980/81', p. 3.

56 Bluth, *The Two Germanies*, p. 192.

57 Zubok, 'New Evidence on the Soviet Factor in the Peaceful Revolutions of 1989', p. 8.

58 Lévesque, *The Enigma of 1989*, p. 53; Fowkes, *The Rise and Fall of Eastern Europe*, p. 178.

59 Crampton, *Eastern Europe*, pp. 348-50; Lévesque, *The Enigma of 1989*, pp. 66-7.

60 Lévesque, *The Enigma of 1989*, pp. 61-3; Zubok, 'New Evidence on the Soviet Factor in the Peaceful Revolutions of 1989', p. 8.

61 Gorbachev, *Memoirs*, pp. 611–7; Gerhard Wettig, 'The Kremlin's Impact on the Peaceful Revolution in East Germany (August 1989–March 1990), in Odd Arne Westad, Sven Holtsmark and Iver B. Neumann (ed.), *The Soviet Union in Eastern Europe 1945–1989* (Basingstoke: Macmillan, 1994) p. 152.

62 Tomasz Goban-Klas and Pål Kolstø, 'East European Mass Media: The Soviet Role', in Westad et al. (ed.), *Eastern Europe*, pp. 126–33.

63 Lévesque, *The Enigma of 1989*, pp. 82–3.

64 Lévesque, *The Enigma of 1989*, pp. 78–9.

65 Zubok, 'New Evidence on the Soviet Factor in the Peaceful Revolutions of 1989', pp. 8, 11.

66 Zubok, 'New Evidence on the Soviet Factor in the Peaceful Revolutions of 1989', p. 14; Zubok, 'Gorbachev and the End of the Cold War: Different Perspectives on the Historical Personality', in Wohlforth (ed.), *Cold War Endgame*, pp. 229–34 ff.

Chapter 4

1 'Minutes of the Meeting of the Politburo of the Central Committee of the Communist Party of the Soviet Union (CPSU, CC), 27–28 December 1988, in *CWIHP Bulletin* #12/13 (fall/winter 2001) pp. 24–6 ff.

2 Bush and Scowcroft, *A World Transformed*, p. 43; Oberdorfer, *From the Cold War to a New Era*, pp. 330–2.

3 Drek H. Chollet and James M. Goldgeier, 'Once Burned, Twice Shy? The Pause of 1989', in Wohlforth (ed.), *Cold War Endgame*, pp. 153, 158.

4 Gates, *From the Shadows*, p. 459.

5 Wohlforth (ed.), *Cold War Endgame*, p. 27; Bush and Scowcroft, *A World Transformed*, pp. 133–4.

6 Zelikow and Rice, *Germany Unified and Europe Transformed*, p. 25; Lévesque, *The Enigma of 1989*, p. 122.

7 Oberdorfer, *From the Cold War to a New Era*, p. 333; Gates, *From the Shadows*, p. 511.

8 Gorbachev, *Memoirs*, pp. 558, 640; Zelikow and Rice, *Germany Unified and Europe Transformed*, p. 27; Walter Isaacson, *Kissinger: A Biography* (London: Faber and Faber, 1992) pp. 726–7.

9 Bush and Scowcroft, *A World Transformed*, pp. 188–9; Oberdorfer, *From the Cold War to a New Era*, p. 348.

10 Bush's speeches on 12 May and 31 May, Lawrence Freedman (ed.), *Europe Transformed: Documents on the End of the Cold War* (London: Tri-Service Press Ltd, 1990) pp. 286–94; Zelikow and Rice, *Germany Unified and Europe Transformed*, pp. 29–32.

11 Margaret Thatcher, *The Downing Street Years* (London: HarperCollins Publishers, 1995) p. 783; Frank Costigliola, 'An "Arm Around the Shoulder": The United States, NATO and German Reunification, 1989–90', *Contemporary European History* 3:1 (1994) p. 95; a 'resulting ceiling' from Bush's speech in Mainz on 31 May see Freedman (ed.), *Europe Transformed*, p. 293.

12 Thatcher, *The Downing Street Years*, p. 463.

13 Robert L. Hutchings, *American Diplomacy and the End of the Cold War: An Insider's Account of U.S. Policy in Europe, 1989–1992* (Washington, DC: The Woodrow Wilson Centre Press, 1997) pp. 12–13.

14 John Dickie, *'Special' No More* (London: Weidenfeld & Nicolson, 1994) p. 209.

15 Thatcher, *The Downing Street Years*, pp. 790, 801; Dickie, *'Special' No More*, p. 209.

16 See Frédérick Bozo, 'Before the Wall: French Diplomacy and the Last Decade of the Cold War 1979–1989', *Nobel Institute Research Seminar Paper* (May 2002) Norwegian Nobel Institute, Oslo, pp. 9–10.

17 Ronald Teirsky, *François Mitterrand: the Last French President* (New York: St Martin's Press, 2000) pp. 181–6; Marie-Pierre Rey, "Europe is our Common Home": A Study of Gorbachev's Diplomatic Concept', *Cold War History* 4:2 (January 2004) pp. 49–53.

18 Beatrice Heuser, 'Mitterrand's Gaullism: Cold War Policies for the Post-Cold War World?', in Antonio Varsori (ed.), *Europe 1945–1990s: The End of an Era?* (Basingstoke: Macmillan, 1995) pp. 352–4; Hutchings, *American Diplomacy*, p. 15; see also Bozo, 'Before the Wall', p. 9.

19 Heuser, 'Mitterrand's Gaullism', pp. 352–5, 360, and p. 349 for 'a pious wish'; see also Bozo, 'Before the Wall', pp. 11–14.
20 Lévesque, *The Enigma of 1989*, pp. 69–74 ff.
21 Brown, *The Gorbachev Factor*, p. 244; Chernyaev, *My Six Years with Gorbachev*, pp. 114–15.
22 Lévesque, *The Enigma of 1989*, p. 73.
23 'Memorandum of Conversation between Egon Krenz and Gorbachev', 1 November 1989, in Hans-Hermann Hertle, 'The Fall of the Wall: The Unintended Self-Dissolution of East Germany's Ruling Regime', *CWIHP Bulletin*, #12/13 (fall/winter 2001) pp. 144–5.
24 Lévesque, *The Enigma of 1989*, p. 145.
25 Bush and Scowcroft, *A World Transformed*, p. 27.
26 Lévesque, *The Enigma of 1989*, pp. 115–19 ff.
27 Lévesque, *The Enigma of 1989*, p. 70.
28 Wettig, 'The Kremlin's Impact on the Peaceful Revolution in East Germany', p. 152.
29 Hertle, 'The Fall of the Wall: the Unintended Self-Dissolution of East Germany's Ruling Regime', pp 132–3.
30 Lévesque, *The Enigma of 1989*, pp. 84–5.
31 Fowkes, *The Rise and Fall of Communism*, pp. 184–5.
32 Mike Denis, *Rise and Fall of the German Democratic Republic, 1945–1990* (London: Longman, 2000) p. 273; Fowkes, *The Rise and Fall of Communism*, pp. 184.
33 Lévesque, *The Enigma of 1989*, p. 144.
34 Denise, *Rise and Fall of the German Democratic Republic*, p. 262; Mazower, *Dark Continent*, p. 387.
35 Zelikow and Rice, *Germany Unified and Europe Transformed*, p. 60.
36 Bluth, *The Two Germanies*, p. 192; Lévesque, *The Enigma of 1989*, p. 147.
37 Zelikow and Rice, *Germany Unified and Europe Transformed*, pp. 33–4; Lévesque, *The Enigma of 1989*, pp. 148–9.
38 Hertle, 'The Fall of the Wall', p. 132.
39 Zelikow and Rice, *Germany Unified and Europe Transformed*, p. 65.
40 Lévesque, *The Enigma of 1989*, pp. 152–3; Zelikow and Rice, *Germany Unified and Europe Transformed*, pp. 66–7.
41 Zelikow and Rice, *Germany Unified and Europe Transformed*, p. 71; Lévesque, *The Enigma of 1989*, p. 153.
42 Loth, *Overcoming the Cold War*, p. 206; Michael G. Huelshoff and Arthur M. Hanhardt, Jr, 'Steps Towards Union: The Collapse of the GDR and the Unification of Germany', in M. Donald Hancock and Helga A. Welsh (ed.), *German Unification: Process and Outcomes* (Boulder: Westview Press, 1994) pp. 77–8.
43 Huelshoff and Arthur M. Hanhardt, Jr, 'Steps Towards Union: The Collapse of the GDR and the Unification of Germany', pp. 75–6; Denise, *Rise and Fall of the German Democratic Republic*, p. 276.
44 Kramer, 'Ideology and the Cold War', p. 571.
45 Lévesque, *The Enigma of 1989*, pp. 155–6.
46 'Soviet Record of Conversation between Gorbachev and Krenz' 1 November 1989, in *CWIHP Bulletin* #12/13 (fall/winter 2001) p. 18.
47 Huelshoff and Hanhardt, Jr, 'Steps Towards Union: The Collapse of the GDR and the Unification of Germany', p. 78.
48 Memorandum of Conversation between Krenz and Gorbachev, 1 November 1989, in *CWIHP Bulletin* #12/13 (fall/winter 2001) p. 144.
49 Manfred Gortemaker, 'The Collapse of the German Democratic Republic and the Role of the Federal Republic', *German Historical Institute London Bulletin*, XXV, no. 2 (November 2003) p. 62.
50 Denise, *Rise and Fall of the German Democratic Republic*, p. 288.
51 Hertle, 'The Fall of the Wall', pp. 136–8.
52 Gorbachev, *Memoirs*, p. 126.
53 Timothy Garton Ash, *We the People: The Revolution of '89 Witnessed in Warsaw, Budapest, Berlin and Prague* (London: Penguin Books, 1990) pp. 62–3.
54 Zelikow and Rice, *Germany Unified and Europe Transformed*, p. 103.
55 Hertle, 'The Fall of the Wall', p. 138.

56   Zelikow and Rice, *Germany Unified and Europe Transformed*, pp. 107–8; Hertle, 'The Fall of the Wall', pp. 138–9.
57   Hertle, 'The Fall of the Wall', p. 139.
58   Hertle, 'The Fall of the Wall', p. 138.
59   Bush and Scowcroft, *A World Transformed*, pp. 190, 191–3.
60   Hertle, 'The Fall of the Wall', p. 140.
61   David H. Shumaker, *Gorbachev and the German Question: Soviet-West German Relations, 1985-1990* (Westport: Praeger, 1995) p. 130.
62   Lévesque, *The Enigma of 1989*, p. 114.
63   Lévesque, *The Enigma of 1989*, p. 115.
64   Timothy Garton Ash, *We the People*, pp. 25–32, 34–5, 39; Beschloss and Talbott, *At the Highest Levels*, p. 87.
65   Crampon, *Eastern Europe*, p. 392, Ash, 39–40.
66   Lévesque, *The Enigma of 1989*, p. 124.
67   Lévesque, *The Enigma of 1989*, pp. 129, 133–5.
68   Geoffrey Swain and Nigel Swain, *Eastern Europe*, p. 198.
69   Crampon, *Eastern Europe*, p. 397; Lévesque, *The Enigma of 1989*, p. 182.
70   Lévesque, *The Enigma of 1989*, pp. 183–4.
71   Crampton, *Eastern Europe*, p. 398; Lévesque, *The Enigma of 1989*, p. 186.
72   Geoffrey Swain and Nigel Swain, *Eastern Europe*, p. 206.
73   Lévesque, *The Enigma of 1989*, pp. 188–9, 190.
74   Crampton, *Eastern Europe*, p. 399.
75   J. Robert Wegs and Robert Ladrech, *Europe since 1945: A Concise History* (4th edn) (Boston and New York: St Martin's Press, 1996) p. 264.
76   Fowkes, *The Rise and Fall of Communism*, p. 187.
77   Lévesque, *The Enigma of 1989*, pp. 165–9 ff.
78   Crampton, *Eastern Europe*, pp. 383–4.
79   Crampton, *Eastern Europe*, pp. 395–7ff.; Wegs and Ladrech, *Europe since 1945*, pp. 264–6.
80   Crampton, *Eastern Europe*, p. 386.
81   Fowkes, *The Rise and Fall of Communism*, pp. 189–90; A record of meeting between Ceauşescu and Gorbachev in Moscow, 4 December 1989, *CWIHP Bulletin*, #12/13 (fall/winter 2001/2) p. 223.
82   Crampton, *Eastern Europe*, p. 386.
83   Fowkes, *The Rise and Fall of Communism*, p. 189; Geoffrey Swain and Nigel Swain, *Eastern Europe*, p. 212.
84   Crampton, *Eastern Europe*, pp. 399–400; Geoffrey Swain and Nigel Swain, *Eastern Europe*, pp. 212–13.
85   Lévesque, *The Enigma of 1989*, pp. 194–9; Micrea Munteanu, 'The Last Days of a Dictator', *CWIHP Bulletin*, #12/13.
86   Thomas Blanton, 'When did the Cold War End?', *CWIHP Bulletin*, #10 (March 1998) pp. 184–6; Munteanu, 'The Last Days of a Dictator', p. 217; Hitchings, *American Diplomacy and the End of the Cold War*, pp. 85–6.
87   Crampton, *Eastern Europe*, p. 400; Lévesque, *The Enigma of 1989*, p. 199; Wegs and Ladrech, *Europe Since 1945*, pp. 268–9.
88   Crampton, *Eastern Europe*, pp. 389, 403–4; Geoffrey Swain and Nigel Swain, *Eastern Europe*, pp. 219–21.
89   Crampton, *Eastern Europe*, p. 38; Fowkes, *The Rise and Fall of Communism*, p. 192.
90   Calvocoressi, *World Politics 1945-2000*, pp. 338–40; Wegs and Ladrech, *Europe Since 1945*, p. 272; Mischa Glenny, *The Balkans, 1804-1999: Nationalism, War and the Great Powers* (London: Granta Books, 2000) pp. 634–62.
91   Lévesque, *The Enigma of 1989*, p. 198.
92   Calvocoressi, *World Politics*, pp. 320–32; Fowkes, *The Rise and Fall of Communism*, pp. xviii–xxii.
93   'Documents on the December 1989 Malta Summit', *CWIHP Bulletin*, #12/13, p. 237; Blanton, 'When did the Cold War End?', p. 185.
94   Lévesque, *The Enigma of 1989*, p. 136.

95   Zelikow and Rice, *Germany Unified and Europe Transformed*, p. 119.
96   Georges-Henri Soutou, *La Guerre de Cinquante Ans: Les Relations Est-Ouest 1943–1990* (Paris: Fayard, 2001) pp. 709–10; Costigliola, 'An "Arm Around the Shoulder"', pp. 98–9.
97   Saki Dockrill, *Britain's Policy for West German Rearmament* (Cambridge: Cambridge University Press, 1991) pp. 121–13 ff. For Stalin's policy towards Germany, see Loth, *Stalin's Unwanted Child*.
98   Bush and Scowcroft, *A World Transformed*, pp. 185–96; Maier, *Dissolution*, p. 252.
99   Costigliola, 'An "Arm Around the Shoulder"', p. 99; Zelikow and Rice, *Germany Unified and Europe Transformed*, pp. 131–4; Bush and Scowcroft, *A World Transformed*, pp. 198–201.
100 Chernyaev, *My Six Years with Gorbachev*, pp. 235–6, 239.
101 Lévesque, *The Enigma of 1989*, p. 222; Zelikow and Rice, *Germany Unified and Europe*, p. 163.
102 Zelikow and Rice, *Germany Unified and Europe*, p. 201.
103 Costigliola, 'An "Arm Around the Shoulder"', p. 103; Maier, *Dissolution*, p. 261.
104 Lévesque, *The Enigma of 1989*, p. 222; Zelikow and Rice, *Germany Unified and Europe*, pp. 159–60.
105 Maier, *Dissolution*, pp. 260–1.
106 Peter H. Merkl, *German Unification in the European Context* (Pennsylvania: The Pennsylvania State University Press, 1993) pp. 318–27; Thatcher, *The Downing Street Years*, pp. 796–99; Shumaker, *Gorbachev and the German Question*, p. 125.
107 Beschloss and Talbott, *At the Highest Levels*, p. 186.
108 Lévesque, *The Enigma of 1989*, pp. 224–9; Zelikow and Rice, *Germany Unified and Europe*, pp. 205, 217, 240–53 ff.
109 Young and Kent, *International Relations*, pp. 625–6; Lévesque, *The Enigma of 1989*, pp. 235–6.
110 Beschloss and Talbott, *At the Highest Levels*, pp. 234–43; Hanns Jurgen Kusters, 'The Kohl-Gorbachev Meetings in Moscow and in the Caucasus, 1990', *Cold War History* 2:2 (January 2002) pp. 195–235; Kai Diekmann and Ralf George Reuth, *Helmut Kohl: Ich Wollte Deutschlands Einheit* (Berlin: Proyläen, 1996) pp. 267–82.
111 Maier, *Dissolution*, p. 278; Loth, *Overcoming the Cold War*, p. 214.
112 'Treaty on the Final Settlement with Respect to Germany, 12 September 1990', in Konrad H. Jarausch and Volker Gransow, *Uniting Germany: Documents and Debates, 1944–1993* (Oxford: Berghahn Books, 1997) pp. 204–8.
113 Costigliola, 'An "Arm Around the Shoulder"', pp. 108–9; For the detailed negotiations leading to the CFE treaty between 1989 and 1990, see Bluth, *Two Germanies*, pp. 211–23 ff.; The International Institute for Strategic Studies (IISS), *Strategic Survey 1990–91* (London: Brassey's, 1991) pp. 28–9.
114 Bluth, *Two Germanies*, p. 216; Lévesque, *The Enigma of 1989*, pp. 240–44.
115 Lévesque, *The Enigma of 1989*, pp. 248–50; Beschloss and Talbott, *At the Highest Levels*, pp. 288–90.
116 Vojtech Mastny, 'Did NATO win the Cold War?', p. 180.
117 Dov Lynch, 'Russia Faces Europe', *Chaillot Papers*, no. 60 (May 2003), Institute for Security Studies, European Union, pp. 32–3; Paul Latawski, 'Central Europe and European Security', in W. Park and G. Wyn Rees, *Rethinking Security in Post-Cold War Europe* (London: Longman, 1998) pp. 81–94.
118 Hutchings, *American Diplomacy*, p. 293.
119 For the reasons why NATO has survived the Cold War, see David S. Yost, *NATO Transformed: The Alliance's New Roles in International Security* (Washington: United States Institute of Peace, 1998) pp. 50–71 ff.
120 Stephen G. Books and William C. Wohlforth, 'Economic Constraints and the End of the Cold War', in Wohlforth (ed.), *Cold War Endgame*, p. 306.
121 For this subject, see Michael Cox, 'Whatever Happened to American Decline?: International Relations and the New United States Hegemony', *New Political Economy* 6:3 (2001) pp. 311–40; Alan P. Dobson, 'The USA, Britain, and the Question of Hegemony', in Geir Lundestad (ed.), *No End to Alliance: the United States and Western Europe-Past, Present and Future* (Basingstoke: Macmillan, 1999) pp. 134–63.

122 Mazower, *Dark Continent*, p. 311.
123 Michael Howard, 'An Unhappy Successful Marriage: Security Means Knowing What to Expect', *Foreign Affairs* 78:3 (May/June 1999) pp. 164–75.
124 Yost, *NATO Transformed*, p. 49; Costigliola, 'An "Arm Around the Shoulder"', p. 109; Lundestad, *The United States and Western Europe*, p. 250.
125 Lundestad, *The United States and Western Europe*, p. 245.
126 Young and Kent, *International Relations since 1945*, p. 648.
127 Latawski, 'Central Europe and European Security', p. 86.
128 Ian Clark, *The Post-Cold War Order: The Spoils of Peace* (Oxford: Oxford University Press, 2001) p. 95.
129 Andrew Cottey, 'NATO Transformed: The Atlantic Alliance in a New Era', in Park and Rees (ed.), *Rethinking Security*, p. 45.
130 IISS, *Strategic Survey 1990–91*, pp. 28, 34; Yost, *NATO Transformed*, pp. 47–50.
131 Young, *Cold War Europe*, pp. 276–7; Janusz Bugaijski, *Nations in Turmoil: Conflict and Cooperation in Eastern Europe* (Boulder: Westview Press, 1993) pp. 203–21.
132 Nina L. Khrushcheva, 'Russia and NATO: Lessons Learned', in S. Victor Papacosma, Sean Kay, Mark R. Rubin (ed.), *NATO: After Fifty Years* (Wilmington: A Scholarly Resources Inc., 2001) pp. 229–41.
133 IISS, *Strategic Survey 2002–3* (Oxford: Oxford University Press, 2003) pp. 109–15.

Chapter 5

1 Erich Hobsbawm, *Age of Extremes* (London: Abacus, 1996) p. 226.
2 Christoph Bluth, 'Strategic Nuclear Weapons and US–Russian Relations: From Confrontation to Co-operative Denuclearisation?', *Contemporary Security Policy* 15:1 (April 1994) p. 80.
3 Garthoff, *The Great Transition*, p. 509.
4 John Lewis Gaddis, *The United States and the End of the Cold War* (New York: Oxford University Press, 1992) p. 173.
5 Bluth, 'Strategic Nuclear Weapons', p. 81.
6 Ronald Reagan, *An American Life* (London: Hutchinson, 1990) p. 13.
7 Gorbachev, *Memoirs*, p. 403.
8 Lawrence Freedman, *The Evolution of Nuclear Strategy* (London: Macmillan, 1981) pp. 383–7.
9 Daniel Calingaert, *Soviet Nuclear Policy under Gorbachev: A Policy of Disarmament* (New York: Praeger, 1991) p. 90.
10 Loth, *Overcoming the Cold War*, pp. 150–5; Lundestad, *The United States and Western Europe*, pp. 205–7.
11 Savel'yev and Detinov, *The Big Five*, pp. 9–11, 55; see also David Holloway, *The Soviet Union and the Arms Race* (New Haven: Yale University Press, 1983) pp. 29–63 ff. According to the USA, strategic nuclear weapons must be intercontinental weapons – ICBM, SLBM and long-range bombers. The Soviet Union insisted that attack on the Soviet homeland from American bases in Europe and the Far East should also be considered strategic. See Donald M. Snow, *Nuclear Strategy in a Dynamic World* (Alabama: The University of Alabama Press, 1981) p. 24. Also note that the term, 'strategic' is often used as meaning 'nuclear', as opposed to non-nuclear (conventional) weapons, i.e. strategic (nuclear) doctrine.
12 Loth, *Overcoming the Cold War*, pp. 163–4.
13 Jonathan Haslam, *The Soviet Union and the Politics of Nuclear Weapons in Europe, 1969–87* (Basingstoke: Macmillan, 1989) pp. 101–5; Fischer, *The Reagan Reversal*, pp. 51–68.
14 'US and NATO Military Planning on Mission of V Corps/U.S. Army during Crises and in Wartime' 16 December 1982 (excerpt), in *CWIHP, Virtual Archive*, http://wwics.si.edu, accessed February 2004; Garthoff, *The Great Transition*, p. 506.
15 Matthew Evangelista, 'Turing Points in Arms Control', in Richard Herrmann and Richard Ned Lebow (ed.), *Ending the Cold War* (Basingstoke: Palgrave Macmillan, 2004) p. 88; Savel'yev and Detinov, *The Big Five*, p. 55.
16 NSDD 32 'US National Security Strategy' May 1982, in Christopher Simpson, *National Security Directives of the Reagan and Bush Administrations: The Declassified History of U.S. Political and*

Military Policy, 1981–1991 (Boulder: Westview Press, 1995) pp. 62–4; Robert Dallek, *Ronald Reagan: the Politics of Symbolism* (Cambridge, MA: Harvard University Press, 1984) pp. 129–42.

17 Pemberton, *Exist with Honor*, pp. 108–9; Loth, *Overcoming the Cold War*, pp. 166–7; Garthoff, *The Great Transition*, p. 505; For the long and controversial history of the B-1 Bomber, see Nick Kotz, *Wild Blue Yonder: Money, Politics and the B-1 Bomber* (Princeton: Princeton University Press, 1988).

18 Walter LaFeber, *America, Russia and the Cold War 1945–1996* (8th edn) (New York: MacGraw-Hill, 1997) p. 314.

19 NSDD 35 (17 May 1982), NSDD 69 (22 November 1982), NSDD 73 (3 January 1983), Simpson, *National Security Directive*, pp. 65, 82, 123, 221, 227, 250. See also *Strategic Survey, 1980–81* (IUSS, 1981) pp. 15, 40; Harry Sauerwein, 'Mobil ICBM and Arms Control', *Survival* 23:5 (September–October 1981), p. 215.

20 Garthoff, *The Great Transition*, p. 505.

21 Reagan, *An American Life*, p. 258; Fischer, *The Reagan Reversal*, pp. 104–5.

22 Garthoff, *The Great Transition*, pp. 511–12; Loth, *Overcoming the Cold War*, p. 168.

23 Young and Kent, *International Relations*, p. 527.

24 Haslam, *The Soviet Union and the Politics of Nuclear Weapons*, pp. 123–4; Loth, *Overcoming the Cold War*, p. 181.

25 Garthoff, *The Great Transition*, p. 512.

26 Oberdorfer, *From the Cold War to a New Era*, p. 25.

27 Reagan, *An American Life*, p. 548; For the SDI, see Edward Reiss, *The Strategic Defence Initiative* (Cambridge: Cambridge University Press, 1992); Frances Fitzgerald, *Way out there in the Blue: Regan, Star Wars, and the End of the Cold War* (New York: Simon & Schuster, 2000).

28 Lawrence Freedman, 'Eliminators, Marginalists and the Politics of Disarmament', in John Baylis and Robert O'Neill (ed.), *Alternative Nuclear Futures: The Role of Nuclear Weapons in the Post-Cold War World* (Oxford: Oxford University Press, 2000) p. 60.

29 LaFeber, *America, Russia and the Cold War*, p. 303; Casper Weinberger, *Fighting for Peace: Seven Critical Years at the Pentagon* (London: Michael Joseph, 1990) 213–20 ff.

30 Lundestad, *The United States and Western Europe*, p. 217.

31 Savel'yev and Detinov, *The Big Five*, pp. 164–6; Garthoff, *The Great Transition*, pp. 518–19.

32 Reagan, *An American Life*, p. 549.

33 Oberdorfer, *From the Cold War to a New Era*, p. 46; Dobrynin, *In Confidence*, pp. 523–7; Raymond Garthoff, 'Foreign Intelligence and the Historiography of the Cold War', *Cold War Studies* 6:2 (spring 2004) p. 40.

34 Beth A. Fischer, 'Reagan's Triumph?: The U.S. and the Ending of the Cold War', *Nobel Institute Research Seminar Paper* (May 2002) Norwegian Nobel Institute, Oslo, pp. 1–19.

35 Gromyko, *Memories*, p. 305; Reagan, *An American Life*, p. 605.

36 Loth, *Overcoming the Cold War*, p. 166; Garthoff, *The Great Transition*, p. 184.

37 Fraser Harbutt, *The Cold War Era* (Oxford: Blackwell, 2002) pp. 302–3.

38 Shultz, *Turmoil and Triumph*, p. 515.

39 Oberdorfer, *From the Cold War to a New Era*, p. 22.

40 Shultz, *Turmoil and Triumph*, pp. 531–3, 577.

41 Garthoff, *The Great Transition*, pp. 242–3.

42 Brown, *The Gorbachev Factor*, p. 272; Savel'yev and Detinov, *The Big Five*, p. 172.

43 Shultz, *Turmoil and Triumph*, p. 573; Garthoff, *The Great Transition*, pp. 201, 222.

44 Kenneth L. Adelman, 'Defense Policy and Arms Control: Discussants', in Eric J. Schmertz, Natalie Datlof and Alexeij Ugrinsky, *President Reagan and the World* (Westport: Greenwood Press, 1997) p. 240.

45 Shultz, *Turmoil and Triumph*, p. 567; Garthoff, *The Great Transition*, p. 219.

46 Young and Kent, *International Relations*, p. 581.

47 Shultz, *Turmoil and Triumph*, p. 583; Thatcher, *Downing Street*, pp. 466–8.

48 Shultz, *Turmoil and Triumph*, p. 575.

49 Dobrynin, *In Confidence* p. 589.

50 Shultz, *Turmoil and Triumph*, p. 594; Garthoff, *The Great Transition*, p. 228.

51 Thatcher, *Downing Street*, p. 470; Garthoff, *The Great Transition*, p. 224.

52 Gorbachev, *Memoirs*, p. 523.

53 Reagan, *An American Life*, p. 640.
54 Oberdorfer, *From the Cold War to a New Era*, pp. 169, 146, 149.
55 Reagan, *An American Life*, p. 646.
56 Garthoff, *The Great Transition*, p. 247.
57 Paul H. Nitze, *From Hiroshima to Glasnost: At the Centre of Decision – A Memoir* (with Ann M. Smith and Steven L. Rearden) (London: Weidenfeld and Nicolson, 1989) p. 421.
58 Shultz, *Turmoil and Triumph*, p. 595.
59 Garthoff, *The Great Transition*, pp. 277, 274–5.
60 Loth, *Overcoming the Cold War*, p. 190.
61 Shultz, *Turmoil and Triumph*, p. 708.
62 Garthoff, *The Great Transition*, pp. 281–5.
63 Nitze, *From Hiroshima to Glasnost*, p. 439.
64 Oberdorfer, *From the Cold War to a New Era*, p. 187.
65 Shultz, *Turmoil and Triumph*, p. 758; Gorbachev, *Memoirs*, pp. 535–7.
66 Shultz, *Turmoil and Triumph*, p. 760; Nitze, *From Hiroshima to Glasnost*, p. 432.
67 Oberdorfer, *From the Cold War to a New Era*, p. 192.
68 Nitze, *From Hiroshima to Glasnost*, pp. 432, 434.
69 Shultz, *Turmoil and Triumph*, p. 769.
70 Oberdorfer, *From the Cold War to a New Era*, pp. 201–2.
71 Reagan, An *American Life*, pp. 677–9; Gorbachev, *Perestroika*, p. 241.
72 Garthoff, *The Great Transition*, p. 291.
73 Shultz, *Turmoil and Triumph*, pp. 773, 778; Lundestad, *The United States and Western Europe*, pp. 228–9.
74 Brown, The *Gorbachev Factor*, pp. 232, 233.
75 Weinberger, *Fighting for Peace*, p. 220; Lundestad, *The United States and Western Europe*, p. 217; Haslam, *The USSR and Nuclear Weapons*, p. 167.
76 Garthoff, *The Great Transition*, pp. 292–4.
77 English, 'The Road(s) Not Taken', p. 259.
78 Garthoff, *The Great Transition*, p. 311; Bluth, *The Two Germanies*, pp. 198–200.
79 Bluth, *The Two Germanies*, pp. 199–204; Richard A. Bitzinger, 'Gorbachev and GRIT, 1985–89: Did Arms Control Succeed because of Unilateral Actions or in spite of Them?', *Contemporary Security Policy* 15:1 (April 1994) pp. 68–79.
80 For European responses, Ivo. H. Daalder, *The Nature and Practice of Flexible Response* (New York: Columbia University Press, 1993) pp. 255–8; Beatrice Heuser, *NATO, Britain, France and the FRG: Nuclear Strategies and Forces for Europe, 1949–2000* (Basingstoke: Macmillan, 1997) pp. 119–20; see also Thomas Halverson, *The Last Great Nuclear Debate: NATO and Short-Range Nuclear Weapons in the 1980s* (Basingstoke: Macmillan, 1995).
81 Haslam, *The Soviet Union and the Politics of Nuclear Weapons*, p. 168; Garthoff, *The Great Transition*, p. 313.
82 Bluth, *The Two Germanies*, p. 98; Garthoff, *The Great Transition*, p. 320.
83 Oberdorfer, *From the Cold War to a New Era*, p. 267; Calingaert, *Soviet Nuclear Policy under Gorbachev*, pp. 109–11.
84 Oberdorfer, *From the Cold War to a New Era*, p. 265; Garthoff, *The Great Transition*, p. 333.
85 Strobe Talbott, 'Why Start Stopped', *Foreign Affairs* (fall 1988), pp. 56–7.
86 Garthoff, *The Great Transition*, p. 339.
87 Oberdorfer, *From the Cold War to a New Era*, p. 277.
88 Jack F. Matlock, Jr, *Autopsy on An Empire: The American Ambassador's Account of the Collapse of the Soviet Union* (New York: Random House, 1995) pp. 122–3.
89 Garthoff, *The Great Transition*, p. 352; Young and Kent, *International Relations*, p. 586.
90 Oberdorfer, *From the Cold War to a New Era*, p. 295.
91 Garthoff, *The Great Transition*, p. 357; Matlock, *Autopsy on an Empire*, p. 125.
92 Evangelista, 'Turning Points in Arms Control', p. 85; Bitzinger, 'Gorbachev and GRIT', p. 69.
93 Gorbachev, *Memoirs*, pp. 592–5; Sakwa, *The Rise and Fall of the Soviet Union*, pp. 461–4.
94 Garthoff, *The Great Transition*, p. 371; Beschloss and Talbott, *At the Highest Levels*, p. 11.
95 Garthoff, *The Great Transition*, p. 372.

Chapter 6

1 Benjamin B. Fischer (ed.), *At Cold War's End: US Intelligence on the Soviet Union and Eastern Europe, 1989-1991* (Washington, DC: Central Intelligence Agency, 1999) NIE 11-23-88, p. 3.
2 Fischer (ed.), *At Cold War's End*, NIE 11-23-88, pp. 21-2.
3 James A. Baker with Thomas M. Defrank, *The Politics of Diplomacy: Revolution, War and Peace, 1989-1992* (New York: G. P. Putnam's Sons, 1995) p. 135.
4 Beschloss and Talbott, *At the Highest Levels*, pp. 115, 117.
5 Baker, *The Politics of Diplomacy*, p. 135.
6 Zubok, 'Gorbachev and the End of the Cold War', p. 215; Gorbachev, *Memoirs*, p. 646.
7 Garthoff, *The Great Transition*, p. 297.
8 Baker, *The Politics of Diplomacy*, p. 135.
9 Beschloss and Talbott, *At the Highest Levels*, p. 35.
10 Bush and Scowcroft, *A World Transformed*, p. 58; Loth, *Overcoming the Cold War*, p. 203.
11 Beschloss and Talbott, *At the Highest Levels*, p. 76.
12 Baker, *The Politics of Diplomacy*, p. 93; Beschloss and Talbott, *At the Highest Levels*, p. 74.
13 Oberdorfer, *From the Cold War to a New Era*, p. 350; Bush and Scowcroft, *A World Transformed*, p. 81.
14 Bush and Scowcroft, *A World Transformed*, p. 60.
15 John Dumbrell, *American Foreign Policy: Carter to Clinton* (Basingstoke: Macmillan, 1997) p. 140.
16 Baker, *The Politics of Diplomacy*, pp. 93-5; Bush and Scowcroft, *A World Transformed*, pp. 58-9.
17 IISS, *Strategic Survey, 1989-1990* (London: Brassey's, 1990) p. 59.
18 Baker, *The Politics of Diplomacy*, p. 151; Garthoff, *The Great Transition*, pp. 384-5, 389.
19 Baker, *The Politics of Diplomacy*, p. 155.
20 Garthoff, *The Great Transition*, pp. 387-8.
21 Beschloss and Talbott, *At the Highest Levels*, p. 123.
22 Fischer (ed.), *At Cold War's End*, NIE 11-18-89, p. 53.
23 Bush and Scowcroft, *A World Transformed*, p. 155; Beschloss and Talbott, *At the Highest Levels*, p. 141.
24 Bush and Scowcroft, *A World Transformed*, p. 163.
25 Documents on the December 1989 Malta Summit, *CWIHP Bulletin*, #12/13 (fall/winter 2001) p. 230.
26 Oberdorfer, *From the Cold War to a New Era*, p. 378; Garthoff, *The Great Transition*, p. 407.
27 Michael Mandelbaum, 'The Bush Foreign Policy', *Foreign Affairs* 70:1 (1990/1991) p. 6; Documents on the December 1989 Malta Summit, *CWIHP Bulletin* #12/13, p. 233.
28 Beschloss and Talbott, *At the Highest Levels*, p. 109; Documents on the December 1989 Malta Summit, *CWIHP Bulletin* #12/13, p. 240.
29 Documents on the December 1989 Malta Summit, *ibid.*, pp. 235, 238; Baker, *Politics of Diplomacy*, pp. 170-1.
30 Gorbachev, *Memoirs*, pp. 665-6; Bush and Scowcroft, *A World Transformed*, p. 173.
31 Bush and Scowcroft, *A World Transformed*, pp. 205, 208.
32 Bush and Scowcroft, *A World Transformed*, p. 493; Evangelista, 'Turning Points in Arms Control', pp. 90-1.
33 Grathoff, *The Great Transition*, p. 423.
34 Beschloss and Talbott, *At the Highest Levels*, pp. 163-4; Baker, *Politics of Diplomacy*, p. 139.
35 Bush and Scowcroft, *A World Transformed*, p. 222.
36 Robert L. Hutchings, *American Diplomacy and the End of the Cold War*, pp. 126-7.
37 Bush and Scowcroft, *A World Transformed*, pp. 227-8; White, *After Gorbachev*, p. 161.
38 Garthoff, *The Great Transition*, p. 426; Beschloss and Talbott, *At the Highest Levels*, p. 119.
39 Bush and Scowcroft, *A World Transformed*, p. 285.
40 Garthoff, *The Great Transition*, p. 447.
41 Bush and Scowcroft, *A World Transformed*, p. 499.
42 Bluth, *Two Germanies*, p. 228.
43 Garthoff, *The Great Transition*, pp. 412-14.
44 Loth, *Overcoming the Cold War*, p. 215.

45   Bluth, *Two Germanies*, p. 220; IISS, *Strategic Survey, 1990–91* (London: Brassey's, 1991) pp. 246–9.
46   Oberdorfer, *From the Cold War to a New Era*, p. 443; Beschloss and Talbott, *At the Highest Levels*, pp. 363–4; *Strategic Survey, 1990–1*, p. 250.
47   Beschloss and Talbott, *At the Highest Levels*, p. 368.
48   Beschloss and Talbott, *At the Highest Levels*, p. 370; IISS, *Strategic Survey, 1991–92* (London: Brassey's, 1992), p. 195.
49   Garthoff, *The Great Transition*, p. 463.
50   Bluth, 'Strategic Nuclear Weapons', p. 81.
51   Bluth, 'Strategic Nuclear Weapons', p. 80.
52   Beschloss and Talbott, *At the Highest Levels*, pp. 370–1, 405.
53   Garthoff, *The Great Transition*, p. 466; Calingaert, *Soviet Nuclear Policy under Gorbachev*, p. 163.
54   Bush and Scowcroft, *A World Transformed*, p. 514.
55   Joseph S. Nye, Jr, 'Arms Control After the Cold War', *Foreign Affairs* 68:5 (winter 1989/90) p. 42; Garthoff, *The Great Transition*, p. 472.
56   Oberdorfer, *From the Cold War to a New Era*, p. 420; Jeremy D. Rosner, 'American Assistance to the Former Soviet States in 1993–1994', in James M. Scott (ed.), *After the End: Making US Foreign Policy in the Post-Cold War World* (Durham, NC: Duke University Press, 1998) pp. 225–9.
57   Beschloss and Talbott, *At the Highest Levels*, p. 377; Bush and Scowcroft, *A World Transformed*, pp. 503–9.
58   Garthoff, *The Great Transition*, pp. 464–7.
59   Baker, *Politics of Diplomacy*, p. 144; Bush and Scowcroft, *A World Transformed*, p. 280.
60   Fischer (ed.), *At Cold War's End*, NIE 11-23-88, 'Gorbachev's Economic Programmes', p. 21.
61   Fischer (ed.), *At Cold War's End*, SINE 11-18.2-91, September 1991 'The Republics of the Former USSR: The Outlook for the Next Year', p. 189.
62   Bush and Scowcroft, *A World Transformed*, pp. 540, 541.
63   Garthoff, *The Great Transition*, p. 471; Bush and Scowcroft, *A World Transformed*, pp. 538–9.
64   Fischer (ed.), *At Cold War's End*, NIE 11-3/8-91, August 1991 'Soviet Forces and Capabilities for Strategic Nuclear Conflict through the Year 2000', p. 361.
65   Bush and Scowcroft, *A World Transformed*, p. 545.
66   Garthoff, *The Great Transition*, p. 491.
67   Oberdorfer, *From the Cold War to a New Era*, p. 468.
68   Garthoff, *The Great Transition*, p. 492; IISS, *Strategic Survey, 1991–2* (Brassey's, 1992) p. 24; *Strategic Survey, 1992–3* (Brassey's, 1993) p. 216.
69   Fischer (ed.), *At Cold War's End*, NIE 11-18.3-91, November 1991 'Civil Disorder in the Former USSR: Can It Be Managed This Winter?', p. 144.
70   Nye, Jr, 'Arms Control After the Cold War', p. 43.
71   Nye, Jr, 'Arms Control After the Cold War', pp. 44–5.
72   Bush and Scowcroft, *A World Transformed*, p. 561.
73   Bluth, *The Two Germanies*, pp. 226–7.
74   *Strategic Survey, 1992–93*, pp. 215–16.
75   See John Prados, 'Open Skies and Closed Minds', in Bischof and Dockrill, *Cold War Respite*, pp. 215–33. For the 1992 Open Sky Treaty, New Scientist (21 April 1992), and B. J. Cutler, 'Fulfilling Ike's Idea for Freer Skies', *Washington Times*, 24 May 1992, p. B4.
76   *Strategic Survey, 1991–92*, p. 24; Bluth, 'Nuclear Weapons and US–Russian Relations', pp. 90–1.
77   Avis Bohlen, 'The Rise and Fall of Arms Control', *Survival* 45:3 (autumn 2003) p. 26.
78   Bohlen, 'The Rise and Fall of Arms Control', p. 27; Lewis A. Dunn and Victor Alessi, 'Arms Control by Other Means', *Survival* 42:4 (winter 2000/1) p. 130.
79   Baker, *The Politics of Diplomacy*, p. 476.
80   Bush and Scowcroft, *A World Transformed*, p. 550.
81   Bluth, 'Nuclear Weapons and US–Russian Relations', pp. 88–9.
82   *Strategic Survey, 1992–3*, pp. 211–13.
83   Bluth, 'Nuclear Weapons and US–Russian Relations', p. 86; Clark, *The Post-Cold War Order*, p. 137.
84   *Strategic Survey, 1992–3*, p. 214.

85   Dunn and Alessi, 'Arms Control by Other Means', p. 130.
86   John Baylis and Robert O'Neill (ed.), *Alternative Nuclear Futures: The Role of Nuclear Weapons in the Post-Cold War World* (Oxford: Oxford University Press, 2000), especially 'The Contemporary Debate about Nuclear Weapons' by Baylis and O'Neill, 'To Confuse Ourselves: Nuclear Fallacies' by Colin Gray, and 'Eliminators, Marginalists and the Politics of Disarmament' by Lawrence Freedman, pp. 1–30, 56–69. See David S. Yost, 'The US and Nuclear Deterrence in Europe', *Adelphi Paper* 326 (London: IISS, 1999) pp. 13–75.
87   *Strategic Survey, 1997-8*, p. 47; Young and Kent, *International Relations*, p. 674.
88   Bluth, 'Nuclear Weapons and US–Russian Relations', p. 82.
89   Yost, 'The US and Nuclear Deterrence in Europe', p. 9.
90   David Shambaugh, *Modernizing China's Military: Progress, Problems, and Prospects* (Berkeley: University of California Press, 2002) p. 90; IISS, *Strategic Survey, 2001/2* (Oxford University Press, 2002) p. 19.
91   Robert S. Litwak, *Rogue States and U.S. Foreign Policy* (Washington, DC: The Woodrow Wilson Centre Press, 2000) pp. 2, 6.
92   Lawrence Freedman, 'Europe and Deterrence', in 'Nuclear Weapons: A New Great Debate' *Chaillot Paper* 48 (Paris: Institute for Security Studies, Western European Union, July 2001) pp. 81–102; Karl-Heinz Kamp, 'Germany and the Future of Nuclear Weapons in Europe', *Security Dialogue* 26:3 (1995) pp. 277–92. See also Brad Roberts, 'From Nonproliferation to Antiproliferation', *International Security* 18:1 (Summer 1993) pp. 139–73; Scott D. Sagan, 'The Perils of Proliferation', *International Security* 18:4 (Spring 1994) pp. 66–107.
93   Bohlen, 'The Rise and Fall of Arms Control', p. 27.
94   Colin Powell with Joseph E. Persico, *My American Journey* (New York: Ballantine Books, 1995) pp. 497–8; Jack Ruina, 'Threats to the ABM Treaty', *Security Dialogue* 26:3 (1995) p. 268.
95   Powell, *My American Journey*, p. 497; Bohlen, 'The Rise and Fall of Arms Control', p. 29.
96   Freedman, *Deterrence* (Cambridge: Polity, 2004) pp. 82–4, 94–5. See also Saki Dockrill, 'After September 11: Globalisation of Security', *Journal of Transatlantic Studies* 1.1 (spring 2003) supplement issue, pp. 1–19.
97   Dunn and Alessi, 'Arms Control by Other Means', p. 130.
98   Bohlen, 'The Rise and Fall of Arms Control', pp. 30–1.
99   'Putin goes Ballistic' Editorial, *The Guardian*, 21 February 2004; *Security Watch*, 23 February 2004 isn-daily – http://www.isn.ethz.ch.

Chapter 7

1   While the term the Third World has increasingly become out of touch with the complex reality which has emerged since the 1980s and before the end of the Cold War, this chapter refers to the Third World in the context of the American–Soviet rivalry, or simply refers to regional conflicts to avoid further confusion. See Iain McLean (ed.), *The Concise Oxford Dictionary of Politics* (Oxford: Oxford University Press, 1996) p. 496; see also Michael Cox, 'International History since 1989', in John Baylis and Steve Smith (ed.), *The Globalization of World Politics* (Oxford: Oxford University Press, 2001) pp. 133–4.
2   Michael Hunt, *Ideology and U.S. Foreign Policy* (New Haven: Yale University Press, 1987) pp. 159–60.
3   S. Neil MacFarlane, 'Successes and Failures in Soviet Policy toward Marxist Revolutions in the Third World, 1917–1985', in Mark N. Katz (ed.), *The USSR and Marxist Revolutions in the Third World* (New York: Woodrow Wilson International Centre for Scholars and Cambridge University Press, 1990) p. 6.
4   MacFarlane, 'Successes and Failures in Soviet Policy', p. 9.
5   Mark Katz, 'Introduction', in Katz (ed.), *The USSR and Marxist Revolutions in the Third World*, p. 2.
6   Wayne P. Limberg, 'Soviet Military Support for Third-World Marxist Regimes', in Katz (ed.), *The USSR and Marxist Revolutions in the Third World*, p. 56.
7   Recent works on the subject, see Mark Kramer, 'Ideology and the Cold War', pp. 359–76; Nigel Gould-Davies, 'Rethinking the Role of Ideology in International Politics during the Cold War', *Journal of Cold War Studies* 1:1 (1999) pp. 92–108.

8   Francis Fukuyama, 'Patterns of Soviet Third World Policy', *Problems of Communism* (September–October 1987) pp. 1–3.
9   Limberg, 'Soviet Military Support', p. 52.
10 Samuel Huntington, 'Patterns of Intervention', *The National Interest* no. 7 (spring 1987) quoted in Fukuyama, 'Patterns of Soviet Third World Policy', p. 2, and also Centre for Defense Information, 'Soviet Geopolitical Momentum: Myth of Menace?', in Robbin F. Laird and Erik P. Hoffmann (ed.), *Soviet Foreign Policy in a Changing World* (New York: Aldine de Gruyter, 1986) pp. 701–12.
11 Constantine Pleshakov, 'Nikita Khrushchev and Sino-Soviet Relations', in Odd Arne Westad (ed.), *Brothers in Arms* (Stanford: Stanford University Press, 1998) p. 227; Constantine Pleshakov, 'Studying Soviet Strategies and Decision Making in the Cold War Years'; Odd Arne Westad (ed), *Reviewing the Cold War* (London: Frank Cass, 2000) pp. 227–8.
12 MacFarlane, 'Successes and Failures in Soviet Policy', p. 9; see also Robert G. Patman, *The Soviet Union in the Horn of Africa: The Diplomacy of Intervention and Disengagement* (Cambridge: Cambridge University Press, 1990) pp. 58–110 ff.; Odd Arne Westad, 'The Fall of Détente and the Turning Tides of History', in Westad (ed.), *The Fall of Détente: Soviet-American Relations during the Carter Years* (Oslo: Scandinavian University Press, 1997) pp. 3–29 ff.; see also Westad, *The Global Cold War: Third World Interventions and the Making of Our Times* (Cambridge University Press, 2005).
13 Limberg, 'Soviet Military Support', pp. 58–9, 60; Vojtech Mastny, *The Cold War and Soviet Insecurity* (Oxford: Oxford University Press, 1996) p. 31.
14 MacFarlane, 'Successes and Failures in Soviet Policy', pp. 22–3.
15 MacFarlane, 'Successes and Failures in Soviet Policy', p. 13.
16 Odd Arne Westad, 'Introduction', in Odd Arne Westad (ed.), *Brothers in Arms* (Stanford: Stanford University Press, 1998), pp. 1–32 ff.
17 For the outbreak of the Korean War, see Kathryn Weathersby, 'Should We Fear This?: Stalin and the Danger of War with America', *CWIHP Working Paper* no. 39 (2002), and Weathersby, 'Soviet Aims in Korea and the Origins of the Korean War, 1945–1950', *CWIHP Working Paper* no. 8 (1994). See also James Hershberg, 'Russian Documents on the Korean War, 1950–1953', *CWIHP Bulletin*, #14/15 (winter 2003–spring 2004) pp. 369–84.
18 Limberg, 'Soviet Military Support', p. 60; Pleshakov, 'Nikita Khrushchev and Sino-Soviet Relations', pp. 227–8.
19 MacFarlane, 'Successes and Failures in Soviet Policy', pp. 28–9.
20 Piero Gleijeses, *Conflicting Missions: Havana, Washington, and Africa, 1959–1976* (Chapel Hill: The University of North Carolina Press, 2002) p. 18.
21 Raymond Garthoff, 'New Evidence on the Cuban Missile Crisis', *CWIHP Bulletin*, #11 (winter 1998) pp. 251–4; Svetlana Savaranskaya, 'Tactical Nuclear Weapons in Cuba: New Evidence', *CWIHP Bulletin*, #14/15, pp. 385–7.
22 Zubok and Pleshakov, *Inside the Kremlin's Cold War*, pp. 211–35; Odd Arne Westad, 'Introduction', in Westad (ed.), *Brothers in Arms*, pp. 7–32 ff.
23 Ilya V. Gaiduk, 'Developing an Alliance: the Soviet Union and Vietnam, 1954–75', in Peter Lowe (ed.), *The Vietnam War* (Basingstoke: Macmillan, 1998) pp. 133–51ff.
24 MacFarlane, 'Successes and Failures in Soviet Policy', pp. 32–3.
25 Patman, *The Soviet Union in the Horn of Africa*, pp. 71–6.
26 Richard Crockatt, *American Embattled: September 11, Anti-Americanism and the Global Order* (London: Routledge, 2003) p. 11.
27 Hunt, *Ideology and U.S. Foreign Policy*, especially chapter 4; Crockatt, *American Embattled*, p. 14.
28 Hunt, *Ideology and U.S. Foreign Policy*, p. 28.
29 Hunt, *Ideology and U.S. Foreign Policy*, p. 123.
30 Ernest May, *Imperial Democracy – the Emergence of America as a Great Power* (New York: Harcourt, Brace and World Inc., 1961), chapters 6–8; Warren I. Cohen, *American Response to China* (New York: Alfred A. Knopf, 1980) pp. 31–60.
31 Crockatt, *American Embattled*, p. 19.
32 Hunt, *Ideology and U.S. Foreign Policy*, p. 133.
33 Hunt, *Ideology and U.S. Foreign Policy*, p. 115; Gaddis, *Russia, the Soviet Union and the United States*, p. 105.

34 Hunt, *Ideology and U.S. Foreign Policy*, p. 148; Saki Dockrill, 'One Step Forward – A Reappraisal of the "Pacific War"', in Saki Dockrill (ed.), *From Pearl Harbor to Hiroshima: The Second World War in Asia and the Pacific, 1941–1945* (London: Macmillan, 1994) pp. 4–5.

35 Robert J. McMahon, 'The Challenge of the Third World', in Peter L. Hahn and Mary Ann Heiss, *Empire and Revolution: The United States and the Third World since 1945* (Columbus: Ohio State University Press, 2001) pp. 8–9; Gaddis, *Russia, the Soviet Union and the United States*, pp. 175–105; Melvyn P. Leffler, *A Preponderance of Power: National Security, the Truman Administration and the Cold War* (Stanford: Stanford University Press, 1992) pp. 15–19; Leffler, 'The American Conception of National Security and the Beginning of the Cold War, 1945–48', *The American Historical Review* 89:2 (April 1984) pp. 346–81.

36 McMahon, 'The Challenge of the Third World', p. 3.

37 Hunt, *Ideology and U.S. Foreign Policy*, p. 159.

38 Dockrill, *Eisenhower's New Look National Security Policy*, pp. 168–70.

39 Herrmann, 'Regional Conflicts as Turning Points', in Hermann and Lebow (ed.), *Ending the Cold War*, pp. 72–3.

40 Hunt, *Ideology and U.S. Foreign Policy*, p. 160; National Security Council meeting, 21 November 1955, *Foreign Relations of the United States* vol.10 (hereafter cited as *FRUS*) (Washington, DC: United States Government Printing Office (USGPO), 1989) pp. 32, 35.

41 State Department Policy Paper (unsigned), 27 November 1953, Box 1, International Meetings Series, *Ann Whitman File*, Dwight D. Eisenhower Library, Abilene, Kansas; *Seminal Report of the Secretary of Defense* (Jan. –June 1956) p. 54.

42 NSC 229th meeting, 21 December 1954, *FRUS 1952–54*, vol. 2, pp. 832–44; NSC 266th meeting, 21 November 1955, *FRUS 1955–7*, vol. 10, p. 34; NSC 214th meeting, 12 September 1954, *FRUS 1952–54*, vol. 14. p. 617.

43 William Rosenau, 'The Eisenhower Administration, US Foreign Internal Security Assistance, and the Struggle for the Developing World, 1954–1961', *Low Intensity Conflict and Law Enforcement* 10:3 (autumn 2001) p. 23.

44 Gary May, 'Passing the Torch and Lighting Fires: The Peace Corps', in Thomas G. Paterson, *Kennedy's Quest for Victory: American Foreign Policy, 1961–1963* (Oxford: Oxford University Press, 1989) pp. 285–6.

45 Harbutt, *The Cold War Era*, p. 145.

46 Lawrence Freedman, *Kennedy's Wars: Berlin, Cuba, Laos, and Vietnam* (Oxford: Oxford University Press, 2000) p. 317.

47 George C. Herring, *America's Longest War* (New York: McGraw-Hill, 1986) esp. chapters 2 and 3.

48 A recent study on the subject, see Howard Jones, *Death of a Generation: How the Assassinations of Diem and JFK Prolonged the Vietnam War* (Oxford: Oxford University Press, 2003).

49 George C. Herring, *LBJ and Vietnam: A Different Kind of War* (Austin: University of Texas, 1994) p. 34.

50 Stanley Karnow, *Vietnam: A History* (Middlesex: Penguin Books, 1987) p. 320.

51 Marilyn B. Young, *The Vietnam Wars, 1945–1990* (New York: Harper Perennial, 1991) p. 237.

52 Harbutt, *The Cold War Era*, p. 222.

53 Stein Tønnesson, 'Tracking Multi-Directional Dominoes', in 77 Conversations between Chinese and Foreign Leaders on the Wars in Indochina, 1964–1967', *CWIHP, Working Paper* no. 22 (1998) p. 22; 'The Mao-Khrushchev Conversations, 31 July–3 August 1958 and 2 October 1959', *CWIHP Bulletin*, # 12/13, pp. 244–72.

54 Chen Jian, *Mao's China and the Cold War* (Chapel Hill: The University of North Carolina Press, 2001) p. 207; Odd Arne Westad, 'History, Memory and the Languages of Alliance-Making', in '77 Conversations' *CWIHP, Working Paper* no. 22 (1998) p. 4.

55 Harbutt, *The Cold War Era*, p. 187.

56 Arthur Marwick, *The Sixties: Cultural Revolution in Britain, France, Italy and the United States, 1968–1974* (Oxford: Oxford University Press, 1998) p. 3.

57 Harbutt, *The Cold War Era*, p. 245.

58 Scott Newton, *The Global Economy, 1944–2000* (London: Arnold, 2004) pp. 79–110.

59 Harbutt, *The Cold War Era*, pp. 237–8.

60 Patman, *The Soviet Union in the Horn of Africa*, pp. 80–7 ff.; for Great Britain's decision to withdraw from east of Suez, see Saki Dockrill, *Britain's Retreat from East of Suez: The Choice between Europe and the World?* (Basingstoke: Palgrave Macmillan, 2002).

61 Chen Jian, *Mao's China and the Cold War*, pp. 242–3; Patman, *The Soviet Union in the Horn of Africa*, pp. 68, 86–7.

62 Westad, 'The Fall of Détente and the Turning Tides of History', p. 19.

63 MacFarlane, 'Successes and Failures in Soviet Policy', p. 35; Westad, 'The Fall of Détente and the Turning Tides of History', p. 11.

64 Patman, *The Soviet Union in the Horn of Africa*, p. 64.

65 Odd Arne Westad, 'Moscow and the Angolan Crisis, 1974–1976: A New Pattern of Intervention', in *CWIHP Bulletin*, #8–9 (winter 1996/7) pp. 21–8 ff.

66 Garthoff, *Détente and Confrontation*, p. 727; Patman, *The Soviet Union in the Horn of Africa*, pp. 113–203 ff.; Steven Jackson, 'China's Third World Foreign Policy: The Case for Angola and Mozambique, 1961–93', *The China Quarterly*, no.142 (June 1995) pp. 388–422.

67 Christopher Andrew, *For the President's Eyes Only*, pp. 411–17; Robert David Johnson, 'The Unintended Consequences of Congressional Reform: The Clark and Tunney Amendments and U.S. Policy toward Angola', *Diplomatic History* 27:2 (April 2003) p. 234; Gleijeses, *Conflicting Missions: Havana, Washington, and Africa, 1959–1976*, pp. 331–3.

68 David Caldwell, 'US Domestic Politics and the Demise of Détente', in Westad (ed.), *The Fall of Détente*, p. 105; see also Jussi Hanhimäki, *The Flawed Architect: Henry Kissinger and American Foreign Policy* (Oxford: Oxford University Press, 2004).

69 Garthoff, *Détente and Confrontation*, pp. 642–3; Zbigniew Brzezinski, *Power and Principle: Memoirs of the National Security Adviser, 1977–1981* (New York: McGraw-Hill Ryerson, 1983) pp. 197–233, 403–414.

70 Brezhnev's conversation with Erich Honecker, 27 July 1979, Westad (ed.), *The Fall of Détente*, p. 235; Westad, 'The Fall of Détente and the Turning Tides of History', in *ibid.*, p. 22.

71 Caldwell, 'US Domestic Politics and the Demise of Détente', p. 109.

72 Garthoff, *Détente and Confrontation*, pp. 923–5, 931.

73 Douglas Little, *American Orientalism: The United States and the Middle East since 1945* (London: I.B. Tauris, 2003) pp. 221–7; Harbutt, *The Cold War Era*, pp. 256–8.

74 Geoffrey Roberts, *The Soviet Union in World Politics* (London: Routledge, 1999) p. 82; Arne Odd Westad, 'Concerning the Situation in "A": New Russian Evidence on the Soviet Intervention in Afghanistan', *CWIHP Bulletin*, #8/9 (winter 1996/7) p. 129.

75 Visiliy Mitrokhin, 'The KGB in Afghanistan' (introduced and ed. by Christian F. Ostermann and Odd Arne Westad), *CWIHP Working Paper*, #40 (February 2002) pp. 17–20.

76 Mitrokhin, 'The KGB in Afghanistan', pp. 25–29; Young and Kent, *International Relations*, pp. 491–2.

77 Mitrokhin, 'The KGB in Afghanistan', p. 82; Odd Arne Westad, 'The Road to Kabul: Soviet Policy on Afghanistan, 1978–1979', in Westad (ed.), *The Fall of Détente*, pp. 129–30.

78 Westad, 'Concerning the Situation in "A"', pp. 130–1.

79 Margot Light, 'Soviet "New Thinking": Soviet Policy in the Third World', *International Affairs* 67:1 (1991) p. 265.

80 LaFeber, *America, Russia and the Cold War*, p. 299; Harbutt, *The Cold War Era*, p. 258.

81 MacFarlane, 'Successes and Failures in Soviet Policy', pp. 40–1; Garthoff, *The Great Transition*, pp. 680–1.

82 William M. Leogrande, *The United States in Central America, 1977–1992: Our Own Backyard* (Chapel Hill: The University of North Carolina Press, 1998) p. 80.

83 C. Andrew, *For the President's Eyes Only*, pp. 370–4.

84 Walter LaFeber, *Inevitable Revolutions: the United States in Central America* (New York: W. W. Norton, 1984) pp. 278–9; Leogrande, *The United States in Central America*, pp. 54–5.

85 Weinberger, *Fighting for Peace*, pp. 94–108 ff.; H. W. Brands, *Into the Labyrinth: the United States and the Middle East, 1945–1993* (New York: McGraw-Hill, 1994) pp. 174–8.

86 LaFeber, *America, Russia and the Cold War*, p. 308.

87 Shultz, *Turmoil and Triumph*, pp. 336–7.

88 Thatcher, *Downing Street*, pp. 330–2.

89 Casper Weinberger, 'U.S. Defense Strategy', *Foreign Affairs* 64:4 (spring 1986) pp. 686–7; Alexander L. George, 'The Role of Force in Diplomacy: A Continuing Dilemma for U.S. Foreign Policy', in H. W. Brands (ed.), *The Use of Force after the Cold War* (College Station: Texas A & M University Press, 2000) pp. 62–3.
90 Shultz, *Turmoil and Triumph*, p. 329; Garthoff, *The Great Transition*, p. 699.
91 *Ibid.*, pp. 681–2, 691–3.

Chapter 8

1 Francis Fukuyama, 'Gorbachev and the Third World', *Foreign Affairs* (spring 1986) pp. 715–16.
2 Wayne P. Limberg, 'Soviet Military Support for Third-World Marxist Regimes', p. 101.
3 Garthoff, *The Great Transition*, pp. 718–19.
4 Fukuyama, 'Gorbachev and the Third World', p. 730.
5 Herrmann, 'Regional Conflicts as Turning Points', p. 74.
6 Limberg, 'Soviet Military Support for Third-World Marxist Regimes', p. 104.
7 Fukuyama, 'Gorbachev and the Third World', p. 720; Mitrokhin, 'The KGB in Afghanistan', p. 109; Young and Kent, *International Relations*, p. 493.
8 Limberg, 'Soviet Military Support for Third-World Marxist Regimes', p. 104; Fukuyama, 'Gorbachev and the Third World', pp. 719–21.
9 Garthoff, *The Great Transition*, p. 720.
10 Fukuyama, 'Gorbachev and the Third World', pp. 724–5.
11 Garthoff, *The Great Transition*, p. 720.
12 Limberg, 'Soviet Military Support for Third-World Marxist Regimes', pp. 93, 110–11; Fukuyama, 'Patterns of Soviet Third World Policy', *Problems of Communism* (September–October, 1987) p. 10.
13 Stephen J. Morris, *Why Vietnam Invaded Cambodia: Political Culture and the Causes of War* (Stanford: Stanford University Press, 1999) pp. 203, 215.
14 Morris, *ibid.*, p. 223; Gaiduk, 'The Soviet Union and Vietnam, 1954–1975', pp. 148–51.
15 Limberg, 'Soviet Military Support for Third-World Marxist Regimes', pp. 63–4, 81; MacFarlane, 'Successes and Failures in Soviet Policy toward Marxist Revolutions in the Third World, 1917–1985', pp. 29–31.
16 Garthoff, *The Great Transition*, p. 720.
17 Chernyaev, *My Six Years with Gorbachev*, p. 62.
18 Calvocoressi, *World Politics*, p. 836.
19 Chernyaev, *My Six Years with Gorbachev*, p. 204; Garthoff, *The Great Transition*, pp. 719–20.
20 Limberg, 'Soviet Military Support for Third-World Marxist Regimes', p. 108; Garthoff, *The Great Transition*, p. 734.
21 Limberg, 'Soviet Military Support for Third-World Marxist Regimes', p. 104; Sakwa, *The Rise and Fall of the Soviet Union*, p. 463.
22 Garthoff, *The Great Transition*, p. 734.
23 Fukuyama, 'Gorbachev and the Third World', p. 730.
24 Garthoff, *The Great Transition*, pp. 648–52.
25 Robert S. Ross, 'The Bush Administration: The Origins of Engagement', in Ramon H. Myers, Michel C. Oksenberg and David Shambaugh, *Making China Policy: Lessons from the Bush and Clinton Administrations* (Lanham: Rowman & Littlefield Publishers, 2001) p. 22; Gorbachev, *Memoirs*, pp. 631–7 ff.
26 Wang Jisi and Wang Yong, 'A Chinese Account: the Interaction of Policies', in *Making China Policy*, p. 270.
27 Garthoff, *The Great Transition*, p. 668.
28 Alvin Rubinstein, 'Moscow's Third World Strategy', in Frederic J. Fleron, Jr, Erik P. Hoffmann and Robin F. Laird (ed.), *Contemporary Issues in Soviet Foreign Policy from Brezhnev to Gorbachev* (New York: Aldine de Gruyter, 1991) p. 689.
29 Fukuyama, 'Patterns of Soviet Third World Policy', p. 8; Melvin A. Goodman and Carolyn McGiffert Ekedahl, 'Gorbachev's "New Directions" in the Middle East', *Middle East Journal* 42:1 (autumn 1988) pp. 574–7.
30 Garthoff, *The Great Transition*, p. 731; Goodman and Ekedahl, 'Gorbachev's "New Directions" in the Middle East', p. 579.

31 MacFarlane, 'Successes and Failures in Soviet Policy toward Marxist Revolutions in the Third World', 1917–1985', p. 41.

32 Goodman and Ekedahl, 'Gorbachev's "New Directions" in the Middle East', pp. 576–81; Garthoff, *The Great Transition*, pp. 731–3 ff.

33 Goodman and Ekedahl, 'Gorbachev's "New Directions" in the Middle East', pp. 573–4; for Great Britain on the Middle East, and the Persian Gulf, see Dockrill, *Britain's Retreat from East of Suez*, pp. 124–7,154–5, 182, 193–6.

34 Fukuyama, 'Patterns of Soviet Third World Policy', p. 11; Fukuyama, 'Gorbachev and the Third World', p. 725; Limberg, 'Soviet Military Support for Third-World Marxist Regimes', pp. 117–18.

35 Chernyaev, *My Six Years with Gorbachev*, pp. 144–5.

36 Rubinstein, 'Moscow's Third World Strategy', p. 689; Limberg, 'Soviet Military Support for Third-World Marxist Regimes', p. 117.

37 Fukuyama, 'Gorbachev and the Third World,' p. 725; Stephen White, *After Gorbachev*, p. 217.

38 Herrmann, 'Regional Conflicts as Turning Points', pp. 67–71.

39 Garthoff, *The Great Transition*, p. 379.

40 Gorbachev, *Perestroika*, p. 222.

41 Rubinstein, 'Moscow's Third World Strategy', p. 691.

42 Rubinstein, 'Moscow's Third World Strategy', pp. 685, 680; Limberg, 'Soviet Military Support for Third-World Marxist Regimes', p. 114.

43 Mark N. Kramer, 'Soviet Arms Transfers to the Third World', *Problems of Communism*, Sept.–Oct. 1987, pp. 66–7.

44 MacFarlane, 'Successes and Failures in Soviet Policy toward Marxist Revolutions in the Third World', p. 47.

45 Christopher Andrew and Oleg Gordievsky, *KGB: The Inside Story of its Foreign Operations from Lenin to Gorbachev* (London: Sceptre, 1991) p. 577; see also Fred Halliday, 'Soviet Foreign Policymaking and the Afghanistan War: from "Second Mongolia" to "bleeding wound", *Review of International Studies* 25:4 (1999) pp. 670–80.

46 Diego Cordovez and Selig S. Harrison, *Out of Afghanistan: the Inside Story of the Soviet Withdrawal* (New York: Oxford University Press, 1995) p. 187.

47 Mitrokhin, 'The KGB in Afghanistan', pp. 17–18; Westad, 'The Road to Kabul', p. 142.

48 The Russian General Staff (trans. and ed. by Lester W. Grau and Michael A. Gress), *The Soviet–Afghan War: How a Superpower Fought and Lost* (Kansas: University Press of Kansas, 2002) pp. 18, 53.

49 Young and Kent, *International Relations*, p. 532; The Russian General Staff, *The Soviet–Afghan War*, p. 19; J. William Derleth, 'The Soviets in Afghanistan: Can the Red Army Fight a Counterinsurgency War?', *Armed Forces and Society* 15:1 (Fall 1988) pp. 33–44 ff.

50 Westad, 'The Road to Kabul', p. 142.

51 Politburo meeting and decisions on Afghanistan, 7 Feb. 1980, *CWIHP, Bulletin #8/9* (winter 1996/7) pp. 165–7.

52 The Russian General Staff, *The Soviet–Afghan War*, p. 53.

53 William Maley, *The Afghanistan Wars* (Basingstoke: Palgrave Macmillan, 2002) pp. 8–17, 60–6; Mark Galeotti, *Afghanistan: the Soviet Union's Last War* (London: Frank Cass, 2001) pp. 3–4.

54 Cordovez and Harrison, *Out of Afghanistan*, p. 61.

55 The Russian General Staff, *The Soviet–Afghan War*, pp. 53–5.

56 The Russian General Staff, *The Soviet–Afghan War*, p. 25; Young and Kent, *International Relations*, p. 533.

57 Gates, *From the Shadows*, p. 149; Bob Woodward, *Veil: The Secret Wars of the CIA 1981–1987* (London: Simon and Schuster, 1987) pp. 78–9, 104.

58 Gates, *From the Shadows*, p. 199.

59 Cordovez and Harrison, *Out of Afghanistan*, p. 70.

60 Maley, *The Afghanistan Wars*, pp. 69–70.

61 Cordovez and Harrison, *Out of Afghanistan*, pp. 65–6; Steve Coll, *Ghost Wars* (New York: The Penguin Press, 2004) pp. 61–2.

62 Gates, *From the Shadows*, p. 252.

63 Cordovez and Harrison, *Out of Afghanistan*, p. 69; Garthoff, *The Great Transition*, p. 713.

64 Derleth, 'The Soviets in Afghanistan: Can the Red Army Fight a Counterinsurgency War?', pp. 44–7.

65 Cordovez and Harrison, *Out of Afghanistan*, pp. 104–5, 156; Coll, *Ghost Wars*, pp. 65–6.

66 Herrmann, 'Regional Conflicts as Turning Points', p. 62.

67 Garthoff, *The Great Transition*, pp. 712–13; John Cooley, *Unholy Wars: Afghanistan, America and International Terrorism* (London: Pluto, 2002) p. 65; The Russian General Staff, *The Soviet-Afghan War*, p. 60.

68 Coll, *Ghost Wars*, p. 65; Cordovez and Harrison, *Out of Afghanistan*, pp. 160–4.

69 Garthoff, *The Great Transition*, p. 712.

70 Cordovez and Harrison, *Out of Afghanistan*, p. 164.

71 Gates, *From the Shadows*, p. 321; Garthoff, *The Great Transition*, p. 714.

72 Maley, *The Afghanistan Wars*, p. 136.

73 A Politburo meeting (excerpt), 10 March 1983, pp. 177–8, see also Westad, 'Concerning the situation in "A"', p. 132, both in *CWIHP, Bulletin #8/9* (winter 1996/7); Sarah E. Mendelson, *Changing Course: Ideas, Politics and the Soviet Withdrawal from Afghanistan* (Princeton: Princeton University Press, 1998) pp. 73–4.

74 Cordovez and Harrison, *Out of Afghanistan*, pp. 92, 102, 152–3.

75 Andrew and Gordievsky, *KGB*, pp. 577–8.

76 Maley, *The Afghanistan Wars*, p. 100.

77 Mitrokhin, 'The KGB in Afghanistan', pp. 138–44 ff.

78 The Russian General Staff, *The Soviet-Afghan War*, pp. 24–5; Cordovez and Harrison, *Out of Afghanistan*, pp. 148–9.

79 Cordovez and Harrison, *Out of Afghanistan*, pp. 187–8.

80 Garthoff, *The Great Transition*, pp. 726–7, 259.

81 Maley, *The Afghanistan Wars*, p. 117–22 ff.; Politburo meeting, 21–22 May 1987 (excerpt), *CWIHP Bulletin, #14/15* (Winter 2003–Spring 2004) p. 148.

82 Cordovez and Harrison, *Out of Afghanistan*, p. 195; Shultz, *Turmoil and Triumph*, p. 692; Overdorfer, *From the Cold War to a New Era*, p. 227.

83 Cordovez and Harrison, *Out of Afghanistan*, p. 199; Mendelson, *Changing Course*, p. 98.

84 Gorbachev's meeting with Italian Minister of Foreign Affairs, Giulio Andreotti, 27 February 1987, p. 147; Politburo meeting, 21–22 May 1987 (excerpt), pp. 148–9, both in *CWIHP Bulletin, #14/15*; Overdorfer, *From the Cold War to a New Era*, p. 227.

85 Gorbachev's meeting with Reagan, 9 December 1987 (excerpt), p. 166; Politburo meeting, 21–22 May 1987 (excerpt), p. 149, both in *CWIHP Bulletin, #14/15*.

86 Politburo meeting, 21–22 May 1987 (excerpt), p. 149; Politburo meeting, 23 February 1987 (excerpt), p. 146, both in *CWIHP Bulletin, #14/15*.

87 Politburo meeting, 21–22 May 1987 (excerpt), pp. 148–9, *CWIHP Bulletin, #14/15*.

88 Shultz, *Turmoil and Triumph*, p. 707.

89 Maley, *The Afghanistan Wars*, p. 138; Cordovez and Harrison, *Out of Afghanistan*, pp. 190–1.

90 Gorbachev's meeting with Reagan, 9 December 1987 (excerpt), *CWIHP Bulletin, #14/15*, p. 166.

91 Garthoff, *The Great Transition*, p. 737.

92 Shultz, *Turmoil and Triumph*, p. 1089.

93 Coll, *Ghost Wars*, p. 186.

94 Maley, *The Afghanistan Wars*, pp. 159, 169.

95 Garthoff, *The Great Transition*, p. 714.

96 Gleijeses, *Conflicting Missions*, pp. 362, 382; Shultz, *Turmoil and Triumph*, p. 1113, and for Tutu's statement see *ibid.*, p. 1115.

97 Shultz, *Turmoil and Triumph*, p. 1113; Gates, *From the Shadows*, p. 337; Garthoff, *The Great Transition*, p. 715.

98 Shultz, *Turmoil and Triumph*, pp. 1116–17.

99 Gleijeses, *Conflicting Missions*, p. 273; Chas. W. Freeman, Jr, 'The Angola/Namibia Accords', *Foreign Affairs* (summer 1989) pp. 128–9.

100 Gleijeses, *Conflicting Missions*, p. 276; Chester A. Crocker, *High Noon in Southern Africa: Making Peace in a Rough Neighbourhood* (New York: W. W. Norton, 1992) pp. 65–70.

101 Freeman, The Angola/Namibia Accords', p. 130; Crocker, *High Noon*, pp. 65–70.

102 Fukuyama, 'Gorbachev and the Third World', p. 724; Gates, *From the Shadows*, pp. 336–7, 347.

103 Gates, *From the Shadows*, p. 346.

104 Herrmann, 'Regional Conflicts as Turning Points', pp. 63–4; Gates, *From the Shadows*, p. 347; Shultz, *Turmoil and Triumph*, p. 1123.

105 Shultz, *Turmoil and Triumph*, pp. 1112–3, 1123.

106 Freeman, 'The Angola/Namibia Accords', p. 133.

107 Crocker, *High Noon*, pp. 347–56.

108 Shultz, *Turmoil and Triumph*, pp. 1124–5.

109 Freeman, 'The Angola/Namibia Accords', pp. 126, 136.

110 Baker, *The Politics of Diplomacy*, p. 599.

111 IISS, *Strategic Survey, 1992–1993* (London: Brassey's, 1993) pp. 204–6; Herrmann, 'Regional Conflicts as Turning Points', p. 64.

112 Garthoff, *The Great Transition*, pp. 741–2; Baker, *The Politics of Diplomacy*, p. 601.

113 Steven Hurst, *The Foreign Policy of the Bush Administration* (London: Cassell, 1999) pp. 80–1.

114 Gates, *From the Shadows*, pp. 151–2 ; Limberg, 'Soviet Military Support for Third World Marxist Regimes', p. 99.

115 LaFeber, *Inevitable Revolutions*, pp. 248–9; Gates, *From the Shadows* p. 152.

116 Leogrande, *The United States in Central America*, pp. 34, 86.

117 LaFeber, *Inevitable Revolutions*, p. 284.

118 *Ibid.*, p. 286; Leogrande, *The United States in Central America*, p. 89.

119 Young and Kent, *International Relations*, p. 562.

120 LaFeber, *Inevitable Revolutions*, pp. 288–9.

121 Limberg, 'Soviet Military Support for Third-World Marxist Regimes', pp. 99–101; Shultz, *Turmoil and Triumph*, p. 287; Lloyd Pettiford, 'Changing Conceptions of Security in the Third World', *Third World Quarterly* 17:2 (1996) p. 290.

122 Leogrande, *The United States in Central America*, pp. 82–4.

123 'Ronald Reagan, Presidential Finding on Covert Operations in Nicaragua, December 1, 1981', in Peter Kornblugh and Malcolm Byrne, *The Iran-Contra Scandal: The Declassified History* (New York: The New Press, 1993) p. 11; Leogrande, *The United States in Central America*, pp. 306–10.

124 'CIA Scope of CIA Activities under the Nicaragua Finding', 19 September 1983, in Kornblugh and Byrne, *The Iran-Contra Scandal*, p. 15; Leogrande, *The United States in Central America*, p. 314.

125 Leogrande, *The United States in Central America*, pp. 330–2.

126 Garthoff, *The Great Transition*, p. 703.

127 'U.S. Congress, Public Law 98–473', 12 October 1984, in Kornblugh and Byrne, *The Iran-Contra Scandal*, p. 20; Herrmann, 'Regional Conflicts as Turning Points', p. 65.

128 Leogrande, *The United States in Central America*, pp. 428–30.

129 Limberg, 'Soviet Military Support for Third-World Marxist Regimes', p. 101; Gates, *From the Shadows*, p. 381.

130 Reagan, *An American Life*, p. 471.

131 Daniel 'Jake' Jacobowitz, 'Public Diplomacy Action Plan: Support for the White House Educational Campaign' 12 March 1985, in Kornblugh and Byrne, *The Iran-Contra Scandal*, pp. 4, 22–3.

132 Leogrande, *The United States in Central America*, p. 409; Kornblugh and Byrne, *The Iran-Contra Scandal*, pp. 3–4.

133 Gates, *From the Shadows*, pp 310–11; Leogrande, *The United States in Central America*, pp. 388, 393.

134 Christopher Andrew, *For the President's Eyes Only*, p. 479.

135 Kornblugh and Byrne, *The Iran-Contra Scandal*, p. 4; Leogrande, *The United States in Central America*, p. 407.

136 Gates, *From the Shadows*, p. 434.

137 Andrew, *For the President's Eyes Only*, pp. 487–9 ff.; Young and Kent, *International Relations*, p. 567.

138 Garthoff, *The Great Transition*, pp. 293–4; Leogrande, *The United States in Central America*, p. 502.

139 Reagan, *An American Life*, p 479.
140 Herrmann, 'Regional Conflicts as Turning Points', pp. 65–6.
141 LaFeber, *America, Russia and the Cold War, 1945–1996*, p. 311.
142 Leogrande, *The United States in Central America*, p. 490; Gates, *From the Shadows*, p. 435.
143 David Mervin, *George Bush and the Guardianship Presidency* (Basingstoke: Macmillan, 1996) pp. 164–5; Baker, *Politics of Diplomacy*, p. 52.
144 Mervin, *George Bush*, p. 166.
145 Baker, *Politics of Diplomacy*, p. 46.
146 Baker, *Politics of Diplomacy*, p. 59.
147 Beschloss and Talbott, *At the Highest Levels*, p. 156; Garthoff, *The Great Transition*, p. 407.
148 Baker, *Politics of Diplomacy*, p. 60.
149 Young and Kent, *International Relations*, p. 575.
150 Pettiford, 'Changing Conceptions of Security in the Third World,' p. 291.
151 Garthoff, *The Great Transition*, pp. 674, 745; Michael Yahuda, *The International Politics of the Asia-Pacific, 1945–1995* (London: Routledge, 1996) p. 214.
152 Garthoff, *The Great Transition*, p. 748; Herrmann, 'Regional Conflicts as Turning Points', pp. 77–8.
153 Henry Kissinger, *Diplomacy* (New York: Simon and Schuster, 1994) p. 773.
154 Pemberton, *Exist with Honor*, p. 156.
155 Adelman, 'United States and Soviet Relations', pp. 82–3.
156 Leogrande, *The United States in Central America*, p. 389; LaFeber, *Inevitable Revolutions*, p. 277.
157 *Ibid.*, p. 303.
158 Garthoff, *The Great Transition*, p. 748; Michael Cox, 'The Soviet-American Conflict in the Third World', in Peter Shearman and Phil Williams (ed.) *The Superpowers, Central America and the Middle East* (London: Brassey's, 1988) p. 181.
159 Schultz-Gorbachev meeting (excerpt), 22 February 1988, *CHIHP Bulletin* #14/15, p. 171.
160 Reagan-Gorbachev meeting (excerpt), 10 December 1987, *CHIHP Bulletin* #14/15 p. 167.
161 Baker, *The Politics of Diplomacy*, p. 1; William C. Wohlforth (ed.), *Cold War Endgame*, pp. 84–5.
162 Baker, *The Politics of Diplomacy*, pp. 1–2.
163 Wohlforth (ed.), *Cold War Endgame*, pp. 78, 87.
164 *Ibid.*, p. 85; Thatcher, *The Downing Street Years*, p. 769.
165 Wohlforth (ed.), *Cold War Endgame*, p. 90.
166 Chernayaev, *My Six Years with Gorbachev*, pp. 283–4; Zubok, 'Gorbachev and the End of the Cold War', p. 226.
167 Wohlforth (ed.), *Cold War Endgame*, pp. 88–9.
168 Baker, *Politics of Diplomacy*, p. 407.
169 Bush and Scowcroft, *A World Transformed*, p. 470; Douglas Little, *American Orientalism*, p. 311.
170 Herrmann, 'Regional Conflicts as Turning Points', p. 79.

Chapter 9

 1 The end of the Cold War is the subject of considerable debate by political scientists. See, for example, Richard K. Herrmann, 'Conclusions: the End of the Cold War – What Have We Learned?', in Richard Ned Lebow and Thomas Risse-Kappen (ed.), *International Relations Theory and the End of the Cold War*, pp. 259–84; William C. Wohlforth, 'Realism and the End of the Cold War', *International Security* 19 (winter 1994/5) pp. 91–129; Paul Shroeder, 'Historical Reality vs. Neo-realist Theory', *International Security* 19:1 (summer 1994) pp. 108–48; John Lewis Gaddis, 'International Relations Theory and the End of the Cold War', *International Security* 17:3 (winter 1992/3) pp. 5–58; Joseph Lepgold, 'Failure or Learning Opportunity? The End of the Cold War and its Implications for International Relations Theory', in William C. Wohlforth (ed.), *Cold War Endgame*, pp. 313–36;. Stephen G. Brooks and William C. Wohlforth, 'Power, Globalization, and the End of the Cold War: Re-evaluating a Landmark Case for Ideas', *International Security* 25:3 (winter 2000/01) pp. 5–53.
 2 Beatrice Heuser, 'Victory in a Nuclear War? A Comparison of NATO and WTO War Aims and Strategies', *Contemporary European History* 7:3 (1998) p. 312. Peter Hennessy, *The Secret State: Whitehall and the Cold War* (London: Allen Lane, The Penguin Press, 2002) p. 5.

3 'East Germany Spy Reports Reveal NATO War Plans', 6 November 2003, *Security Watch*, http://www.isn.ethz.ch, accessed 18 Nov. 2003; Robert G. Patman, *The Soviet Union in the Horn of Africa*, p. 69.

4 Kramer, 'Ideology and the Cold War', pp. 552–3.

5 Wohlforth, 'Realism and the End of the Cold War', p. 97.

6 Bush and Scowcroft, *A World Transformed*, p. 286.

7 Zubok, 'Gorbachev and the End of the Cold War', p. 233.

8 Odd Arne Westad, 'Moscow and the Angolan Crisis', p. 28.

9 English, 'The Road(s) Not Taken', p. 260.

10 Alex Nove, 'The Fall of Empires – Russia and the Soviet Union', in Geir Lundestad (ed.), *The Fall of Great Powers: Peace, Stability, and Legitimacy* (Oslo: Scandinavian University Press, 1994) p. 136.

11 Andrei Shleifer and Daniel Treisman, 'A Normal Country', *Foreign Affairs* (March/April 2004) http://www.foreignaffairs.org, p. 1.

12 Ivo H. Daalder and James M. Lindsay, *America Unbound: The Bush Revolution in Foreign Policy* (Washington, DC: Brookings Institution Press, 2003) p. 43.

13 Howard, 'An Unhappy Successful Marriage', pp. 164–75; Lundestad, *The United States and Western Europe since 1945*, p. 236.

14 Georges-Henri Soutou, 'Convergence Theories in France in the Sixties and Seventies', in Wilfried Loth (ed.), *Eastern Europe and Western Europe in the Cold War (1965–1975)* (forthcoming).

15 Klaus Larres, 'Germany and the West: The "Rapallo Factor" in German Foreign Policy from the 1950s to the 1990s', in Larres and Panikos Panayi (ed.), *The Federal Republic of Germany since 1949: Politics, Society and Economy before and after Unification* (London: Longman, 1996) p. 322.

16 William Wallace, 'Rethinking European Order: West European Responses, 1989–97 – Introduction', in Robin Niblett and William Wallace (ed.), *Rethinking European Order: West European Responses, 1989–1997* (Basingstoke; Palgrave, 2001) p. 20.

17 English, 'The Road(s) Not Taken', p. 251; Mastny, 'The New History of Cold War Alliances', p. 79; Celeste A. Wallander, 'Western Policy and the Demise of the Soviet Union', *Journal of Cold War Studies* 5:4 (fall 2003) pp. 168–9.

18 Maier, *Dissolution*, p. 216.

19 Imanuel Geiss, 'Great Powers and Empires: Historical Mechanisms of their Making and Breaking', in Lundestad (ed.), *The Fall of Great Powers*, pp. 35–6.

20 Nove, 'The Fall of Empires – Russia and the Soviet Union', p. 136.

21 Imanuel Geiss, 'The Federal Republic of Germany in International Politics Before and After Unification', in Larres and Panayi (ed.), *The Federal Republic of Germany*, pp. 157, 159–60.

22 Maier, *Dissolution*, p. 216; Michael Cox, Book Reviews, *Journal of Cold War Studies* 4:2 (spring 2002) p. 112.

23 Hartmut Mayer, 'Central Power, Central Debate? The German Foreign Policy Community and the Rethinking of European Order', in Niblett and Wallace, *Rethinking European Order*, pp. 72–3; Larres, 'Germany and the West', pp. 322–3.

24 Lundestad, *The United States and Western Europe since 1945*, p. 292.

25 Strobe Talbott also discusses the dynamics of arms control; see his 'Why Start Stopped', pp. 53–4. See also Saki Dockrill, 'Détente and Deterrence: Optimum Security for Western Europe and the Ending of the Cold War', in Yegorova (ed.), *Cold War and the Policy of Détente*, pp. 107–43.

26 Crockatt, *America Embattled*, p. 161.

27 Bush and Scowcroft, *A World Transformed*, p. 564.

28 Robert Kagan, *Paradise and Power: America and Europe in the New World Order* (London: Atlantic Books, 2004) pp. 55, 58; Ian Clark, *Globalization and Fragmentation: International Relations in the Twentieth Century* (Oxford: Oxford University Press, 1997) p. 177; John Lewis Gaddis, *The United States and the End of the Cold War*, p. 26.

29 Cox, 'International History since 1989', pp. 113–18; John J. Mearsheimer, *The Tragedy of Great Power Politics* (New York: W. W. Norton, 2001) pp. 377–80; see also Mearsheimer, 'Back to the Future: Instability after the Cold War', *International Security* 15:1 (summer 1990) pp. 5–56, and 15:2 (fall 1990), pp. 191–222.

30 David C. Kang, 'Getting Asia Wrong', *International Security* 27:4 (spring 2003) pp. 58–63; Samuel P. Huntington, *The Clash of Civilizations and the Remaking of World Order* (London: Touchstone Books, 1998) pp. 218–45.

31 R. E. Williams (ed.), *A Century of Punch* (London: William Heinemann, 1956) p. 142.

32 Clark, *Globalization and Fragmentation*, p. 172.

33 Oberdorfer, *From the Cold War to a New Era*, p. 223; Shultz, *Turmoil and Triumph*, p. 892.

34 Marin Van Creveld, *The Rise and Decline of the State* (Cambridge: Cambridge University Press, 1999) p. 383.

35 Clark, *Globalization and Fragmentation*, p. 1.

36 An excellent study on the subject, see Clark, *Globalization and Fragmentation*.

37 Crockatt, *The Fifty Years War*, p. 375; Cleveld, *The Rise and Decline of the State*, p. 86; Jan Aart Sholte, 'The Globalization of World Politics', in Baylis and Smith, *The Globalization of World Politics*, pp. 13–24.

38 Arnold Beichman (ed.), *CNN's Cold War Documentary: Issues and Controversy* (Stanford: Hoover Institution Press, 2000) p. 24.

39 Crokatt, *The Fifty Years War*, p. 368.

40 Cox, 'International History since 1989', p. 134.

41 John Baylis, 'International and Global Security in the Post-Cold War Era', in Baylis and Smith (ed.), *The Globalization of World Politics*, p. 254.

42 Creveld, *The Rise and Decline of the State*, p. 400.

43 S. Neil MacFarlane, 'Intervention in Contemporary World Politics', *Adelphi Paper* 350 (London: The IISS, 2002) p. 51.

44 MacFarlane, 'Intervention in Contemporary World Politics', pp. 50, 52.

45 *Ibid.*, p. 53.

46 Nicholas J. Wheeler and Alex J. Bellamy, 'Humanitarian Intervention and World Politics', in Baylis and Smith (ed.), *The Globalization of World Politics*, pp. 473–4; Mats Berdal, 'Lessons Not Learned: The Use of Force in "Peace Operations" in the 1990s', *International Peacekeeping* 7:4 (winter 2000) p. 58.

47 Adam Roberts, 'The Crisis in UN Peacekeeping', *Survival* 36:3 (autumn 1994) p. 103.

48 Young and Kent, *International Relations*, p. 618.

49 Crokatt, *The Fifty Years War*, p. 375.

50 Ole R. Holsti, 'Public Opinion and U.S. Foreign Policy after the Cold War', in Scott (ed.), *After the End*, pp. 143–5.

51 Cox, *US Foreign Policy after the Cold War*, p. 5.

52 Andrew Kohut, 'Post-Cold War Attitudes towards the Use of Force', in H. W. Brands, *The Use of Force after the Cold War* (College Station: Texas A & M University Press, 2000) pp. 170–1.

53 Kagan, *Paradise and Power*, pp. 83, 85.

54 James M. Scott and A. Lane Crothers, 'Out of the Cold: The Post-Cold War Context of U.S. Foreign Policy', in Scott (ed.), *After the End*, pp. 5–8.

55 Cox, *US Foreign Policy after the Cold War*, p. 13, 11; Scott and A. Lane Crothers, 'Out of the Cold', pp. 8, 13.

56 Scott and Crothers, 'Out of the Cold', pp. 7–8.

57 Cox, *US Foreign Policy after the Cold War*, p. 17; Lundestad, *The United States and Western Europe since 1945*, p. 250.

58 John Dumbrell, *American Foreign Policy*, pp. 181–90.

59 Scott and Crothers, 'Out of the Cold', p. 1; Sidney Blumenthal, *The Clinton Wars* (New York: Viking, 2003) pp. 60–1, 632; Jonathan Mermin, 'Television News and American Intervention in Somalia: The Myth of a Media-Driven Foreign Policy', *Political Science Quarterly* 112:3 (1997) pp. 385–403.

60 Tony Smith, 'Good, Smart, or Bad Samaritan: A Case for U.S. Military Intervention for Democracy and Human Rights', in Brands (ed.), *The Use of Force after the Cold War*, pp. 31–45.

61 Cox, *US Foreign Policy after the Cold War*, pp. 14–15.

62 Kagan, *Paradise and Power*, p. 47; Wesley K. Clark, *Waging Modern War: Bosnia, Kosovo, and the Future of Combat* (Oxford: Public Affairs, 2002) p. 453.

63 IISS, *Strategic Survey, 1999–2000* (Oxford: Oxford University Press, 2000) p. 73; Philip H.

Gordon, 'NATO after 11 September', *Survival* 43:4 (winter 2001) p. 92; Anthony Forster and William Wallace, 'What is NATO for', *Survival* 43:4 (winter 2001) p. 110; Frédéric Bozo, 'Continuity or Change: the View from Europe', in Victor Papacosma, Sean Kay and Mark R. Rubin (ed.), *NATO after Fifty Years* (Wilmington: A Scholarly Resources Inc. Imprint, 2001) pp. 64–9.

64 Crokatt, *The Fifty Years War*, p. 377.

65 Litwak, *Rogue States*, pp. 2–3, 7, 149–50.

66 MacFarlane, 'Intervention in Contemporary World Politics', pp. 72–3.

67 Maley, *The Afghanistan Wars*, pp. 248–9.

68 Saki Dockrill, 'Britain's Grand Strategy and Anglo-American Leadership in the War Against Japan', in Brian Bond and Kyoichi Tachikawa (ed.), *British and Japanese Military Leadership in the Far Eastern War 1941–1945* (London: Frank Cass, 2004) pp. 6–13.

69 'After September 11: A Conversation' (a record of a one-day symposium at the Nixon Centre, Washington, DC on 4 October 2001), *The National Interest* (Thanksgiving 2001) p. 67; G. John Ikenberry, 'Getting Hegemony Right', *The National Interest* (spring 2001) pp. 18–19.

70 Daalder and Lindsay, *America Unbound*, p. 120.

71 Jeremy D. Rosner, 'American Assistance to the Former Soviet States in 1993–1994', p. 242.

72 Michael Cox, 'Meanings of Victory: American Power after the Towers', in Ken Booth and Tim Dunne (ed.), *Worlds in Collision: Terror and the Future of Global Order* (Basingstoke: Palgrave Macmillan, 2002) p. 156; Ikenberry, 'Getting Hegemony Right', pp. 17–18.

73 Crockatt, *America Embattled*, p. 161.

74 Daalder and Lindsay, *America Unbound*, p. 42.

75 *Ibid.*, p. 43; Kagan, *Paradise and Power*, p. 90.

76 Dockrill, 'After September 11: Globalization of Security', pp. 1–19; Bob Woodward, *Plan of Attack* (New York: Simon & Schuster, 2004) p. 27.

77 John Kampfner, *Blair's Wars* (London: The Free Press, 2003) pp. 191–284 ff.; James K. Wither, 'British Bulldog or Bush's Poodle? Anglo-American Relations and the Iraq War', *Parameters* (winter 2003–4) pp. 67–82.

78 IISS, *Strategic Survey, 2002–3* (Oxford: Oxford University Press, 2003) pp. 152–3.

79 IISS, *Strategic Survey, 2003–4* (Oxford: Oxford University Press, 2004) p. 9; see John Prados, *Hoodwinked: Documents that Reveal How Bush Sold Us a War* (New York: The New Press, 2004).

80 'The National Security Strategy of the United States of America' (hereafter cited as NSS), 17 September 2002, p. 27; http://www.whitehouse.gov/nsc/nss.html George W. Bush, 'Introduction' to NSS, and also see NSS, pp. 1, 13.

81 Bush's introduction to NSS, and p. 6.

82 Daalder and Lindsay, *America Unbound*, p. 122.

83 Michael M. Gunter, 'Dealing with Terrorism: The Regan Record', in Eric J. Schmertz, Natalie Datlof and Alexej Ugrinsky (ed.), *President Reagan and the World* (Westport: Greenwood Press, 1997) p. 170.

84 MacFarlane, 'Intervention in Contemporary World Politics', p. 53; Philip H. Gordon and Jeremy Shapiro, *Allies at War: America, Europe and the Crisis over Iraq* (New York: McGraw-Hill, 2004) p. 217. Author's emphasis.

85 Gareth Evans, 'When is it Right to Fight?', *Survival* 46:3 (autumn 2004) p. 58.

86 Kagan, *Paradise and Power*, pp. 108–13.

87 NSS, p. 5.

88 See the Office of the Under-Secretary of Defense, 'Report of the Defence Science Board Task Force on Strategic Communication', September 2004.

89 *Washington Post*, 18 January 2005, p. 12.

90 Peter S. Canellos, 'Despite Cabinet Shuffle, Neocon Ideology Remains', *Boston Globe*, 7 December 2004; John Lewis Gaddis, *Surprise, Security and the American Experience* (Cambridge, MA: Harvard University Press, 2004) pp. 93–4.

91 Mats Berdal, 'The UN after Iraq', *Survival* 46:3 (autumn 2004) pp. 83–102.

92 Kagan, *Paradise and Power*, p. 115.

Select Bibliography

Scholars in the West have debated the Cold War for over 40 years. This literature has been recently enriched by new evidence from the former Eastern bloc, as well as by the newly declassified documents in the USA and other major Western European countries under the 30-year rule. The literature of the Cold War is vast and still growing. It includes research monographs, documents, memoirs, oral histories, and general accounts of some specific aspects, such as intelligence, nuclear weapons, external policies, culture and domestic responses to the Cold War.

Despite the opening of some archival documents from the former Communist bloc after 1989, the literature of the Cold War in English in the USA, Great Britain and Western Europe is far more substantial (currently up to the early 1970s), in terms of both quality and quantity, than that of the Soviet Union, China and the rest of the former Communist countries. While this gap is inevitable, there exists no single key book that covers all the aspects of the Cold War as seen from both East and West throughout the period. Students must, therefore, be prepared to read several key books before going into in-depth analysis of each specific subject.

This book draws on source material and new evidence, which can be found in http://cwihp.si.edu/ for the Cold War International History Project (CWIHP), in the form of bulletins (with the latest issue 14/15 published in winter 2003–spring 2004), working papers and the virtual archive. *Diplomatic History* has its own discussion forum (the H-NET Discussion) at http://www.h-net.org/~diplo/. The Parallel History Project on NATO and the Warsaw Pact (PHP), organized by the Centre for Security Studies and Conflict Research in Zurich, Switzerland, has its own website and publishes some documents and brief notes relevant to the subject at http://www.isn.ethz.ch/php. The National Security Archive based at George Washington University, USA, publishes primary documents on the Cold War at http://www.gwu.edu/~nsarchiv/.

The literature of the post-Cold War period is still sketchy, but articles and annual survey volumes published by the International Institute of Strategic Studies (IISS) are useful. Most publications from IISS, such as *Survival, Adelphi Papers, Military Balance*, and *Strategic Survey*, are also available online at www.iiss.org. At the same time, students can also investigate major government policies and those of international organizations (such as the US Department of Defense at www.defenselink.mil/, The White House at www.whitehouse.gov/,

Whitehall at www.number-10.gov.uk, NATO at www.nato.int/docu/home.htm), and international news briefs ISN Security Watch at http://www.isn.ethz.ch/, The *Washington Post* at www.washingtonpost.com, the *New York Times* at www.nytimes.com; and for (US) policy making and international security aspects see, for example, *Foreign Affairs* at www.foreignaffairs.org, and *International Security* from www.mitpress.mit.edu.

The following are important general studies on the subject, and are also used in this book. Unless otherwise stated the place of publication is England.

General Books on the Contemporary History of International Relations (1945–2004)

Covers generally since 1945

Calvocorressi, Peter, *World Politics since 1945* (Longman, 2002) 8th edition – now a classic study of world politics.

Young, John W., and Kent, J., *International Relations since 1945: A Global History* (Oxford University Press, 2004) – an excellent and comprehensive survey of historical and contemporary debates about the issues in global history.

Covers the Cold War period

Ball, Simon, *The Cold War* (Arnold, 1997) – a well researched book.

Crockatt, Richard, *The Fifty Years War: The United States and the Soviet Union in World Politics, 1941–1991* (Routledge, 1996) – a sound analysis of superpower relations.

Gaddis, J. L., *We Now Know* (Oxford University Press, 1997) – an interpretive account of the Cold War between 1945–63.

Hanhimäki, Jussi M. and Westad, Odd Arne, *The Cold War: A History in Documents and Eyewitness Accounts* (Oxford University Press, 2003) – a useful collection of documents and witness history.

LaFeber, Walter, *America, Russia and the Cold War* (New York: McGraw-Hill, 1996) – a readable account with emphasis on American perspectives.

The end of the Cold War

Garthoff, Raymond L., *The Great Transition: American-Soviet Relations and the End of the Cold War* (Washington, DC: The Brookings Institution, 1994) – a detailed and fascinating account of the end of the Cold War.

Herrmann, Richard K. and Lebow, R. N. (ed.), *Ending the Cold War: Interpretations, Causation, and the Study of International Relations* (Palgrave Macmillan, 2004) – a number of key case studies, theories and ideas which shaped the end of the Cold War.

Wohlforth, William C. (ed.), *Cold War Endgame: Oral History, Analysis and Debates* (Pennsylvania: The Pennsylvania State University Press, 2003) – based on the 1996 conference at Princeton University, a lively account.

Covers the post-Cold War period

Brands, H. W., *The Use of Force after the Cold War* (College Station; Texas A & M University Press, 2003) – a collection of excellent essays on American foreign and national security policy after the Cold War.

Clark, Ian, *The Post-Cold War Order: The Spoils of Peace* (Oxford University Press, 2001) – a stimulating account of the subject.

Unpublished and Published Official Documents (which are cited in the text)

A Micro Film Project of University of Publications of America Inc., Washington, DC, *Diaries of Dwight D. Eisenhower, 1953–61* (1986).

Dwight D. Eisenhower Library, Abilene, KS, Ann Whitman File.

Küsters, Hans Jürgen and Hofmann, Daniel (ed.), *Dokumente zur Deutschlandpolitik: Deutsche Einheit Sonderedition aus den Akten des Bundeskanzleramtes, 1989–90* (München: Oldenbourg, 1998).

Simpson, Christopher, *National Security Directives of the Reagan and Bush Administration: The Declassified History of U.S. Political and Military Policy, 1981–1991* (Boulder: Westview Press, 1995).

United States Defense Department, *Seminal Report of the Secretary of Defense,* (Jan. –June, 1956).

United States Government Printing Office, Washington, DC, *Foreign Relations of the United States [FRUS].*

Secondary Sources (books, articles and working papers which are cited in the text)

Adelman, Kenneth L., 'Defense Policy and Arms Control: Discussants', in Eric J. Schmertz, Natalie Datlof and Alexeij Ugrinsky, *President Reagan and the World* (Westport: Greenwood Press, 1997).

Aldrich, Richard (ed.), *British Intelligence, Strategy and the Cold War, 1945–1951* (Routledge, 1992).

Alexander, Michael, *Managing the Cold War: A View from the Front Line* (London: The Royal United Services Institute for Defence and Security Studies (RUSI), 2005).

Andrew, Christopher, *For the President's Eyes Only: Secret Intelligence and the American Presidency from Washington to Bush* (HarperCollins, 1996)., and Gordievsky, O., *KGB: The Inside Story of Its Foreign Operations from Lenin to Gorbachev* (Sceptre, 1991).

Ash, Timothy Garton, *We the People: The Revolution of '89 Witnessed in Warsaw, Budapest, Berlin and Prague* (Penguin Books, 1990); *In Europe's Name: Germany and the Divided Continent* (Jonathan Cape, 1993).

Baker, James A. with Defrank, Thomas M., *The Politics of Diplomacy: Revolution, War and Peace, 1989–1992* (New York: G. P. Putnam's Sons, 1995).

Baylis, John and O'Neill, R. (ed.), *Alternative Nuclear Futures: The Role of Nuclear Weapons in the Post-Cold War World* (Oxford University Press, 2000), and Smith, Steve (ed.), *The Globalization of World Politics* (Oxford University Press, 2001).

Beichman, Arnold (ed.), *CNN's Cold War Documentary: Issues and Controversy* (Stanford: Hoover Institution Press, 2000).

Berdal, Mats, 'Lessons Not Learned: The Use of Force in "Peace Operations" in the 1990s', *International Peacekeeping* 7:4 (winter, 2000); 'The UN after Iraq', *Survival* 46:3 (autumn 2004).

Beschloss, Michael R. and Talbott, S., *At the Highest Levels: The Inside Story of the End of the Cold War* (Warner Books, 1994).

Bischof, Günter and Dockrill, S. (ed.), *Cold War Respite: The Geneva Summit of 1955* (Baton Rouge: Louisiana State University Press, 2000).

Bitzinger, Richard A., 'Gorbachev and GRIT, 1985–89: Did Arms Control Succeed because of Unilateral Actions or in spite of Them?', *Contemporary Security Policy* 15:1 (April 1994).

Blanton, Thomas, 'When Did the Cold War End?', *CWIHP Bulletin #* 10 (March 1998).

Blumenthal, Sidney, *The Clinton Wars* (New York: Viking, 2003).

Bluth, Christoph, *New Thinking in Soviet Military Policy* (The Royal Institute of International Affairs/Pinter Publishers, 1990); 'Strategic Nuclear Weapons and US-Russian Relations: From Confrontation to Co-operative Denuclearisation?', *Contemporary Security Policy* 15:1 (April 1994); *The Two Germanies and Military Security in Europe* (Palgrave Macmillan, 2002).

Bohlen, Avis, 'The Rise and Fall of Arms Control', *Survival* 45:3 (autumn 2003).

Bond, Brian and Tachikawa ,K. (ed.), *British and Japanese Military Leadership in the Far Eastern War 1941–1945* (Frank Cass, 2004).

Books, Stephen G. and Wohlforth, W. C., 'Economic Constraints and the End of the Cold War', in William C. Wohlforth (ed.), *Cold War Endgame* (Pennsylvania: The Pennsylvania State University Press, 2003).

Booth, Ken and Dunne, T. (ed.), *Worlds in Collision: Terror and the Future of Global Order* (Palgrave Macmillan, 2002).

Bozo, Frédérick, 'Continuity or Change: the View from Europe', in Victor Papacosma, Sean Kay and Mark R. Rubin (ed.), *NATO after Fifty Years* (Wilmington: A Scholarly Resources Inc. Imprint, 2001)., 'Before the Wall: French Diplomacy and the Last Decade of the Cold War 1979–1989', *Nobel Institute Research Seminar Paper* (May 2002), Norwegian Nobel Institute, Oslo.

Brands, H. W., *Into the Labyrinth: the United States and the Middle East, 1945–1993* (New York: McGraw-Hill, 1994).

Brooks, Stephen G. and Wohlforth, W. C., 'Power, Globalization, and the End of the Cold War: Re-evaluating a Landmark Case for Ideas', *International Security* 25:3 (winter 2000/01).

Brzezinski, Zbigniew, *Power and Principle: Memoirs of the National Security Adviser, 1977–1981* (New York: McGraw-Hill Ryerson, 1983).

Bugaijski, Janusz, *Nations in Turmoil: Conflict and Cooperation in Eastern Europe* (Boulder: Westview Press, 1993).

Bush, George and Scowcroft, B., *A World Transformed* (New York: Alfred A. Knopf, 1998).

Brown, Archie, *The Gorbachev Factor* (Oxford University Press, 1996).

Bullock, Alan, *Hitler and Stalin: Parallel Lives* (HarperCollins, 1991).

Calingaert, Daniel, *Soviet Nuclear Policy under Gorbachev: A Policy of Disarmament* (New York: Praeger, 1991).

Chen, Jian, *Mao's China and the Cold War* (Chapel Hill: The University of North Carolina Press, 2001).

Chernyaev, Anatoly, *My Six Years with Gorbachev* (Pennsylvania: The Pennsylvania State University Press, 2000).

Clark, Ian, *Globalization and Fragmentation: International Relations in the Twentieth Century* (Oxford University Press, 1997).

Clark, General Wesley K., *Waging Modern War: Bosnia, Kosovo, and the Future of Combat* (Oxford: Public Affairs, 2002).

Cohen, Warren I., *American Response to China* (New York: Alfred A. Knopf, 1980).

Coll, Steve, *Ghost Wars* (New York: The Penguin Press, 2004).

Cooley, John, *Unholy Wars: Afghanistan, America and International Terrorism* (Pluto, 2002).

Cordovez, Diego and Harrison, Selig S., *Out of Afghanistan: the Inside Story of the Soviet Withdrawal* (Oxford University Press, 1995).

Costigliola, Frank, 'An "Arm Around the Shoulder": The United States, NATO and German Reunification, 1989–90', *Contemporary European History* 3:1 (1994).

Cox, Michael, *US Foreign Policy after the Cold War: Superpower Without a Mission?* (London: The Royal Institute of International Affairs, 1995); 'Whatever Happened to American Decline?: International Relations and the New United States Hegemony', *New Political Economy* 6:3 (2001).

Crampton, R. J., *Eastern Europe in the Twentieth Century and After* (Routledge, 1997).

Creveld, Marin Van, *The Rise and Decline of the State* (Cambridge University Press, 1999).

Crockatt , Richard, *American Embattled: September 11, Anti-Americanism and the Global Order* (Routledge, 2003).

Crocker, Chester A., *High Noon in Southern Africa: Making Peace in a Rough Neighbourhood* (New York: W. W. Norton, 1992).

Cutler, B. J., 'Fulfilling Ike's Idea for Freer Skies', *Washington Times* (24 May 1992).

Daalder, Ivo. H., *The Nature and Practice of Flexible Response* (New York: Columbia University Press, 1993), and Lindsay, James M., *America Unbound: The Bush Revolution in Foreign Policy* (Washington, DC: Brookings Institution Press, 2003).

Dallek, Robert, *Ronald Reagan: the Politics of Symbolism* (Cambridge, MA: Harvard University Press, 1984).

Denis, Mike, *Rise and Fall of the German Democratic Republic, 1945–1990* (Longman, 2000).

Derleth, William, 'The Soviets in Afghanistan: Can the Red Army Fight a Counterinsurgency War?', *Armed Forces and Society* 15:1 (Fall 1988).

Dickie, John, *'Special' No More* (Weidenfeld & Nicolson, 1994).

Diekmann, Kai and Reuth, R. G., *Helmut Kohl: Ich Wollte Deutschlands Einheit* (Berlin: Proyläen, 1996).

Dobrynin, Anatoly, *In Confidence: Moscow's Ambassador to America's Six Cold War Presidents* (New York: Random House, 1995).

Dobson, Alan P., 'The USA, Britain, and the Question of Hegemony', in Geir Lundestad (ed.), *No End to Alliance: the United States and Western Europe-Past, Present and Future* (Macmillan, 1999).

Dockrill, Saki R., *Britain's Policy for West German Rearmament* (Cambridge University Press, 1991). (ed.); *From Pearl Harbor to Hiroshima: The Second World*

War in Asia and the Pacific, 1941–1945 (London: Macmillan, 1994); *Eisenhower's New Look National Security Policy, 1953–1961* (Macmillan, 1996); (ed.), *Controversy and Compromise: Alliance Politics between Britain, the Federal Republic of Germany and the United States* (Philio, Germany, 1998); 'The Eden Plan and European Security', in Gunter Bischof and S. Dockrill (ed.), *Cold War Respite: The Geneva Summit of 1955* (Baton Rouge: Louisiana State University Press, 2000); *Britain's Retreat from East of Suez: The Choice between Europe and the World?* (Palgrave Macmillan, 2002); 'After September 11: Globalisation of Security', *Journal of Transatlantic Studies* 1.1 supplement issue (spring 2003); 'Détente and Deterrence: Optimum Security for Western Europe and the Ending of the Cold War', in N. I. Yegorova (ed.), *Cold War and the Policy of Détente: Problems and Discussions* (Moscow: Russian Academy of Sciences, Institute of Universal History, 2003).

Donnelly, Thomas, 'Rebasing, Revisited', *National Security Outlook* (December 2004).

Dumbrell, John, *American Foreign Policy: Carter to Clinton* (Macmillan, 1997).

Dunn, Lewis A. and Alessi, V., 'Arms Control by Other Means' *Survival* 42:4 (winter 2000/1).

Dyker, David A., *Restructuring the Soviet Economy* (Routledge, 1997).

English, Robert, *Russia and the Idea of the West: Gorbachev, Intellectuals, and the End of the Cold War* (New York: Columbia University Press, 2000).

Evangelista, Matthew, 'Turing Points in Arms Control', in Richard Herrmann and Richard Ned Lebow (ed.), *Ending the Cold War* (Palgrave Macmillan, 2004).

Evans, Gareth, 'When is it Right to Fight?', *Survival* 46:3 (autumn 2004).

Filitov, Alexei, 'Victory in the Post War Era: Despite the Cold War or Because of It?', *Diplomatic History* 16:1 (winter 1992).

Fischer, Benjamin B. (ed.), *At Cold War's End: US Intelligence on the Soviet Union and Eastern Europe, 1989–1991* (Washington, DC: Central Intelligence Agency, 1999); 'More Dangerous than We Thought? New Evidence on the Soviet War Scare', *Nobel Institute Research Seminar Paper* (May 2002) Norwegian Nobel Institute, Oslo.

Fischer, Beth A., *The Reagan Reversal: Foreign Policy and the End of the Cold War* (Columbia: University of Missouri Press, 1997)., 'Reagan's Triumph?: The U.S. and the Ending of the Cold War', *Nobel Institute Research Seminar Paper* (May 2002) Norwegian Nobel Institute, Oslo.

Fitzgerald, Frances, *Way out there in the Blue: Regan, Star Wars, and the End of the Cold War* (New York: Simon & Schuster, 2000).

Fleron, Frederic J., Jr, Hoffmann, E. P., and Laird, R. F. (ed.), *Contemporary Issues in Soviet Foreign Policy from Brezhnev to Gorbachev* (New York: Aldine de Gruyter, 1991).

Forster, Anthony and Wallace, William, 'What is NATO for', *Survival* 43:4 (Winter 2001).

Fowkes, Ben, *The Rise and Fall of Communism in Eastern Europe* (Macmillan, 1995).

Freedman, Lawrence, *The Evolution of Nuclear Strategy* (Macmillan, 1981); (ed.), *Europe Transformed: Documents on the End of the Cold War* (Tri-Service Press Ltd,

1990); *Kennedy's Wars: Berlin, Cuba, Laos, and Vietnam* (Oxford University Press, 2000); 'Europe and Deterrence', in 'Nuclear Weapons: A New Great Debate' *Chaillot Paper* 48 (Paris: Institute for Security Studies, Western European Union, July 2001); *Deterrence* (Polity, 2004).

Fukuyama, Francis, 'Gorbachev and the Third World', *Foreign Affairs* (spring 1986); 'Patterns of Soviet Third World Policy', *Problems of Communism* (Sept. –Oct. 1987); *The End of History and the Last Man* (Hamish Hamilton, 1992).

Freeman, Chas. W., Jr, 'The Angola/Namibia Accords', *Foreign Affairs* (summer 1989).

Gaddis, John Lewis, 'Hanging Tough Paid Off', *Bulletin of the Atomic Scientists* 45:1 (January 1989). *Russia, the Soviet Union and the United States: An Interpretive History* (New York: McGraw Hill, 1990); *The United States and the End of the Cold War: Implications, Reconsiderations, Provocations* (Oxford University Press, 1992); 'International Relations Theory and the End of the Cold War', *International Security* 17:3 (winter 1992/3); *Surprise, Security and the American Experience* (Cambridge, MA: Harvard University Press, 2004).

Gaiduk, Ilya V., 'Developing an Alliance: the Soviet Union and Vietnam, 1954-75', in Peter Lowe (ed.), *The Vietnam War* (Basingstoke: Macmillan, 1998).

Galeotti, Mark, *Gorbachev and his Revolution* (Macmillan, 1997)., *Afghanistan: the Soviet Union's Last War* (Frank Cass, 2001).

Garthoff, Raymond, 'New Evidence on the Cuban Missile Crisis', *CWIHP Bulletin* #11 (winter 1998); 'Foreign Intelligence and the Historiography of the Cold War', *Journal of Cold War Studies* 6:2 (spring 2004).

Gates, Robert M., *From the Shadows: The Ultimate Insider's Story of Five Presidents and how they Won the Cold War* (New York: Touchstone, 1996).

Geiss, Imanuel, 'Great Powers and Empires: Historical Mechanisms of their Making and Breaking', in Geir Lundestad (ed.), *The Fall of Great Powers: Peace, Stability, and Legitimacy* (Oslo: Scandinavian University Press, 1994); 'The Federal Republic of Germany in International Politics Before and After Unification', in Larres, K. and Panayi, P. (ed.), *The Federal Republic of Germany since 1949: Politics, Society and Economy before and after Unification* (Longman, 1996).

George, Alexander L., 'The Role of Force in Diplomacy: A Continuing Dilemma for U.S. Foreign Policy', in H. W. Brands (ed.), *The Use of Force after the Cold War* (College Station: Texas A & M University Press, 2000).

Gleijeses, Piero, *Conflicting Missions: Havana, Washington, and Africa, 1959–1976* (Chapel Hill: The University of North Carolina Press, 2002).

Glenny, Mischa, *The Balkans, 1804–1999: Nationalism, War and the Great Powers* (Granta Books, 2000).

Goban-Klas, Tomasz and Kolstø, Pål, 'East European Mass Media: The Soviet Role', in Arne Odd Westad, S. Holtsmark and Iver B. Neumann (ed.), *The Soviet Union in Eastern Europe 1945–89* (Macmillan, 1994).

Goodman, Melvin A. and Ekedahl, C. M., 'Gorbachev's "New Directions" in the Middle East', *Middle East Journal* 42:1 (autumn 1988).

Gorbachev, Mikhail, *Memoirs* (Bantam Books, 1995); *Gorbachev on my Country and the World* (New York: Columbia University Press, 1999).

Gordon, Philip H., 'NATO after 11 September', *Survival* 43:4 (winter 2001), and Shapiro, J., *Allies at War: America, Europe and the Crisis over Iraq* (New York: McGraw-Hill, 2004).

Gortemaker, Manfred, 'The Collapse of the German Democratic Republic and the Role of the Federal Republic', *German Historical Institute London Bulletin* XXV, no. 2 (November 2003).

Gould-Davies, Nigel, 'Rethinking the Role of Ideology in International Politics during the Cold War', *Journal of Cold War Studies* 1:1 (1999).

Gray, Colin, 'To Confuse Ourselves: Nuclear Fallacies', in John Baylis and R. O'Neill (ed.), *Alternative Nuclear Futures: The Role of Nuclear Weapons in the Post-Cold War World* (Oxford University Press, 2000).

Gromyko, Andrei, *Memories* (London: Hutchinson, 1989).

Hahn, Peter L. and Heiss, M. A., *Empire and Revolution: The United States and the Third World since 1945* (Columbus: Ohio State University Press, 2001).

Halliday, Fred, 'Soviet Foreign Policymaking and the Afghanistan War: from "Second Mongolia" to "Bleeding Wound" ', *Review of International Studies* 25:4 (1999).

Halverson, Thomas, *The Last Great Nuclear Debate: NATO and Short-Range Nuclear Weapons in the 1980s* (Macmillan, 1995).

Hancock, M. Donald and Welsh, H. A. (ed.), *German Unification: Process and Outcomes* (Boulder: Westview Press, 1994).

Hanhimäki, Jussi, *The Flawed Architect: Henry Kissinger and American Foreign Policy* (Oxford University Press, 2004).

Harbutt, Fraser, *The Cold War Era* (Blackwell, 2002).

Haslam, Jonathan, *The Soviet Union and the Politics of Nuclear Weapons in Europe, 1969–87* (Macmillan, 1989); 'Collecting and Assembling Pieces of the Jigsaw: Copying with Cold War Archives', *Cold War History* 4:3 (April 2004).

Hennessy, Peter, *The Secret State: Whitehall and the Cold War* (Allen Lane, The Penguin Press, 2002).

Herring, George C., *America's Longest War* (New York: McGraw-Hill, 1986); *LBJ and Vietnam: A Different Kind of War* (Austin: University of Texas, 1994).

Herrmann, Richard K., 'Regional Conflicts as Turning Points', in Herrmann and Richard Ned Lebow (ed.), *Ending the Cold War: Interpretations, Causation, and the Study of International Relations* (Palgrave Macmillan, 2004).

Hershberg, James, 'Russian Documents on the Korean War, 1950–1953', *CWIHP Bulletin #14/15* (winter 2003/spring 2004).

Hertle, Hans-Hermann, 'The Fall of the Wall: The Unintended Self-Dissolution of East Germany's Ruling Regime', *CWIHP Bulletin #12/13* (fall/ winter 2001).

Heuser, Beatrice, 'Mitterrand's Gaullism: Cold War Policies for the Post-Cold War World?', in Antonio Varsori (ed.), *Europe 1945–1990s: The End of an Era?* (Macmillan, 1995); *NATO, Britain, France and the FRG: Nuclear Strategies and Forces for Europe, 1949–2000* (Macmillan, 1997); 'Victory in a Nuclear War? A Comparison of NATO and WTO War Aims and Strategies', *Contemporary European History* 7:3 (1998).

Hobsbawm, Erich, *Age of Extremes* (Abacus, 1996).

Hogan, Michael J. (ed.), *The End of the Cold War: Its Meaning and Implications* (New York: Cambridge University Press, 1994).

Holloway, David, *The Soviet Union and the Arms Race* (New Haven: Yale University Press, 1983).

Howard, Michael, 'An Unhappy Successful Marriage: Security Means Knowing What to Expect', *Foreign Affairs* 78:3 (May/June 1999).

Hughes, Thomas L., 'Up From Reaganism', *Foreign Policy* no. 44 (fall, 1981).

Hunt, Michael, *Ideology and U.S. Foreign Policy* (New Haven: Yale University Press, 1987).

Hurst, Steven, *The Foreign Policy of the Bush Administration* (Cassell, 1999).

Hutchings, Robert L., *American Diplomacy and the End of the Cold War: An Insider's Account of U.S. Policy in Europe, 1989–1992* (Washington, DC: The Woodrow Wilson Centre Press, 1997).

Huntington, Samuel, 'Patterns of Intervention', *The National Interest* no. 7 (spring 1987); *The Clash of Civilizations and the Remaking of World Order* (Touchstone Books, 1998).

Ikenberry, G. John 'Getting Hegemony Right', *The National Interest* (spring 2001).

Jackson, Steven, 'China's Third World Foreign Policy: The Case for Angola and Mozambique, 1961–93', *The China Quarterly* no. 142 (June 1995).

Jarausch, Konrad H. and Gransow, Volker, *Uniting Germany: Documents and Debates, 1944–1993* (Berghahn Books, 1997).

Johnson, Robert David, 'The Unintended Consequences of Congressional Reform: The Clark and Tunney Amendments and U.S. Policy toward Angola', *Diplomatic History* 27:2 (April 2003).

Jones, Howard, *Death of A Generation: How the Assassinations of Diem and JFK Prolonged the Vietnam War* (Oxford University Press, 2003).

Kagan, Robert, *Paradise and Power: America and Europe in the New World Order* (Atlantic Books, 2004).

Kamp, Karl-Heinz, 'Germany and the Future of Nuclear Weapons in Europe', *Security Dialogue* 26:3 (1995).

Kampfner, John, *Blair's Wars* (London: The Free Press, 2003).

Kanet, Roger E. and Kolodziej, E. A. (ed.), *The Cold War as Cooperation* (Macmillan, 1991).

Kang, David C., 'Getting Asia Wrong', *International Security* 27:4 (spring 2003).

Karnow, Stanley, *Vietnam: A History* (Penguin Books, 1987).

Katz, Mark N. (ed.), *The USSR and Marxist Revolutions in the Third World* (New York: Woodrow Wilson International Centre for Scholars, 1990).

Kay, Mark and Rubin, R. (ed.), *NATO: After Fifty Years* (Wilmington: A Scholarly Resources Inc., 2001).

Kennedy, Paul M., *The Rise and Fall of the Great Powers* (New York: Random House, 1987).

Khrushcheva, Nina L., 'Russia and NATO: Lessons Learned', in S. Victor Papacosma, et al. (eds), *NATO: After Fifty Years* (Wilmington: A Scholarly Resources Inc., 2001).

Kissinger, Henry, *Diplomacy* (New York: Simon & Schuster, 1994)., *Does America Need a Foreign Policy? – toward a Diplomacy for a Twenty-first Century* (Simon & Schuster, 2002).

Kohut, Andrew, 'Post-Cold War Attitudes towards the Use of Force', in H. W. Brands, *The Use of Force after the Cold War* (College Station: Texas A & M University Press, 2000).

Kornblugh, Peter and Byrne, M., *The Iran-Contra Scandal: The Declassified History* (New York: The New Press, 1993).

Kotz, Nick, *Wild Blue Yonder: Money, Politics and the B-1 Bomber* (Princeton: Princeton University Press, 1988).

Kramer, Mark, 'Soviet Arms Transfers to the Third World', *Problems of Communism*, Sept.-Oct. 1987; 'Jaruzelski, the Soviet Union, and the Imposition of Martial Law in Poland: New Light on the Mystery of December 1981', *CWIHP Bulletin #11* (winter 1998); 'Ideology and the Cold War', *Review of International Studies* 25:4 (October 1999).

Kusters, Hanns Jurgen, 'The Kohl-Gorbachev Meetings in Moscow and in the Caucasus, 1990', *Cold War History* 2:2 (January 2002).

LaFeber, Walter, *Inevitable Revolutions: the United States in Central America* (New York: W. W. Norton, 1984).

Laird, Robbin F. and Hoffmann, E. P. (ed.), *Soviet Foreign Policy in a Changing World* (New York: Aldine de Gruyter, 1986).

Lane, Ann, *Yugoslavia: When Ideals Collide* (Palgrave Macmillan, 2004).

Larres, Klaus, 'Germany and the West: The "Rapallo Factor" in German Foreign Policy from the 1950s to the 1990s', in Larres and P. Panayi (ed.), *The Federal Republic of Germany since 1949: Politics, Society and Economy before and after Unification* (Longman, 1996).

Latawski, Paul, 'Central Europe and European Security', in W. Park and G. Wyn Rees, *Rethinking Security in Post-Cold War Europe* (Longman, 1998).

Lebow, Richard Ned and Risse-Kappen, T. (ed.), *International Relations Theory and the End of the Cold War* (New York: Columbia University Press, 1995).

Leffler, Melvyn P., 'The American Conception of National Security and the Beginning of the Cold War, 1945–48', *The American Historical Review* 89:2 (April 1984); *A Preponderance of Power: National Security, the Truman Administration and the Cold War* (Stanford: Stanford University Press, 1992).

Leogrande, William M., *The United States in Central America, 1977–1992: Our Own Backyard* (Chapel Hill: The University of North Carolina Press, 1998).

Lévesque, Jacques, *The Enigma of 1989: The USSR and the Liberation of Eastern Europe* (California: University of California Press, 1997).

Light, Margot, 'Soviet "New Thinking": Soviet Policy in the Third World', *International Affairs* 67:1 (1991).

Limberg, Wayne P., 'Soviet Military Support for Third-World Marxist Regimes', in Mark N. Katz (ed.), *The USSR and Marxist Revolutions in the Third World* (New York: Woodrow Wilson International Centre for Scholars, 1990).

Little, Douglas, *American Orientalism: The United States and the Middle East since 1945* (I. B. Tauris, 2003).

Litwak, Robert S., *Rogue States and U.S. Foreign Policy Containment after the Cold War* (Washington, DC: The Woodrow Wilson Centre Press, 2000).

Logevall, Fredrik, 'A Critique of Containment', *Diplomatic History* 28:4 (September 2004) pp. 473–99.

Loth, Wilfried, *Stalin's Unwanted Child: The Soviet Union, the German Question and the Founding of the GDR* (Macmillan, 1998); *Overcoming the Cold War* (Palgrave Macmillan, 2001); 'Moscow, Prague and Warsaw: Overcoming the Brezhnev Doctrine', *Cold War History* 1:2 (January 2001).

Lowe, Peter (ed.), *The Vietnam War* (Macmillan, 1998).

Lundestad, Geir, 'The End of the Cold War, the New Role for Europe, and the Decline of the United States', *Diplomatic History* 16:2 (spring 1992); (ed.), *The Fall of Great Powers: Peace, Stability, and Legitimacy* (Oslo: Scandinavian University Press, 1994); (ed.), *No End to Alliance: the United States and Western Europe – Past, Present and Future* (Macmillan, 1999); *The United States and Western Europe since 1945: From 'Empire' by Invitation to Transatlantic Drift* (Oxford University Press, 2003).

Lynch, Dov, 'Russia faces Europe', *Chaillot Papers,* no. 60 (May 2003) Institute for Security Studies, European Union.

MacFarlane, S. Neil, 'Successes and Failures in Soviet Policy toward Marxist Revolutions in the Third World, 1917–1985', in Mark N. Katz (ed.), *The USSR and Marxist Revolutions in the Third World* (New York: Woodrow Wilson International Centre for Scholars, 1990); *Intervention in Contemporary World Politics*, Adelphi Paper, 350 (IISS, 2002).

Maier, Charles S., *Dissolution: The Crisis of Communism and the End of East Germany* (Princeton: Princeton University Press, 1997).

Mandelbaum, Michael, 'Ending the Cold War', *Foreign Affairs* 68:2 (spring 1989); 'The Bush Foreign Policy', *Foreign Affairs* 70:1 (1990/1991).

Maley, William, *The Afghanistan Wars* (Palgrave Macmillan, 2002).

Marwick, Arthur, *The Sixties: Cultural Revolution in Britain, France, Italy and the United States, 1968–1974* (Oxford University Press, 1998).

Mastny, Vojtech, *Helsinki, Human Rights, and European Security: Analysis and Documentation* (Durham: Duke University Press, 1986); *The Cold War and Soviet Insecurity* (Oxford University Press, 1996); 'The Soviet Non-invasion of Poland in 1980/81 and the End of the Cold War', *CWIHP Working Paper #23* (September 1998); ' "We are in a Bind" Polish and Czechoslovak Attempts at Reforming the Warsaw Pact, 1956–1969', *CWIHP Bulletin #11* (winter 1998); 'Did NATO win the Cold War?: Looking over the Wall', *Foreign Affairs* 78:3 (May/June 1999); 'The New History of Cold War Alliances', *Journal of Cold War Studies* 4:2 (spring 2002).

Matlock, Jack F., Jr, *Autopsy on An Empire: The American Ambassador's Account of the Collapse of the Soviet Union* (New York: Random House, 1995).

May, Ernest, *Imperial Democracy – the Emergence of America as a Great Power* (New York: Harcourt, Brace and World Inc., 1961).

Mazower, Mark, *Dark Continent: Europe's Twentieth Century* (New York: Vintage Books, 2000).

McAdams, A. James, *Germany Divided: From the Wall to Reunification* (Princeton: Princeton University Press, 1993).

McMahon, Robert J., 'The Challenge of the Third World', in Peter L. Hahn and Mary Ann Heiss, *Empire and Revolution: The United States and the Third World since 1945* (Columbus: Ohio State University Press, 2001).

Mearsheimer, John J., 'Back to the Future: Instability after the Cold War', *International Security* 15:1 (summer 1990) and 15:2 (fall 1990); *The Tragedy of Great Power Politics* (New York: W. W. Norton, 2001).

Mendelson, Sarah E., *Changing Course: Ideas, Politics and the Soviet Withdrawal from Afghanistan* (Princeton: Princeton University Press, 1998).

Merkl, Peter H., *German Unification in the European Context* (Pennsylvania: The Pennsylvania State University Press, 1993).

Mermin, Jonathan, 'Television News and American Intervention in Somalia: The Myth of a Media-Driven Foreign Policy', *Political Science Quarterly* 112:3 (1997).

Mervin, David, *George Bush and the Guardianship Presidency* (Macmillan, 1996).

Mitrokhin, Visiliy, 'The KGB in Afghanistan' (introduced and edited by Christian F. Ostermann and Odd Arne Westad), *CWIHP Working Paper* no. 40 (February 2002).

Morris, Stephen J., *Why Vietnam Invaded Cambodia: Political Culture and the Causes of War* (Stanford: Stanford University Press, 1999).

Mueller, John, 'Quiet Cataclysm: Some Afterthoughts about World War III', *Diplomatic History* 16:1 (winter 1992).

Munteanu, Micrea, 'The Last Days of a Dictator', *CWIHP Bulletin* #12/13 (fall/winter, 2001).

Myers, Ramon H., Oksenberg, Michel C. and Shambaugh, David, *Making China Policy: Lessons from the Bush and Clinton Administrations* (Lanham: Rowman & Littlefield Publishers, 2001).

Narinskii, Mikhail M., 'The Soviet Union and the Marshall Plan', in Antonio Varsori and Elena Calandri (ed.), *The Failure of Peace in Europe, 1943–1948* (Palgrave Macmillan, 2002).

Newton, Scott, *The Global Economy, 1944–2000* (Arnold, 2004).

Niblett, Robin and Wallace, W. (eds), *Rethinking European Order: West European Responses, 1989–1997* (Basingstoke: Palgrave, 2001).

Nitze, Paul H. (with Ann M. Smith and Steven L. Rearden), *From Hiroshima to Glasnost: At the Centre of Decision – A Memoir* (Weidenfeld and Nicolson, 1989).

Nove, Alex, 'The Fall of Empires – Russia and the Soviet Union', in Geir Lundestad (ed.), *The Fall of Great Powers: Peace, Stability, and Legitimacy* (Oslo: Scandinavian University Press, 1994).

Nye, Joseph S., Jr, 'Arms Control After the Cold War', *Foreign Affairs* 68:5 (winter 1989/90).

Oberdorfer, Don, *From the Cold War to a New Era: The United States and the Soviet Union, 1983–1991* (Baltimore: The Johns Hopkins University Press, 1991).

Odeen, Philip, 'Domestic Factors in US Defence Policy', *Adelphi Paper* no. 173 (London: International Institute for Strategic Studies, 1982).

Oye, Kenneth A., 'Explaining the End of the Cold War: Morphological and Behavioural Adaptations to the Nuclear Peace?', in Richard Ned Lebow and Thomas Risse-Kappen (eds), *International Relations Theory and the End of the Cold War* (New York: Columbia University Press, 1995).

Papacosma, S. Victor, Kay, S. and Rubin, Mark R. (eds), *NATO: After Fifty Years* (Wilmington: A Scholarly Resources Inc., 2001).

Park, W. and Rees, G. W., *Rethinking Security in Post-Cold War Europe* (Longman, 1998).

Paterson, Thomas G. (ed.), *Kennedy's Quest for Victory: American Foreign Policy, 1961–1963* (Oxford University Press, 1989).

Patman, Robert G., *The Soviet Union in the Horn of Africa: The Diplomacy of Intervention and Disengagement* (Cambridge University Press, 1990).

Pedaliu, Effie G. H., *Britain, Italy and the Origins of the Cold War* (Palgrave Macmillan, 2003).

Pemberton, William E., *Exist with Honor: the Life and Presidency of Ronald Reagan* (M. E. Sharpe, 1998).

Pettiford, Lloyd, 'Changing Conceptions of Security in the Third World', *Third World Quarterly* 17:2 (1996).

Pleshakov, Constantine, 'Nikita Khrushchev and Sino-Soviet Relations', in Odd Arne Westad (ed.), *Brothers in Arms* (Stanford: Stanford University Press, 1998)., 'Studying Soviet Strategies and Decision Making in the Cold War Years', in Odd Arne Westad (ed.), *Reviewing the Cold War* (London: Frank Cass, 2000).

Powell, Colin with Joseph E. Persico, *My American Journey* (New York: Ballantine Books, 1995).

Prados, John, 'Open Skies and Closed Minds', in Bischof Günter and S. Dockrill (eds), *Cold War Respite: The Geneva Summit of 1955* (Baton Rouge: Louisiana State University Press, 2000)., *Hoodwinked: Documents that Reveal How Bush Sold Us a War* (New York: The New Press, 2004).

Reagan, Ronald, *An American Life* (Hutchinson, 1990).

Reiss, Edward, *The Strategic Defence Initiative* (Cambridge University Press, 1992).

Rey, Marie-Pierre, 'Europe is our Common Home: Gorbachevian USSR and Western Europe, 1985–1991', *Nobel Institute Research Seminar Paper* (June 2002), Norwegian Nobel Institute, Oslo; 'Europe is our Common Home': A Study of Gorbachev's Diplomatic Concept', *Cold War History* 4:2 (January 2004).

Roberts, Adam, 'The Crisis in UN Peacekeeping', *Survival* 36:3 (autumn 1994).

Roberts, Brad, 'From Nonproliferation to Antiproliferation', *International Security* 18:1 (summer 1993).

Roberts, Geoffrey, *The Soviet Union in World Politics* (Routledge, 1999).

Rosenau, William, 'The Eisenhower Administration, US Foreign Internal Security Assistance, and the Struggle for the Developing World, 1954–1961', *Low Intensity Conflict and Law Enforcement* 10:3 (autumn 2001).

Rosner, Jeremy D., 'American Assistance to the Former Soviet States in 1993–1994', in James M. Scott (ed.), *After the End: Making US Foreign Policy in the Post-Cold War World* (Durham, NC: Duke University Press, 1998).

Rubinstein, Alvin, 'Moscow's Third World Strategy', in Frederic J. Fleron Jr, Erik P. Hoffmann and Robin F. Laird (eds), *Contemporary Issues in Soviet Foreign Policy from Brezhnev to Gorbachev* (New York: Aldine de Gruyter, 1991),

Ruina, Jack, 'Threats to the ABM Treaty', *Security Dialogue* 26:3 (1995).

Sakwa, Richard, *Gorbachev and His Reforms, 1985–1990* (New Jersey: Prentice Hall, 1991); *The Rise and Fall of the Soviet Union 1917–1991* (Routledge, 2002).

Sauerwein, Harry, 'Mobil ICBM and Arms Control', *Survival* 23:5 (September-October 1981).

Savaranskaya, Svetlana, 'Tactical Nuclear Weapons in Cuba: New Evidence', *CWIHP Bulletin #* 14/15 (winter 2003/spring 2004).

Savel'yev, Aleksandr G. and Detinov, Nikolay N. (trans. by Dmitriy Trenin and ed. by Grefoy Varhall), *The Big Five: Arms Control Decision-Making in the Soviet Union* (Westport: Praeger, 1995).

Sagan, Scott D., 'The Perils of Proliferation', *International Security* 18:4 (spring 1994).

Schmertz, Eric J., Datlof, N. and Ugrinsky, A., *President Reagan and the World* (Westport: Greenwood Press, 1997).

Schulzinger, Robert D., 'The End of the Old World Order', *Diplomatic History* 20:4 (Fall 1996).

Schweizer, Peter, *Victory: The Reagan Administration's Secret Strategy that Hastened the Collapse of the Soviet Union* (New York: The Atlantic Monthly Press, 1994).

Scott, James M. (ed.), *After the End: Making US Foreign Policy in the Post-Cold War World* (Durham, NC: Duke University Press, 1998).

Shambaugh, David, *Modernizing China's Military: Progress, Problems, and Prospects* (Berkeley: University of California Press, 2002).

Shearman, Peter and Williams, P. (eds), *The Superpowers, Central America and the Middle East* (Brassey's, 1988).

Shroeder, Paul, 'Historical Reality vs. Neo-realist Theory', *International Security* 19:1 (summer 1994).

Shultz, George P., *Turmoil and Triumph: My Years as Secretary of State* (New York: Charles Scribner's Sons, 1993).

Shumaker, David H., *Gorbachev and the German Question: Soviet-West German Relations, 1985–1990* (Westport: Praeger, 1995).

Sjursen, Helene, *The United States, Western Europe and the Polish Crisis* (Palgrave Macmillan, 2003).

Snow, Donald M., *Nuclear Strategy in a Dynamic World* (Alabama: The University of Alabama Press, 1981).

Soutou, Georges-Henri, *La Guerre de Cinquante Ans: Les Relations Est-Ouest 1943–1990* (Paris: Fayard, 2001); Dockrill, Saki, Frank, R. and Varsori, A. (eds), *L'Europe: de l'Est et de l'Ouest dans la Guerre Froide, 1948–1953* (Paris: Presses de L'Université Paris-Sorbonne, 2002); 'Convergence Theories in France in the Sixties and Seventies', in Wilfried Loth (ed.), *Eastern Europe and Western Europe in the Cold War (1965–1975)* (forthcoming).

Swain, Geoffrey and Swain, N., *Eastern Europe since 1945* (Macmillan, 1993).

Talbott, Strobe, 'Why Start Stopped', *Foreign Affairs* (fall 1988).

Taylor, Brian D., 'The Soviet Military and the Disintegration of the USSR', *Cold War Studies* 5:1 (winter 2003).

Teirsky, Ronald, *François Mitterrand: the Last French President* (New York: St Martin's Press, 2000).

Thatcher, Margaret, *The Downing Street Years* (HarperCollins Publishers, 1995).

The Russian General Staff (trans. and ed. by Lester W. Grau and Michael A. Gress), *The Soviet-Afghan War: How a Superpower Fought and Lost* (Kansas: University Press of Kansas, 2002).

Tønnesson, Stein, 'Tracking Multi-Directional Dominoes', in '77 Conversations between Chinese and Foreign Leaders on the Wars in Indochina, 1964–1967', *CWIHP Working Paper* no. 22 (1998).

Ulam, Adam B., *Understanding the Cold War* (New Brunswick: Transaction Publishers, 2002).

Varsori, Antonio (ed.), *Europe 1945–1990s: The End of an Era?* (Macmillan, 1995), and Calandri, E. (ed.), *The Failure of Peace in Europe, 1943–1948* (Palgrave Macmillan, 2002).

Walker, Rachel, *Six Years that Shook the World: Perestroika – the Impossible Project* (Manchester University Press, 1993).

Wallander, Celeste A., 'Western Policy and the Demise of the Soviet Union', *Journal of Cold War Studies* 5:4 (fall 2003).

Weathersby, Kathryn, 'Soviet Aims in Korea and the Origins of the Korean War, 1945–1950', *CWIHP Working Paper* no. 8 (1994); "Should We Fear This?": Stalin and the Danger of War with America', *CWIHP Working Paper* no.39 (2002).

Wegs, J. Robert and Ladrech, R., *Europe since 1945: A Concise History* (4th edn) (Boston and New York: St Martin's Press, 1996).

Weinberger, Casper, 'U.S. Defense Strategy', *Foreign Affairs* 64:4 (spring 1986); *Fighting for Peace: Seven Critical Years at the Pentagon* (Michael Joseph, 1990).

Westad, Arne Odd, 'Moscow and the Angolan Crisis, 1974–1976: A New Pattern of Intervention', in *CWIHP Bulletin* #8–9 (winter 1996/7); 'Concerning the situation in "A": New Russian Evidence on the Soviet Intervention in Afghanistan', *CWIHP Bulletin* #8/9 (winter 1996/7); (ed.), *The Fall of Détente: Soviet-American Relations during the Carter Years* (Oslo: Scandinavian University Press, 1997); 'The Road to Kabul: Soviet Policy on Afghanistan, 1978–1979', in Odd Arne Westad (ed.), *The Fall of Détente: Soviet-American Relations during the Carter Years* (Oslo: Scandinavian University Press, 1997); (ed.), *Brothers in Arms* (Stanford: Stanford University Press, 1998); 'History, Memory and the Languages of Alliance-Making', in '77 Conversations', *CWIHP Working Paper* no. 22 (1998); (ed.), *Reviewing the Cold War* (Frank Cass, 2000); *The Global Cold War: Third World Interventions and the Making of Our Times* (Cambridge University Press, forthcoming); and Holtsmark, S. and Neumann, Iver B. (eds), *The Soviet Union in Eastern Europe 1945–89* (Macmillan, 1994).

Wettig, Gerhard, 'Stalin's Note of 10 March 1952: Historical Context', in Georges-Henri Soutou et al. (eds), *L'Europe: de l'Est et de l'Ouest dans la Guerre Froide*, p. 137–49; 'The Kremlin's Impact on the Peaceful Revolution in East

Germany (August 1989-March 1990)', in Odd Arne Westad et al. (eds), *The Soviet Union in Eastern Europe 1945–1989* (Macmillan, 1994).

Wheeler, Nicholas J. and Bellamy, A. J., 'Humanitarian Intervention and World Politics', in Baylis and Smith (eds), *The Globalization of World Politics* (Oxford University Press, 2001).

White, Stephen, *After Gorbachev* (Cambridge University Press, 1993).

Wither, James K., 'British Bulldog or Bush's Poodle? Anglo-American Relations and the Iraq War', *Parameters* (winter 2003–4).

Wohlforth, William C., 'Realism and the End of the Cold War', *International Security* 19 (winter 1994/5).

Woodward, Bob, *Veil: The Secret Wars of the CIA 1981–1987* (Simon & Schuster, 1987); *Plan of Attack* (New York: Simon & Schuster, 2004).

Yahuda, Michael, *The International Politics of the Asia-Pacific, 1945–1995* (Routledge, 1996).

Yegorova, N. I. (ed.), *Cold War and the Policy of Détente: Problems and Discussions* (Moscow: Russian Academy of Sciences, Institute of Universal History, 2003).

Yeltsin, Boris, *Against the Grain* (New York: Summit Books, 1990).

Yost, David S., *NATO Transformed: The Alliance's New Roles in International Security* (Washington: United States Institute of Peace, 1998); 'The US and Nuclear Deterrence in Europe', *Adelphi Paper* 326 (IISS, 1999).

Young, John W., *Cold War Europe, 1945–1991: A Political History* (Arnold, 1996).

Young, Marilyn B., *The Vietnam Wars, 1945–1990* (New York: Harper Perennial, 1991).

Zelikow, Philip and Rice, Condoleezza, *Germany United and Europe Transformed: A Study in Statecraft* (Cambridge, MA: Harvard University Press, 1995).

Zlotnik, Marc, 'Yeltsin and Gorbachev: The Politics of Confrontation', *Cold War Studies* 5:1 (winter 2003).

Zubok, Vladislav M., 'Soviet Policy Aims at the Geneva Conference, 1955', in Günter Bischof and Saki Dockrill (eds), *Cold War Respite: The Geneva Summit of 1955* (Baton Rouge: Louisiana State University Press, 2000) pp. 55–74; 'New Evidence on the End of the Cold War: New Evidence on the "Soviet Factor" in the Peaceful Revolutions in 1989', *CWIHP Bulletin*, Issue # 12–13 (fall/winter 2001); 'The Brezhnev Factor in Détente, 1968–1972', in N. I. Yegorova (ed.), *Cold War and the Policy of Détente: Problems and Discussions* (Moscow: Russian Academy of Sciences, Institute of Universal History, 2003); 'Gorbachev and the End of the Cold War: Different Perspectives on the Historical Personality', in William C. Wohlforth (ed.), *Cold War Endgame: Oral History, Analysis, and Debates* (Pennsylvania: The Pennsylvania State University, 2003); and Pleshakov, C., *Inside the Kremlin's Cold War: From Stalin to Khrushchev* (Cambridge, MA: Harvard University Press, 1996).

Index

Aden 156
Afghanistan
  Soviet invasion (1979) 7, 9, 18, 159–62,
    168, 176–7
  Soviet war 177–84
  Soviet withdrawal 184–5
  Taliban 222
  United States involvement 178–80,
    182–5, 224
Africa, United States involvement 185–90
Akhromeyev, Sergei Fedorovich 45,
    111–12, 126
Albania 49, 85–6
Albright, Madeleine 220
Allen, Richard 106
Allende, Salvador 162–3
Amin, Hafizullah 161
Andreeva, Nina 28–9
Andropov, Yuri 10, 18–19, 52, 55, 58,
    157, 168–9
Angola, conflict 157, 158, 165, 185–9
Anti Ballistic Missile (ABM) Treaty 105,
    108, 112, 139
Arab-Israeli war (1967) 51
Arias, Oscar 195–6
arms reduction
  conventional 122–3, 129
  see also nuclear weapons
arms trade 169, 174, 175–6, 179, 196–7
Asia
  post-Cold War 213
  and Soviet Union 144–6, 172
Aziz, Tariq 202

Baker, James 12, 68, 122, 124–5, 196,
    200–1
Baklanov, Oleg 39
Balkans, Communism collapse 83–7
Baltic Republics 32, 37–9, 126–7, 132

Belarus, nuclear weapons 135–6
Berlin Wall, fall of 32–3, 67, 75–9, 210
Bessmertnykh, Aleksandr 129
Bin Laden, Osama 222
Blair, Tony 224
Bosnia 97
Brandt, Willy 6, 57, 69
Brezhnev, Leonid 6, 17–19, 24, 44, 49
  and Czechoslovakia 51, 52
  and Poland 55–6
  Third World policies 141
Britain
  end of Cold War 70–1
  Iraq invasion 224–5
  and Soviet Union 3
Brzezinski, Zbigniew 158–9
Bukharin, Nikolai 24
Bulgaria 83–4
Bush, George
  end of Cold War 12, 68–70, 118
  and Nicaragua 196–7
  nuclear weapons policy 121–35
  and Soviet Union 87
Bush, George W. 16, 139, 222–7

Cambodia 167, 197–8
Carlucci, Frank 116
Carter, Jimmy 8, 101, 158–9, 162, 190
Casey, William (Bill) 8, 114, 178–9, 192
Castro, Fidel 146, 162, 168, 170, 188–9
Ceauşescu, Nicolae 64, 84–5
Central America 162–3, 190–8
Charter 77 group 53, 82
Chebrikov, Viktor Mikhailovich 21, 25,
    30
Chechnya 207
chemical weapons 128
Cheney, Dick 68, 124, 132, 227
Chernenko, Constantine 10, 19

Chernobyl disaster 23, 110
Chernyaev, Anatoly 22, 46, 63
Chiang Kai Shek 144
Chile 162-3
China
  Communist 4, 144
  nuclear weapons 138
  post-Cold War 213
  and Soviet Union 18, 146, 156-7, 172
  and United States 6, 158
Churchill, Winston 3
Clinton, Bill 138, 139, 219-22
Cold War
  end of 11-14, 92-3, 200-1, 203-12
  European perspective 207-11
  origins (1917-46) 2-3
  outbreak of (1946-8) 3
  post-Cold War 94-8, 212-22
  progress of (1948-79) 4-7
  'Second Cold War' (1979-84) 7-11
  Soviet perspective 93-4, 205-7
  United States perspective 211-12
Combined Joint Task Forces (CJTF)
  97
Commonwealth of Independent States
  (CIS) 42
Communism
  Eastern Europe 52-3, 79-87
  Third World 142-7
Comprehensive Test Ban Treaty (CTBT)
  137
Conference on Security and Cooperation
  in Europe (CSCE) 9, 60, 92-3
Contras, Nicaragua 164, 190, 193-6
Conventional Forces in Europe (CFE)
  Treaty 92-3, 122-4, 129, 134
Council for Mututal Economic Assistance
  (CMEA - COMECON) 60-1, 169
Crimean Tartars 28
Croatia 56, 86-7, 211
Crocker, Chet 188
Cruise missiles 101-2
Cuba 10, 146, 157, 159, 168, 170
  Angola involvement 186-9
  Nicaragua involvement 192-3
Cuban Missile Crisis 99, 146
Czech Republic 83
Czechoslovakia
  Communism collapse 82-3
  Communist coup 4
  East German refugees 76
  and Soviet Union 51-2, 64, 82

Daniloff, Nicholas 110
Dashichev, Vyacheslav 72
decolonization 216
Deng Xiaoping 172
détente
  Europe (1970s) 6-7, 53, 209
  Gorbachev's policies 171-3
Diego Garcia 156
Dobrynin, Anatoly 22, 106, 108
Dos Santos, Jose Eduardo 185
Duarte, José Napoleón 190
Dubček, Alexander 51-2, 82
Dulles, Allen 150

Eagleburger, Lawrence 10
East Germany see German Democratic
  Republic
Eastern Europe
  Communism collapse 79-87
  post-Cold War 96-8
  and Soviet Union 49-54, 62-6
Egypt 158, 172-3
Eisenhower, Dwight D. 6, 151
El Salvador 162, 190-2, 197
Ethiopia 157, 159, 168
Europe
  détente (1970s) 6-7, 53, 209
  see also Eastern Europe; Western
    Europe
European Defence Community (EDC) 4
European Economic Community (EEC)
  and CMEA 60-1
European Monetary Union (EMU) 71
European Union (EU) 96

Federal Republic of Germany
  (FRG)
  Cold War 208-9
  formation of 4
  and German Democratic Republic 57,
    73-5
  and NATO 5
  nuclear weapons 115
  'Finlandization' 9
Ford, Gerald 158
Fowkes, Ben 49
France
  Cold War 208
  end of Cold War 70-1
  nuclear weapons 138
freedom fighters 198-9
Fukuyama, Francis 13, 142

Gaddis, John Lewis 13
Galeotti, Mark 27
Garthoff, Raymond 133
Gates, Robert 124
General Agreement on Tariffs and Trade (GATT) 125
Geneva Conference (1955) 4, 5
Geneva summit (1985) 100, 106–9
Genscher, Hans-Dietrich 89
German Democratic Republic (GDR)
  collapse of 75–9
  economy 51
  formation of 4
  unification with West 87–92
  and West Germany 57, 73–5
  see also Berlin Wall
Germany
  nuclear weapons 138
  and Soviet Union 2–3, 4–5, 71–3
  unification 32–3, 67, 73–5, 79, 87–92, 210–11
  see also Federal Republic of Germany; German Democratic Republic
Gierek, Edvard 54
globalization 171, 214–16
Gomulka, Wladyslaw 52, 54
González, Felipe 43
Gorbachev, Mikhail
  comes to power 19, 20–2
  democratization process 27–33, 61, 206–7
  and East Germany 76–7, 78–9
  and Eastern Europe 62–6
  economic policies 33–6
  end of Cold War 12, 67–75, 203–7
  European policy 59–62
  fall from power 36–42
  foreign policy 45
  German unification 73–5, 89–92
  Gulf War 201–2
  image of 7
  legacy of 42–8
  nuclear weapons policies 100, 106–19, 121–34
  reform policies 22–7, 121–2
  resignation 42
  Third World policies 167–76, 198–202
  and United States 68–70, 121–2, 211–12
Gordievsky, Oleg 108
Grachev, Andrey 40

Grenada 162, 163–4
Grishin, Viktor 20
Gromyko, Andrei 20, 22, 52, 106, 181
Grósz, Károly 64, 81, 87
Gulf War (1990–1) 139, 201–2

Haig, Alexander 106, 179, 192–3
Havel, Václav 82
Hay, John 148
Helsinki Act 53
Hitler, Adolf 3
Ho Chi Minh 145
Honecker, Erich 19, 57, 73–4, 76
Hungary
  Communism collapse 81–2
  East German refugees 75–6
  economy 51, 54
  and Soviet Union 18, 64
Hunt, Michael 149
Husák, Gustáv 64, 82
Hussein, Saddam 12, 128, 201–2, 222, 224

Iliescu, Ion 85
India 171–2
Indian Ocean, Soviet presence 156–7
Intermediate-range Nuclear Forces in Europe (INF) 100, 103–4, 109, 112–17, 123
Iran
  Iran-Contra affair 114, 194–5
  revolution (1979) 159
  and Soviet Union 173
Iraq
  Iran war 173
  Kuwait invasion 12, 201–2
  US-UK invasion (2003) 224–6
  weapons 138, 139, 222
Islam, and United States 179
Israel 51, 158, 163, 173

Jakeš, Miloš 82
Japan 148–9, 172
Jaruzelski, Wojciech 56, 64, 80
John Paul II, Pope 54
Johnson, Lyndon B. 6, 153

Kádár, János 64
Kania, Stanislaw 55
Karmal, Babrak 177
Kazakhstan 28, 135–6
Kennedy, John F. 6, 146, 151–3

KGB 18–19, 30, 39–40
Khomeini, Ayatollah 159
Khrushchev, Nikita 5–6, 24, 44, 145–6, 151
Kim Il Sung 145
Kim Jong Il 227
Kirkpatrick, Jean 163
Kissinger, Henry 69, 141, 158
Kohl, Helmut 10, 74–5, 78–9, 87–92, 104
Korea, and Soviet Union 144–5
Korean War 4, 5, 145
Kosovo 57, 86, 221
Krenz, Egon 76–7
Kryuchkov, Vladimir 30, 39, 40
Kuklinski, Ryczard 58
Kuwait, Iraq invasion 12, 201–2
Kvitsinskiy, Yuli 104

Lake, Anthony 221
Laos 145–6
Le Peng 172
Lebanon 163
Lenin, Vladimir Ilyich 24
Ligachev, Yegor Kuzmich 21, 25, 30
Lithuania 38, 127
Lukyanov, Anatoly 32

Maastricht Treaty (1992) 96
MacFarlane, Neil 143
Machel, Samora 186
Mahan, Alfred Thayer 147–8
Malta summit (1989) 124–6
Mandelbaum, Michael 12
Mao Zedong 4, 6, 144
Marshall Plan 3
Matlock, Jack 40, 68, 106
Mazowiecki, Tadeusz 80–1
McFarlane, Robert 108
McLean, Donald 145
Mearsheimer, John 138, 213
Medvedev, Vladim 21–2, 30
Meese, Edwin 195
Middle East 158, 163, 172–3
Milošević, Slobodan 86, 221
Mitterand, François 10, 70–1
Mladenov, Petar 84
Mongolia 144
Morrow, Hans 77
Moscow summit (1988) 118
Moscow summit (1991) 130
Moscow summit (2002) 140

Mozambique 157, 168, 186, 190
Mueller, John 12
Mutual and Balanced Force Reductions (MBFR) 9–10, 123

Nagorno-Karabakh 28
Nagy, Imre 81
Najibullah (Najib), Mohammed 182–3
Namibia 186–9
National Missile Defence (NMD) project 140
Nicaragua 162, 164, 168, 190–7, 199
Nicholson, Arthur 108
Nitze, Paul 104, 111–12
Nixon, Richard 6, 154
North Atlantic Treaty Organization (NATO)
    'Able Archer' exercise 9, 204
    formation of 4
    and Germany 5, 89–92
    membership 97–8
    nuclear weapons 123–4, 138
    post-Cold War 94–8
    and Warsaw Pact 204–5
North Korea 138, 139, 144, 227
North, Oliver 114, 194–5
Novotný, Antonin 51
Nuclear Non-Proliferation Treaty (NPT) 99, 136
nuclear weapons 8–9, 10, 26, 44, 99–119, 121–40, 211

oil prices 53–4
Olympic Games
    1980 (Moscow) 162
    1984 (Los Angeles) 9, 19
Open Sky Treaty 134
Organization of Security and Cooperation in Europe (OSCE) 93–4
Ostpolitik 6, 57, 71, 209

Pakistan, and Afghan war 179–82
Paris Accords (1973) 154
Pavlov, Valentin 36, 39, 40
Perle, Richard 106, 111
Pershing missiles 101–2, 115
Pinochet, Augusto 163
Pleshakov, Constantine 143
Poindexter, Admiral 114
Poland
    Communism collapse 80–1
    crisis (1980–1) 54–9

economy 51
Solidarity movement 55-6, 80-1
and Soviet Union 64
Ponomarev, Boris Nikolaevich 157
Powell, Colin 94, 116
Pozsgay, Imre 81
Prague Spring 52-3
Pugo, Boris 38, 39, 40
Putin, Vladimir 139, 207

Quayle, Dan 124-5

Reagan, Ronald
Central America policies 190-7
economic policies 13
nuclear weapons policies 100-19
and Poland 58-9
Reagan Doctrine 190, 198-9
rearmament programme 10
and Soviet Union 8, 12, 198-9
Third World policies 162-5, 198-202
refugees 217
Reykjavik summit (1986) 60, 110-13
Rice, Condoleezza 207
'rogue states' 138, 139, 221-2
Romania
Communism collapse 84-5
economy 51
and Soviet Union 49, 64, 65, 85
Romanov, Grigoriy 20
Roosevelt, Franklin D. 149
Roosevelt, Theodore 147-8
Rumsfeld, Donald 16, 224, 227
Russian Republic 37, 134-40, 207
Ryzhkov, Nikolai 21, 36

Sadat, Anwar 158
Sakharov, Andrei 23, 31
SALT see Strategic Arms Limitation Talks
Saudi Arabia 179
Savimbi, Jonas 185
Schabowski, Gunter 77
Schmidt, Helmut 101, 102
Scowcroft, Brent 12, 68, 122, 125, 130-1
Second World War 3
security, concept of 216-18
September 11 attacks 139, 203, 222-4
Serbia 57, 86-7
Shakhnazarov, Georgy 22
Shatalin, Stanislav 35-6
Shevardnadze, Eduard 22, 38, 39, 59, 75, 107, 124, 126, 200-1

Short-Range Intermediate Nuclear Forces (SRINF) 114-16
Shultz, George 12, 106, 107-8, 113, 163, 164, 183-4, 214
Single European Act (SEA) 61
Slovak Republic 83
Slovenia 86, 211
Socialist Unity Party of Germany (SED) 73-4, 76
Solidarity movement 55-6, 80-1
South Africa 185-8
South East Asian Treaty Organization (SEATO) 150
Soviet Union
'acceleration' period 22-3
Afghanistan war 7, 9, 18, 159-62, 168, 176-85
Angola involvement 185-90
arms trade 169, 174, 175-6, 196-7
Brezhnev era 17-19
and China 18, 146, 156-7, 172
collapse of 13, 36-42, 134-5
Communist Party 21, 29-33
coup attempt (1991) 39-41, 131-2
and Czechoslovakia 51-2, 64, 82
democratization 27-33
and Eastern Europe 49-54, 62-6
economic crisis 33-6
end of Cold War 93-5, 205-7
and Europe 59-62
foreign relations 2-3, 7
and German unification 71-5, 89-92
Glasnost 23-5, 42-3, 206-7
Gorbachev era 20-2, 42-8
nationalism 27, 37-8
and NATO 204-5
and Nicaragua 194
nuclear weapons 8-9, 26, 44, 99-119, 121-34
Perestroika 23, 25-7, 33-4, 42-3, 65, 118-19, 121-2, 126-7, 206-7
and Poland 54-9
and Romania 49, 64, 65, 85
Third World policies 18, 141-7, 156-62, 167-76, 198-202
troop withdrawals 128-9
stagflation 156
Stalin, Josef 2-3, 4-5, 24, 27-8, 143-5
START see Strategic Arms Reduction Talks

Stinger missiles 182–3
Strategic Arms Limitation Talks (SALT I) 6, 7, 99
Strategic Arms Limitation Talks (SALT II) 99–100, 103, 107–8, 158–9
Strategic Arms Reduction Talks (START) 12, 100, 104, 112, 117, 122, 124, 126, 130–1, 211
  START II 133–40
Strategic Defence Initiative (SDI) (Star Wars) 8–9, 100, 104–5, 107–14, 116–17, 211
Strategic Offensive Reductions Treaty (SORT) 140
Suslov, Mikhail 18, 55
Syria 163

Taraki, Nur Mohammed 161
television 65
terrorism, threat of 216–17
Thatcher, Margaret 8, 10, 12, 43, 59, 70
Third World
  and Soviet Union 18, 141–7, 156–62, 167–76
  and United States 147–65, 198–202
Tocqueville, Alexis de 2
Truman Doctrine (1947) 3

Ukraine 41–2, 135–6
Ulbricht, Walter 52
United Kingdom see Britain
United Nations 3
United States
  and Afghanistan war 178–80, 182–5
  Angola involvement 185–90
  and China 6, 158
  economy 155–6
  end of Cold War 68–70, 94–6, 211–12
  and German unification 89
  Iraq invasion 224–6
  and Japan 148–9
  nuclear weapons 99–119, 121–40
  and Poland 58–9
  post-Cold War 218–22
  Second World War 2–3
  Third World policies 147–65, 198–202
  Vietnam War 151–5

USSR see Soviet Union
Ustinov, Dmitry 20, 55

Vance, Cyrus 159
'velvet revolution' 82–3
Vietnam
  and Soviet Union 167, 170
  Vietnam War 151–5
  'Vietnam syndrome' 156

Wałęsa, Lech 55, 80–1
Walker, Rachel 21
Waltz, Kenneth 138
Warsaw Pact 5, 63, 93, 96–7, 204–5
Washington summit (1990) 127–8
Watergate scandal 156
weapons of mass destruction (WMD) 138–40, 221–2, 224–5
Weinberger, Caspar 8, 105, 106, 108, 114, 163, 164, 193
Weizsacker, Richard von 7
West Germany see Federal Republic of Germany
Western Europe
  Cold War 207–11
  nuclear weapons 100–2, 115
  post-Cold War 96–7
  see also Europe
Wilson, Charles 179
Wilson, Woodrow 148
Wolfowitz, Paul 227

Yakovlev, Alexander 22, 30, 39, 59
Yanayev, Gennady Ivanovich 39
Yasov, Dmitri 39, 40
Yeltsin, Boris 25–6, 31–2, 40–1, 42, 135–40, 207
Yemen 157, 168, 173–4
Yugoslavia
  collapse of 86–7, 97
  nationalism 56–7
  and Soviet Union 49

Zakharov, Genmady 110
Zhdanov, Andrei 144
Zhivkov, Todor 83–4
Zia ul-Haq, Muhammad 179
Zimbabwe 157
Zubok, Vladislav 63, 66, 143